The Pursuit of Criminal Justice

Edited by
Gordon Hawkins and
Franklin E. Zimring

The Pursuit of Criminal Justice

*Essays from the
Chicago Center*

The University of Chicago Press
Chicago and London

GORDON HAWKINS is associate professor of
criminology and director of the Institute of
Criminology at Sydney University Law School.
He is also a fellow of the Center for Studies in
Criminal Justice at the University of Chicago
Law School.

FRANKLIN E. ZIMRING is the Karl N. Llewellyn
Professor of Law at the University of Chicago
Law School and director of the Center for
Studies in Criminal Justice.

THE UNIVERSITY OF CHICAGO PRESS, CHICAGO 60637
THE UNIVERSITY OF CHICAGO PRESS, LTD, LONDON

© 1984 by The University of Chicago
All rights reserved. Published 1984
Printed in the United States of America
93 92 91 90 89 88 87 86 85 84   1 2 3 4 5

LIBRARY OF CONGRESS CATALOGING IN PUBLICATION DATA
Main entry under title:

The Pursuit of criminal justice.

  (Studies in crime and justice)
  Bibliography: p.
  Includes index.
  1. Criminal justice, Administration of—United States—
Addresses, essays, lectures. 2. Criminal law—United
States—Addresses, essays, lectures. I. Hawkins,
Gordon, 1919–   II. Zimring, Franklin E.   III. Series.
HV9950.P87 1984   364'.973   84-12
ISBN 0-226-32001-4

To H.W.M.

Contents

Preface

This volume celebrates nearly two decades in the life of the Center for Studies in Criminal Justice at the University of Chicago. In these pages, the reader will find a variety of essays, topics, and authors, and perspectives that we regard as representative of the eclectic character of the center. There are two further components of the volume. First, Gordon Hawkins sets out in his introductory essay to place the center in the historical and intellectual context of the history of criminological research at the University of Chicago. Second, we provide a comprehensive bibliography, by topic, of the center's publications over the period 1965–82.

Is such a project worthy of independent publication? In discussing this question with colleagues, we began by noting that library shelves are already groaning under the weight of volumes of self-congratulation and institutional boosterism that have not left the world of ideas a better place. To organize a volume around the contribution of a single research institution is often parochial and occasionally unseemly. But the arguments that developed in favor of the enterprise persuaded us to go forward. The first consideration was the essays themselves. Diverse in scope and perspective, most of them seem to us to have stood the test of time quite well and to be of potential value to future students of criminology, criminal justice reform, and criminal law. Many were scattered beyond the reach of a student or academic researcher—episodically published, misclassified, and fugitive literature in a disorganized field. We felt that individually the essays deserved a wider audience. Collectively, these contributions portray a broader vision of the study of law and legal institutions than has been fashionable in academic American law.

Second, these essays and their supporting bibliography are intended as an introduction to the much broader literature in each topic. Our own researches have suggested that such guidance is frequently unavailable to nonspecialists.

Criminal justice is a set of topics, not a discipline. For those who view problems as opportunities for reform, it is a field of opportunity without limit. Knowledge and change are achieved through slow and incremental processes. In the life of institutions, seventeen years is a long time. We have not, in that time, developed a cure for crime or reduced the squalor of even one Chicago courtroom of first instance. But some seeds were sown, and some light was shed on the interrelated problems of crime, its control, and the path to criminal justice.

Franklin E. Zimring

Introduction

Gordon Hawkins

"Chicago is the great American city," wrote Norman Mailer in 1968, "Perhaps it is the last of the great American cities."[1] Yet the features of the city he noted—the decaying Loop with its screeching El, the malodorous carnage in the slaughterhouses, "the largest gang of juvenile delinquents on earth," and "the people [who] had great faces, carnal as blood, greedy, direct, too impatient for hypocrisy, in love with honest plunder"[2]—are not the kind that figure in the guidebooks. Nor would they usually be regarded as sources of civic pride.

But cities, like the people who build and inhabit them, are often loved and celebrated for their defects as much as for their virtues. This is certainly true of Chicago. For most of the world the name of the city is still a byword for lawlessness, underworld violence, and organized crime. It is known, affectionately, as the city where Capone reigned, Dillinger died, and the St. Valentine's Day Massacre occurred, rather than the place where Dreiser wrote, Sullivan and Miës van der Rohe built, and where Fermi fathered the self-sustaining nuclear chain reaction. The rare distinction of its architecture, its unequaled collection of nineteenth-century French paintings, the preeminence of its symphony orchestra under Reiner and Solti are ignored in favor of the squalid and lethal operations of not-particularly-well-organized organized criminals during and after the Prohibition era of the 1920s and early 1930s.

Ironically, it is by no means certain that Chicago's reputation for inordinate crime and corruption is entirely deserved. The city has had a long and vigorous tradition of investigative reporting; reformers have been remarkably effective at conducting exposés; and Chicago sociologists were more diligent than scholars in any other city in analyzing organized crime, juvenile delinquency, and political corruption. As a result, crime and corruption in Chicago were exposed to public scrutiny to a degree unparalleled anywhere else. Historian Mark Haller has suggested that "Chicago deserves a reputation for the vigor of its newspapers and scholars; instead it has a world-wide reputation for crime and corruption."[3]

However that may be, the city has undoubtedly made a substantial and sometimes spectacular contribution to the volume of crime in America, not merely organized crime, but crime of all varieties. What is less well known

1

outside a fairly narrowly defined circle, however, is that Chicago has also been the home of two separate, sustained major attempts to contribute to the enlargement of knowledge of crime and delinquency and also of the operation of the criminal justice system. Both of these exercises originated in and were supported by the University of Chicago, although they developed independently at different periods of time and in different departments of the university—specifically, in the Department of Sociology in the 1920s and in the Law School in the 1960s.

The Chicago School of Criminology

This volume is the product of and reflects the work of those associated with the second of these two enterprises—the Center for Studies in Criminal Justice at the University of Chicago Law School, established in 1965 with the support of the Ford Foundation. But it seems appropriate by way of introduction to say something about that earlier undertaking, which played a part of major significance in the development of criminological scholarship and research. This is of more than merely antiquarian interest. The authors of one criminological textbook observe in relation to some of those earlier Chicago studies of juvenile crime how "quaint its delinquents seem to us today, in their knickerbockers and cloth caps and pre-atomic innocence." But they add that no subsequent work on the subject "has been accompanied by a body of data comparable in quantity or relevance to that of the Chicago school."[4] Moreover, as James F. Short has noted, "among research traditions most basic to both continuity and change in criminological thought, perhaps none has been so important to research, theory, and social action with respect to crime and delinquency as that associated with Clifford A. Shaw and Henry D. McKay and the 'Chicago school.'"[5]

The fact is that in Chicago in the 1920s not only did crime flourish to such a degree that "all the statistics of the time suggested a crime wave of major proportions,"[6] but there also developed in this period the first serious attempts at the empirical study of urban crime. The Chicago school of criminology, sometimes referred to as the "Chicago Ecological School," pioneered the investigation of social factors affecting urban delinquency and crime and laid the foundation of sociological criminology in America.

A remarkable series of works, which have become sociological classics, appeared within a period of six years—Frederic M. Thrasher's *The Gang* (1927); Clifford Shaw's *Delinquency Areas* (1929), *The Jack-roller* (1930), and *The Natural History of a Delinquent Career* (1931); Shaw and Henry D. McKay's *Social Factors in Juvenile Delinquency* (1931); John Landesco's *Organized Crime in Chicago* (1929); Harvey W. Zorbaugh's *The Gold Coast and the Slum* (1929); and Walter C. Reckless's *Vice in Chicago* (1933). One could also add as belonging to that era Edwin Sutherland's *The Professional*

Thief (1937) for which the original manuscript which forms the core of the book was complete in 1930.

These books were the work of students and former students of the Department of Sociology at the University of Chicago, which, under the leadership of Ernest W. Burgess, W. I. Thomas, and Robert E. Park, dominated the intellectual and professional development of sociology for a period of almost half a century.[7] The textbook that Burgess and Park coauthored, *Introduction to the Science of Sociology*, largely determined the direction and content of American sociology after 1921, when it first appeared.[8]

In the 1920s, the Chicago sociology department did a great deal of highly original research in urban ecology, ecology in this context meaning the interrelationship of social phenomena and their environment. The rapid growth of cities in nineteenth-century America had led to the concentration of interest in the city as a sociological phenomenon. Chicago was a rapidly expanding city. Professors in the department were interested in the city and closely connected to it. Ernest Burgess had a large number of contacts with community agencies. Robert Park saw the favorable opportunity for urban study. As early as 1915 he urged the department to take advantage of the research opportunities to use "the city as its laboratory."[9] Under their joint influence "the scholarly output in [urban ecology] was in fact so abundant that the department . . . acquired the reputation for almost exclusively concentrating on spatial distributions in its own city."[10]

In these early years, Burgess developed what later became known as his "zonal hypothesis." He distinguished five zones typically found within a city: (1) a central business zone, (2) a zone of transition (some industry, slums, and first settlement areas), and (3–5) progressively more desirable residential areas. At least for modern, industrial, expanding cities, he hypothesized that newly migrating populations poured into the slums because they were close to available work and were all they could afford. His research showed that as each racial or national group moved into the slum areas—the zones of transition—it experienced severe social disorganization. The characteristic extremes of poverty, disease, and social and behavioral pathology were a product of this social disorganization and not, as was widely believed, a demonstration of the inferior genetic quality of the immigrants.

It is not difficult to see the implications of this approach for the study of criminal behavior or to understand the proliferation of studies dealing with this aspect of urban life. In the 1920s "perhaps the most conspicuous aspect of the reputation of the city of Chicago . . . was the magnitude of its crime."[11] And it was precisely in the zones of transition or "interstitial zones," as Frederic Thrasher called them, that the highest rates of crime and delinquency were found.

Initially research centered on juvenile delinquency. Frederic Thrasher had done a master's thesis on Boy Scouts in 1918. He then began a study of boy gangs, culminating in his 1926 dissertation, "The Gang: A Study of 1,313 Gangs in Chicago." He found a marked tendency for urban juvenile delinquency to occur in groups of boys and for delinquency to be especially prevalent in the interstitial zones of the city.

At about the same time, Clifford Shaw and his associates at the Illinois Institute for Juvenile Research were also doing work on juvenile delinquency. Shaw had done graduate work in the Chicago sociology department, and his work at the institute was a continuation of this effort. He and Henry McKay collaborated closely with Burgess and the Chicago graduate students for almost thirty years.[12]

Burgess characterized Shaw as "the father of modern scientific research in juvenile delinquency."[13] Shaw published several books on the subject, including three which were lengthy life histories of juvenile delinquents. Empirical American sociology was "popularized and transmitted to all corners of the world by the Shaw monographs more than by any other examples of this brand of social research."[14]

Shaw's writings were also based on the "zonal" hypothesis of Burgess. He mapped Chicago and found areas of particularly high incidence of delinquency in the slums.[15] In addition to research, Shaw helped to create the Chicago Area Project in 1934. This was an effort to get members of a community to rebuild community organization in high-delinquency neighborhoods. It was hoped that organized activity and indigenous leaders would lessen the influence of gangs.

While Thrasher, Shaw, and McKay studied the incidence and distribution of juvenile delinquency, John Landesco, a graduate student in the Department of Sociology and a protégé of Ernest W. Burgess, concentrated his attention on adult criminals, in particular those involved in organized crime. His research in this area occupied the major part of his time for nearly eight years and resulted in *Organized Crime in Chicago*, which Mark Haller said in 1967 still stood "alone as a scholarly attempt to understand the social roots of organized crime in an American city."[16] Landesco found that adult criminals were recruited from juvenile gangs in the same slum neighborhoods that had been the focus of attention for Thrasher, Shaw, and McKay. "The gangster," he wrote, "is a product of his surroundings in the same way in which the good citizen is a product of his environment."[17]

The other work carried out at this time that provided important hypotheses and data about a major form of criminal behavior was Edwin Sutherland's *The Professional Thief*, not published until 1937.[18] This work begins with a description of the profession as experienced by one professional thief, but it differs from the "case history" or "life history" documents produced by Clifford Shaw and his associates in a number of significant respects.[19]

In the first place, the structure and organization of the description is determined by the fact that it was elicited in response to questions prepared by Sutherland. Second, the material thus obtained was supplemented by the incorporation of other material derived by Sutherland from some eighty-five hours of discussion with his informant. Third, the resulting document is liberally annotated by Sutherland on the basis of information derived from supplementary sources such as other professional thieves and the representatives of municipal and private police systems. Finally, the descriptive material is followed by two chapters in which certain hypotheses and generalizations suggested by that material are elaborated and discussed.

For the scholar reviewing the work of these pioneers, two curious features emerge. First, this "first fine careless rapture" of seminal ideas was not followed by consolidation and further growth. It is true that Shaw and McKay continued their work, adding to their "massive documentation of empirical regularities,"[20] revising and updating their original material in *Juvenile Delinquency and Urban Areas*, published in 1942; and that after Shaw's death this work too was revised and updated and issued in a new edition in 1969.

But although in the later editions more data, including comparative data and case materials, were added and some changes in theoretical perspective were made, this represented the tending of land already under cultivation rather than the breaking of new ground. Although some work in what is called "the Chicago tradition" has continued in other places, focusing on various theoretical and empirical issues raised in the early years, from Chicago itself no other substantial criminological work in that tradition has emerged since those early years.

The second puzzling thing is that, although the influence of the Chicago pioneers is frequently and even fulsomely acknowledged in innumerable articles and books, no full survey, much less a systematic analysis and evaluation of their work and the nature of their influence on research, theory, and social action, has ever appeared. Indeed, in his introduction to the revised 1969 edition of Shaw and McKay's *Juvenile Delinquency and Urban Areas*, James F. Short draws attention to the piecemeal character of such critical examination as their work has attracted. In a reference to the theoretical continuity and the empirical, logical, and operational adequacy of that work, he remarks: "While attempts have been made to assess one or another of these aspects of Shaw and McKay's work and are scattered in the literature, no comprehensive assessment has been published."[21]

This is not the place nor have we the temerity to take up the challenge implicit in that statement. In this context, it will be sufficient to note some of the salient characteristics of the criminological work carried out during that golden age of Chicago sociology. First, the most striking and pervasive feature is the emphasis on empiricism. Indeed, this aspect of their studies has by some critics been regarded as the Chicago school's greatest weakness.[22] Edward Shils has noted that such works as Thrasher's *The Gang*, Zorbaugh's *The Gold Coast and the Slums*, Reckless's *Vice in Chicago*, and Landesco's *Organized Crime in Chicago* "did not set out to demonstrate any explicitly formulated sociological hypothesis."[23] He points out that they were not engaged in building or testing hypotheses but rather that "they attempted to illustrate with direct, firsthand reports some process or interrelationship which appeared . . . to be of crucial significance in the modern world or in human behavior in general."[24]

There is some truth in this criticism. Yet reluctance to embark on hypotheses, coupled with stress on firsthand observation, accurate description, and careful verification of facts is surely preferable to what is more frequently encountered in the social and behavioral sciences: theory tottering on stilts of sparse facts and gratuitous assumptions. Nor can it be said that any of the writers under consideration were crassly or narrowly empiricist in the sense that they were indifferent to theoretical reasoning and engaged in the mere compilation of factual information guided by no principles of selection.

For example, the notion of the city as a mosaic of separate neighborhoods and cultures enabled them to observe these cultures as others before them had not done. They could view seriously and objectively the culture of gangs or professional thieves, or organized criminals, and analyze each in its own terms. They did not see criminal cultures as necessarily pathological and were able to analyze criminal careers much as other sociologists might analyze legitimate careers. This was a liberating contribution to criminological theory.

Although they appear to have been relatively abstemious when it came to speculative construction, this was not because they were engaged in what Shils calls "aimless and enthusiastic botanizing."[25] It was due to the fact that in their case, theory was controlled by observation rather than observation by theory. As Howard Becker puts it, "The research scheme did not grow out of a well-developed axiomatic theory, but rather from a vision of the character of cities and city life. . . . Everything was material for the developing theory. And studies of all kinds done by a variety of methods, contributed to its development."[26] In relation to social history, J. H. Hexter has remarked that those who "would rather arrive at conclusions than start with them may see some small virtue in a work plan that places the conclusion at the end rather than at the beginning of an investigation."[27] The Chicago work plan possessed that virtue.

It also possessed a corollary virtue—theoretical formulations when achieved were not treated as immutable inscriptions on the tablets in the Ark of the Covenant. Harold Finestone has clearly brought out the way in which Shaw and McKay made shifts in their theoretical perspective as their work progressed because their data resisted analysis in terms of their earlier hypotheses. Thus, beginning with an emphasis on social change and social disorganization as factors in the genesis of delinquency, they moved toward a functionalist position which emphasized relationships between delinquency and more stable features of social structure.[28]

But it is not because of their conceptualizations, suggestive as some of them have proved to be, that the work of Shaw and McKay and their colleagues is so significant; it is because they observed the facts. To give just one example, the importance of association in groups in the genesis of juvenile delinquency, which Thrasher and Shaw and McKay emphasized, was derived from simple observation; yet it is of major significance. Shaw and McKay found that of 5,480 offenders, more than 80 percent had committed their crimes in association with others.[29] The implications of that discovery, both for the interpretation of criminal statistics and the framing of criminal justice policy, have still not been fully recognized.[30]

The second characteristic of the Chicago school is one described by Shils as having fulfilled "a momentously important function in the development of social science."[31] The Chicago scholars pioneered the method of research now known as participant-observation within sociology. Despite their failure to make a "direct contribution to a systematic theory of human behavior and social organization," says Shils, they established "an unbreakable tradition of firsthand observation, a circumspect and critical attitude toward sources of information and the conviction that the way to the understanding of human behavior lies in the study of institutions in operation and of the concrete individuals through whom they operate."[32]

It is impossible to exaggerate the importance of this method. The pursuit of a general theory of human behavior in society made up of "hypotheses fitted into a general system of propositions, internally consistent with one another," may be legitimate exercise, but it frequently leads to the construction of systems in which "the chief intellectual content is an elaborate terminology."[33] Often they are so tenuously related to reality that determining the nature of the relationship becomes itself a new field for study and scholarly research.

At a lower level of abstraction this is no less important. One of the principal reasons Landesco's *Organized Crime in Chicago* stood "alone as a scholarly attempt to understand the social roots of organized crime in America" is that, unlike the vast majority of studies of this topic, it was based on firsthand observation.[34] Landesco had been an immigrant boy on Chicago's West Side, and it was on the basis of extensive contacts with criminal groups in the city that he was able to recognize the roots of organized crime in the culture and social structure of the neighborhoods in which the gangsters had been raised and to reject implicitly the view (held not only by early sociologists but also by members of a presidential task force forty years later) that it represented an exotic import from Southern

Italy. Similarly, Thrasher's *The Gang* had remained for over half a century the most comprehensive and thorough analysis of the phenomenon of juvenile gangs ever written. It is significant that when it was reissued in 1963, James F. Short remarked, "Recent enthusiasm for abstract conceptualization, particularly of varieties of delinquent subcultures, has outstripped the data at hand, and we are badly in need of new empirical studies."[35]

Third, in addition to empiricism and insistence on the importance of firsthand observation, the work of the Chicago school was characterized to a remarkable degree, both in respect to methodology and to the selection of subjects for investigation, by eclecticism. This seems to have been due in part to the fact that Albion Small, who founded the sociology department in 1892 and remained head of it until 1925, unlike other leading sociologists of the time, "had no *idée maîtresse* about the nature of society; he was not committed to any substantive view about the constitution and working of society, and he did not require that his colleagues agree with him about anything other than the need to improve sociology."[36] As a result, Small was an extremely open and flexible head of department and made no attempt to impose or encourage any kind of homogeneous consensus. It is not surprising, therefore, that, as Morris Janowitz notes, "the style of scholarship of the leading members of the Chicago School was exceedingly diverse [and the] school contained theoretical viewpoints and substantive interests which were extremely variegated."[37]

This diversity in style, theoretical orientation, and substantive interest was matched by equal variety in methods of investigation. In addition to quantitative data like census, police and court figures, commitment and recidivism statistics, a great variety of other material, such as cartographic data, official and unofficial documentary evidence, reports of participant observation and interviewing, case histories, and autobiographies, was assembled. Landesco's citation of lists of attendants and pallbearers— including senators, congressmen, aldermen, and judges—at the funerals of gangsters (designed to demonstrate the intimate relations between politics and organized crime) provides a striking example of the utilization of unconventional material. At times it seems almost as though they were collecting data for an exercise in "total history" by some future Le Roy Ladurie. In fact, they produced, as Edward Shils puts it, "a body of knowledge of one large-scale society such as exists for no other society in history."[38]

Finally and, for many of those involved, most importantly, there was from the beginning a firm commitment to social policy issues and social action. "Chicago's poverty and wealth, filth and luxury, agitation and crime, attracted international attention, as did its ill-managed and corrupt municipal government. . . . Albion Small hoped the new discipline of sociology would ultimately serve to improve society. Chicago was an excellent place in which to begin."[39] This commitment was reflected in the early years in such things as Charles Henderson's involvement nationally in prison reform, Robert Park's active role in the Illinois Commission on Race Relations, and W. I. Thomas's membership in the Chicago Vice Commission. The most striking example of the movement "from the ivory tower of academia to the workaday world of high crime-rate neighborhoods" was the Chicago Area Project (or projects), the principal activity of which was the development of youth welfare organizations among residents of delinquency areas and direct work with delinquent individuals and groups.[40]

Writing of McKay, Shaw, and Burgess, Daniel Glaser says, "Not only had these men pioneered in theory and research on juvenile delinquency, but they had also moved via the Chicago Area Project to do something significant about it."[41] It was in these projects that there originated the concept of the marginal worker, which Glaser refers to as "the most important idea in the field of crime prevention and protection."[42] Originally, the marginal workers were people like Shaw and McKay integrating social science with crime prevention activity. But Glaser describes the "ideal marginal worker in delinquency prevention, as originally conceived in the Area Projects" as being "a person who had been involved in delinquency and crime, had been helped by residents in the Area Project in obtaining self-sufficiency in a noncriminal life, and felt committed thereafter to help others make this transition."[43] The marginal worker idea has since been adopted in a variety of delinquency prevention projects under such titles as "gang worker," "extension youth worker," and "street worker."

The decline of criminological studies in the Department of Sociology coincided with the temporary decline of the department itself. The reasons for that decline have never been precisely determined. Edward Shils says, "In the course of time the original vision vanished, and there was left behind a tendency toward the repetition of disconnected investigations . . . busy work, done simply because the data and the labor power were available . . . never acquired the dignity of relevance or significance."[44] Faris, in *Chicago Sociology, 1920–1932*, is, as Janowitz remarks, "politely circumspect about the ending of the period of preeminence."[45] Faris writes of "the aging of the principal members of the second-generation faculty, . . . the pressures and distractions incident to the great depression and the Second World War" and says that "leadership in sociology has become shared more widely with other universities as a more balanced distribution of sociological effort prevails."[46] According to Steven Diner, writing about "the eclipse of the department of sociology" in a final footnote to his account of the first three decades of the department's history,

> Whereas in the first thirty years it had consensus without homogeneity, the next quarter of a century saw the heterogeneity dissolve into conflict which was as temperamental as it was intellectual.[47]

Janowitz writes of "institutional exhaustion . . . partial intellectual exhaustion . . . a failure of self-renewal," and adds, "in part the decline must have been due to personality clashes and to personal rigidities."[48] Janowitz also describes returning to the University of Chicago in 1961 after a decade's absence to find that basic materials had been removed, and that "in other cases, the files were purged of embarrassing materials—that is, revealing documents—by jealous wives."[49] This suggests that any future account of the factors that were at work is likely to be less than fully comprehensive.

Mark Haller has suggested that the strange discontinuity which makes early Chicago criminology appear intellectually stillborn may have been related to a general movement in sociology toward the collection of masses of quantitative data and a growing belief that being scientific meant being statistical. Sociologists came to believe that studies based upon participant-observation could never generate good hypotheses because one never knew whether the cases were typical. Sociologists in general ceased being sympathetic to the methods of the Chicago school, believing them not sufficiently rigorous.[50]

However that may be, the fact is that after the end of the thirties the initial impetus which gave birth to the Chicago school of criminology seems to have been exhausted and the cohesiveness that held so many disparate elements together dissolved. Apart from the revisions and expansions of Shaw and McKay's original work noted earlier, the last work which belongs specifically to that era is Sutherland's *The Professional Thief*.

Sutherland had received a doctorate in sociology at Chicago in 1913 and returned there as a research professor from 1929 to 1935. He went on to become one of the world's leading criminologists, and the influence of his studies in sociological criminology at Chicago is apparent in much of what he subsequently wrote. Karl Schuessler puts it as follows:

> His training there [in Chicago] was largely in the hands of Charles Anderson, Albion Small and W. I. Thomas, whose collective influence is quite evident in Sutherland's earlier writing, with its emphasis on social process. It is also evident in his theory of criminal behavior, which may be regarded as an adaptation of interactional sociology as expounded by W. I. Thomas; it is further evident in his empirical research, which is based on those techniques of careful investigation that came to be known as the hallmark of the Chicago school of sociology.[51]

Yet in an important respect Sutherland's later work represented a substantial break with the past. At some time in the 1930s he became "committed to the principle that the goal of science is general theory applicable to all events of a given class."[52] He therefore set out to devise a complete and full explanation of crime—a general hypothesis that would "fit every case in the defined universe."[53]

The theory he produced—the theory of differential association—seems to have been modeled on physical science, with the process of association being analagous to the action of some form of energy on matter. Human agents are represented as being in a condition of passive plasticity, mechanically responsive to increments of association. Ultimately he found himself in a theoretical impasse from which he candidly admitted he could find no escape. Critics contended that his theoretical model could not accommodate a patently obvious feature of human experience: the existence of individual variations in responsiveness to criminal associations. "In view of the extent of the disagreement," he wrote, "I must be wrong. In fact, I am fairly convinced that the hypothesis must be radically changed. . . . My difficulty is that I do not know what to change it to."[54]

Another student who left the Chicago Department of Sociology, where he did his master's degree in the twenties, to become "one of the towering figures in American criminology" was George Bryan Vold.[55] Vold, whose *Theoretical Criminology* (1958) was quickly accepted as the standard work on theories of criminality and a quarter of a century later is regarded as a classic, was also interested in the possibility of some kind of general criminological theory.

Vold concluded that group conflict theory, which emphasized "the role of the normal antagonisms and conflicts of human groups to one another as the setting for or condition generally explanatory of large areas of criminal activity,"[56] was the most plausible general theory of crime causation. But he was more cautious than Sutherland and more cautious than many contemporary conflict theorists who have used conflict theory to explain all crime.[57] Vold specifically noted that "many kinds of impulsive, irrational acts of a criminal nature" and some "ordinary common-law [offenses] involving persons and property" were unrelated to any conflict between different interest groups in organized society.[58]

Walter C. Reckless, whose *Vice in Chicago* (1933; reprint ed., Montclair, N.J.: Patterson Smith, 1969) was one of the original Chicago "classics," also deserves mention as an alumnus who went on to achieve distinction. His *Crime Problem*, first published in 1950, went into five editions and became recognized as one of the principal American criminological textbooks. It is interesting to note that in the third edition of the book he too (somewhat tentatively) proposed a general etiological theory. "*If criminology must have a general theory*," he wrote, "containment theory is proposed as a theory of best fit to explain the bulk of crime and delinquency" (emphasis added).[59] The theory lacks the clarity and precision of Sutherland's formulation and, unlike the differential association theory, has received little attention from other scholars.

Sutherland, Vold, and Reckless are possibly the most outstanding of those students who finally left Chicago to continue careers in teaching and research elsewhere. But the list of what James Short calls " 'Old Chicagoans' in the sense that they were intellectually nurtured at the University of Chicago and in that city's streets and institutions" would contain the names of a substantial proportion of the leading contributors to the field of criminology in this century.[60]

In 1977, Gilbert Geis and Robert Meier conducted a survey of a sample of persons who had written books or articles heavily cited in the criminological literature during the period 1945 through 1972. Among the half dozen open-ended questions they addressed to these "highly-cited elders in criminology" was one which ran "What academic book/article made the greatest impression on you?" It is significant that "by far the leading response focused on the works of Edwin H. Sutherland . . . and volumes by members of the Chicago school, such as Robert Park and Ernest Burgess."[61]

But while the influence of the Chicago school was diffused and disseminated throughout other centers of teaching and research around America, in Chicago itself there was something of a hiatus until the establishment of the Center for Studies in Criminal Justice at the Law School, which brought about a renaissance of interest and activity in the field of criminology. Between the two ventures, separated in time by more than a quarter century, there was no formal connection, although both in theory and practice some parallels can be discerned.

The Center for Studies in Criminal Justice

In 1937, when the last of the "classic" works from the Chicago school of criminology was published, Norval Morris was attending an Australian grammar school, and the University of Chicago Law School was blissfully innocent of empirical criminology. It was not until the early 1960s that an expanding definition of law-related studies and optimism about the Academy's capacity to change the world generated the center which brought Morris to Chicago.

The 1960s, like the 1920s, were seen as a period of explosive increases in urban crime and violence after some years of relative stability. Crime was becoming an urgent national concern, and in 1965 the Ford Foundation responded by funding a number of university-connected centers to do research on reform and change in the criminal justice system. The Center for Studies in Criminal Justice at the University of Chicago Law School was one of the first to be funded, with an initial grant of $1 million for five years, followed in 1970 by an additional grant at a level of 70 percent of the original grant for a further five years. The initiative in Chicago came principally from Dean Phil C. Neal and Professor Francis A. Allen. Professor Allen was to be closely involved with the center until his departure from Chicago in 1966 to become dean of the Law School of the University of Michigan, Ann Arbor.

The general grant terms indicated that all centers were to use "the capacity of legal education and other disciplines to experiment in the community laboratory with various approaches to needed reforms."[62] There is an interesting echo here of Robert Park's injunction in 1915 that the Chicago sociology department should use "the city as its laboratory." William Pincus, who was with the Ford Foundation when the first grants were made, recalled later: "We hoped applied research would test an idea, come up with a hypothesis, test that out, leave it or adopt it, and move on to something else."[63] Beside the general grant terms, which applied to all the centers, the Ford Foundation expected that Chicago would "at least in the beginning be oriented more heavily toward research and training."[64]

Norval Morris was invited to Chicago in 1964 to found the center and to serve as its first director and as Julius Kreeger Professor of Law and Criminology—the first such joint appointment in the history of the Law School. The author of a number of books and many articles in the fields of criminal law and criminology, he had an international reputation as an authority in both fields.

Morris was born in New Zealand in 1923 and educated at an English public school. After service in the armed forces in World War II he graduated in law at the University of Melbourne, Australia, in 1946. He then did a Ph.D. in criminology at the London School of Economics, where he won the Hutchinson Medal in 1950. Subsequently he taught at the Universities of Harvard, Melbourne, and also Adelaide, where he was dean of the Law School from 1958 and 1961. He had been a member of the United Nations standing committee of experts on the prevention of crime and the treatment of offenders since 1955, and in 1958–59 he served as chairman of the Commission of Inquiry into Capital Punishment in Ceylon. From 1962 to 1964 he was director of the U.N. Asia and Far East Institute for the Prevention of Crime and Treatment of Offenders in Tokyo.

This sparse chronology gives only the skeletal structure that supported an enormous variety of interests and activities in the criminal justice field up to 1964. From 1965, as founding director of the center, Morris shaped its development through the first decade of its existence until his resignation in 1975 to become dean of the University of Chicago Law School. For the benefit of those to whom he is known only through his published works, it is necessary to give some more information about him.

His publications reflect his intellectual vitality, creativity, and range of reference in lucid, lively, and elegant prose. They also display a remarkable ability, not only to deal with current questions, but also to anticipate emerging problems and future developments. In addition, he has combined scholarship with the adoption of a conspicuous public position as a reformer in the fields of law and penology. In that role his unrivaled fluency and skill as a public speaker enable him to capture and hold any audience and to ensure that he is always heard (if not always heeded).

Perhaps the qualities which most impress themselves on those who have worked with him are his immense vitality and buoyancy, the total absence of animus or rancor in disagreement or dispute, and his instant and generous recognition of distinction in others. His commitment to the achievement of efficiency, decency, and humanity in the criminal justice system is unmarked by the humorless unction or insistence on ideological purity that too often disfigure the reformist stance.

Nor is his concern with these matters limited to the production of prospectuses for change. Thus in the course of a study of the Menard State Penitentiary Psychiatric Division in Illinois, he discovered eighteen men who were illegally confined there—in some cases twenty-five years beyond the time they should have been released. It is characteristic of him that he not only sought and obtained their prompt release but also accepted appointment as chairman of a task force to advise the director of the Illinois Department of Corrections on the treatment of psychiatric patients under the jurisdiction of the Department of Corrections.

One of Morris's earliest acts as director of the center was to recruit Hans Mattick, who is the subject of a brief memorial essay at the end of this volume, as associate director. Mattick, as one of his contributions to this volume demonstrates, was inclined on occasion to pessimism. Morris by contrast was, and remains today, essentially optimistic. This difference in temperament led to occasional disagreements—so that a few privileged witnesses now know what does happen when an irresistible force meets an immovable object—but for the most part they were at one, and together made a formidable team.

From the start, as a matter of policy, the administrative staff of the center was kept to a minimum. Here one of the most striking parallels with the Department of Sociology in the 1920s emerges. Just as Robert Park and Ernest Burgess had used students, both graduate and undergraduate, to carry out research into urban crime and delinquency, so Morris and Mattick recruited students to engage in research. Mattick was later to describe the situation as follows:

> [The] Center was located in the law school, the kind of law school with students who are also residential students who, after their first two years of law studies, don't know what to do with themselves and are very eager to gain clinical or field kind of experiences to get away from books and classroom studies. So we had an enormous pool of potential research assistants there, who were bright and highly qualified.[65]

For the first four years of operation Morris and Mattick, together with an administrative assistant and secretarial help, constituted the only full-time staff of the center. During that period, just under one hundred paid students worked for or with the center.

In the fifth year, 1970, one of these students, Wayne Kerstetter, was appointed research associate and administrator of the center. He remained in that position until 1972, when he left to become special assistant to the New York City police commissioner. In the meantime, Franklin Zimring, who as a student had worked with the center from its inception, had been in 1971 appointed associate director. Hans Mattick, codirector of the center since 1968, resigned from that position in 1972 to become professor of criminal justice and director of the Research Center in Criminal Justice at the University of Illinois, Chicago Circle. In 1973, Zimring succeeded him as codirector. Finally, in 1975, when Norval Morris resigned to become the seventh dean of the Law School, Zimring took over as director of the center.

When an institution of this character has been in existence for seventeen years and for the last seven years has been operating successfully under a director of the "second generation," it may be said to have come of age. In the circumstances, it is interesting to consider whether it is possible to discern the development of a tradition or pattern of common ideas comparable with the tradition that grew up in connection with earlier explorations of the criminal justice field in the sociology department.

One resemblance that is apparent is a pervasive emphasis on empiricism in so far as that means a general tendency to regard systems of ultimate answers and great truths with suspicion and a preference for the search for solutions to particular problems. This has been reflected in the fact that research has mostly taken the form of fairly narrowly defined investigations of a highly specific character. It is reflected also in the fact that such policy proposals as have from time to time been made by center scholars have lacked the sovereign sweep of calls for total revolutionary reconstruction of the social order and have rather had the character of piecemeal social engineering programs often referred to pejoratively as "band-aid" measures.

An essentially empiricist approach is also reflected in such studies as Mattick's monumental work on jails, much of Jacobs's writing on prisons, Haller's studies relating to organized crime and the police, Alschuler's pioneering work on plea bargaining, Zeisel's work on sentencing, and Zimring's investigations in the area of firearms and violence. In almost every case, the primary aim has been to find out the facts and consider what inferences can be legitimately drawn from them rather than to seek evidence to support some a priori hypothesis. The parallel with the old Chicago school is close.

This is not to suggest that in any of these cases was the accumulation of evidence achieved by "pure" observation or the totally random collection of data. Both observation and the collection of data are inevitably selective to some degree and are guided by theoretical considerations, however rudimentary. The essential point is, as we have said in relation to the earlier observers, theory was controlled by observation rather than observation being controlled by theory.

Another immediately striking resemblance is that Norval Morris did not espouse any grand, comprehensive theory of a general and systematic nature. Nor did he require that his colleagues or students agree with him about anything beyond the need to enlarge and develop knowledge in the field of crime and criminal justice. This was precisely analogous to Albion Small's attitude in the sociology department, as was his hope that any knowledge achieved might have some practical application and ultimately lead to social improvement.

Morris believed neither that there was any uniquely correct method of investigation nor that absolute priority should be assigned to a particular area of inquiry. He was ready to consider any imaginative proposal or hypothesis, and this is reflected in the considerable diversity in style, subject, and method of treatment in the studies listed in the center's bibliography. The essays included in this volume alone reflect the fact that the center's pattern of thought and action has been no less eclectic than the earlier tradition.

Finally, the parallel between the two enterprises is exemplified in the continuation of what Edward Shils saw as of momentous importance in the development of social science: the tradition of firsthand observation and participant-observation. Morris's active participation in the administration of both state and federal penal institutions, Jacobs's participant-observation studies in Stateville Penitentiary, Keller's work on halfway houses, Alschuler's and also Kerstetter's work in connection with plea bargaining and both the Legal Services to Youth and the Cook County Jail Legal Aid project—all these in different ways entailed the kind of direct involvement with "institutions in operation and the concrete individuals through whom they operate" to which Shils refers.[66]

While these similarities are significant, collation of this kind may give a misleading impression. It was not the case that the center stood for a revival of the old-time sociological religion nor did its output consist merely of a réchauffé of earlier insights. What it did stand for can perhaps best be defined by considering it in relation to the dominant ideology or orthodoxy in criminological circles in the mid-1960s when the center was set up.

The nature of that orthodoxy is well described by James Q. Wilson in *Thinking about Crime*, and it is, as he says, clearly reflected in the 1967 report of the President's Commission on Law Enforcement and Administration of Justice together with the task force reports dealing in detail with the topics covered in the main report.[67] In describing what he refers to as "the criminological perspective" or "the general perspective of criminologists" in that period, Wilson notes three dominant themes.

First there was a shared belief in the importance of "searching for the causes of crime . . . a commitment to causal analysis." Second, there was an almost entirely uncritical acceptance of "the rehabilitative (or reformation) theory of corrections," or "the treatment ideology." Third, there was the failure to give serious attention to deterrence and, on the part of many criminologists, the repudiation of "deterrence (usually described as 'punishment') [as] of no value."[68]

It is significant that in his inaugural lecture for the Julius Kreeger Chair of Law and Criminology delivered at the University of Chicago on 16 May 1966, Norval Morris challenged each of these canons of orthodoxy. He spoke ironically of "the expensively outfitted and numerous safaris that have searched for the source of criminality."[69] He discussed at length the limits of the rehabilitative ideal, reminding his audience that five years previously "at this law school . . . I tried to sketch the dangers of abuse of human rights from assumptions of power for rehabilitative purposes."[70] He opened his "broad theoretical statement of position" by stating, "We need more knowledge of the efficacy of our various penal sanctions in their deterrent and educative roles" and went on to emphasize the "compelling need" for deterrence research.[71]

This was more than inaugural rhetoric. At the time of Morris's speech, a series of studies and empirical soundings in deterrence was already under way with Franklin Zimring as principal investigator having been initiated a few days after the center was established in 1965. Work in this area resulted in a variety of publications listed in the Cumulative Bibliography.[72]

Morris later developed the case against criminological research into the causes of crime more fully and explicitly, and no searches for that particular Holy Grail were ever supported by the center.[73] In subsequent articles and finally in a book *The Future of Imprisonment* (Chicago: University of Chicago Press, 1974) he developed and refined his ideas on the "rehabilitative ideal" (in his words, "coerced cure") and the theory and practice of imprisonment. The book included a chapter detailing a plan for an institution for repetitively violent criminals in the drafting of which many center scholars assisted. In 1976 a federal correctional institution was opened at Butner, North Carolina, with a program incorporating key elements of the Morris model.[74]

Another area in which prevailing views were challenged was that of organized crime. Orthodox ideas on the subject centered around the notion of a nationwide Italian crime syndicate known as the Mafia operating in the major American cities and controlling the most lucrative rackets. As the report of the President's Commission on Law Enforcement and Administration of Justice put it:

Today the core of organized crime in the United States consists of 24 groups operating as criminal cartels in large cities across the Nation. Their membership is exclusively Italian. . . . Recognition of the com-

mon ethnic tie of the 5,000 or more members of organized crime's
core groups is essential to understanding the structure of these groups.
. . . Organized crime in its totality thus consists of these 24 groups
allied with other racket enterprises to form a loose confederation
operating in large and small cities."[75]

Those who worked on this subject at the center reviewed the evidence and
reached very different conclusions. In the first year of the center's existence,
historian Mark Haller began the research into organized crime, the products
of which are listed in the Cumulative Bibliography and exemplified in two
articles in this volume.

It was not the case, of course, that all criminologists at that time accepted
the conventional wisdom or that there were no exceptions to the general
perspective. The new, or radical, criminologists were developing a critique
of current criminology on ideological grounds. Their view is expressed in
Richard Quinney's *Criminology: Analysis and Critique of Crime in America*:

Contemporary criminology is closely tied to the state's interests. . . .
Seeking a critical understanding and questioning the legal system have
traditionally fallen outside the dominant ideological and scientific interests of most criminologists. The liberal ideology underlies most research and theory in contemporary criminology. These liberal values
are translated into the kinds of research criminologists conduct, the
theories they construct and the way in which they are ideologically
tied to the state. Criminologists then are the ancillary agents of political power.[76]

The center by contrast supported a quite different type of questioning on
scholarly grounds.

Mark Haller has suggested that if the center scholars were guided by any
common idea it is simply that they were all engaged in "an interdisciplinary
questioning of received wisdom."[77] Certainly there was no common manner
or content of thinking that characterized those who came together at the
center. No systematic body of concepts or series of integrated assertions
ever emerged. And although there was considerable collaboration in ideas,
there was a large degree of specialization in subject matter.

It has to be said that in the early years there were some concessions to
fashion and current vogues. What was called "action research" in some
cases might better have been termed "inaction research." The Probation
Officer—Case Aid Project, the center's longest and most extensive demonstration and research project, did not produce results commensurate with
the investment in time and resources. Two other unsuccessful projects—
Cook County Jail Legal Aid and Legal Services to Youth—demonstrated
that the provision of legal aid services does little to ameliorate fundamental

social inequity. It also proved that measurement of the consequences of introducing those services was beyond the center's capacity. The truth is, while it is no part of the function of universities and similar institutions to celebrate the status quo or encourage complacent conformism, they are ill equipped for curing social ills.

However, examination of the center's second annual report, dated 31 August 1967, makes it clear that the pursuit of criminological chic was not an overriding preoccupation. The projects mentioned were only three out of a total of sixteen listed in the report as either in process or having been completed. The list included, as well as the research activities into jails, halfway houses, deterrence, and organized crime already noted in passing, work on capital punishment, compensation to victims of crimes of violence, continuances in criminal courts, the operation of the 1964 Criminal Justice Act in the federal district courts, indigent appeals, and misdemeanor arrests. The report also records Dr. Georg Stürup's stay at the center in the 1966–67 academic year as a visiting scholar. During his stay, in addition to participating in research and teaching programs relating to mental illness and criminal law and delivering the 1966 Issac Ray Lectures at the University of Pennsylvania, Dr. Stürup wrote *Treating the Untreatable* (Baltimore: Johns Hopkins Press, 1968) and *Treatment of Sexual Offenders in Herstedvester, Denmark* (Copenhagen: Munksgaard, 1968).

Nineteen sixty-seven also saw the beginning of research into violence and into the use of the death penalty. This led to the publication in 1968 of the first of a series of studies on gun control by Franklin Zimring and the first of Hans Zeisel's studies on capital punishment. In 1967, too, Professor Johannes Andenaes came from the University of Oslo to collaborate with Zimring in the deterrence project. I came to the center for the first time from the University of Sydney in that year for the same purpose and began a series of biennial visits which has continued to the present day. Albert Alschuler also joined the center for a year from the University of Texas to work on a study of plea bargaining, which was to be the subject of further research by Wayne Kerstetter in the 1970s.

By the end of the first five years, the center had been involved in a total of twenty major research projects reflected in all the subject headings in this volume, with one exception, sentencing, which did not become a major preoccupation until the 1970s. In addition, more than a hundred books, monographs, articles, reviews, and other fugitive pieces written by persons associated with the center had appeared. By 1982, the total publications had risen to three hundred fifty.

This proliferation of papers and books is itemized by topic in the Cumulative Bibliography. The headings reflect the areas in which the center has been involved in research, in many cases from the very beginning. The Bibliography is included not in the belief that bulk is beautiful or that quantity is an acceptable substitute for quality, but so the reader whose interest is stimulated by any of the pieces reprinted here may pursue that interest further.

The way in which the center has developed over the years cannot plausibly be presented as the fulfillment of a master plan. The center's current mode of operation owes something to fortuity. It is also the outcome of institutional evolution which, like biological evolution, depends on adaptation to environmental conditions to ensure survival.

The crucial problem is to assemble the critical mass necessary to sustain the kind and scale of criminal law–related research so far carried on at the center. This would not be possible if the only source of interested and qualified research professionals were the Law School faculty. At the same time, without major foundation support, the permanent full-time employment of resident professionals is not possible.

Since 1965, however, a formidable body of criminal justice scholars have spent periods in residence as research associates, research fellows, visiting fellows, and visiting scholars engaged in a number and variety of research projects which defy the systematizer's ordering skill. Many of those who first came to the center as research associates in the course of or after completing doctoral work in law or social science have gone on to faculty positions at other universities and have since returned here for varying periods as fellows. Those who have "graduated" in this way include Albert Alschuler (Colorado), Richard Block (Loyola), Richard Frase (Minnesota), James Jacobs (Cornell), Wayne Kerstetter (Illinois), Michael Tonry (Maryland), Thomas Weigend (Max Planck Institute), and Franklin Zimring (Chicago).

At a more senior level, overseas practitioners and scholars from all round the world have come to the center as visiting scholars and fellows for periods from three months to a year. Such visitors have included, in addition to those already mentioned, Mr. Atushi Nagashima from the Ministry of Justice, Tokyo; Dr. Dusan Cotic from the Institute for Criminology and Criminological Research, Belgrade; Dr. Kurt Weiss from the Sociological Institute at the University of Saarland, Germany; Professor Richard Harding from the University of Western Australia; Jan van Rooyen from the University of South Africa, Pretoria; and Mr. Zen Tokoi, director of the United Nations Asian and Far East Institute for the Prevention of Crime and Treatment of Offenders, Tokyo.

Not all of those who have visited and worked at the center continue to be associated with it. But many have maintained close and continuous research ties, and it is this group of affiliates who constitute the body of fellows of the center. They are physically in residence only on an occasional and sporadic basis, so there is no group photograph. But in so far as an institution consists of the individuals who compose it, they together with the faculty fellows are the center.

Since the termination of Ford Foundation funding in 1975, the center's financial position, in a period of considerable fiscal difficulty for all institutions of higher education and research, has not been notably secure. But a combination of public and private support and assistance from the university have ensured the center's continued existence. A good deal of work has been done in cooperation with other research and policy planning agencies (e.g., the Vera Institute of Justice, the National Institute of Mental Health, the Twentieth-Century Fund, the National Institute of Law Enforcement and Criminal Justice, the National Institute of Corrections, the Police Foundation, and the Rand Corporation). Without such interinstitutional collaboration, the scale of the center's activities would have required a large permanent staff and space needs inconsistent with living within the Law School.

This vignette would be incomplete without brief mention of two publishing ventures. In 1971 the center established with the University of Chicago Press a series of book-length publications devoted to criminology and criminal justice entitled "Studies in Crime and Justice." The series was established so that significant contributions of lasting value to scholarship in this area would achieve maximum impact. To date sixteen books have been published, and they are listed at the back of this volume, which is itself the sixteenth in the series.

The other venture, *Crime and Justice: An Annual Review of Research*, is a series dealing with research developments in the field of criminal justice which commenced publication in 1979. Edited by Michael Tonry and Norval Morris, guided by a distinguished editorial board, funded by the National Institute of Justice, and published by the University of Chicago Press, five volumes have so far appeared. For each volume, essays by leading scholars, including many center fellows, are commissioned. In the main, they have been summaries of the "state of the art" on defined topics together with the author's views on policy and research implications. But the review is intended also to include essays of a more idiosyncratic, speculative nature dealing with analytic or conceptual topics and novel lines of enquiry. The contents of the volumes in this series are also set out at the end of this book.

The selection for inclusion in this volume of a mere handful of items from the mass of material produced over seventeen years by persons associated with the center is inevitably an invidious task. Even if all those persons are insusceptible to envy or resentment, it should be said that inclusion in this selection is not intended as an accolade for the authors whose work is represented. Little familiarity with academic life is required to raise doubts about the association between publication and wisdom, as well as that between wisdom and social significance.

In the process of selection no attempt has been made to ensure conformity with a unitary theme or synthetic editorial vision. What is present here is a sampler of specimens that, despite their common provenance, reflect no shared social philosophy or ideological commitment. If there is a discernible affinity of attitude or style, it derives from a common concern with matters of social policy rather than from an agreed agenda for social action.

The reader who hopes to find here definitive answers to key problems posed by crime and the operations of the criminal justice system will be disappointed. On the other hand, he or she may be relieved at the absence of suggestions that the development of a "new consciousness" or the "negation of the established order" would provide a certain solution for all social problems.

The contributions to this volume deal in the main with concrete particulars rather than elevated generalities. They are principally concerned with factual enquiry and the search for knowledge at the empirical level. In the pursuit of criminal justice the attainment of such knowledge is no less important a precondition of effective action than in any other field of human endeavor.

Notes

1. Norman Mailer, *Miami and the Siege of Chicago* (New York: New American Library, 1968), 85.

2. Ibid., 90.

3. Personal communication from Professor Mark H. Haller, Dept. of History, Temple University, 23 November 1980.

4. Donald R. Taft and Ralph W. England, Jr., *Criminology*, 4th ed. (New York: Macmillan Co., 1964), 180.

5. James F. Short, Jr., ed., "On Criminology and Criminologists: Continuity, Change, and Criticism," in *Delinquency, Crime, and Society* (Chicago: University of Chicago Press, 1976), 1.

6. Mark H. Haller, Introduction to John Landesco, *Organized Crime in Chicago*, (1968; Chicago: University of Chicago Press, Midway reprint, 1969), vii. It should be added that Haller now says, "Today I am not so trusting of available statistics as I was when I wrote that. The statement may well be true, but I'm more agnostic" (see note 3 above).

7. Morris Janowitz, Introduction to W. I. Thomas, *On Social Organization and Social Personality* (Chicago: University of Chicago Press, 1966), vii.

8. Robert E. L. Faris, *Chicago Sociology, 1920–1932*, with a Foreword by Morris Janowitz (Chicago: University of Chicago Press, 1970), 37.

9. Robert E. Park, "The City: Suggestions for the Investigation of Human Behavior in the Urban Environment," *American Journal of Sociology* 20 (1915): 577.

10. Short, "On Criminology and Criminologists," 51.

11. Ibid., 72.

12. Ernest W. Burgess and Donald J. Bogue, eds., *Contributions to Urban Sociology* (Chicago: University of Chicago Press, 1964), 591.

13. Ibid.

14. Ibid.

15. See especially Clifford R. Shaw and Henry D. McKay, *Juvenile Delinquency and Urban Areas*, rev. ed. (Chicago: University of Chicago Press, 1969), 171–75.

16. Haller, Introduction to Landesco, *Organized Crime*, vii.

17. Landesco, *Organized Crime*, 221.

18. Edwin H. Sutherland, *The Professional Thief* (Chicago: University of Chicago Press, 1937).

19. E. G. Clifford, R. Shaw, and Maurice E. Moore, *The Natural History of a Delinquent Career* (Chicago: University of Chicago Press, 1931); Clifford R. Shaw, Henry D. McKay, and James F. McDonald, *Brothers in Crime* (Chicago: University of Chicago Press, 1938); Clifford R. Shaw, *The Jack-Roller* (1930; reprint, Chicago: University of Chicago Press, 1966).

20. James F. Short, Jr., Introduction to Shaw and McKay, *Juvenile Delinquencies*, xxvii.

21. Ibid., xxvi.

22. James F. Short, Jr., Introduction to Frederic M. Thrasher, *The Gang*, abridged ed. (Chicago: University of Chicago Press, 1963), xxi.

23. Edward Shils, *The Present State of American Sociology* (Glencoe, Ill.: Free Press, 1948), 10.

24. Ibid.

25. Ibid., 64.

26. Becker, Introduction to Shaw, *The Jack-Roller*, vii.

27. J. H. Hexter, *Reappraisals in History*, 2d ed. (Chicago: University of Chicago Press, 1979), 25.

28. H. Finestone, "The Delinquent and Society: The Shaw and McKay Tradition," in *Delinquency, Crime, and Society*, 23–49.

29. Clifford R. Shaw and Henry D. McKay, "Social Factors in Juvenile Delinquency," in National Commission on Law Observance and Enforcement (Wickersham Commission), *Report on the Causes of Crime*, vol. 2 (Washington: U.S. Government Printing Office, 1931), 195–96.

30. See, however, Franklin E. Zimring, "Kids, Groups and Crime: Some Implications of a Well-Known Secret," *Journal of Criminal Law and Criminology* 72 (1981): 867–85, reprinted here as chap. 18.

31. Shils, *The Present State*, 11.

32. Ibid., 11–12.

33. Ibid., 55, 57.

34. Haller, Introduction to Landesco, *Organized Crime*, vii.

35. Short, Introduction to Thrasher, *The Gang*, xxiii.

36. Steven J. Diner, "Department and Discipline: The Department of Sociology at the University of Chicago, 1892–1920," *Minerva* 13 (1975): 550.

37. Janowitz, Introduction to Thomas, *On Social Organization*, vii.

38. Shils, *The Present State*, 11 n. 8.

39. Diner, "Department and Discipline," 521–22.

40. Daniel Glaser, "Marginal Workers: Some Antecedents and Implications of an Idea from Shaw and McKay," in Short, *Delinquency, Crime, and Society.* Solomon Kobrin, "The Chicago Area Project: a 25-Year Assessment," *Annals of the American Academy of Political and Social Science* (March 1957): 19–29.

41. Glaser, "Marginal Workers," 154.

42. Ibid.

43. Ibid., 260.

44. Shils, *The Present State*, 11.

45. Morris Janowitz, Introduction to Faris, *Chicago Sociology*, x.

46. Faris, *Chicago Sociology*, 132.

47. Diner, "Department and Discipline," 553 n. 78.

48. Janowitz, Introduction to Faris, *Chicago Sociology*, x.

49. Ibid., xii.

50. Haller, personal communication, 23 November 1980. On this see also Fred H. Matthews, *Quest for an American Sociology: Robert E. Park and the Chicago School* (Montreal: McGill-Queens University Press, 1977), 179–80.

51. Karl Schuessler, Introduction to Edwin H. Sutherland, *On Analyzing Crime* (Chicago: University of Chicago Press, 1973), x–xi.

52. Schuessler, editorial note in ibid., 6.

53. Sutherland, *On Analyzing Crime*, 17.

54. Ibid., 25.

55. Donal E. J. Macnamara, "George Bryan Vold, 1895–1967," in George B. Vold, *Theoretical Criminology*, 2d ed., prepared by Thomas J. Bernard (New York: Oxford University Press, 1979), ii.

56. Thomas J. Bernard, in ibid., 282.

57. Richard Quinney, *The Social Reality of Crime* (Boston: Little, Brown, 1970).

58. Vold, *Theoretical Criminology*, 292, 296.

59. Walter C. Reckless, *The Crime Problem*, 3d ed. (New York: Appleton-Century-Crofts, 1961), 356.

60. Short, "On Criminology," 1.

61. Gilbert Geis and Robert F. Meier, "Looking Backward and Forward: Criminologists on Criminology, as a Career," in *Criminology: New Concerns* (Beverly Hills, Cal.: Sage Publications, 1979), 179.

62. Robert B. Goldman, "Helping the Law Do Its Job," Centers of Criminal Justice Project Evaluation (New York: Ford Foundation, 1970, mimeographed), 2.

63. Ibid., 1.

64. Ibid., 5.

65. John H. Laub, "Dialogue with Hans W. Mattick," *University of Toledo Law Review* 10 (Winter 1979).

66. Shils, *The Present State*, 11–12.

67. James Q. Wilson *Thinking about Crime* (New York: Basic Books, 1975), 43–63. See also President's Commission on Law Enforcement and Administration of Justice *The Challenge of Crime in a Free Society* (Washington, D.C.: U.S. Government Printing Office, 1967).

68. Wilson, *Thinking about Crime*, 53, 54, 55, 60.

69. Norval Morris, "Impediments to Penal Reform," *University of Chicago Law Review* 33 (1966): 631.

70. Ibid., 638.

71. Ibid., 627–28, 631–35.

72. See in particular Franklin E. Zimring, *Perspectives on Deterrence* (Washington, D.C.: National Institute of Mental Health, 1971); Franklin E. Zimring and Gordon Hawkins, *Deterrence: The Legal Threat in Crime Control* (Chicago: University of Chicago Press, 1973); and Johannes Andenaes, *Punishment and Deterrence* (Ann Arbor: University of Michigan Press, 1974).

73. Norval Morris and Gordon Hawkins, *The Honest Politician's Guide to Crime Control* (Chicago: University of Chicago Press, 1970), 45–53.

74. U.S. Department of Justice, Federal Prison System, *Federal Correctional Institution, Butner, North Carolina* (Washington, D.C.: U.S. Department of Justice, 1981).

75. President's Commission on Law Enforcement, *The Challenge of Crime*, 192–93.

76. Richard Quinney, *Criminology: Analysis and Critique of Crime in America* (Boston: Little, Brown, 1975), 13.

77. Haller, personal communication, 23 November 1980.

One   Corrections

1 Street Gangs behind Bars
James B. Jacobs (1974)

Social Organization of the Prison

The social organization of the prison has attracted the attention of sociologists since Clemmer (1958) published *The Prison Community* in 1940. In that work he emphasized the isolation of the "fish" arriving at prison and the gradual socialization into the inmate subculture through association with primary groups. Later students confirmed the identity stripping impact of the total institution upon the convicted individual and pointed to the functional importance of participation in primary groups as a solution to crucial situational problems, material and psychological (Garabedian, 1963; Goffman, 1961; McCorkle and Korn, 1954; Sykes, 1958).

Sykes and Messinger (1960) account for the structure and character of the inmate organization by reference to the special problems of adjustment found behind the walls. Three crucial problems are noted: social rejection, material deprivation, and sexual frustration. In response to these institutional pressures there emerges an inmate organization characterized by a code which embraces a deviant perspective in "solidary opposition" to conventional values and institutional goals. This code allows the individual to maintain a favorable image of self and to avoid identity collapse by providing a rationale which enables him to reject his rejectors (McCorkle and Korn, 1954). The inmate social system is also described as a system of interrelated roles and functions which enables the inmate to order and to classify experience within the walls in terms which deal specifically with the problems of prison life (Sykes, 1966).

In recent years, however, several students have shown that the solidary opposition theorists have paid too little attention to the importance of organizational goals in accounting for the uncooperative and oppositional character of the inmate code (Grusky, 1959; Berk, 1966; Street, Vintner, and Perrow, 1966). They have demonstrated that where organizational goals have shifted from custody to treatment, the inmate normative system

"Street Gangs behind Bars" appeared in *Social Problems* 3, no. 21 (Winter 1974): 359–409. Reprinted with permission of the Society for the Study of Social Problems and the author.

The research was carried out under a Ford Foundation grant. Grateful acknowledgment is made to Norval Morris and Barry Schwartz for their enthusiasm and guidance in this research.

would also shift to a perspective favorable to staff and organizational goals. Rather than being socialized within the prison to reject the formal organization, those inmates committed to smaller treatment institutions would become socialized into an increasingly favorable orientation.

While this suggestion of "solidary cooperation" contradicted the solidary opposition theory, it was easily subsumed under the more general theory of "indigenous influence." The proponents of solidary cooperation, like those of solidary opposition, accepted the fact that socialization through primary groups into inmate perspective based upon situational variables was the standing explanation for inmate attitudes, values, and behavior.

An alternative to the indigenous influence theory itself was offered by Irwin and Cressey (1964), who found some support in Clemmer and Schrag for the proposition that criminal dispositions and behavioral patterns before prison have strong explanatory power in accounting for inmate behavior. These authors urge us to focus great attention upon pre-institutional behavior patterns.

> Like thieves, legitimate people are not necessarily stripped of outside statuses and they do not play the prison game. They bring a set of values to prison and don't leave them at the gate . . . it seems a worthy hypothesis that thieves, convicts and do-rights all bring certain values and behavior patterns to prison with them, and that total "inmate culture" represents an adjustment or accommodation of these three systems within the official administrative system of deprivation and control. (Irwin and Cressey, 1964:241)

This exploration of inmate norms and behavior in terms of extra-prison variables has been termed a theory of "cultural drift" (Schwartz, 1971). Further force has been lent to this theory by the work of Giallombardo (1966), who explains sexual adjustment in a woman's prison by the sex roles prevalent in the wider society. Both Irwin and Cressey and Giallombardo make use of the Becker-Geer (1960) distinction between manifest and latent culture. Those authors argue that latent culture develops in anticipation of a social system in which the individual is not currently participating. An individual may therefore orient his behavior inside prison according to norms internalized while on the street.

The indigenous influence theory of inmate culture informs the rehabilitative model of the prison in much the same way as Merton's anomie theory provides a theoretical rational for "welfare state" programs of crime prevention through expansion of economic opportunity (Gouldner, 1970). If the behavior of the prisoner can be entirely explained in terms of the institutional environment in which he is placed, then the right mix of institutional policies and programs would produce a rehabilitated individual whose favorable disposition toward formal organizational goals would augur well for his later return to the community.

The policy implications flowing from the theory of cultural drift are far more pessimistic. The cultural drift theory casts doubt upon the potential of penal institutions for converting their clients. General acceptance of this theory would force the society to support its prison system with a rationale other than that of rehabilitation. The study reported here lends further support to the cultural drift theory. It suggests that in Illinois prisons the inmate organization is best understood as an extension of an identical organization imported from the streets of Chicago.

The Study

This study was undertaken at Stateville Penitentiary between June and October, 1972. Located 30 miles from Chicago, Stateville is a typical walled-in maximum security penitentiary holding approximately two thousand inmates. The writer operated as a known observer for the entire peirod of the study. Contact was established with many gang leaders as well as with independents or "off brands." Formal interviews were conducted with key members of prison staff and of the Illinois Department of Correc-tions. Most of the time was spent interacting informally with inmates on their jobs, in their cells, and in the prison yard.[1] The most basic division of the inmate population is by race. Blacks account for 70 percent of the population; Latins contribute 10 percent; and whites 20 percent. From the outset of the fieldwork, special focus was placed upon the most salient aspect of the informal organization—the existence of four Chicago street gangs as viable organizations behind the walls.

Three of the gangs are black; one in Latin. Among the black gangs, the Black P. Stone Nation is undoubtedly the best known to the public due to the extensive publicity given to the trials of the leadership for extortion of federal anti-poverty funds. The Stones are extremely well organized and of the four gangs comes closest to constituting a professional criminal syndi-cate. On the streets of Chicago's South Side, as well as within the prison, the Disciples are the chief rivals of the Stones. At Stateville both groups claim some 400 adherents. The Disciples are far more loosely organized than the Stones, having fewer members in their late 20's and 30's, and account for more disciplinary infractions than any of the other gangs. The conservative Vicelords is an old gang associated with Chicago's West Side and especially with the Lawndale area (Keiser, 1969). In the late 1960's the Vicelords earned national attention for their efforts to clean up their community and to pioneer various small business ventures. Within Stateville there are between 150 and 200 Vicelords. Their organization is well disciplined; authority has remained firmly in the hands of several of the older original members. Rarely are Vicelords involved in serious disciplinary violations. The latter finding also holds true for the Latin Kings, which despite small numbers within the prison (30), is one of the largest gang federations in Chicago. At Stateville the Kings are extremely closely knit and at times also serve as spokesmen for all Latin inmates.

The Gangs

The four gangs active at Stateville are parts of the largest street gangs in Chicago. All of them can be characterized as lower class gangs, territorially associated with Chicago's most dilapidated slum areas. Consistent with Thrasher's (1926) observations of one-half century ago, we find that on the streets these gangs are simultaneously involved in a wide variety of activities, including gang fighting, mugging, armed robbery, extortion, drug trafficking and, more recently, various legitimate business ventures and involvement in anti-poverty programs.

There can be no doubt that the existence of the gangs in the prison is inextricably tied to their continued viability on the street. Informants repeatedly emphasized that, were the gangs to dissolve on the streets, they would immediately disappear from the prison. It was recalled that various other gangs, having small followings at Stateville, evaporated when the parent gang became absorbed by a different group.

Gang fights on the streets are immediately felt behind the walls. A news report of a killing involving Disciples and Stones on Chicago's South Side at once raised the tensions of members at Stateville. Visits from ranking gang members, often under disguise, are frequent. Even more frequently, families carry information about the gang to and from the prison. In the last five years the influx of gang members has been so great that a communication link between street and prison has been established merely through the steady commitment of members.

Within the prison the visibility of the gangs is extremely high. Each gang vigorously affirms its own identity through symbolic representation. Members "represent" to one another by esoteric salutes and verbal greetings. Gang colors and insignias are won on sweat shirts, t-shirts, and as tattoos.

Under the rubric of "political prisoners," "revolution," and "white racism," the four gangs demonstrate a rudimentary solidarity opposed to white society, white administration, and white inmates. While the young gang members have for the first time placed the older cons in fear of physical security, they have also brought into the prison a rebellious attitude toward all authority. Little distinction is made between various control agents. In fact, within the prison the security staff is referred to as the "police." Black (and Latin) consciousness and the political implications of incarceration have become salient issues. In contributing to the transformation of a group of inmates "in itself" to a group "for itself," the gangs can be said to have begun to politicize the prison.

Socialization and Recruitment

The "gang thing" is the most significant reality behind the walls. The unaffiliated convict enters prison fearing that his life may be in danger from the gangs. Even if he is not immediately concerned with survival, he will face the prospect of being shaken down for commissary and sex. The security staff can be of little help in protecting him. In one way or another, a strategy must be carved out for dealing with the gang situation. Often the young white inmate may become a "punk" for one of the gangs. Some whites, the "crazy motherfuckers," have been able to maintain physical security because of demonstrated fighting ability; others because of supposed connections with organized crime.

The Latin Kings and Vicelords, skeptical of penitentiary members, do not recruit in the prison, but the Stones and Disciples recruit vigorously (as they do on the streets). Frequently solicitation will be forceful; it is often highly sophisticated. The fish will be confronted by both a "hard" and a "soft" sell.

In contrast to the recruitment pressures experienced by the unaffiliated convict, the gang member from the street has no trouble whatever in adjusting to the new environment. As the warden of Pontiac Penitentiary told me: "When a new guy comes up here it's almost a homecoming—undoubtedly there are people from his neighborhood and people who know him."[2] The chief of the Disciples claims to have known 75 Disciples upon arrival at Stateville. A young leader of the Latin Kings explained that because of his position in the Kings he knew all but two of the Kings upon arrival. The first afternoon he received a letter from the ranking chief welcoming him into the family.

B.P., chief of the Vicelords, explains that when a young Vicelord is spotted coming into the prison, he will see to it that the man is set up immediately with coffee, tea, deodorant, and soap. Visitors and correspondents will be arranged for those Vicelords deserted by their families. Normally the gang member will have the situation run down for him by his cell house chief. This orientation can be quite elaborate. Evidence the following written rules circulated by the Disciples:

    I. Degradation of another Disciple will not be tolerated at any time.
    II. Disrespect for any Governing body of said cell house will not be permitted.
    III. There will not at any time be any unnecessary commotion while entering the cell house.
    IV. Homosexual confrontation toward another Disciple will definitely not be tolerated.
    V. Dues will be paid up on time at any designated schedule.
    VI. Fighting another Disciple, without consulting a Governing chief will result in strict disciplining.

  VII. Upon greeting another Disciple, proper representation will be ascertained.

 VIII. There will never be an act of cowardice displayed by any Disciple, for a Disciple is always strong and brave.

   IX. There will not be any cigarettes upon entering the hole for those who relentlessly obstruct the rules and regulations of the organization, or the institution.

    X. Anyone caught perpetrating the above rules and regulations with disorder and dishonesty, will be brought before the committee and dealt with accordingly.

The parallel between these rules and "inmate code," often described as prescribing solidarity among cons and opposition to staff, is striking. That the inmate code can be accounted for by reference to the norms of certain criminal subcultures is precisely the thesis advanced by Irwin and Cressey (1964).

Services Performed by the Gang for its Members

Besides physical security, the gang in prison, as on the street, serves important material and psychological functions for its members. To some degree the organizations function as buffers against poverty within the institution. Each gang has a poor box. Cell house chiefs in each of the gangs collect cigarettes from the members and store them for those who have legitimate need. When a member makes a particularly good "score" or deal, he is expected to share the bounty with the leaders and to donate to the poor box. While skeptical independents claim that these boxes are often depleted and that many benefits do not filter down to the soldiers, this observer has often seen the leaders giving away cigarettes. Furthermore, when a gang member is placed in isolation, he can always expect cigarettes and food to be passed to him.

    The organizations function as a communication network. If McCleery (1960) is correct in asserting that a crucial concern of the convicted man is the lack of information about institutional decisions, then the organizations do function to keep their members informed and to place a coherent definition on the situation on all events within the institution. By having their soldiers assigned to jobs in the administration building, as runners, as yard gang workers, and as house help, the gangs insure that information can flow from front to back with great precision.

    The gangs provide a convenient distribution network for contraband goods. One Latin King informant explained that where an independent might hesitate to attempt a score fearing that he might be unable to secrete the stolen items, a gang member knows that within a number of minutes he can divest himself of the major share of the contraband.

The role of the gangs in organizing illicit activities is unclear. What is clear is that no illicit activities operate within the prison without the tacit approval of the gang leaders. Gang affiliation enables the young inmate to establish connections in the illegal trafficking and to muscle in on any independents not already paying off to one of the other gangs.

By far the most important function which these four organizations play at Stateville is the psychological support they provide for their members. Whether one subscribes to the theories of Cohen (1955) or Miller (1958) in accounting for the origin of delinquent gangs, the important point here is, as Thrasher (1963) noted, that the gang serves as a membership and reference group providing the delinquent with status and a positive view of self, G.B., leader of the Disciples, explained:

> These guys in my branch [of the Disciple federation] are closer to me than my own family. Anything I do around them is accepted—for stuff that my parents would put me down for, these guys elevate me to a pedestal.

Over and over again inmate informants, gang members and off brands, expressed the opinion that the gangs provide a source of identification, a feeling of belonging and an air of importance.

> It's just like a religion. Once a Lord, always a Lord. Our people would die for it. Perhaps this comes from lack of a father figure or lack of guidance or from having seen your father beaten up and cowering from the police. We never had anything with which to identify. Even the old cons like me—they are looking for me to give them something they have been looking for for a long time.

Gang members consistently explained that on the street and within the prison, it is the same—the gang allows you to feel like a man; it is a family with which you can identify. Several informants soberly stated that the organization is something, the only thing, worth dying for.

The organizations, with their insignias, colors, salutes, titles, and legendary histories provide the only meaningful reference group for their members. Within the organizational framework the soldiers are allocated definite roles and can aspire to successive levels of status.

Soldiers and Indians

For soldier, or "indian," incarceration is not a career break. To the contrary, role requirements are more stringent in the prison than they were on the street, since in the prison the indians are under the 24 hour scrutiny of their leaders. Indeed, they are in some cases presented with their first opportunity for associating with the revered chiefs. This highly open or visible situation transforms the prison setting into an especially fateful field of action, when status can be more easily won and lost. The indian who represents well and "takes care of business" can earn a title or promotion in rank (to cell house chief's assistant, for example). He is also rewarded by access to the inner circles, where he will be close to the chiefs, privy to inside information, and even come to be recognized as a kind of chief himself by his peers. B.P. explained to me:

> Last week one of our chiefs was caught with a knife in his cell. Since we needed him out in the population one of the young Vicelords volunteered to take the weight for it. He went before the Disciplinary Court and was given 15 days isolation time, a Blue Shingle, and recommended to staff for loss of good time. Because of the Blue Shingle he cannot go to the commissary to buy the stuff he needs, but all he's got to do is ask because we're going to see to it that he gets anything he wants.

An indian may be rewarded for carrying out such tasks as providing starched clothes for the chief or being reliable in conveying messages. Much depends upon the particular organization. The Vicelords would not accord status to the senseless use of violence against inmates or staff but would reward a member who was helping his brothers learn to read. In the Disciples, status might be otherwise allocated.

Indians do not and are not expected to relate to the staff. Extensive interaction with security or professional personnel would be suspect for an indian, although expected behavior for a chief. The rank-and-file members are simply not responding to the administration. Instead, the prison experience is more likened to a game where status is accorded to the individual who continues to act in prison the part he was playing on the streets.

"Gang banging" is a popular activity for gang members on the street as well as in the prison. This activity, as defined by whites and off brands, refers to "rip offs," extortion, bullying, and general harassment by groups of gang members.

While the leadership does not necessarily approve of gang banging and often discourages it, they do not like to be placed in the position of policing their followers. To do so places the leader in an uneasy position. On the one hand, the administration questions their sincerity with respect to advancing prison reforms when their followers are involved in gang banging activities. On the other hand, the indians are doubtful about their leaders' effort to bridge the gap with the administration and are restless with the politics of negotiation. To be sure, the leaders cannot altogether afford to disregard the attitudes of their followers. The latter must be indulged or the chief may find his own influence waning at the expense of an ambitious rival.

Leaders and Chiefs

Leadership is of crucial importance for the gangs. The leaders form the nucleus without which the group would cease to exist. They provide role models for the indians and serve as the most significant others, both inside and outside the prison. In practical matters too, the leaders play an important part in the day-to-day life of the average member.

In contrast with the indigenous influence theory, which explains prison leadership as arising within the context of situational contingencies, Irwin and Cressey (1964) argue that each of the inmate subcultures, do-rights, convicts, and thieves, generate their own leadership. The thief leader has the most influence on the behavior patterns of the institution because the norms and values which he brings into the prison from the criminal subculture are respected by convicts and thieves alike. When it comes to exerting influence with respect to institutional concerns, however, the convict leader runs things. The important point is that this view shows leadership being imported into the prison.

At Stateville no clearcut division of the informal organization into do-rights, thieves, and convicts was observed. Yet it is clear that the leaders among the inmates are the same individuals who held high positions within the gangs on the street. There is no example at Stateville of an inmate leader who is not also a gang leader. It is also true that when a higher ranking chief is committed to the institution, he must immediately assume command. There is no doubt in the mind of any informant, for example, that if Jeff Fort, supreme leader of the Black P. Stone Nation, were to be transferred to Stateville, the other chiefs of the Stones would step aside.

The chiefs of the four organizations tend to be older than the rank-and-file member. B.P. of the Vicelords, for example, is 37. He was one of the founders of the organization and an almost legendary figure in the eyes of the younger Vicelords. Several of the chiefs have chosen to remain in the shadows and to assert their authority only during private conservations with their inner council. This strategy is thought necessary in order to prevent harassment from the prison officials. Of course, in the case of celebrities like Jeff Fort, rank in the gang is already well known.

Berk (1966) has found that inmate leaders within the maximum security prison tend to be more aggressive individuals. Schrag (1954:139) noted that the "institutional adjustments of leaders are marked by significantly greater numbers of rule infractions, including escapes, fights and assaults." At Stateville neither of these propositions is supported. The chiefs are distinguished by their reliance upon wits rather than fists. For visible and invisible leaders alike, involvement in serious disciplinary infractions is rare. Indeed, their disciplinary records are in many cases exemplary. This underscores the sophistication of their leadership and their lack of concern for such prison luxuries as can be illicitly procured.

The gang leaders evince little interest in those rewards, legal or illegal, which can be gained in prison.[3] Many times the leaders have explained that there is nothing within the penitentiary which they want. Extra commissary, pressed clothes, and movies are not taken seriously. As one old con remarked: "From the administration's point of view, what's wrong with these young gang bangers is that they do not program."

In summary, the patterns of leadership exhibited behind the walls have been directly imported from the streets. The leadership among the inmates at Stateville is in no way dependent upon accommodation with staff or upon a good job within the formal organization. Nor, as Clemmer found, is the influence of leadership merely restricted to small primary or friendship groups.[4] On the contrary, the most salient characteristics of inmate leadership at Stateville is its autonomy from situational variables and its influence over large secondary groups.

Inter-Gang Relations

Unaffiliated inmate observers have found it remarkable that gangs which have been killing one another for years on the Chicago streets have been able to cooperate under the extraordinarily demanding prison conditions. G.B., leader of the Disciples, has told me that the murderer of his mother is reputed to be among the inmates at Stateville but that he has taken no action to learn the individual's identity. For him to pursue a personal vendetta against a member of a rival gang could only result in the most disastrous consequences under the present circumstances of total confinement. There is an absolute consensus among the leadership that "international war" must be avoided at all costs. The victors of such a confrontation could only be the custodial staff, thought to be anxiously awaiting the day on which they can drag out their heaviest artillery. Quarrels among inmates or between inmates and staff have been repeatedly quelled by the gang leaders in an attempt to forestall what is foreseen as another Attica. Even those off brand observers hostile to the gangs have attributed the absence of a major riot at Stateville to the coolness of the gang leadership.

Any fight beween two or more members of rival gangs can have explosive repercussions. Thus, the leaders have developed a list of international rules to which all of the gangs have pledged to abide.The rules include the following:

I.   There will be no rip-offs between organization members.
II. Each organization must stay out of the other organizations' affairs. In a dispute between members of two organizations, members of a third are to stand clear and to attract no attention.

III. No organization will muscle in on a dealer already paying off to another organization.

IV. Organizations will discipline their own members in the offended party's presence.

V. Organizations cannot extend their protection to non-members.

At the time of this study (a long hot summer), the Disciples did not feel that the international rules had been equally supported. In two cases Disciple chiefs disciplined (by administering beatings) their own members who were wrongfully involved in disputes with members of other organizations. But when the situation was reversed and the Disciples were the offended party, the Stones did not discipline their members. Consequently the rules held only ambiguous authority.

Most of the disputes within the prison occur between the Stones and the Disciples, the rival street gangs on Chicago's South Side. When such conflicts do occur, the leaders have been extremely effective in forging solutions, often by agreeing to give up their members for a head-to-head fight. During the negotiations, the chief of the Vicelords often plays an important mediating role, acting as go-between for the two sides. To both sides is stressed the need to prevent the indians from jumping off and initiating a major riot.

Impact of the Gangs upon Informal and Formal Organizations

While the basis for the gang leader's authority is his position on the street, neither he nor his lieutenants and followers remain aloof from institutional concerns. The chiefs attempt to control or to receive recognition from every area of the prison society. Actually the gang leaders have no coherent program and no real objectives which they seek to achieve within the prison. A clinical counselor at Stateville explained:

> What the gang leaders want is a moderately confortable existence for their people within the prison and an opportunity to maintain their ties with the gang on the street as well as to promote their gang identity within the prison.

No area of prison life has remained unaffected by the mass influx of gang members. In contrast to the rational control exercised by the gangs and their leaders in preventing the outbreak of a gang war is the displacement of the old informal organization dominated by Stateville's old politicians and merchants. Given the prospect of cutting the gang members in or going out of business, many of the old cons active in the prison rackets chose to retire. To date the gangs themselves have not stepped in to organize these rackets. Dealers explain that this is due to a lack of finesse in gang members who do not know how to manuever inside the prison. They further claim that there has been an absolute decline in the quantity of contraband trafficking since the gangs have taken over.

Moreover, the smooth running accommodation system formerly existent at Stateville, as elsewhere (Sykes, 1966), has broken down. Since influence within the informal organization is no longer dependent upon formal organizational support, the staff's leverage has deteriorated. That one of the most powerful gang leaders cannot get into the T.V. college program is evidence of the demise of the accommodation system. Furthermore, in attempting to understand this situation, it should be emphasized that the values of the white rural staff and the black urban gang member may also contribute to breakdown in communication and accommodation.

Life for the off brands have also been considerably altered by the presence of the gangs. A young, tough, and aggressive black inmate noted:

> You must respect what the hierarchy says. If they ask for a work stoppage, for example, you'd have to stop work or be badly beaten.

A 50 year old con-wise black inmate echoed the same opinion:

> The gang leaders have absolute control. T could just have told his men to tear it [Stateville] down and they would—a lot of these guys would die for their gang—dying doesn't mean anything to them. They'd rather die than let it be said that they wouldn't go all the way.

The rising importance of the gangs in the late 1960's was not lost upon several old cons who chose to join them as the best means of adaptation. The gangs accepted these men for their knowledge of prison ways and their readiness to be "fronted off." That is to say that these individuals were willing to serve as spokesmen for the gangs and to mediate with staff. The exchange provided the gangs with visible fall guys in case of an administrative crackdown and provided the old cons security, some degree of status, and an opportunity to continue exploiting the prison situation. However much importance these members appear to have in the prison, they have no regular rank within the organizations and could claim no place within the organization on the street.

Where the chiefs feel that their organizations and members will be benefitted by prison policies, they have not hesitated to support and work with the administration. B.P., Vicelord chief, points out that many of his people are deficient in reading and arithmetic skills. Remedial programs in that direction have been strongly supported by the organizations. The Stones have been particularly active in encouraging their members to get into the high school program. ALAS, a bilingual program for Spanish inmates, is the most advanced and successful program at Stateville today. The federal monies and academic talent assembled for this program were originally obtained through the efforts of a leading Latin King. Only the vigorous support of the Kings' leadership accounts for the success of ALAS.

As has been traditional at maximum security institutions, Stateville inmates are assigned to jobs in such areas as prison industry, yard maintenance, barber shop, laundry, and hospital. The smooth functioning of these work assignments is dependent upon the support and approval of the gang leadership. Each gang assigns one member on each job assignment the responsibility for reporting on all inmate and staff developments. The Disciples require these reports to be in writing and utilize a code to refer to Disciples, rival gang members, and staff. Where voluntary rehabilitation programs in such areas as drug abuse, vocational training, and education are evaluated negatively, they will not be patronized. One professor from a nearby junior college, who brought an automotive training program into the prison, reports that in the first few months he was approached by various gang members who candidly told him that they were checking out his program. The much touted group therapy program at Stateville had not attracted a single gang member at the time this study was carried out. This is not surprising. To the extent that the individual turns his attention inward, his commitment to the group is undermined. Group therapy shores up the definitions of the prison as an experience of *individual* adjustment, adaptation, introspection, and rehabilitation. Contrariwise, the gang promotes the definition of prison experience as a group response and group adaptation.

The dominance of the gangs at Stateville has posed grave challenges for the administration and especially for the security officers. The authority of the line officer has been sharply undermined. Today it requires a lieutenant to carry out responsibilities which a line officer could have handled five years ago. When, for example, an officer decides to "walk" an inmate to isolation for a disciplinary infractions, it is not uncommon for the inmate gang member to refuse to go.

> The inmate will say "fuck you, Jack, I'm not going." Then several members of his gang will gather around him. I'll have to call a lieutenant. Often one of the gang leaders will just come over and tell the man to go ahead.

The custodial staff see their influence eroding in inverse proportion to the increasing influence of the gang leaders. This is a cause for low staff moral and increased tension.

To date the administration had not formally recognized the existence of the gangs (for example, by assigning them a role within the formal organizational structure), although informally it has been essential to take them into consideration. One key administrator of the reform administration stated:

> I tried to deal with the gangs when I was superintendent. The gangs are here and they must be recognized. The leaders have tremendous power. No doubt they could inflict terrible damage upon the place if they wanted to. They have not done it so far because there is nothing to get out of that kind of thing.

Custodial and administrative personnel, as individuals, have also had to deal with the gangs. In numerous cases the chief guard has called the leaders to his office to discuss problems with one of their soldiers. In one situation he called to his office one of the Latin King chiefs to discuss the difficulties which a Spanish inmate (not a King) in the commissary was having with inmates pressuring him to steal for them. The chief was able to speak with several other leaders, and the problem was resolved in a couple of days. In another case a Disciple refused to go to isolation and locked himself in his cell. The chief guard called the Disciple leader to his office and discussed the potentially explosive consequences of the situation. Subsequently the leader went to the cell of the irate soldier and talked to him about the pros and cons of provoking a violent confrontation with staff: "If you think it's important enough, then we won't let them take you." The next morning the gang member went peaceably to isolation.

The point is that the gangs have been able to force their definition of the situation onto the lower levels of the staff. What the gangs are demanding is recognition of the legitimacy of their organizations and leadership hierarchies. The chiefs want it to be formally recognized that they have the right and the responsibility to intercede and speak in the name of their followers. When for several months a rudimentary inmate council, Project ABLE, was operating, the gang leaders agreed that the most important aspect of Project ABLE was that is allowed them the mobility to circulate through the prison, collecting information from their people which could be brought to the attention of the staff. The functioning of Project ABLE, thoroughly dominated by the gang leaders, certainly marked the high water point of the gangs' efforts to force their definition of the situation onto the formal organization of the prison.

The full ramifications of the mass jailing of Chicago street gang members and leaders have still not been felt on the streets of Chicago. Within the prison bitter enemies with long histories of warfare have learned to cooperate with one another. Certain leaders speculate about the development of a grand alliance and the rise of a Black Mafia to challenge the syndicate for control of Chicago vice. Other leaders have become increasingly convinced of the need to channel the energy of the gangs into political action. From behind Stateville's walls, the Latin Kings hammered out a treaty which produced six months of peace among all Latin gangs in Chicago in 1971. The details of that treaty were many months in the drafting, and the final execution of the agreement involved the coordinated visits of numerous gang leaders to Stateville. Such episodes underscore the need for further research on the relationships between prison and community.

Conclusion

Mathiessen (1966) has criticized the sociological literature of the prison for its inordinate concentration upon the similarities of all total institutions and for its inattention to the interrelationship between total institution and wider society. This exploratory report has highlighted an unusual development within Illinois prisons. It suggests that the inmate organization cannot be understood in terms of "indigenous prerequisites." By emphasizing the *importation* of organization, roles, and norms from the streets of Chicago, support has been offered for the Irwin-Cressey theory of cultural drift.

Within Stateville Penitentiary, gang members remain oriented toward the same membership group and leadership hierarchy as they did before having been committed to prison. Rather than experiencing a collapse upon passing through the gates, they have maintained the same self-identity conception as they held upon the streets. To the extent that adjustment needs to be made to the contingencies of incarceration, the adjustment is a group rather than an individual phenomenon.

No conclusion should be drawn from the above description of Stateville's social organization that similar developments have occurred in other states with different social, economic, and ethnographic patterns. Indeed, it is a central argument of this paper that the relationship between the social organization of the total institution and the surrounding society needs to be much more deeply explored. Comparative research on the prisons of states in other regions remains to be done.

Notes

1. The difficulties encountered by a white researcher attempting to carry on participant observation within the tense and racially charged atmosphere of a maximum security prison cannot be minimized. The fact that access to the prison had been arranged by Professor Norval Morris, a strong advocate of prison reform whose liberal positions were well known to the inmate leadership, was a considerable advantage. From the outset the researcher maintained a position of complete honesty about the purposes of his research. Contacts with the security guards were cordial but kept to a minimum. Every effort was made to earn the confidence of the gang leadership. The legal background of the research proved to be a valuable asset in establishing an informal exchange relationship with key informants. In addition, several times during the research the writer was able to intercede with the administration on behalf of inmates, thereby enhancing his credibility.

2. Contrast this statement with Goffman's (1961:14) sober view of initiation into the total institution.

> The recruit comes into the establishment with a conception of himself made possible by certain stable social arrangements in his home world. Upon entrance, he is stripped of the support provided by these arrangements. In the accurate language of some of our oldest total institutions, he begins a series of abasements, degradations, humiliations and profanations of self. His self is systematically, is often unintentionally, mortified. He begins some radical shifts in his moral career, a career composed of the progressive changes that occur in the beliefs that he has concerning himself and significant others.

3. Compare this with Goffman's (1961:48–60) discussion of the privilege system which is said to structure the routine of the total institution.

4. Clemmer (1958) characterized leadership as unstable and as emerging only within the context of the primary group.

References

American Friends Service Committee. *Struggle for Justice.* New York: Hill and Wang

Becker, Howard S., and Blanche Geer. 1960. "Latent Culture: a note on the theory of latent social roles." *Administrative Science Quarterly* 5 (September): 304–13.

Berk, Bernard. 1966. "Organizational goals and inmate organization." *American Journal of Sociology* 71 (March): 522–24.

Bettleheim, Bruno. 1947. "Individual and mass behavior in extreme situations." In *Readings in Social Psychology.* Edited by Eleanor Maccoby et. al. New York: Holt, Rinehart, and Winston.

Clemmer, Donald. 1958. *The Prison Community.* New York: Rinehart and Co.

Cohen, Albert K. 1955. *Delinquent Boys: The Culture of the Gang.* Free Press.

Erickson, Gladys. 1957. *Warden Ragen of Joliet.* New York: E. P. Dutton and Co.

Galtung, Johan. 1961. "Prison: the organization of dilemma." In *The Prison.* Edited by Donald R. Cressey. New York: Holt, Rinehart and Winston.

Garabedian, Peter G. 1963. "Social roles and processes of socialization in the prison community." *Social Problems* 11 (Fall): 139–52.

Garrity, Donald L. 1961. "The prison as a rehabilitating agency." In *The Prison.* Edited by Donald R. Cressey. New York: Holt, Rinehart and Winston.

Giallombardo, Rose. 1966. *Society of Women: A Study of the Women's Prison.* New York: Wiley.

Goffman, Erving. 1961. *Asylums.* Garden City, New Jersey: Anchor.

Gouldner, Alvin W. 1970. *The Coming Crisis of Western Sociology.* New York: Basic Books.

Grossner, George P. 1958. "The role of informal inmate groups in change of values." *Children* 5 (January–February): 25–29.

Grusky, Oscar. 1959. "Organizational goals and the behavior of informal leaders." *American Journal of Sociology* 65 (July): 59–67.

Irwin, John, and Donald Cressey. 1964. "Thieves, convicts, and the inmate culture." In *The Other Side.* Edited by Howard S. Becker. New York: The Free Press.

Keiser, Lincoln. 1969. *The Vice Lords: Warriors of the Streets.* New York: Holt, Rinehart and Winston.

Mathiessen, Thomas. 1966. "The sociology of prisons: problems for future research." *British Journal of Sociology* 17 (December): 36–379.

McCleery, Richard. 1960. "Communication patterns as bases of systems of authority and power." In *Theoretical Studies in Social Organization of the Prison.* New York: Social Science Research Council.

McCorkle, Lloyd, and Richard Korn. 1954. "Resocialization within the walls." *The Annals of the American Academy of Political and Social Sciences* 293 (May): 88–98.
Miller, Walter B. 1958. "Lower class culture as a generating milieu of gang violence." *Journal of Social Issues* 14 (Summer): 5–19.
Morris, Norval, and Gordon Hawkins. "Attica Revisited: The Prospect for Prison Reform." *Arizona Law Review* 14 (1972): 747–63.
Reckless, Walter. 1956. "The impact of correctional programs on imates." *British Journal of Delinquency* 6:138–147.
Roebuck, Julian. 1963. "A critique of 'Thieves, Convicts, and the Inmate Culture.'" *Social Problems* 11 (Fall): 193–200.
Royko, Mike. 1971. *Boss*. New York: The New American Library.
Schrag, Clarence. 1954. "Leadership among prison inmates." *American Sociological Review* 3 (Fall): 11–16.
———. 1961. "Some foundations for a theory of corrections." In *The Prison*. Edited by Donald R. Cressey. New York: Holt, Rinehart and Winston.
Schwartz, Barry. 1971. "Pre-institutional vs. situational influence in a correctional community." *Journal of Criminal Law, Criminology and Police Science* 62:532–43.
Short, James. 1963. "Introduction" In *The Gang*. By Frederick M. Thrasher. Chicago: The University of Chicago Press.
Short, James, Ray Tennyson, and Kenneth Howard. 1963. "Behavioral dimensions of gang delinquency." *American Sociological Review* 28 (June): 411–28.
———. 1972. *Emerging Rights of the Confined*. South Carolina Department of Corrections.
Street, David, Robert Vinter, and Charles Perrow. 1966. *Organization for Treatment*. New York: The Free Press.
Sykes, Gresham. 1958. *The Society of Captives*. New York: Atheneum.
Sykes, Gresham, and Sheldon Messinger. 1960. "The inmate social system." *Theoretical Studies in Social Organization of the Prison*. New York: Social Sciences Research Council.
Thrasher, Frederick M. 1963. *The Gang* Chicago: The University of Chicago Press.
Tittle, Charles R. 1969. "Inmate organization: sex differentiations and the influence of criminal subcultures." *American Sociological Review* 34 (August): 492–505.
Wheeler, Stanton H. 1961. "Social organization in a correctional community." *American Sociological Review* 26 (October): 697–712.
Wilson, Thomas P. 1968. "Patterns of management and adaptations to organizational roles: a study of prison inmates." *American Journal of Sociology* 74 (September): 146–57.
Yablonsky, Lewis. 1970. *The Violent Gang*. Baltimore: Penguin Books.

2 The Prosaic Sources of Prison Violence

Hans W. Mattick (1972)

It is, perhaps, gratuitous to assert that those who have been convicted of breaking the law are most in need of having respect for the law demonstrated to them. We are, moreover, a generous people who are fond of the notion that the law includes more than a narrow legalism—" . . . for the letter killeth, but the spirit giveth life." In that view, which we all share in our more virtuous moments, the law approaches the Platonic ideal of the good, the true and the beautiful. It is a wonderful vision where the law embodies all that is moral, all that is humane, all that is decent and all that is civilized. But, in the age of Pendleton, Attica, San Quentin—and all the tragic rest, it may be instructive to inquire how some of those who act on our behalf have sometimes demonstrated respect for the law to those who have been convicted of breaking the law.

It may also be instructive to try to trace some of the correlates of prison violence—what are popularly referred to as "the causes" of violence—and to do it in such a way as to transcend the usual banalities. Neither the simpleminded conspiracy theories, involving inside or outside agitators, that the old-line penal administrators are so quick to espouse, nor the standard complaints that inmates put forward during the course of riots, are in themselves, sufficient explanations. These are important and, perhaps, necessary conditions, but they are secondary because they are constants in the prison situation. They have been present from the beginning of our experience with incarceration, and they are present today, but prison violence fluctuates sporadically and independently of these constants. Much more fundamental is a contradictory complex of utilitarian and religious ideas of 18th and 19th century origin, which have been slowly debased into a melange of 20th Century "high school thought," and now serve as the basis for our penal policy. It is, for the most part, a policy of isolation and punishment, accompanied by the rhetoric of rehabilitation, which results in the chronic underfinancing, inadequate staffing, deflected sexuality, and

"The Prosaic Sources of Prison Violence" first appeared as number 3 of *Occasional Papers*, published by the Law School of the University of Chicago (1972).

This paper is based upon a presentation made by Hans W. Mattick at a symposium, "Law and Order," held 1 February 1972 in Los Angeles. The symposium was organized by the Law Alumni Association of Los Angeles.

general lack of resources and poverty of imagination that characterizes our prisons and jails. But, these too have been constants for the past 200 years and cannot, of themselves, explain sporadic fluctuations in prison violence. If such conditions were both necessary and sufficient, the Nazi concentration camps would have been less one-sided in their violence, and in a continuous state of revolt. We know that was not the case. To try to explain prison violence, we must penetrate below the surface and get to more fundamental structures and processes.

The massacre at Attica has captured the public imagination, at least for a little while; but as bloody as it was, it is by no means the most calculated use of deadly force in a prison disturbance in recent years. That dubious distinction belongs to Pendleton. One can understand the fear, anger and disorganization at Attica, with the lives of hostages seemingly at stake and no clear chain of command to control the situation, without condoning the tragic consequences; but there can be no moral justification for what happened at Pendleton. A short account of "the Pendleton incident" was given in the January-Feburary 1970 issue of the *N.C.C.D. News*, an organ of the National Council on Crime and Delinquency:

> According to Bruce Nelson, of the *Los Angeles Times*, on September 26, 1969, "12 white men fired repeated volleys of buckshot through a fence [at the Indiana State Reformatory] at young black men who were lying on their stomachs. They killed one and wounded 46. Very few people around the country seemed to notice." Shortly before the shooting, several hundred inmates had congregated in a fenced-in recreation area. They had several demands, including the right to read black literature and to wear their hair in the "Afro" style. Their most important demand was the release of four black inmates who, for unclear reasons, had been isolated. . . . The guards told inmates in the recreation area to leave the vicinity. Many, including all the white inmates, did so. The black inmates asked to present their grievances to [the Superintendent who] refused to talk to the inmates. On the other side of a chain-link fence were 11 white guards and at least one vocational teacher, dressed in riot helmets and carrying loaded shotguns, according to Nelson. The confrontation continued for about 10 to 15 minutes. No attempt was made to disperse the crowd with tear gas, smoke bombs or nearby fire equipment. The guards fired warning shots and then, at the command of the Captain . . . the guards began firing through the fence. . . . One witness said that some of the men were trying to rise from the ground, raising their hands in a gesture of surrender, but were told by the guards, "you've had your chance," and were shot down. After the shooting, the men were told to leave the blood-spattered court, and did so, carrying the wounded. Two men were left lying on the pavement. One of the two . . . was dead. Of the 46 wounded, estimates of those seriously injured run from eight to twenty.

It may be added that a second inmate died about five months later and, although this story was covered in the *Los Angeles Times*, some 3,000 miles away, the Chicago newspapers, only 170 miles away, failed to mention it. For sheer coldbloodedness, Pendleton far surpasses the emotion-packed atmosphere of Attica.

Such seemingly one-sided incidents of prison violence, unless they are directed against the authorities, receive very uneven news coverage and slip easily from the memory if, indeed, they ever entered it. But that does not mean they are rare occurrences. Perhaps a more recent "incident," that happened after Pendleton and before Attica, will help reinforce this point. The following account was given in the April 1971 issue of *Civil Liberties*, an organ of the American Civil Liberties Union:

> The mass beatings and shootings of inmates at a Florida prison have led to a massive A.C.L.U. lawsuit alleging violations of federal civil rights law and state law. . . . On February 12, about 500 prisoners were peacefully assembled in the prison yard by order of the prison officials. Guards and other officers, according to the complaint, fired on them "at point blank range," with absolutely no warning or provocation. The guards then fired into the windows of occupied cells. Five days of beatings and tear gassing of prisoners followed. At one point, officers opened fire into the windows of the prison hospital.

It might be added that February 12th in 1971 was a Friday, followed by a weekend of Saturday and Sunday, which, combined with an "emergency," is the best of all reasons to close down an institution and keep all outsiders out. A great deal can be done to prepare an institution for public scrutiny in three days.

Again, not a very pretty story and, like the affairs at Pendleton and Attica, not yet finally resolved in the courts. But, if we waited upon court determination before such matters received any comment, some of the most significant events of our time would have years of silence before they came to public notice. The Chicago Panther Party raid, the Kent and Jackson State killings and the My Lai incident, are typical examples. However the blame for violence at Pendleton and Attica may ultimately be fixed, prison violence is clearly not a simple one-sided affair, with the inmates always aggressing against their keepers. Moreover, although we had serious prison disturbances in both Ohio and Oregon in 1968, and two earlier cycles in the early 1950s and the late 1920s, the massive use of deadly force against groups of prisoners in the last three or four years seems to be a new development.

One would have thought that we could have taken notice sooner that something was seriously amiss in the prison system of the United States when such clear desperation signals as the following were manifest to many public and private observers over the past forty years: (1) In 1968, the celebrated Davis "Report on Sexual Assaults in the Philadelphia Prison System and Sheriffs' Vans" was published. (2) In 1967, the President's Crime Commission, among other things, again revealed the appalling state of American prisons and jails. (3) Earlier in the 1960s, there was some desultory, but subterranean, discussion at the Congresses of the American Correctional Association, of the novel punishment methods being used in Arkansas, Florida and Illinois prisons. In Arkansas, the infamous "Tucker Telephone," a hand-operated electric generator that was attached to the genitals of prisoners for punishment purposes, was in frequent use. In Florida, at Raiford Prison, a new use for salt was discovered. Nude inmates, cuffed hand and foot through their cell bars were seated in piles of salt for periods of 72 hours without relief. In Illinois' Sheridan Reformatory, the members of the inmates boxing team were being used as an indirect disciplinary method, while "shock-therapy" was being converted into punishment at the Menard Psychiatric Division. (4) In the 1950s, the inmates at Rock Quarry Prison in Georgia were breaking each other's legs with 20 pound sledgehammers to achieve transfers, and at Angola Penitentiary in Louisiana, prisoners were crippling themselves for life by cutting their Achilles' tendons in a vain attempt to call attention to their conditions of imprisonment. (5) In 1931, the Wickersham Commission revealed the appalling state of American prisons and jails. (6) That was the year after 317 inmates of the Ohio State Penitentiary died, locked into their cells, in the course of a fire, said to have been set by rioting inmates, although there is some debate about whether the riot began before or after the fire. But, enough is, perhaps, too much. It is clear that violence is no stranger to the prison environment.

With the potential for violence being such a characteristic feature of prison life, it may be a vain pursuit to seek for developmental patterns and explanations in what appears to be a constant. If there is a "pattern," it is a subtle and emergent process that must be stated in tentative terms. Nevertheless, looking back over the past 40 years, prison violence, like a huge, malignant amoeba, seems to have both shape and direction.

There is, to begin with, a change in the proportionate distribution of violence among the wounders and the wounded. In the earlier period (1930–1960), most of the violence was more securely contained within the walls and consisted, for the most part, of assaults between inmates. Then, in descending order of frequency, there were assaults between keepers and kept, self-mutilations by inmates and a few suicides. Except for a few mass disturbances that came to public notice, with few casualties but some property damage, little systematic information about intramural violence exists for the early period.

In the later period (since 1960), self-mutilations seem to have diminished and both suicides and ambiguous deaths, and the proportion of altercations beween inmates and guards, have increased. Rebellious inmates have also had more strenuous and self-conscious attempts to communicate their grievances beyond the walls and have begun to find a constituency there. This is, in part, a natural development of the more general civil rights movement and the reflection on the cumulative number of ex-prisoners in the free community who maintain an interest in prison affairs, e.g., every year about 70,000 prisoners leave the prisons and about 3,000,000 persons pass through local jails; to these must be added the increasing numbers of convicted persons being placed on probation, residents of halfway houses and pre-release centers, persons in community treatment programs, and organized groups of ex-prisoners, like the Fortune Society, which are multiplying rapidly. The guards, too, have begun to seek extramural support for their grievances in the form of incipient unionization, associational alliances with police organizations and attempts to influence civil service regulations.

Population shifts and changes in sentencing procedures have also had an impact on prison violence. Geographically, there seems to have been a slow migration of prison violence in a northerly and westerly direction, as white racism has manifested itself in heretofore less tested regions. The southern prisons, in the earlier period, had a much greater tolerance for violence and a more apathetic public audience for what went on among the nether classes in the prisons, while violence that came to public notice in the north tended to generate more public indignation in passing. Thus, while northern prisons got blacker and blacker, incident to Negro migration, and as the increasing use of probation tended to weed out the less violence-prone and more stable prisoners of both races, an exacerbated level of racial conflict was added to the normal level of violence in the northern prisons while southern prisons were still segregated and able to shield their normal level of violence from adverse public scrutiny. The net effect of these population shifts, changes in sentencing practices and differences in public attitudes was to increase the actual and perceived amount of violence in northern and western prisons, while the amount of violence, actual and perceived, in southern prisons, was largely masked. Moreover, while racial conflict between guards and prisoners has a long contributory history to prison violence, with the inmates getting much the worst of it, as active recruitment of Negro prison staff belatedly gets under way, some interesting and unanticipated cross-alliances become possible. It is too early to try to determine what the relation of these new staffing patterns will be to prison violence; all contingencies are possible, but it will be a period of stress for all concerned.

Thus far, we have taken an external view of prison violence by citing some historical examples, pointing out the changing racial composition of prison inmates, indicating some regional differences and referring to changes in sentencing practices, e.g., non-institutional alternatives, like probation, that also change the character of the residual prison population. Such factors, in themselves, do not explain" prison violence, but they must be understood as contributory elements. We must now place these factors in context and take an internal view of prisons as unisexual, age-graded, total institutions of social control. They are closed communities where real human beings interact in both formal and informal ways, as keepers and kept go through their daily routines. It is in the real humanity of prisoners and guards, and in their mundane routines, that we will find the sources of prison violence.

In any situation where a relatively small group of men control and direct a much larger group, the controllers depend, in a very real sense, on the passive acquiescence of the controlled. Such passivity is purchased by an effective sharing of power. The maintenance of absolute controls requires such implacable social relations that few men are willing to impose them, and even fewer will abide them, for they convert life into death. Prisons are characterized by caste relations where every member of the dominant caste, regardless of personal qualifications, formally rules every member of the subordinate caste, regardless of personal qualifications. Since such personal qualities as intelligence, sophistication, experience, age, strength and energy are differentially distributed among men, regardless of legal status, the formal rules designed to preserve caste relations tend to be subverted. And yet, unless the smaller ruling caste is willing live in a Hobbesian "state of nature," where the hand of every man is potentially raised against every other, and this for every minute of the day, they know they must come to terms, and do so, with some of the conditions set by the more numerous subordinate caste. It is somewhat like the "social contract" that early philosophers said was necessary for men to emerge from the "state of nature."

Thus the prisoners and their keepers strike a complex bargain. It is a tacit, implicit and informal bargain, somewhat ambiguous as to its precise limits and level, and somewhat variable as to time, place, circumstance and personalities, but one that is unmistakably present. Like the exercise of police discretion in the free community, or plea-bargaining in the criminal courts, such informal arrangements tend to be unacknowledged in daily practice, and are denied altogether when their legitimacy is brought into question by the formal requirements of the criminal justice system, but their weight is disproportionate in the normal prison community. If the average penal administrator or guard were asked, "Who's running this prison, anyway?" they would reply with some degree of self-righteous assertiveness, "Why, we are, of course." In the last analysis, they are right; but the last analysis could mean every prisoner is locked in his cell, gagged and straitjacketed; and then some would be perverse enough to breathe at a rhythm of their own choosing. Few penal administrators want to run a prison that way, for in that direction lies inhumanity and death. It is a question of where the line is drawn, and the line must not only be drawn but accepted. Most penal administrators know where the line is drawn, some will acknowledge it, but a few entertain the delusion of absolute control.

Different prisons strike this bargain at different levels of tolerance, depending upon such factors as the kinds of work or programs the administration wants the prisoners to participate in; the amount of intramural mobility imposed by prison architecture on the routine tasks of prison life; the intelligence and sophistication of guards and inmates; corruption through sentimentality, stupidity, laziness, or venality; the external political climate, custom, tradition and the like. These are the human factors in prison life that make life minimally tolerable for all concerned. Once the level of this power-sharing bargain has been fairly well established, it is difficult to change its terms and limits because very complex social relations, and mutual expectations and obligations come to depend upon it. To disrupt these informal relations by sudden or extensive social changes, affecting either staff or inmates, is to disrupt prison life; and such disruptions increase the probability violence.

In the past, when southern prisons were more strictly segregated, and the northern and western prisons still had a racial balance that favored white inmates, prison violence could usually be accounted for in terms of an inadvertent or unavoidable change in the power-sharing bargain. Political elections were followed by key staff changes; groups of prisoners were transferred without notice; the normal turnover of staff and the receipt and discharge of prisoners; the implementation or discontinuance of work assignments or treatment programs; in short, many of the things that had the appearance of the routine could also have very fateful consequences for the informal set of social relations organized around the existing power-sharing bargain. When such routine changes affected important pressure points in the closed prison community, the expectations and obligations of many persons, most of whom were indirectly related to each other, were suddenly disappointed. This would raise the level of tension in an already tense environment, and a precipitating incident that would ordinarily be more easily contained, would be the occasion for a sudden flaring of violence.

How was anyone to know that among the inmates who were discharged a few days ago was, for example, inmate "X," who worked in the officer's dining room and was stealing food which he sold, traded or gave away to others who, in turn, were trading or paying off gambling debts to still others, and so on, *ad infinitum?* Similarly, when Captain "A," a grizzled veteran who knew how to survive the prison environment, finally retired and was replaced by Lieutenant "B," who tried to run the cell-house "by the book," a subterranean chain reaction took place, affecting both guards and prisoners, that required many adjustments. Suddenly a whole host of guards who had been having their civilian clothes cleaned, repaired and pressed in the tailor shop, had to turn to outside cleaning shops. Moreover, the tailor shop inmates who had been rewarded in a variety of ways for their extracurricular work, were denied the capital that enabled them to participate in the internal economy.

Such individual examples are only indicative, and necessarily limited in their ramifications. When group transfers, staff shifts, prison industry contracts, elections that affect the upper echelons of prison administration, or too rapid attempts are made to either "tighten up" or "loosen up" the *status quo*, the results can be very serious. Gambling debts go unpaid, borrowed goods are out of control, lovers are separated, incompetent people lose competent help, political or friendship alliances are broken up, mutual service and communication links are disrupted; in short, the social fabric, real and symbolic, is badly torn.

To an outsider, such events have a pedestrian appearance because he is used to the available alternatives and free choices that a free man can make. If a firm's bookkeeper quits his job, another can be hired; if a grocery store closes, there is another in the next block. Some of the routine disruptions of prison life are somewhat akin to the breakdown of utilities or a transportation strike in the free world. Some persons are affected at once, others experience delayed and indirect effects, but only a few have the resources or alternatives to make long-run substitutions. In the closed prison community, life is driven in on itself; there are fewer alternatives and choices, and people are more directly and intensely related, whether they wish it or not. If the routine changes of prison administration, or external politics, press too frequently or too rapidly on the crucial nerve centers, and disrupt the social fabric in such a way that the power-sharing bargain is threatened at too many points for too many people, the potential for violence is escalated. Moreover, the actual eruption of violence is likely to be delayed because the latent effects of routine changes take time to ramify through the prison's social structure. Much of what has been considered random or "irrational" prison violence is traceable to such routine prison processes that are simply allowed to happen instead of being carefully planned for and skillfully managed. Invariably, when the violence was "explained," the administration invoked conspiracies and the inmates voiced the ordinary grievances about food, sentences, parole policies and the like. Both were right to some degree, because both the conspiracies and the grievances were real; but they were just as real six months ago and, more than likely, would be just as real six months hence. Such "explanations" are more in the nature of rationalizations than a reflection of actual and proximate "causes."

As we approach the present and consider contemporary prison violence, everything that has been said about the power-sharing bargain still has general applicability, but with some important differences. Perhaps most important is the fact that there is a lesser willingness to bargain, and the bargain that is struck, is struck at a much lower level, with fewer benefits for fewer inmates. As, in process of time, the prison population got blacker and blacker, and more Chicano and Puerto Rican as well, the parties to the traditional bargain became more hostile to each other. Much has been said in recent years about a "new breed" of prisoners, and that they are the source of recent violence. A much better case can be made, however, for the existence of an "old breed" of prison guard and penal administrator who have been sheltered, much more than their prisoners, from social changes taking place in the free community. Prisons are isolated, rural, resistant to change and, for the most part, content to remain so. Prisoners are transients who are always upsetting the *status quo*. Moreover, they are more urban, more influenced by current events, more socially aware and naturally concerned about civil rights and the condition of man; but this too is a part of a much wider social movement concerned with equality and justice. Not even the most secure prison can keep it out. A generation ago, penal administrators were deploring the presence of a "new breed" of spoiled and overindulged youthful offenders who were the offspring of permissive parents, and bemoaning the absence of the old, professional safecrackers and con-men who "knew how to do time."

In this perspective, every generation of prisoners has been a "new breed" of prisoners. In addition, in recent years, as an accompaniment to the civil rights movement and dissent over the war in Vietnam, we have responded to social dissent by defining a part of it as criminal. The result has been a new mixture of prisoners, and a new kind of exchange of information among them. Radical ideologists have been thrown together with traditional criminal types, and each has taken something from the other at the margin. Thus, the prisons have been "politicalized," and some of the prisoners convicted of traditional crimes have been furnished with a radical critique of imprisonment and all of society, while some of the more radical social dissidents have been furnished with traditional criminal techniques that may be useful in the furtherance of their objectives. It is a stupid arrangement that the older European countries have learned to handle more astutely by wiser separations among these classes of prisoners. And this new mixture of prisoners is regularly delivered into the hands of a predominantly white, rural, conservative, ruling caste in the prisons; a ruling caste which, for the financial, numerical and philosophical reasons mentioned earlier, is wholly inadequate to the task.

No wonder, then, that there is more intransigence and less willingness to compromise in the informal bargaining processes that make prison life minimally tolerable for all concerned. For a while, the guards and penal administrators were still able to bargain in the traditional way with the decreasing proportion of white prisoners, but that form of power-sharing has come to an end. In the prison situation, where outside race relations are reversed, the white minority feels the mouting pressure of the darker majorities. The choice is getting narrower and the potential for violence is increasing; soon the choices will be only open hostility, repression or compromise. This is one interpretation of what the prisoners at the Tombs, at Attica, and elsewhere, meant when the cry went up: "We want to be treated like human beings." It is also one interpretation of what President Nixon meant when he sent his 13 point directive to Attorney General Mitchell on November 13, 1969, and said, "The American system for correcting and rehabilitating criminals presents a convincing case of failure."

There is today, as there was in 1870, some evidence that we are, at long last, ready to face the prison problem. When such an unlikely group as President Nixon, Chief Justice Burger, Attorney General Mitchell and Senator Hruska, on the one hand, and Senators Kennedy and McGovern and Congressman Mikva and former Attorney General Clark, on the other, can agree on the current necessity for penal reform, there might be some hope. Chief Justice Burger, in his State of the Federal Judiciary message last July said, "If any phase of the administration of justice is more neglected than the courts, it is the correctional systems." Attorney General Mitchell, citing the recommendations of the National Congress on Penitentiary and Reformatory Discipline of 1870, citing the Wickersham Commission of 1931, and referring to the findings of the President's Commission on Law Enforcement and Administration of Justice of 1967, at the National Conference on Corrections held at Williamsburg, Virginia on December 6, 1971, was moved to ask: "What was the result of this century of recommendations?" And he answered: "In state after state, most of the prisons have no programs for correcting prisoners."

So there is recognition in high places that a problem exists. Moreover, recent U.S. Court decisions in Arkansas (*Holt* v. *Sarver*, 2/18/70), Rhode Island (*Morris* v. *Travisino*, 3/11/70), California (*Clutchette* v. *Procunier*, 6/21/71) and Virginia (*Landman* v. *Royster*, 10/30/71), have held longstanding prison practices unconstitutional. Even the Quakers, who had such an enormous influence on the form of American imprisonment, have returned to the drawing board after 200 years. A working party of the American Friends Service Committee recently published a report on crime and punishment in America, entitled *Struggle for Justice* (Hill & Wang, Inc., 1971), in which they said, in effect, "We were wrong and must begin again with a different set of premises."

Santayana has admonished that "Those who cannot remember the past are condemned to repeat it." We have been through such a repetitious cycle once before. In 1870, the National Congress on Penitentiary and Reformatory Discipline has held at Cincinnati, Ohio. It was clear to the best penal minds in the country that we had already reached a serious impasse in our methods of imprisonment. Accordingly, after a thorough review of what was wrong with American penology, this National Congress published the famous Declaration of Principles which was to give rise to a New Penology. We can ascertain some measure of what the participants of the National Congress felt they had accomplished by adverting to the sentiments of Zebulon Brockway, the foremost penal administrator of his day, who was present and active. In 1876 he was appointed Warden of the Elmira Reformatory, the "wonder prison" of the western world. Some seventeen years after the National Congress of 1870, he reflected on its accomplishments and was still able to describe it as "an experience similar to that of the disciples of Our Blessed Lord on the Mount of Transfiguration." Last December, just one hundred years later, we held the National Conference on Corrections at Williamsburg, Virginia. Seventeen years hence, will we, as Santayana admonished, have remembered the past, or will we reflect with Goethe that "There is nothing so frightful as ignorance in action?"

Two   Courts

3   The Offer That Cannot Be Refused
Hans Zeisel (1980)

It is the number of cases that go to trial that primarily determine the workload of a criminal court system. Time spent on cases that are pleaded guilty is measured in fractions of an hour; time spent on preparing and conducting a trial is measured in days and weeks. From the managerial point of view guilty pleas are clearly preferable. From that point of view, the criminal court system of New York City did splendidly in 1973. Altogether, only 2.2% of the arrests were disposed of by trial, an exceptionally low proportion by any comparison. Figure 1 shows how this average varies by the type of crime charged.

Homicide cases were most likely to go to trial, followed by charges of assault and grand larceny. In none of the remaining categories did trial reach the average of 2% of all dispositions. These low trial figures suggest that the system during that year tried hard to obtain guilty pleas. How was that done?

As a rule, as we have seen, the prosecutor offers defendant and his counsel a reduction of the charge and often also a certain sentence. The defendant and his counsel must then decide whether to accept the offer or reject it and go to trial. The calculus involved in this decision is the comparison between what is offered for a guilty plea, the expected sentence after trial if it should end in conviction, and the chance of conviction:

$$\begin{bmatrix} \text{Sentence} \\ \text{after} \\ \text{guilty plea} \end{bmatrix} \quad \text{vs.} \quad \begin{bmatrix} \text{Sentence} \\ \text{after} \\ \text{trial} \end{bmatrix} \quad \times \quad \begin{bmatrix} \text{Likelihood of} \\ \text{being found} \\ \text{guilty at} \\ \text{trial} \end{bmatrix}$$

If the likelihood of being found guilty at trial is high, the difference between the two sentences is all that will matter. If, on the other hand, the defendant considers his chances of acquittal at trial good, then he will choose trial despite the large sentence differential.

What is likely to happen after trial (the right side of the formula) is of

"The Offer That Cannot Be Refused" first appeared in *The Criminal Justice System*, edited by Franklin E. Zimring and Richard S. Frase (Boston: Little, Brown and Co., 1980), 568–71. Reprinted by permission of Little, Brown and Co, Inc.

FIGURE 1
Percent of Arrests Reaching Trial by Type of Crime

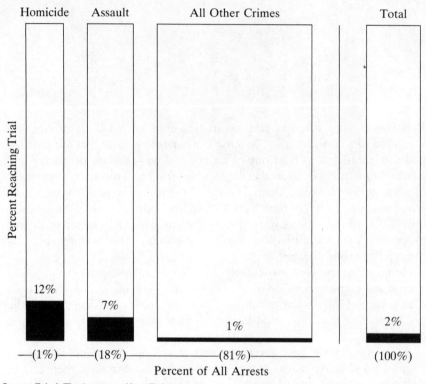

Source: Zeisel, The Anatomy of Law Enforcement,
figure 12-1.

course not part of the negotiation; it is an expectation informed, as a rule, by experienced defense counsel.

Our interviews are replete with references to this sentence differential: "After the trial jury was hung, I guess I'd rather have gone to trial again, but my lawyer said I faced up to eight years if I was convicted. So I took the offered plea to a misdemeanor." (Defenant in case #195)

On the whole, the greater the difference between the offered sentence and the sentence expected after conviction at trial, the more defendants will plead guilty and avoid trial. That sentence differential, therefore, is a figure of importance. It determines the proportion of defendants who will demand trial; it also determines the sentencing level of the system.

In spite of its importance, however, the size of that sentence differential is known only intuitively to judges, prosecutors, and lawyers in the system; it is never publicized and has never been measured with any precision. The data in the present study allow a first step toward such measurement. In some cases that went to trial and eventually ended in conviction we know the sentence that had been offered in the course of plea negotiations.

Figure 2 contains the eight cases for which we know the sentence after conviction at trial and the sentence offered for a guilty plea, which the defendant had refused:

If both the offered and the eventual sentence after trial are prison sentences, their length provides a natural yardstick for comparison. In the four cases for which we have such pairs of sentences, the average increase of the eventual over the offered sentence was 61%.

If the offered sentence was probation and the eventual sentence involved

FIGURE 2
Sentence Offered for (Refused) Guilty Plea and Sentence after Trial (Eight Cases)

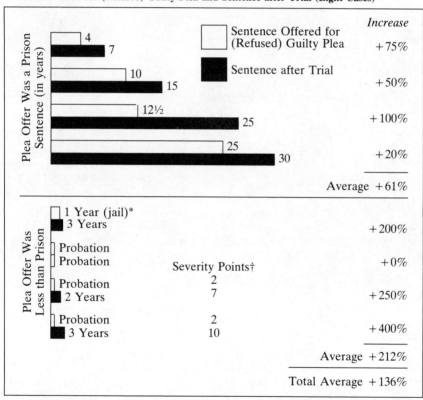

Source: Zeisel, The Anatomy of Law Enforcement, figure 12-2.
*Offer was for an E felony.

†On the scale used by the Administrative Office of the U.S. Courts to compare the severity of prison and nonprison sentences.

custody, an artificial yardstick is required. For this purpose we used the point scale developed by the Administrative Office of the U.S. Courts. We found that in the lower sentencing ranges, the differential was higher. The average sentence increases somewhat over 200%.

The average increase for all eight cases was 136%. Note that the cases in Figure 2 form a biased sample, in as much as some of these defendants went to trial *because* the difference between the offered guilty plea and the expected sentence after trial was too small. This means that the sentencing differentials in Figure 2 are likely to be on the low side, as compared to the (unknown) average for all cases.

Three   Death Penalty

4

Hans Mattick and the Death Penalty
Sentimental Notes on Two Topics
Norval Morris (1979)

I first met Hans Mattick in 1964, soon after I came to this country from a two-year stint for the United Nations in Japan. Within a matter of months we were working together in the Center for Studies in Criminal Justice at the University of Chicago; we remained close friends until his death in January of 1978. Like all who worked with Hans and learned from him, I have a sense of being privileged far beyond my deserts; none who had experienced it would wish to be free of his tutelage. The ripples of decency and of the informed humanism of his life will, I hope, continue to spread.

Here was how I saw the pattern of his life, insofar as the experiences he spoke of to me seemed to influence his attitude to crime and punishment. A wandering childhood, his father absent, six grade schools, three high schools, periods on and off welfare, periods in welfare and "reformatory" institutions, and periods on the road, in the sense known to a young hobo of the depression, all brought the child and youth, Hans Mattick, into a wider contact than is common among our leading criminologists with social adversity and with those who find their various ways to jails and prisons. There followed four years in the army, of which two were in the European theatre, and then back to, of all places, the University of Chicago—its college, its department of sociology, and its Committee on Social Thought. It was a wildly unusual academic background, a fortuity; but like so many other examples of good fortune, it was, as you will see, far from the product of chance alone.

In 1973 Hans Mattick had occasion to write some of his reactions to one experience of his youthful years. I offer a lengthy extract for two reasons: it tells so much about Mattick, and it poses, yet again for us, despite our plethora of good intentions, the plight of the institutionalized child.

Hans received a letter from a private "School for Boys" which I shall call "XYZ," an institution for neglected, rejected, orphaned and delinquent boys. The letter solicited funds, suggesting that "a small amount of voluntary help will accomplish miracles in a boy's life." Hans was an alumnus of the XYZ School. I have his reply. Here are some extracts addressed to "Dear Well-Intentioned People":

"Hans Mattick and the Death Penalty" is an abridged version of an article that appeared in the *University of Toledo Law Review* 10, no. 2 (1979): 299–316.

After I left XYZ, I continued to be a wayward boy and a member of the undeserving classes. But, whereas I had been a dumb, put-upon brute before XYZ, the course of my life had been changed, for people like you had made it possible for me to have the dubious benefit of the XYZ experience: I was now a maddened animal. I will not detail the malicious and predatory life I led for some years after XYZ. The war intervened and, after the war, the resumption of my education at a good university, and on to my present station in life. It took me about fifteen years to bring the benefits of XYZ under control, before I could take up the fragments of my life again. XYZ—you almost succeeded in ruining me forever!

Looking back on that period of my life—and there is so much I cannot take the space and time to tell you—I shudder to think what a malevolent effort the staff of XYZ (unconsciously, but actively, added by my fellow victims—poor things, we were like scorpions on a hot stove, stinging each other and ourselves in the blind, nameless rage inspired in us) made to forever muddle my "life's prospects," and what Herculean effort it took, on my part, to cleanse my soul, my mind and my body from the experience that had been XYZ. Now that I look back from the vantage point of a relatively successful life—a good marriage, a treasured family, an interesting profession, the respect of my peers and all the other trappings of worldly self—I find I can be objective about XYZ, but I am not detached. Deep, deep in my soul there is an encapsulated carcinoma that will always be XYZ. A part of me will always weep for the poor, dumb beasts that misguided good intentions tend to produce. I was better off—I say it without qualification—as a truant, a runaway, a thief, a vulnerable young victim in the alleys of the city, than what XYZ tried its best to make of me.

Do not comfort yourselves that I am unusual, or exceptional, or disgruntled, or irrational: I am speaking to you as a XYZ boy would speak had he the freedom to speak and the insight of hindsight. When you have a boy from a disorganized family, perhaps an alternative commitment to the court disposition, or some poor punk kid who is simply more put upon by this world than he can defend himself against, and you ask him: "Don't you like it here? Aren't we treating you well?", what does he know, and what can he say? He's stuck, poor dumb brute—and you can tell yourself you are doing him and society a favor. It is a cheap and false victory! To test it, just give each boy over the age of twelve an absolute free choice: (1) We will give you the money it costs to support you here, every month, and you can go live where you please; or (2) decide on the merits that you will stay will us. YOU WOULD NOT DARE TO MAKE THAT OFFER; it would be the end of XYZ!

I ask you to earnestly consider, at the next meeting of the Board of Trustees, whether the difference is one of the degree or kind between XYZ and Buchenwald. I submit it is a question of degree and not kind. Whatever your intentions, you did me nothing but harm. The whole machinery, from the Board, to the staff, to the institutionalized inmates; it is an amalgam designed to maladjust people. You are fortunate that most young boys have enough flexibility in their nature to absorb a great deal of mental and physical abuse so that they can emerge from the XYZ experience with some species of survivability— but they are bent more severely and scarred more deeply than if they had been left alone. Don't be taken in by your own good motives and the easy assumption that you know better than another what is good for them. It is not true. By that logic I would clap the lot of you into the nearest insane asylum as public nuisances.

It is a sobering thought that another Hans Mattick—if we were blessed to find one—probably would not be admitted to the University of Chicago and certainly would lack the opportunities for accelerated study that helped to shape Mattick's mind. We should have more wildcards to play. For Mattick, the wild card was held by Joseph Lohman, a teacher at this university, later Sheriff of Cook County and then the first Director of the Berkeley School of Criminology. The wild card came into Lohman's hand because he had the perception to be fascinated by an aggressive youth he met by chance one night, behaving on the uncertain edge of delinquency but with a copy of *The Origin of Species* poking out of his hip pocket! Why did he have it, Lohman enquired? For the compelling reason that the young Mattick liked it, and what business was that of anyone else? And Lohman had the sensitivity to understand Mattick's potential and later the energy to support his growth.

Mattick's thesis combined his studies and his experience. Entitled *Parole to the Army*,[1] it launched his career as a professional criminologist, a professional criminologist with a most unusual personality and an extraordinary range of interests.

Hans Mattick mastered one subject better than anyone else in the world— the American jail. He came to know it from administrative experience (again under the influence of Joseph Lohman), from earlier brief visits as a client to an occasional lock-up, from research and from study. It was a subject appropriate to Han's pervading concern for the diminution of human suffering. In the jails is collected, as he often told us, a vast array of the victims of adversity, the socially incompetent, the physically and mentally ill, the retarded, the luckless waifs and strays of a harsh society, as well as a powerful admixture of the wicked and the evil. He was moved by his heart, of course, but his mind always held a steady regard for political and social realities and achieved a firm adherence to scholarly range and precision. His Illinois Jails Survey[2] is a model of these qualities, carrying forward the great traditions of accuracy and controlled fervor for reform of John Howard, the first of the penal reformers outside the church to care for minimum decencies even in the jail cell.

Few feel the lash on another's back; we all have blinkers to the suffering of others; but Mattick more than anyone else I have ever known managed without sentimentality to empathize with the downtrodden. He often risked himself on the line of principle—his resignation offered if the child remained in the jail; his resignation completed as a protest against an impending execution at the jail. And you always knew in dealing with Mattick that he expected similar principled behavior from you. Hence, he elevated and developed his colleagues and friends as carping critics never can.

For six years, as co-director of the Center for Studies in Criminal Justice at the University of Chicago, he taught us daily. His formidable intellectual and aesthetic range of interests, combined with an utter seriousness of purpose, made him a great teacher. He launched a series of studies which shape the lives of more than a few contemporary criminologists; they will continue to dominate our scholarly and community efforts—studies in violence, in sentencing, in the work of the police, in prisons, and, of course, in jails. He was, for those graduate students and colleagues who fell within his powerful concern, a lasting influence. He was exhaustive but never dull; a tough critic but one who always suggested a way out or a way around. He knew a very great deal, and what was constantly surprising was that so much that he knew turned out to be true!

Mattick had an earthy strength, the chest of the long distance swimmer, a vigorous physical presence. And the inner strength of unqualified integrity was almost equally apparent. That integrity pervaded his teaching and his scholarship.

The focus of his own research turned often to areas not noted for their rigor, topics characterized by faddish commentary rather than by analytic precision. Who else than Hans, with such utter lack of self-deception, would publish a report revealing, with brutal accuracy, the unfulfilled expectations of his own demonstration project?

Hans had a fierce impatience of cant and hypocrisy. I would watch his shoulders hunch forward, moving to the kill, as he bore in on the affected or condescending arguments of those who so clearly knew the comforting values of imposing suffering on others.

Hans, as you saw in his letter to the trustees of the XYZ School, had a direct, firm, and abrasive side to his nature. But he also recognized, more than is the modern fashion, the pervasive need for warmth and emotion in human relations. I have Mrs. Mattick's permission, in support of that statement, to quote a letter from Hans to Lloyd Ohlin. Lloyd had written to Hans expressing gratitude for his hospitality and saying how difficult he found it to express the sincerity and warmth of his feelings for Hans. Hans replied, in part:

> We are trapped in a society where the expression of warm, tender, nostalgic and positive emotions between men must be reserved for

occasions when one or the other is physically absent. Nevertheless, I must develop emotional relations with people (men or women) who I appreciate intellectually or I get to feeling alienated. And if I do not feel some return of sentiment, no matter how attenuated, flowing back to me, the relationship becomes progressively estranged, and brittle to the breaking point. I need both mental stimulation and emotional warmth from people (and am quite sure that others require the same) or I feel a sense of incompleteness about the relationship.

Those of you who did not know Hans Mattick may gain from that extract some flavor of the good fortune of those of us who did.

But Hans was moved by principle and firm beliefs which never genuflected to the claims of friendship. He gave a good deal of time and energy to setting his closer colleagues and students straight. He chose his ground carefully, and, like others who risked argument with Hans, I often had wounds to lick. He did, however, make the mistake of attending my course in criminal law, which gave me, at least on occasion, the sense of the upper hand; but even that was evanescent since, after each class, he would drag me away from the law teacher's penchant for conceptual analysis—the calm of what he saw as the lawyer's remote approach to the problems of crime—and thrust me into the turbulent, political realities of crime and its control where, somewhat ruefully, one felt the dominant force of his informed instruction.

It is, therefore, peculiarly painful to be commenting on a topic he concerned himself with throughout his professional life—capital punishment—without being afforded the response of his incisive, sometimes devastating, but always affectionate criticism.

Mattick wrote and spoke a great deal about capital punishment, but the article he saw as most completely capturing his views was *The Unexamined Death: An Analysis of Capital Punishment.*[3] The detailed arguments of the pamphlet are intensified and expanded in his last writing on capital punishment which he entitled "An Unsentimental View of Capital Punishment"[4] to encompass later data, the decision of the Supreme Court in *Furman v. Georgia*[5] in 1972 and the Gilmore execution in Utah in 1977; but the dominant themes appropriately remain the same.

I do not propose to rehearse those themes; they are well known; *The Unexamined Death* and "An Unsentimental View" are available. Let me offer rather a pespective on the capital punishment controversy, suggesting why it seems to me no longer possible, responsibly, to advocate the reintroduction of capital punishment as an ordinary, functioning instrument of government in this country. An obvious preambulatory apology is appropriate: to seek originality here would be folly, but a new weaving of some established strands of argument may be of value.

Issue is joined on many fronts. The conflict is characterized by overstatement, opinions often masquerading as facts. Each side, with cause, accuses the other of letting either the heart or the spleen rule the head. In this situation, is the topic appropriate at all in the context of a memorial tribute to a fine scholar and a generous friend? I think so. Not because of the details of many of these arguments, but because capital punishment defines principle in the balance between the State and the citizen. It is a fundamental political question, an inexorable problem for the morally sensitive citizen.

The topic is inescapable, though its discussion contributes nothing to social safety nor to the quality of social intercourse. The executioner acts for us, and his actions, more than any other, define both the power relationship and the proper limits of respect between State and Citizen. It is a topic plagued by sentimentality, where sensibility, balance, and social sentiment are often confused by maudlin and excessive concern for the murderer or by a simplistic reliance on condign punishment, no matter what its social disadvantages.

For this discussion, at least, let me try to be clear. I am not personally touched by the death of the murderer. Regrettably, most people's deaths do not touch me, nor, if I observe correctly, does the death of another sadden many, apart from a small circle of close friends—some, on unguarded occasions, even seem quite pleased. It is not the death of the murderer that should attract emotion; no, it is for us, for whom the prison authorities and the executioner act vicariously—for our values, our culture, our future as a society—that I find sentiment in this debate entirely appropriately, Hence, some sentimental notes on capital punishment.

The Current Controversy: or, Conclusions from Inadequate Evidence

The arguments hunt in pairs: capital punishment is a uniquely effective deterrent; not so, is the reply, the available data indicate that the death penalty is no greater deterrent to murder than the usual alternative severe punishments. It is man's innate sense of justice that the punishment should bear a just proportion to the crime, and, hence, capital punishment is the only fit punishment for the deliberate murderer; not so, is the reply, for it is morally wrong for the State, in the name of the Law, deliberately to take life, absent immediate necessity to protect life. And so goes the point and the counterpoint, rebuttal and surrebuttal, ranging over categories of homicide; through retributive, moral, and economic analysis; and to problems of the administration of the law relating to capital punishment and the viability of alternative sanctions. A fine collection of these arguments is found in Bedau's *The Death Penalty in America*.[6]

I wish to confirm where we are with two aspects of the current controversy—the deterrence question and the question of the constitutionality of the death penalty—to link the two, and then to offer three joint themes that lead me to a firm and unreconstituted abolitionist position.

Striving to avoid the tendentious on a topic of heated partisanship, a panel of the National Academy of Sciences recently concluded that "the deterrent effect of capital punishment is definitely not a settled matter, and this argument is the strongest social scientific conclusion that can be reached at the present time."[7] Further, they argued, contrary to the usual academic position that everything ought to be the subject of further research, "research on this topic is not likely to produce findings that will or should have much influence on policy makers."[8]

I am aware that Daniel Glaser, in his excellent article,[9] reaches a somewhat different conclusion on what might be termed the Sellin v. Ehrlich debate,[10] a conclusion tending to the rejection of the Ehrlich differential deterrence hypothesis.[11] Glaser's view seems to me preferable to that of the panel of the National Academy of Sciences (committees often have to reach consensual conclusions where the caution of the lowest common denominator predominates), but the difference is inconsequential for my present purpose. Can anything, then, be teased out, for policy decisions, from the cautious "conclusion" of the National Academy panel?

First, one must be careful to note what issues the Academy's conclusion does not reach. It does not suggest that capital punishment is not a deterrent to those crimes which are punishable by execution. Almost certainly, capital punishment does deter such crimes. What is at issue is whether the death penalty is a marginally *more* effective deterrent than the alternative punishment it would replace. *That* is what is not settled; to be blunt about the matter, whether capital punishment saves lives of potential victims even if one discounts as of zero value the lives taken by the executioner.

Is that a weak and unhelpful conclusion for the formulation of punishment policy? I think not. The death penalty is no novelty. It has been used somtimes and in some places with vigor, expenditure, range, imagination and cruelty; elsewhere and at other times, cautiously, rarely and confined to particularly brutal homicides or particular types of homicide. And still we are at sea about the deterrent relationship between detection, conviction, this ultimate punishment and life saving. One can at least conclude that any marginal life-saving effects escape our present capacities to measure them; they are not manifest; they cannot be relied upon. At the very least, this conclusion would seem relevant to the burden of proof of policy decision, even though not determinative of the substance of that decision. Later, I will return to this contention.

What of the other major question in the current controversy about capital punishment—its constitutionality?

As commentators since de Tocqueville have monotonously noted, in the United States social and ethical issues of national significance are often converted into constitutional questions. The judiciary, in particular the members of the Supreme Court, have supplanted theologians, moralists, philosophers, and political scientists as the high priests of political and social morality. How have they fared with the capital punishment question?

A review of the decisions of the Supreme Court from *Furman v. Georgia*[12] to the present suggests that they have not fared very well at all. A reading of the case laws sheds little light on the fundamental question of who, if anyone, may constitutionally be executed.

What would appear to be a retentionist majority on the Supreme Court so vacillates on constitutionally permissible procedures and guidelines for its application that the retentionists in state legislatures are, to my satisfaction, gradually being drawn to a sense of helpless impotence. To find just the right blend of procedures and practices to avoid the arbitrary imposition of capital punishment is no easy task, but such is the necessary and sound constitutional command. In a punishment system already skewed generally on racial lines, the avoidance of arbitrariness and, indeed, of constitutionally objectionable discrimination is particularly difficult.

Difficult though that task is, the Court has had less difficulty in the area of procedural due process than in that of substantive due process in invoking the death penalty. Orderly fact-finding, even in situations battered by the emotions of racial prejudice, is far easier to define than are the lines between criminality and illness, just punishment and cruelty, and aggravating and mitigating circumstances of punishment. Indeed, one wonders whether such issues can ever be made satisfactorily justiciable, they have such a necessary arbitrary quality; but inexorably the courts must address them within our constitutional structure.

At the root of the Supreme Court's decision making in this difficult and complex area of constitutional litigation is a principle of proportion between the punishment, on the one hand, and the circumstances of the offense taken together with the character and propensities of the offender, on the other. This principle is underscored by the Court's recognition of the unique and irreversible nature of the punishment of death. In *Woodson v. North Carolina*,[13] the plurality of the Court stressed that "the penalty of death is qualitatively different from a sentence of imprisonment, however long,"[14] and, pursuing this principle, the Court held two years later that capital punishment for even heinous non-lethal rape is impermissible.[15] Presumably, it is impermissible for all other non-lethal crimes as well, though hijacking, kidnapping children for ransom, and similar particularly outrageous non-lethal crimes have not been passed upon.

Although the Court has been able to formulate a reasonably bright line rule for cases in which the death penalty is *not* applicable, it has been far from successful in delineating when it *is* applicable. Earlier it had been conceded by the Court that the predetermination of which crimes should be capitally punished is an impractical if not impossible task. In the often overlooked case of *McGautha v. California*,[16] Justice Harlan, speaking for the Court, noted that "[t]o identify before the fact those characteristics of criminal homicides and their perpetrators which call for the death penalty, and to express these characteristics in language which can be fairly understood and applied by the sentencing authority, appear to be tasks which are beyond present human ability."[17] Unfortunately, the wisdom of this concession was later forgotten.

It is against this background of the difficulty of predetermination of cases constitutionally suitable for the executioner's gentle attentions that the Court's rejection of mandatory capital punishment schemes in *Woodson* is best understood. The judge or jury must be entrusted with the discretion to apply the death penalty to a given offender in a specific case. This discretion, however, is not unbridled; it must be "directed and limited,"[18] in a consistent and rational manner, by legislative definition of aggravating and mitigating circumstances, within categories of capital crimes, they are, in each case, to be balanced before any determination of the appropriate sanction is reached.

The problem that arises, however, is that the task of defining statutory guidelines for aggravating and mitigating circumstances is not substantially easier than the task judged to be "beyond present human ability"[19] by Justice Harlan in *McGautha*. Hence, much of the recent and current death penalty litigation has been mired in definitional questions concerning the constitutionality of the guidelines.[20] What can be gleaned from the case law is that the legislative guidelines can be quite broad, provided that they give some rational guidance to the sentencing authority. What degree of vagueness is permissible remains in doubt.

The Court's overreaching requirement for any set of aggravating or mitigating circumstances is that they must tend to avoid "arbitrariness or caprice,"[21] and result in a decision "based upon reason rather than upon caprice or emotion."[22] But reason itself, as I shall suggest, may be inadequate to the enunciation of a sense of justice.

The Supreme Court has approved the definition of an aggravating circumstance as "especially heinous, atrocious, or cruel," in *Proffitt v. Florida*;[23] this definition, however, is neither conclusive nor exclusive. The Court has struggled somewhat more with the problem of acceptable guidelines for mitigating circumstances. Obviously, the circumstances of the crime must be considered. And it is further clear that mitigating circumstances flowing from the personal circumstances of the killer have to be taken into account—his criminal career, his youth, his psychopathology.

Mental illness, for example, or retardation cannot be ignored. I believe, as a matter of principle, that there should be no special defense of insanity to a criminal charge; but it is entirely appropriate, indeed unavoidable, in determining the appropriate, fair and just, quantum of punishment. Certainly, when the death penalty is a possible penalty, mental illness must be a relevant, mitigating circumstance.

That which is obvious found its expression in *Lockett v. Ohio.*[24] There, the Chief Justice concluded that

> the Eighth and Fourteenth Amendments require that the sentencer, in all but the rarest kind of capital case, not be precluded from considering as a mitigating factor, any aspect of a defendant's character or record and any of the circumstances of the offense that the defendant proffers as a basis for a sentence less that death.[25]

The question of the appropriate degree of open-endedness of the range of mitigating circumstances is at present before the Supreme Court in *Spinkellinik v. Wainwright.*[26] But even if limiting the jury to a list of seven mitigating circumstances is constitutionally permissible, the seven listed in the Florida statute[27] at issue in *Spinkellinik* require such broad and imprecise judgments to be made by the jury that the thrust of the present argument is not weakened.

There thus remains a fundamental tension between the grant of discretion to a sentencing authority, judge or jury, and the need for guidelines for the exercise of that discretion sufficiently precise to fulfill the Supreme Court's requirement of sufficient "reliability," which must mean predictability, the quality of treating like cases alike, "in the determination that death is the appropriate punishment in a specific case"[28] bearing in mind the "qualitative difference" in reliability required for this decision as distinct from other lesser decisions about punishment.

What a tangled web we weave when we try to take on the task biblically attributed to St. Peter—the precise quantification of guilt. Guilt or innocence may have to be based on an assumption of free-will, making concession to determinist values in only the clearest cases. By contrast, as regards the assessment of the degree of guilt, the relative quantities of wickedness, such a simple relationship between mind and consequences is obviously inadequate. The entire existential reality must be assessed if we are striving for a just hierarchy of degrees of fair punishability, with death at the pinnacle—the personal and situational totality must be considered. Considered, yes; but we are too ignorant to do much more. There is a reach to this whole assessment which I find, to put no fine phrase upon it, morally pretentious.

All punishment under the criminal law is imprecise if more than a rough and ready hierarchy of severity related to social harm, wickedness, deterrence and clemency are to be calibrated; but in our search for substantive sentencing principle in the context of the death penalty, the arbitrariness becomes starkly manifest. St. Peter's task here is so clearly beyond man's capacity. We see so imprecisely through the fogs of malice, fear, intent and mental disturbance. I would agree, with great respect, with Professor Black, that, in these decisions, caprice and mistake are inevitable;[29] but for my present submission, I do not need to go so far. All that is now required seems ineluctably to emerge even from these early post-*Furman* wrestlings with guiding discretion in the decision to execute: "this most irrevocable of sanctions should be reserved for a small number of extreme cases"[30] and, be it noted, extreme cases within a few categories of capital crime.

Is any conclusion relevant to policy decision available at this obviously interstitial and complex stage of the constitutional litigation? I think so. The conclusion for purposes of my present argument is this: it ill not be possible to draft a constitutionally acceptable capital punishment statute and give it constitutionally acceptable implementation that will cover other than a relatively few murderers. The requirement of statutorily defined hierarchies of gravity of homicides that are to be related to hierarchies of positive and negative qualities in the killer to justify the particular severity of this punishment will produce a grid that will, in the realities of heightened conflict attending all cases where capital punishment may be involved, lead to relatively few executions. The carrying out of an execution will remain a rare event.

Briefly putting the above two themes together: we lack knowledge of the marginal deterrent efficacy of capital punishment; the Constitution precludes executions at a rate to acquire that knowledge. The battle will have to be fought on other grounds. If it is, my belief is that the retentionist majority on the Supreme Court (an apologetic group, in the main) will attentuate and disappear. Lacking the justification of an assumed life-saving quality, the logical structure of the retentionist decision is severely strained.

Let me then move on to three themes which seem to me to prevail in the above context of an unestablished differential deterrence by capital punishment and only a few executions:

A. The Burden of Proof and the Execution
B. Capital Punishment and Crime Control
C. The Media Circus: The Carnival Execution.

A. The Burden of Proof and the Execution

The death of the murderer is not the central issue; killing him is. The execution is an act of high symbolism—the execution of the political or religious dissenter is, of course, as the world's religions testify, the very highest symbolism—but every execution is the largest expression of the relationship between the state and the citizen. It should not be undertaken without a high degree of confidence in the need.

On the evidence we have, capital punishment as murder control is unsubstantial, as crime control it is ridiculous. The United States' return to capital punishment would, on the state of the evidence, be a sin against those distinctive values which are the unique American contribution to cultural evolution—the most careful balancing of the rights of the citizen as against the state. As a life-saving mechanism, capital punishment might be appropriately weighed in those scales, but its efficacy and the need to use it must be shown.

Early in my own involvement in this topic, as Chairman of a Commission of Inquiry into Capital Punishment in the country then called Ceylon, I decided to track for myself the precise processes of an execution in that country. As a governmental inquiry, we had ample powers of subpoena and of access to penal institutions. I followed the procedures carefully and tried to identify with the prison staff who must carry out the execution. Thereafter, I had no doubt where lay the burden of proof in the capital punishment controversy.[31] Camus has made the point well,[32] but for me, it is most gracefully phrased by George Orwell in his superb essay, "A Hanging."[33] Here is an extract:

> We set out for the gallows. Two warders marched on either side of the prisoner, with their rifles at the slope; two others marched close against him, gripping him by arm and shoulder, as though at once pushing and supporting him. The rest of us, magistrates and the like, followed behind. . . .
>
> It was about forty yards to the gallows. I watched the bare brown back of the prisoner marching in front of me. He walked clumsily with his bound arms, but quite steadily, with that bobbing gait of the Indian who never straightens his knees. At each step his muscles slid neatly into place, the lock of hair on his scalp danced up and down, his feet printed themselves on the wet gravel. And once, in spite of the men who gripped him by each shoulder, he stepped slightly aside to avoid a puddle on the path.
>
> It is curious, but till that moment I had never realized what it means to destroy a healthy, conscious man. When I saw the prisoner step aside to avoid the puddle I saw the mystery, the unspeakable wrongness, of cutting a life short when it is in full tide. This man was not dying, he was alive just as we are alive. All the organs of his body

were working—bowels digesting food, skin renewing itself, nails growing, tissues forming—all toiling away in solemn foolery. His nails
would still be growing when he stood on the drop, when he was falling through the air with a tenth of a second to live. His eyes saw the
yellow gravel and the grey walls, and his brain still remembered, fore-
saw, reasoned—even about puddles. He and we were a party of men
walking together, seeing, hearing, feeling, understanding the same
world; and in two minutes, with a sudden snap, one of us would be
gone—one mind less, one world less.[34]

Absent cogent proof of need, even at a level of balance of probability, the
duty to kill should be imposed on no man. That there is no lack of volunteers
to act as executioners merely strengthens the point. If someone must act for
me in this killing—and such is surely the case, for in a democracy he does act
for me—I would reject the volunteer.

In practice, the execution will be the business of the prison administration, sometimes fancifully called the correctional administration. To one
who, like Hans Mattick, takes seriously the eighth amendment's injunction
to avoid cruel and unusual punishments even within the prison's walls,
capital punishment is a symbolic punishment of particular evil in the present
context of our overcrowded, understaffed, ancient and huge prisons where
too frequently the gangs rule and the predator brutalizes the weak and
unprotected. Capital punishment reinforces these attitudes of staff and
prisoners alike that are antipathetic to making our prisons safe and secure
institutions of necessary punitive banishment from society; it is particularly
antipathetic to such efforts as are pursued in prison to assist prisoners, if they
wish it, to self-development towards less criminous lives.

I have been in prison at times of an execution; the prisoners see it clear; it
is no necessity of social defense; it is conscious social revenge; it is the
archetypal evil in man ascendant. Capital punishment is a denial of the long
passage to minimum decencies in our cultural inheritance. Unjustified by
necessity, it is not otherwise justifiable.

The relevant doctrine is the doctrine of necessity and its foundations are
not laid. Nor can they be. It is grossly unlikely that we will execute with such
frequency that the hypothesis of differential deterrence, if it reflects reality,
can be achieved, and even more unlikely that it can be measured. Given the
constitutional, political and social realities of this country, capital punishment will not reach a level at which its utilitarian justification can be
established.

Executions in the United States have never exceeded the rate of 200 per
year for all offenses,[35] with executions for homicide presumably comprising
the great bulk of this two hundred. Even in the 1930's, the peak decade of
the application of this penalty in this country, the busy years for the executioner, murderers were executed at an average rate of 170 per year—thus,

perhaps, one in fifty murderers were so punished. By the mid-1960's the execution rate had declined to the point of disappearance with the last execution being in 1967, unless one counts the "consensual" Gilmore execution in Utah in 1977.

With executions taking place at these low levels we could not test the marginal deterrence hypothesis. The consitutional restraints ensure that no such numbers will recur. The available evidence tends, in my judgment, to refute that hypothesis rather than to favor it; but, certainly, knowing what we do not know, a due respect for the sanctity of life precludes justifying executions on the grounds of necessary protection of society.

I put aside, for another day which I hope will never come, Kantian arguments of an inexorable obligation to execute the murderer to redress the wrong he has done, independently of any social utility to be gained thereby. Such values are far removed from the political strife of the legislator and the court; they seem wildly irrelevant in the context of the wearisome delays of the American trial and appellate processes by which the execution responds in that equation to an existential event far removed from the circumstances of the convicted killer.

In summary, the burden of proof of need to execute lies, in the reality situation in which we find ourselves, on those who favor capital punishment. They have not, and, on utilitarian grounds, they cannot carry that burden of proof.

B. Capital Punishment and Crime Control

I have two further brief addenda to offer, one on crime control, one on the media. First, a reaction to the astonishing suggestion that capital punishment is an appropriate national response to the very serious and pervasive problems of violent crime in this country.

This must surely be placing undue reliance on symbolism. After all, not even the most perfervid retentionist now believes capital punishment will be imposed on more than a few categories of aggravated homicide. How then can it have impact on other crimes? There are links, of course, risks of capital killings in some classes of violent crimes, but a measurable reduction of violent crimes generally to be achieved by executions at the rate the constitution will permit seems a considerable flight of fancy.

Hugo Bedau describes the death penalty as "a unique symbol in the endless struggle of society to control and comdemn violent crime."[36] But if we ask what that symbol represents in the context of that endless struggle, the answer is that for the most part it stands for morbid satisfaction with a penal method that has become increasingly rare, arbitrary and discriminatory in its application and almost completely irrelevant to the problem of controlling violent crime. And C. H. Rolph some years ago described the existence of the death penalty as "overshadowing every subsidiary problem in crime and punishment."[37] Yet, in practical terms, the significance of the availability or nonavailability of the death penalty as a sanction could hardly be *under*estimated.

This unwarranted preoccupation with capital punishment evidenced by these writers may, in part, explain why, in a decade which has seen the rate of criminal homicide nearly doubled, that of aggravated assault more than doubled, that of robbery more than tripled, and the number of prison inmates expanded to an unprecedented three hundred thousand, public attention can be so easily diverted and focused on an issue of such singular inconsequence. It is as though a man whose home stood in the path of an approaching tornado were to worry about the proper alignment of his picket fence.

The priority accorded to the topic of the death penalty is out of all proportion to its significance to the promotion of public welfare. It is a distraction from the serious and important task of reducing violence, particularly criminal violence, in this country.

C. The Media Circus: The Carnival Execution

Finally, a note on a theme I heard frequently when the bizarre circumstances attending the Gilmore execution titillated all that is worst in public interest. "I am in favor of capital punishment in certain cases," the cocktail party contention went, "but only if it is *not* accompanied by an appalling media circus like the Gilmore execution." It is a delusion; television, the newspapers, the radio and the weeklies have joined the executioner and will sensationalize the last months, weeks and days of the condemned man. Every execution in this country and the antecedent capital trials and appeals will go beyond the more gory details of crime and any ordinary aspects of the lives of the victims and witness to include the digestive and amatory processes of the murderer; all will be media events, the carnival execution is show business at its nadir, at its most vulgar.

Add the first amendment to the constitutional controls, earlier discussed, which will limit the number of executions, and every potential execution becomes a debasement of what is best in this society, an elevation of our affection for the sensational. Crime, it is said, does not pay. Sometimes it does, sometimes it doesn't. On the other hand, executions certainly pay the lords of television and the barons of the press and pay them well. Crocodile tears and mock sympathy for the executioner's client is part of the stock in trade of some; others stimulate sales by exaggerated outrage at the crime and by vehemently expressed satisfaction in the execution. And all for no established social advantage.

It is those favoring the death, finally, who exhibit sentimentality in this debate. If there is a linguistic distinction between "sentiment" and "sentimental" on the one hand, and "sentimentality" on the other—and the Oxford English Dictionary does define sentimentality to include the "affection of sensibility"—then in this culture, given the constitutional realities, the attitudes of the media and the limits on our knowledge of deterrence, it is not the abolitionists who are the sentimentalists.

In brief, on the known facts, we lack the purity of heart for a just, fair and appropriate invocation of the death penalty.

Notes

1. H. Mattick, *Parole to the Army* (August 1956) (unpublished M.A. thesis, Department of Sociology, University of Chicago).
2. H. Mattick & R. Sweet, *Illinois Jails: Challenge and Opportunity for the 1970's*, A Survey Conducted for the Center for Studies in Criminal Justice, the Law School, U. of Chicago (1969) (with financial support from the Ford Found. and Ill. Law Enforcement Comm.).
3. H. Mattick, *The Unexamined Death: An Analysis of Capital Punishment* (rev. ed. 1966).
4. Mattick, "An Unsentimental View of Capital Punishment," 36 *Community* 7 (Summer 1977).
5. 408 U.S. 238 (1972).
6. *The Death Penalty in America* (2d ed. H. Bedau 1967). See also *Capital Punishment in the United States* (H. Bedau & C. Pierce eds. 1976).
7. *Deterrence and Incapacitation: Estimating the Effects of Criminal Sanctions on Crime Rates* (A. Blumenstein ed. 1978).
8. Id. at 62–63.
9. Glaser, "Capital Punishment—Deterrent or Stimulus to Murder?: Our Unexamined Deaths and Penalties," 10 *U. Tol. L. Rev.* 317 (1979).
10. See Baldus & Cole, "A Comparison of the Works of Thorsten Sellin and Isaac Ehrlich on the Deterrent Effect of Capital Punishment," 85 *Yale L.J.* 170 (1975); Bowers & Pierce, "The Illusion of Deterrence in Isaac Ehrlich's Research on Capital Punishment," 85 *Yale L.J.* 187 (1975); Ehrlich, "Deterrence: Evidence and Inference," 85 *Yale L.J.* 209 (1975); Peck, "The Deterrent Effect of Capital Punishment: Ehrlich and His Critics," 85 *Yale L.J.* 359 (1976).
11. Id
12. 408 U.S. 238 (1972).
13. 428 U.S. 280 (1976).
14. Id. at 305.
15. Coker v. Georgia, 433 U.S. 584 (1977).
16. 402 U.S. 183 (1971).
17. Id. at 204.
18. Gregg v. Georgia, 428 U.S. 153, 189 (1976).
19. 402 U.S. at 204.

20. See, e.g., Lockett v. Ohio, 98 S. Ct. 2954 (1978); Gardner v. Florida, 430 U.S. 349 (1977); Gregg v. Georgia, 428 U.S. 153 (1976); Woodson v. North Carolina, 428 U.S. 280 (1976); Proffitt v. Florida, 428 U.S. 242 (1976); and Spinkellenik v. Wainright, 578 F.2d 582 (1978).

21. Gregg, 428 U.S. at 201.

22. Gardner, 430 U.S.

23. Proffitt, 428 U.S. at 255–56.

24. 98 S. Ct. 2954 (1978).

25. Id. at 2995.

26. 578 F.2d 582 (1978), cert. denied, 47 U.S.L.W. 3637 (1979).

27. Id. at 587 n.7.

28. Woodson v. North Carolina, 428 U.S. 280, 305 (1976).

29. C. Black, *Capital Punishment: The Inevitability of Caprice and Mistake* (1974).

30. Gregg v. Georgia, 428 U.S. 153, 182 (1976).

31. And as an impropriety, to be justified in the accounting only by the passage of the years, let me confess that I arranged for my two fellow commissioners, who came to the enquiry tending to support capital punishment, to be led through the same sequence of protracted and close relationships with the prisoner to be executed, culminating in the squalid formalities of the killing.

32. A. Camus, *Reflections on the Guillotine: An Essay on Capital Punishment* (1960).

33. 1 *Orwell, The Collected Essays, Journalism and Letters* 44 (S. Orwell & L. Angus eds. 1968).

34. Id. at 45–46.

35. *Capital Punishment 1975*, Nat'l Crim. Just. Information and Statistics Service, Law Enforcement Assistance Ad., U.S. Dep't of Just., No. SD-NPS-CP-4, at 22–23 (July 1976).

36. Bedau, "Foreword" to W. Bowers, *Executions in America*, at xx (1974).

37. C. H. Rolph, *Common Sense about Crime and Punishment* 102 (1961).

Four   Deterrence

5   The Morality of Deterrence

Johannes Andenaes (1970)

I. The Problem

Deterrence, both general and special, is one of the traditionally accepted aims of the criminal law. This article will consider only general deterrence: the deterrent effect of the threat of punishment. This concept will be used in its broad sense, including the so-called moral or educative effects of criminal law,[1] thus corresponding to the continental term "general prevention."

Legislators as well as criminal courts often base their decisions on considerations of general deterrence. But punishment on this ground has been attacked time and again in the literature as unjust. Bittner and Platt, for example, contend that "punishment on the basis of deterrence is inherently unjust. For if an example is made of a person to induce others to avoid criminal actions then he suffers not for what he has done but on account of other people's tendency to do likewise."[2] This criticism, frequently raised, seems to rest on Kant's moral principle that man should always be treated as an end in himself, not only as a means for some other end.[3]

Ethical questions cannot be conclusively resolved by analysis and argument. In the last resort we have to take a stand based on personal sentiment, or, in more lofty terms, personal values. There is no possibility of empirical verification of these values. All we can do is discuss the implications and consistency of our principles.

The Kantian principle has a persuasive ring, but can hardly be treated as a binding rule without closer scrutiny. As with other abstract principles it lends itself to different interpretations, and it is difficult to evaluate the validity of the principle without examining its practical applications. Realistically, societies often treat people in ways designed to promote the good of society at the expense of the individual concerned. Military conscription may be the prime example of this phenomenon which also finds expression in quarantine regulations, confinement of dangerous mentally ill patients, and detention of enemy citizens in wartime. Thus, the Kantian principle, in practical application, is of doubtful value. Moreover, even if we accept the

"The Morality of Deterrence" first appeared in the *University of Chicago Law Review* 37 (1970): 649–64.

principle, it hardly leads to a general conclusion that punishment based on deterrence in contrary to the demands of justice.

The theory of general deterrence has, however, often been stated in terms which make it a rewarding target of attack on ethical grounds.[4] Reverend Sydney Smith's statement of the theory in the 1830's provides a good example.

> When a man has been proved to have committed a crime, it is expedient that society should make use of that man for the diminution of crime; he belongs to them for the purpose. Our primary duty, in such a case, is to treat the culprit that many other persons may be rendered better, or prevented from being worse, by dread of the same treatment; and, making this the principal object, to combine with it as much as possible the improvement of the individual.[5]

This statement considers only the application of punishment in the individual case and does not relate punishment to the general rule of law. For a closer analysis of this relationship it may be useful to distinguish between general preventive considerations as a basis for *legislation* and as a basis for *sentencing*.[6]

II. Considerations of General Prevention in Lawmaking

The legislature's prescriptions, for example, of life imprisonment for murder, thirty days imprisonment for tax evasion or drunken driving, or a heavy fine for speeding, are general provisions directed toward everyone. They attempt to motivate every potential violator to conform. Infliction of punishment for one of these violations is a consequence of the legal provision; it does not require special justification in each case. Punishment is essential to the law's effectiveness; without its application the law would be an empty letter. Thus, if it is ethically justifiable to issue penal laws in order to regulate human conduct, it cannot be ethically unjust to apply the law in the individual case. It cannot be said that the offender "suffers not for what he has done but on account of other people's tendency to do likewise."[7] He suffers for what he has done in the measure prescribed by the legislature. As H. L. A. Hart has put it, the primary operation of criminal punishment consists of announcing certain standards of behavior and attaching penalties for deviation, and then leaving individuals to choose. This, he asserts, is a method of social control which maximizes individual freedom within the framework of the law.[8]

The connection between the criminal provision and its application was stated forcefully by Feurbach.[9] The aim of the penal law, he says, is deterrence. The aim of the application of punishment is to fulfill the command of the law so that it does not contradict itself. Feuerbach discussed and accepted Kant's principle; he argued that this principle does not conflict with the application of punishment as a consequence of the law.

Acceptance of this proposition does not mean that legislation based on the principles of deterrence is exempt from criticism. The basis for the criticism, however, must derive from a different source. Such criticism could be based on a deterministic view of human life. If every act is the product of heredity and environment, the choice between conforming to the law and breaking it is somewhat illusory. To say that a person *could* have acted differently is merely to state in another way that *if* he had possessed a different personality, or *if* the external situation had been different, the action, too, would have been different. The person makes a choice, to be sure, but with this given personality in this given situation, the choice could only be what it was. The Swedish law professor Vilhelm Lundstedt, one of the best known proponents of general prevention, considered punishment a necessary means to inculcate moral standards in the populace; but recognizing the force of the deterministic position, he characterized the convicted offender as "a kind of martyr to the maintenance of the social order."[10]

I do not intend to discuss the free will problem, which easily leads to a tangle of metaphysics and semantics.[11] Suffice it to say that in practical life we all tend to differentiate between those who can and those who cannot control their actions and that it is a generally accepted proposition that every normal person has to face the moral and legal responsibility for his voluntary acts. On the other hand, many thoughtful men feel a certain ambivalence, a lurking doubt, towards the concepts of guilt and responsibility. The tendency of the modern, enlightened mind to look for the individual and social causes of the criminal act makes moral indignation evaporate and may even turn it into compassion and pity. At the very least there is a feeling that many of the persons who break the law and consequently are subjected to prosecution and punishment were poorly equipped to resist the temptation. Without moral indignation, punishment is inflicted only reluctantly. For this reason, Bittner and Platt are right when they assert that the execution of punishment has become less and less compatible with prevailing moral sentiment[12]—prevailing, that is, among the well-educated and liberal-minded. As a Norwegian Supreme Court judge once said: "Our grandparents punished, and they did it with a clear conscience. We punish too, but we do it with a bad conscience." Although the institution of punishment is necessary, it is a sad necessity.

As long as legislation is restricted to achieving deterrence through economic sanctions, few people will find any moral objection. The same holds true for the threat of losing one's driver's license as a deterrent to traffic offenses. The morality of deterrence can be reasonably discussed only in relation to penalties which inflict a serious suffering, humiliation, and degradation on the offender.

The question has been most thoroughly explored in the context of the death penalty imposed for murder. Some defend the death penalty on retributive grounds irrespective of its deterrent value. Others accept it on utilitarian grounds, because they believe that the supreme penalty has a substantial deterrent effect. Of the opponents, many take the position that they will oppose capital punishment as long as it is not proven to have a more substantial deterrent effect than other forms of punishment. Others take the more absolute moral position asserting that the death penalty is unjustifiable regardless of its effect. For example, in 1902, a member of the Norwegian parliament stated during the debates on the new Penal Code: "Even if it were so that capital punishment were necessary to deter people, I cannot accept it. I cannot accept it because it runs counter to the moral principles a society ought to be built upon."[13]

In our society there would be widespread agreement that the death penalty ought not be imposed for minor offenses, and the same feeling is expressed toward long prison terms which are considered too harsh for the offense for which they are imposed. A threat of punishment which would be considered justifiable for the hijacking of an airliner would be considered excessive for car theft or shoplifting. In 1969 a twenty-year-old Virginia student without a previous criminal record was sentenced to 25 years in prison (with five years suspended for good behavior) for the possession of marijuana.[14] In Virginia the minimum penalty for possession of more than 25 grains (about half a teaspoonful) of marijuana is twenty years, the same minimum penalty as for first degree murder. This is a clear example of punishment which is excessive in relation to the nature of the crime.

Thus, the decisive point does not seem to be whether the law is based on considerations of deterrence, but rather whether it can be accepted as a *reasonable means* to a *legitimate end*. The German courts have declared that the constitutional principle of the dignity of man requires (1) that only culpable offenders be punished, and (2) that the punishment be in just proportion to the gravity of the offense and the culpabilty of the offender.[15] The first restriction rules out strict liability and vicarious liability in criminal law. I shall not discuss these problems but will deal only with the second proposition.

Punishment in relation to the gravity of the offense and the culpability of the offender provides an elastic formula. Opinions as to the gravity of the offense and the culpability of the offender may differ, but the formula seems to express the essence of the common sense of justice. The formula is valid also with regard to penalties imposed on the basis of considerations other than general deterrence. The Norwegian Penal Code has a provision which prescribes a minimum penalty of two years imprisonment for aggravated larceny, provided the defendant has had at least three previous convictions for that crime. The motivation behind this provision was a desire to insure a more efficient treatment of professional thieves. However, from time to time cases have arisen where the two-year minimum has been applied to petty thieves who happen to have committed a burglary to obtain small quantities of food. Such cases have provoked strong criticism because of the lack of proportion between crime and punishment. The legislature responded to this criticism with a 1967 amendment to the Penal Code providing that the court can disregard the minimum sentence if special circumstances are present.

Where the probability of detection of criminal behavior is low, legislatures are sometimes inclined to compensate by increasing the severity of penalties. In the history of criminal law this has been a recurrent theme. The brutality of penal law in former times is more easily understood when one considers the weakness of state organization and the absence of an organized police force.[16] No doubt a moderate level of penal sanctions combined with widespread and effective enforcement is more acceptable to the moral sentiment than harsh penalties with only sporadic enforcement. Compensating for weak enforcement with harsh penalties may also lead to severe treatment of one type of offense in relation to another offense which, although more reprehensible, is more easily detected. Such discrepancies may be justfiable from a utilitarian point of view, and if the discrepancies are glaring they might violate the widely accepted principle of reasonable proportion between crime and punishment.

III. Considerations of General Prevention in Sentencing

The preceding discussion has been concerned solely with situations where a sentence based on considerations of deterrence is prescribed by the legislature, as when a penal provision prescribes a fixed sentence (for example, imprisonment for life for murder) or a minimum penalty binding on the courts (as in the original version of the Norwegian aggravated larceny law). However, this is seldom the prevailing pattern in modern legislation. Typically the law gives the judge broad discretion to make the sentence fit the offense and the offender. The relationship between the threat of sanction and the application of punishment thus becomes more complex. The role of the court is not only to carry out the prescriptions of the law but also to exercise its own judgment. The law could, of course, require that the judge in sentencing consider only the rehabilitation of the individual offender. In such a system a murderer might receive a suspended sentence or probation if the judge determines that there is no danger of recidivism, and, in contrast, the petty but incorrigible thief might be imprisoned for life. But most criminal codes leave the task of weighing the different purposes of punishment, including general prevention, to the judge. For example, the Norwegian Penal Code states in section 52 that the court may suspend the punishment "unless the concern for general law-abidance or for restraining the convict from further offenses requires execution of the punishment." The "concern for general law-abidance" is meant to cover the general preventive aspects of punishment.

In practice, it seems that judges in all countries give weight to general preventive considerations as long as the penalty remains reasonably proportionate to the crime. For a meaningful discussion of the moral aspect of the consideration of general prevention in sentencing, it is necessary to distinguish between different situations. The court, in meting out the penalty, may consider the potential deterrent effect of *each particular sentence.* Or the court may consider the foreseeable effects of *this level of punishment for this type of offense.* Both types of considerations may be applied in the same case, and it is not easy to draw a clear line between them. Nevertheless, the distinction is important for analysis.

If the sentencing judge wishes to attach weight to the general preventive effect of a particular sentence, he should consider the publicity which the decision will receive and the possible reactions of those people who will hear or read about the decision. If a case has for some reason attracted great publicity, a severe sentence could be expected to have a great deterrent effect. If, on the other hand, the publicity is minimal and the sentence probably will be known only to the defendent himself and the officials involved with the case, the judge could let the offender off with a light sentence without sacrificing any general preventive effects. In a system of this kind it is a fair generalization that the offender is used as a means for the public good, and most people would find the system unjust because it would violate the principle of equality before the law. It may, to be sure, often be difficult to determine what equality means, or, in other words, what differences between two similar cases justify a different treatment, but few would disagree that differences in the amount of publicity ought to be irrelevant. For this reason, the system might also be self-defeating since a system of criminal justice which is exposed as capricious and unjust will be unable to act as an educative force. I shall not go so far as to assert that it is unjust under all circumstances to attach weight in sentencing to the deterrent effects of the particular sentence, but at least we are in an area which demands extreme caution.

The situation is different when general prevention is taken into consideration in determining the general level of penalties for different types of offenses. This seems to me both legitimate and necessary. If the Penal Code gives the court freedom to determine the sentence (for example, within the limits of one year and twenty years of imprisonment), this means that the legislature has abstained from developing a fixed and detailed system of penalties. The threat of the law has a certain indefiniteness, and the task of specifying the exact extent of the threats falls to the courts. In countries with efficient judical review of sentencing, the supreme court established guidelines for the lower courts. In systems where sentencing is viewed as the exclusive, or almost exclusive, province of the trial court, the discrepancies between these courts will necessarily be greater. But in relation to the legislative enactment the task is, in principle, the same. The sentencing is simply a continuation of the evaluations begun by the legislature; and it would be arbitrary and contrary to the public interest to exclude motivations or general prevention.

What of the Kantian principle in this case? When the structure of penalties is fixed by the legislature it could not reasonably be said that the individual offender serves as a means to deter others. I tend to see it the same way when the level of penalties is fixed by the courts. But whether one agrees with these propositions is of little consequence for the moral judgment.

I shall illustrate the use of general preventive considerations in sentencing by some cases from the Norwegian Supreme Court, chosen somewhat randomly. The Court has power to alter sanctions of lawbreakers, on appeal by the prosecutor or the defendant, and it states its reasons for doing so.

1. *1947 Norsk Retstidende 368.* A Norwegian guard in a German camp in Norway for Yugoslavian prisoners had, at the instigation of a superior, brutally killed a prisoner. The trial court sentenced the defendant to death, and the Supreme Court upheld the sentence. Justice Skau for the majority declared: "Public international law has strict rules for the treatment of prisoners of war and accepts the highest penalties for serious crimes against them. Prisoners of war, civil as well as military, are in an especially vulnerable position and have no other defense than that which a strong legal protection can give. But a strong legal protection in this relationship supposes not only strict rules of law but also strict enforcement." Chief Justice Stang added: "As conditions have been under this war and may become under a new one it is necessary that guards and supervisors in prisons and concentration camps [learn] that to maltreat or kill a prisoner is a crime which will be severely punished. For general preventive reasons it is therefore necessary to apply the ultimate penalty of the law."

2. *1947 Norsk Retstidende 271.* This case concerned the question of drunken driving. The law has a fixed limit of blood alcohol content (0.05 per cent) and for general preventive reasons the courts have established a practice of not suspending sentences in such cases in the absence of extraordinary circumstances. Sometimes the trial court, consisting of one judge and two lay assessors, suspends the prison sentence out of pity for the defendant. In this case the lay assessors outvoted the judge and suspended a 21-day prison sentence. They argued that this case was an isolated instance of drunken driving by an otherwise law-abiding citizen. On appeal by the prosecution the Supreme Court imposed a 30-day prison sentence without

92   DETERRENCE

suspension. The Court emphasized the great danger represented by drunken drivers and the increasing number of such drivers.

3. *1947 Norsk Retstidende 269*. The defendant, a thirty-year-old man with no previous record, had been drunk in a public place and struck a policeman. In the trial court the lay assessors, outvoting the judge, suspended a 30-day sentence. On appeal by the prosecution the Supreme Court reversed. Judge Gaarder spoke for the court: "I find the appeal justified and, in accord with the previous practice of this court in similar cases, the penalty should be reinstated. Considerations of general prevention speak against suspending the penalty in this type of case."

4. *1953 Norsk Retstidende 1312*. The defendant was the captain of a Bristol trawler that had been fishing illegally in Norwegian territorial waters. The trial court imposed the harshest sentence ever meted out for this offense. The captain's appeal was unsuccessful, Judge Thrap, speaking for the majority, stated that the purpose of the law forbidding trawling was to protect the vital interests of the coastal population. Illegal fishing by Norwegian and foreign trawlers caused the coastal population considerable loss and inconvenience. The trawling not only adversely affected local fishing interests, but also endangered their fishing tackle. Judge Thrap pointed out that the law had time and again been made more rigorous, and he quoted official statements regarding the need for stringent sanctions. In conclusion he stated: "Because of the strong, general preventive considerations in this field, I take as my starting point that fines and confiscations shall be in amounts which, in each individual case, are adequate for efficient enforcement of the law." Experience had shown that the previous penalties had been insufficient. Under these circumstances, the Supreme Court saw no reason to reduce the sentence imposed by the trial court. One judge dissented. He agreed that it was justifiable to introduce stricter penalties, but was unwilling to go as far as the majority because he felt that the resulting sanction would vary too much from previous practice.

As these cases show, the Court is concerned not with the effect of the individual sentence, but rather with the effect of varying penalties for different types of offenders. It seems difficult to find valid objections to a judge taking deterrence into consideration in the same manner as a legislator does. However, we may sometimes question the beliefs of the courts with regard to the effects of a certain sentencing policy. For example, is it realistic to assume that the war crime sentences imposed in Norway after World War II will have any deterrent effect in a future wartime situation? There may also be differences in value judgments. With regard to the drunken driving cases we may ask: How many prison sentences are we willing to accept in order to save one life or save one person from crippling injury? Similar questions confront the legislature.

Considerations of general prevention are frequently mentioned by a court in deciding whether to suspend a sentence. While principles of general deterrence seem to weigh against suspension, special circumstances of the specific case may warrant suspension of sentence. For example, in the drunken driving cases the court may be motivated to suspend the sentence because of the bad health of the offender;[17] the suicidal tendencies of the offender's wife;[18] or by the lapse of time since the act was committed.[19]

Questions may arise as to which circumstances can properly be considered in determining the extent of the penalties. The next two cases serve as examples.

5. *1962 Norsk Retstidende 517.* The defendant, a nineteen-year-old man, followed an elderly woman and snatched her bag containing 750 kroner (about $100). He had no previous convictions and the trial court imposed a ninety-day suspended sentence. On appeal by the prosecution, the Supreme Court reduced the sentence to forty-five days but denied suspension. Speaking for the Court, Judge Bendiksby stated: "The prosecution had produced evidence that recently there has been a great increase in 'bag-snatching.' Since September 25, 1961, there have been eighteen cases in Oslo. The victims, according to a list which was produced in the case, are generally elderly women; the victim in this case was eighty years old. Crimes of this kind are difficult for the police to solve; in only four of the eighteen cases has the offender been found. There is obviously a strong need to support effectively the work of the police who are trying to protect citizens who are especially exposed to this kind of attack and who have little capacity to defend themselves. When the culprit is caught, the sanction ought to be severe. I therefore find that considerations of general deterrence weigh heavily in favor of denying suspension in this type of crime."

6. *1969 Norsk Retstidende 1048.* On several occasions, the defendant, an eighteen-year-old boy, had purchased moderate quantities of hashish, sometimes with friends as partners. The trial court stated that he had actively taken part in creating a milieu of narcotics in his home town. The court imposed a sixty-day prison sentence, the last thirty-five of which were suspended. On appeal the defendant sought to have the entire sentence suspended, arguing that he was now engaged in vocational training and had broken with the narcotics milieu. Speaking for the majority, Judge Boelviken conceded that it was unnecessary to require the defendant to serve the sentence in order to prevent him from further criminal activity. However, referring to general preventive considerations and the Court's previous practice in such cases, she held that the defendant's crime was sufficiently serious to require him to serve at least part of his sentence. Judge Hiorthoy, dissenting, believed that since the defendant bought and imported hashish only for personal use, rather than being a professional narcotics importer,

principles of general deterrence should not be decisive. He felt that considerations of general deterrence should give way when imprisonment would have greatly adverse effects on the defendant. After discussing the particular circumstances of the defendant, he added that he did not feel bound by the previous rigorous practice of the Court in narcotics cases: "Conditions have changed, and the recommendation of the prosecution as well as the sentence of the court below shows that a different and milder course of sentencing is now followed in cases in which the defendant made only personal use of the narcotics. Such a policy expresses a view, which I share, that the general deterrent effects of punishment are questionable in relation to personal use of marijuana [hashish], and that this ought to be taken into consideration when determining whether a sentence should be suspended."

The other three judges agreed with Judge Boelviken, adding that it would be contrary to previous practice of the Court to suspend the entire sentence, and that conditions had not changed so as to justify changing that practice.

The bag-snatching case presents the question whether it is ethically defensible to increase the penalty because of changes in the crime rate or in other social conditions. I agree with the court's affirmative answer to this question. Just as the legislature considers social conditions in legislating against certain conduct, the court should have the power to adjust sentencing policy to the changing needs of society. Such adjustment may lead to less severe sentences for some crimes and to harsher sentences in others. This was the argument of the dissenting judge in the hashish case. Infanticide is an example of a crime for which there has been mitigation of former harsh sentencing practices. Since this crime no longer represents a frequent problem in the Scandinavian countries, penal sanctions for it have become much more lenient, and in the few cases which have recently been heard, the sentence has almost always been suspended.

Perhaps one exception, illustrated by a German case from the Nazi era,[20] should be made regarding the factors which the court should consider when determining a penalty. The defendant was convicted of violating a law which prohibited sexual intercourse between people of Jewish and "Aryan" nationality. The Supreme Court considered it proper to take notice that the number of such violations had greatly increased *after the commission of the act of the defendant.* While the character of the charge makes this decision especially repugnant, it seems that in any case subsequent developments should be excluded as an aggravating factor in sentencing. However, this problem will rarely arise.[21]

In Norway, the question has recently arisen as to whether it is unjust to establish two levels of sentences: one for Norwegians and a different one for foreigners. Norway is a small, peaceful country with a modest crime rate. Compared to those of other nations, punishments are mild, with few prison sentences of more than two or three years. Recently there have been several cases in which foreign, professional criminals have taken advantage of Norway's relatively lax law enforcement to engage in armed robbery, check forgery and narcotics smuggling. Thus, the Norwegian legal system must deal with professional criminals who are accustomed to much more severe penalties in countries in which they have previously operated. It is against national interests to make Norway a tempting base for international narcotics dealers or other professional criminals drawn there by the mild criminal penalties. On the other hand, there is no wish to change the present penalties imposed on Norwegian citizens. Nevertheless, such a dual system seems objectionable, especially when a Norwegian and a foreign national are involved in the same crime.

Sentencing practices vary from one country to another; for example, sentencing in the Scandinavian countries differs in many respects from that in the United States. With the exception of penalties for drunken driving, sentencing in the Scandinavia countries is much more uniform and more lenient. It is therefore dangerous to generalize. A study of sentencing practice in Norway leads to the conclusion that when general deterrence considerations are part of the grounds of a judgment, the general penalty level, not the effect of the particular sentence, is determinative. However, this is not necessarily the case in other countries.

Nigel Walker's exposition on "exemplary sentences," for example, seemingly reveals a willingness of English courts to adjust a sentence to the needs of deterrence felt in the particular case. "A judge who believes that more severe sentences will influence potential offenders, but who cannot ensure that his colleagues will adopt his policy, will sometimes impose sentences which are markedly more severe than the norm for the express purpose of increasing their deterrent effect."[22] Exemplary sentences, Walker explains, are usually imposed to deal with a specific offense which has suddenly become more frequent or which has attracted much publicity, especially if the instances of the offense are limited to a certain locality.

A famous example of this system at work is the use of harsh sentences to suppress attacks on blacks in the Notting Hill district of London in 1958.[23] Nine boys, six only seventeen years old and all but one with no police record, were sentenced to four years imprisonment. This imposition of exemplary sentences was upheld by the Court of Criminal Appeal. Other trials follwed, in which offenders received lighter sentences; and the race riots waned after the exemplary sentences. But it is extremely difficult to ascertain the role of the exemplary sentences in ending the turmoil.

Walker supports using criminal penalties as a deterrent but argues against the occasional exemplary sentence, not for ethical reasons but because he questions the effectiveness of the exemplary sentence. However, there may be fields where the exemplary sentence works effectively; white collar crime may be such a field. A high official of the Antitrust Division of the United States Justice Department stated some years ago:

> No one in direct contact with the living reality of business conduct in the United States is unaware of the effect the imprisonment of seven high officials in the electrical Machinery Industry in 1960 had on the conspiratorial price fixing in many areas of our economy; similar sentences in a few cases each decade would almost completely cleanse our economy of the cancer of collusive price fixing and the mere prospect of such sentences is itself the strongest available deterrent to such activities.[24]

Even assuming that unusually heavy penalties of the Notting Hill type have the desired effect, such penalties may be objectionable from an ethical standpoint because they are arbitrary, imposing unequal treatment on one actor but not on another who may be equally blameworthy. But it will not always be easy to tell whether an exemplary sentence is being imposed. As mentioned above, the distinction between the two points at which considerations of general prevention can enter the sentencing process (in calculating the effects of a certain *level of penalties* or of a *particular sentence*) is not a sharp one. A judge in deciding the right level of penalties for a specific crime at a specific time and place comes close to considering the effects of the particular sentence. And it may happen that the judge, in pronouncing a sentence harsher than previous practice would dictate, does not himself know whether he is changing to a new level of penalties or only temporarily parting from the standard sentence to impose an exemplary sentence.

Sometimes it may seen fictitious to talk about determining a level of sentencing, because the case under consideration is more or less unique. The *Quisling* case may serve as an example. The Norwegian Supreme Court sentenced Quisling to death for treason, apparently motivated by a belief that it was necessary to apply the supreme penalty for reasons of general prevention.[25] If it is granted that the death penalty is permissible, the decision is not objectionable. There is no disproportion between crime and punishment and no breach of the principle of equality before the law.

IV. Proof of Deterrent Effect

The result of our discussion so far can be summed up in this statement: Punishment on the basis of general prevention is ethically defensible, both in legislation and sentencing, if the penalty is in reasonable proportion to the gravity of the offense and does not violate the principle of equality before the law. However, the question may be raised from another angle. It is often asserted that there is no scientific proof for the general preventive effects of punishment, and it may be argued that it is morally unjustifiable to inflict punishment on the basis of a belief which is not corroborated by scientific evidence. The burden of proof, it is sometimes said, is on those who would invoke punishment. Others may answer that the burden of proof is on those who would experiment at the risk of society by removing or weakening the protection which the criminal law now provides.

Two points should be made. First, our lack of knowledge of general prevention may be exaggerated. In some areas of criminal law we have experiences which come as close to scientific proof as could be expected in human affairs. In many other areas it seems reasonably safe to evaluate the general preventive effects of punishment on a common sense basis. Modern psychology has shown that the pleasure-pain principle is not as universally valid as is assumed, for instance, in Bentham's penal philosophy. Nevertheless, it is still a fundamental fact of social life that the risk of unpleasant consequences is a very strong motivational factor for most people in most situations.

Second, even in questions of social and economic policy we rarely are able to base our decisions on anything which comes close to strict scientific proof. Generally we must act on the basis of our best judgment. In this respect, the problems of penal policy are the same as problems of education, housing, foreign trade policy, and so on. The development of social science gradually provides a better factual foundation for decisions of social policy, but there is a long way to go. Besides, research always lags behind the rapid change of social conditions.

However, it is undeniable that punishment—the intentional infliction of suffering—is a special category among social policies. It contrasts sharply with the social welfare measures which characterize our modern state. This calls for caution and moderation in its application. I do not think the legal concept of "burden of proof" is very useful in this context. The balance that should be struck between defense of society and humaneness towards the offender can hardly be expressed in a simple formula. The solution of the conflict will depend on individual attitudes. Some people identify more with the values threatened by criminal behavior; others identify more with the lawbreaker. But certainly punishment should not be imposed precipitously. History provides a multitude of examples of shocking cruelty based on ideas of deterrence, often in combination with ideas of just retribution.

One conclusion ought to be beyond controversy. As long as society feels obliged to use punishment for general preventive reasons, it is important for researchers to attempt to evaluate the accuracy of the assumptions that lawmakers, courts and law enforcement agencies make about general prevention. This is a badly neglected field of research. It may be necessary and ethically justifiable to base policy decisions on common sense reasoning, often amounting to sheer guesswork, as long as no other alternative exists.

But it is morally indefensible to continue to punish other human beings without making real efforts to replace speculation with scientific facts.

Notes

1. See Andenaes, "The General Preventive Effects of Punishment," 114 *U. Pa. L. Rev.* 949 (1966); Hawkins, "Punishment and Deterrence: The Educative, Moralizing, and Habituative Effects," 1969 *Wis. L. Rev.* 550.

2. Bittner & Platt, "The Meaning of Punishment," 2 Issues in *Criminology* 79, 93 (1966).

3. Kant, "Metaphysische Anfangsgrunde der Rechtslehre," zweiter Teil, erster Abschnitt, *Das Staatsrecht Allgemeine Anmerkung E.* (1797). The question has been thoroughly discussed in German literature since World War II as a reaction to the extreme application of general deterrence under the Nazi regime. See Bruns, "Die 'Generalpraevention' als Zweck und Zumessungsgrund der Strafe?" *Festschrift fur Hellmut von Weber zum 70. Geburtstag* (1963). Several authors have expressed the opinion that the acceptance of general prevention as an aim of punishment violates article 1 of the new German Constitution, which declares the dignity of man inviolable. Some also adduce the European Convention of Human Rights in support of their position. The German courts, however, have not accepted these views. See 1968 *Deutsche Juristenzeitung* 388; Judgment of May 6, 1954, 6 *Entscheidungen des Bundesgerichtshofs in Strafsachen [BGHSt.]* 125; Judgment of Aug. 4, 1965, 20 *BGHSt.* 264.

4. It should be noted in passing that the other traditional justifications for punishment are also subject to attack. Retribution as a goal of criminal justice is generally condemned by modern authors. And reform and rehabilitation, long the goals of reformers, have been increasingly criticized in recent years. Experience has shown how even the best of intentions can lead to oppressive results. Thus, efforts at reform and rehabilitation, according to critics, should not exceed the limits established by the other purposes of punishment. Norval Morris, for instance, states as a leading principle of criminal policy: "*Power over a criminal's life should not be taken in excess of that which would be taken were his reform not considered as one of our purposes. The maximum of his punishment should never be greater than that which would be justified by the other aims of our criminal justice.*" Morris, "Impediments to Penal Reform," 33 *U. Chi. L. Rev.* 627, 638 (1966) (emphasis in original). Restraint of dangerous offenders seems to be the only traditional justification of punishment still meeting with general approval, and this justification applies to only a small segment of offenders.

Generally the controversy over punishment reflects differences of opinion with regard to the justification of an institution considered indispensable. But there are also voices which question the institution of punishment itself. Bittner and Platt state that "while the punitive approach has, to all appearances, no future, psychologically oriented treatment is in ascendance." Bittner & Platt, supra note 2, at 98–99. Their explanation for this shift is that the execution of punishment has become less and less compatible with prevailing moral sentiment. "Thus, it appears that in the long run it could not possibly matter whether punishment works or not, for it has been going out of use, not gracefully, but inexorably." Id.

5. As quoted by Radzinowicz and Turner in "A Study on Punishment: Introductory Essay," 21 *Can. B. Rev.* 91, 92 (1943).

6. We shall leave aside the problem of whether general prevention does play or ought to play a role in the execution of sentences and in decisions about release on parole.

7. Bittner & Platt, supra note 2, at 93.

8. H. L. A. Hart, *Punishment and Responsibility* 23 (1968).

9. Feuerbach, *Revision der Grundsatze und Grundbegriffe des positiven peinlichen Rechts*, erster Teil, at 48–58 (1799).

10. As quoted in 31 *Svensk Juristtidning* 373 (1946).

11. A detailed analysis of the problem is given in H. Ofstad, *An Inquiry into the Freedom of Decision* (1961). For a brief discussion see Andenaes, "Determinism and Criminal Law," 47 *J. Crim. L.C. & P.S.* 406 (1956).

12. Bittner & Platt, supra note 2.

13. 1902 *Odelstingsforhandlinger* 438.

14. *Life*, Nov. 10, 1969, at 24.

15. 1968 *Deutsche Juristenzeitung* 388.

16. See E. Schmidt, *Einfuehrung in die Geschichte der deutschen Strafrechtspflege* 63–64, 93–94 (2d ed. 1951); L. Radzinowicz, *A History of English Criminal Law* (1948); E. Anners, *Humanitet och rationalism* 14–15 (1965).

17. 1968 *Norsk Retstidende* 737.

18. Id. at 705.

19. Id. at 707.

20. 1937 *Juristische Wochenschrift* 3083.

21. In the Norwegian bag-snatching case cited above, it is not clear from the judgment whether the Court made any distinction according to whether the change in the crime rate had taken place before or after the commission of the crime.

22. N. Walker, *Sentencing in a Rational Society* 68–69 (1969).

23. Id. at 69–70; Wootton, *Crime and the Criminal Law* 100–1 (1963); Andenaes, supra note 1, at 953, 982.

24. Spivack, as quoted in D. Cressey & D. Ward, *Delinquency, Crime, and Social Process* 210 (1969).

25. 1945 *Norsk Retstidende* 109 (quoted in Andenaes, supra note 1, at 953).

6 The Legal Threat as an Instrument of Social Change

Franklin E. Zimring

and

Gordon Hawkins (1971)

Law and Behavior

There exist two contrasting views on the relationship between legal precepts and public attitudes and behaviour. According to the one, law is determined by the sense of justice and moral sentiments of the population, and legislation is a vehicle through which programmed social evolution can be brought about [Aubert, 1969, p. 69].

At one extreme then is the view expressed in Dicey's lectures (1905) at Harvard Law School in 1896 and a few years later in Sumner's celebrated pioneer study (1906): Law is a dependent variable determined and shaped by current mores and the opinion of society. At the other extreme, the view is exemplified by Soviet jurists like Kechekyan (1956) who see the law as an instrument for social engineering. It is also true, as Aubert (1969) points out, that some sociologists "try, in a limited way, to confront the two views and determine the conditions under which the law may change social relationships [p. 69]." Yet none of those who have addressed themselves to this problem appear to have made any systematic attempt to consider the factors which militate for any systematic attempt to consider the factors which militate for and against the success of law to induce change in customary behavior. This is not to say that no attempt has been made to take account of the variables which determine the effectiveness of law as a means to socialize change. The truth is rather that such attention has been limited to the significance of particular variables in specific situations. Thus Aubert (1966) in his study of the Norwegian Housemaid Law of 1948 emphasizes the importance of the level of information and the process of communicating norms. Gorecki (1966) has drawn attention to the way in which such conditions as the socio-economic structure of the Polish rural areas and social pressures of a customary and religious nature have prevented the realization of the legislative aim of the Polish divorce rules. Dror (1959) has commented on the failure of law to change family life and marriage habits in Turkey and Israel. Indeed on the basis of the Israeli and Turkish experience he formulates a "basic hypothesis" to the effect that "changes in law have more effect

"The Legal Threat as an Instrument of Social Change" appeared first in *Journal of Social Issues* 27, no. 3 (1971): 33–48.

on emotionally neutral and instrumental areas of activity than on expressive and evaluative areas of activity [Dror, 1959, p. 801]." Yet while it is conceivable that such an hypothesis—though the distinction between "instrumental" and "expressive" activities is by no means clear—may have some validity, it can hardly be regarded as doing much more than focusing attention on one aspect of an extremely complex problem.

One other matter deserves comment by way of introduction. Aubert (1966) remarks on what he calls an "ambivalence" or "curious dualism" which ran through the legislative debates on the Housemaid Law:

> It was claimed, on the one hand that the law is essentially a codifica-
> tion of custom and established practice, rendering effective enforce-
> ment inessential. On the other hand, there was a tendency to claim
> that the Housemaid Law is an important new piece of labour legisla-
> tion with a clearly reformatory purpose attempting to change an un-
> acceptable *status quo* [p. 110].

We too have noticed an ambivalence or dualism, although of a rather different character, in discussions of the efficacy of legal attempts to control behavior. Thus is casual conversations we have noted a reluctance on the part of friends and colleagues to formulate objective principles about the extent to which the threat of punishment conveyed by law can change customary behavior. In particular, there seems to be a failure to recognize a distinction between issues relating to the *morality* or *expediency* of prohibiting particular types of behavior and issues relating to the *efficacy* of such prohibitions. Thus there is a tendency for the views expressed to vary as the subject changes from alcohol to marijuana to firearms to racial discrimination, and to vary according to the speaker's view of the rightness or wrongness of prohibiting the particular behavior under discussion. Commonly, the conclusion to such discussions is the comforting one that the law can succeed in doing right but will inevitably fail when authorities attempt to prohibit what should not be prohibited. Unfortunately, since there is a wide variation in moral views among our acquaintances, this general principle leads to contradictory conclusions about the efficacy of particular attempts to control behavior. In the preliminary note that follows, we attempt to discuss in objective terms the use of the legal threat of punishment to induce social change. Our emphasis is more on the narrow issue of the deterrent effect of threat of punishment than on the great variety of other mechanisms associated with compliance to legal commands. Yet we feel a discussion of the narrow topic will inform the general topic of law as an agent of social change.

Threat as a Socializing Mechanism

By definition, the threat of sanctions cannot achieve a deterrent effect unless the presentation of that threat results in some individuals acting differently from the way they would in the absence of the legal threat. In this sense at least the legal threat can always be seen as an attempt to change patterns of behavior. Yet in our view it is important to distinguish between cases where the main thrust of the threat of punishment is aimed at preserving the status quo in social relations from isolated temptations to deviation, and the increasing number of cases in which the legal threat is used in the attempt to change social customs.[1] When the threat of punishment is aimed at preserving the status quo, the formal legal command is usually only one of many forces pushing socialized potential offenders toward conformity. Other social norms will usually exist to complement the behavioral command of the law. Thus knowledge of the law prohibiting burglary is preceded in the socilization process by messages about the wrongness of stealing and home invasion. By the time a citizen reaches adulthood, he has monitored a consistent stream of messages about burglary—messages which, with the specific legal threat, form a network of restraining influences probably stronger than the sum of its separate components. And for most people, when the legal threat is directed at reinforcing a long standing and important social norm, it is usually correct to view a demand for compliance as not requiring the learning of new patterns of behavior. In most cases the traditional habit of imagining that threats are directed by the legal system at each individual in his separate capacity also seems justified.

When the law is used as an instrument of social change, it is more likely that the achievement of acceptable rates of compliance will require an active reorientation of the values and behaviors of the significant part of a threatened audience that has previously followed the outlawed custom. Under these circumstances it would not be surprising to find that the behavior which such threats seek to restrain will have acquired positive social meaning for members of a threatened audience far more often than in the case of traditional crimes. Further, there is reason to suppose that when the law seeks to restrain customary behavior, those whose responses are most important in predicting rates of compliance will be, not individuals, but groups among whom the forbidden behavior has been customary (Massell, 1968; Stjernquist, 1963).

If these assertions are correct, it will be important to note, in any analysis seeking to predict and understand the operation of legal threats, whether the aim of the law is change or stability, because there are differences between the two types of situation that can lead to differences in threat effectiveness. But before elaborating somewhat on the use of threats to achieve social change, a few qualifications are in order.

Some of the conditions associated with the use of legal threats to promote social change occur in other situations where law and custom are not synchronized. In particular, the same kind of circumstances can obtain when the law has not changed but the social values and customs that traditionally supported a law have changed. A change in social conditions without change in legal rules creates much the same kind of disequilibrium between custom and rule that is created by altering the law, and it is this disequilibrium between custom and rule that makes it necessary to consider separately legal threats aimed at social change. In fact, in the contest between an old rule and a new custom, the attempt to return social relations to a prior state can be seen as a subcategory of law as an instrument of social change, albeit a special subcategory, because the legitimacy of the old rule at least will have the support of a tradition of lip service in the community. For this reason there is a basis for viewing America's experiences with alcohol in the 1920s and marijuana in the 1960s as similar attempts to legislate social change. However, it is important to distinguish the cases because, among other reasons, we ordinarily expect the new-law-versus-old-custom contest to provoke more widespread resistance than the old-law-versus-new-custom; the tradition of lip service mentioned above is an inertial force of some consequence.

There are important similarities as well as differences between deterrent threats used to reinforce existing social conventions and those aimed at social change. It would be naive to suppose that the lessons learned about the operation of threats in other settings can have no relevance to the analysis of threats directed at changing customary behavior. The motive force of deterrence in each case is the fear of unpleasant consequences, and many of the same factors that are important in predicting the outcome of threats that reinforce traditional prohibitions will bear significantly on the ability of threats to achieve social change. The vocabulary of deterrence—stressing threat credibility, the severity of sanctions, and modes of communication—will thus be a necessary, if inadequate, tool for analyzing this special class of laws.

There are important differences among threats aimed at social change, and these differences can lead to substantial variations in threat effectiveness. If this is the case, it is a mistake to base general conclusions about the effectiveness of threats as instruments of change on single observations. To deny, for instance, that stateways can change folkways on the basis of "our experience with Prohibition" is to operate from an insufficient inductive basis, unless it can be demonstrated that all attempts to change social behavior through the use of legal threats are similar in all important respects. The essence of this note is that this is not the case. We hope to suggest some of the variations in situations that might explain why some attempts to change customary behavior through legal sanctions succeed while others fail dismally. Among the factors that appear to be most important are variations in the nature of the custom, variations in the social characteristics of the individuals and groups that have adhered to the custom before it was forbidden, and variations in the way in which the threat of punishment is carried out.

Variations in the Nature of the Custom

Differences in the nature of the custom that appear to influence the probability that a custom will be successfully suppressed include: (a) the utilitarian and moral significance of a custom to its adherents, (b) the extent to which a custom enjoys popular support, (c) the degree to which practice of the custom is visible to enforcement agencies, (d) the extent to which the custom is of such a nature that a general change may extinguish individual drives to follow it, and (e) the degree to which the change in custom meets current community needs.

The Significance of Customs

Of obvious importance in predicting the effect of threatening customary behavior is the degree of commitment to a particular custom on the part of members of a threatened audience. Public religious observance and burning high-sulphur coal for home-heating are both social customs of some popularity in the United States, but the two customs are poles apart if the first is a central expression of deeply held religious convictions, while the second persists by reason of casual tradition and convenience. Behavior that is perceived as satisfying important drives is more difficult to extinguish than behavior that satisfies less compelling drives, and this axiom provides us with one basis for ranking the differential significance of customary behavior. A second index for ranking the importance of customs is the extent to which adherents of a particular custom perceive that legitimate alternatives to the prohibited custom exist which can fulfill the drives associated with the customary behavior. Thus, while high-sulphur coal is associated with the admittedly important aim of keeping warm during winter, the availability of other heat sources makes this custom less important than it would be if those who ordinarily heat their houses with this type of coal can be persuaded that practicable heating alternatives exist. Clearly, some forms of customary behavior are more amenable to substitution than others. It would seem difficult, for instance, to persuade a group associated with a suppressed religion that belief in a nonforbidden dogma would yield the satisfaction they associate with their present faith.

When the law seeks to prohibit behavior that has been customary, it is also possible that the prohibited behavior will have acquired a *moral* significance for many of its adherents (as, for example, was the case for Mormons who practiced polygamy in the nineteenth century). The possibility of normative support for a custom introduces a problem that traditional criminal law prohibitions do not often encounter. The moral dimension of adherence to custom is an important element to consider when trying to predict the effect that threatening behavior might have, because the prohibition of conduct that is considered morally right or even morally imperative may give an entirely different character to the reactions of a threatened audience.

Variations in the importance of a custom play a significant role in the simple utilitarian calculus that has long been accepted as a major explanation of the deterrent effect of threats. The more important a custom, the more severe and more certain must be the punishment threatened, if the legal policy is to prove effective as a means of social change. Yet, while this simple formulation might accurately state the relationship between variations in the purely utilitarian value of customary behavior and the effect of legal prohibitions, the situation is somewhat more complex when we consider the ways in which variations in the moral significance attached to customary behavior affect the prospects for prohibition. To be sure, the greater the moral importance of a custom, the greater the unpleasantness of the penalty that must be attached to that custom to secure a change in behavior. But moral support for a prohibited custom can further inhibit the preventive effect of threats by rendering ineffective two usually powerful reasons for complying with legal threats—respect for law and law-abidingness, and the negative social connotations normally conveyed by punishment. Most groups in society believe in the legitimacy of law as a system of social control, which is one important explanation of why so many people obey so many laws. Yet the belief that violation of any law is wrong may be overwhelmed by a specific moral sense when individuals feel that a customary behavior is of greater moral importance than whatever force a general respect for law brings to bear on a particular situation. Thus a man who finds it difficult to commit a petty crime, such as illegal parking for minor pecuniary advantage, because of his feelings—not about parking but about violations of the law—might feel different when the motives he has for law violation are altruistic. Those who continue to place a higher moral value on prohibited behavior may feel more like the doctor exceeding the speed limit to visit a patient than like the petty law violator mentioned above, and even if they continue to express respect for law in general terms, this respect will not be seen as a barrier to violation of the prohibition of the valued custom.

At the same time, the moral significance of a prohibited custom may act to make the consequences of conviction and punishment less worthy of avoidance than they would be otherwise. For the majority of people the most degrading aspect of punishment is the social message it conveys. Conviction and punishment for serious offenses carry social stigma, and the fear of stigma is a significant aspect of the unpleasantness that constitutes the deterrent stimulus. The moral value of customary behavior may result in the would-be offender rejecting the negative significance of punishment for himself if he is punished in a worthy cause. Indeed, he may invert the moral value of the ordinary symbols of degradation by viewing the discomfort and disrepute he suffers as signs of personal dedication. Moreover, if most of his peers share his moral views about a particular type of law violation, their perception of the negative value of punishment may also be inverted and the effects of severe punishment may include positive status for the person subjected to that punishment.

Extent of Popular Support for the Custom

The popularity of a prohibited custom is an important element in predicting the effects of attempting its abolition. At the outset, information about the number of people in society who have supported a now-prohibited custom should help define the sheer size of the social-control task that faces those attempting to enforce the new law. In addition, information about the number of individuals who adhere to the custom can also provide clues as to the types of person the legal threat must reach. The more widespread adherence to a custom has been, the more it will be the case that the legal threat is aimed at normally socialized individuals. The smaller the number of individuals adhering to a custom threatened by law, the more the legal system is on notice that potential violators of the legal prohibition may differ from the general population in ways that might make predicting their responses to threat a special problem.

The extent to which a forbidden custom has adherents in society is also important in predicting how difficult the new law will be to enforce. The more widespread the support for a forbidden custom, the greater the probability that judges, juries, and other administrative personnel will identify with the custom itself or the type of people who adhere to it, and this can undermine enforcement of the law against all offenders or against a class of offenders with which the rest of the community identifies.

One might question whether there are many occasions in which customs with a degree of public acceptance sufficient to generate forces that might inhibit enforcement are outlawed in democratic societies. Yet, while it is certainly the case that authoritarian and "occupation" regimes more commonly institute laws against popular customs, the democratic process can produce such attempts at social change when groups or even regions are in sharp disagreement over the moral propriety of a particular customary behavior. For this reason, any time that the power to declare law is more centralized than, or otherwise removed from, the responsibility of enforcing it, the law itself may not compel the sympathy of the enforcement agencies. Moreover, as long as the group adhering to a particular custom is not thought of as unambiguously deviant, the attempt to maintain customary behavior may attract the sympathies of members of the community who do not identify with the custom, but have no strong scruples against it.

The fact that it is more difficult successfully to prohibit customary behavior should not be interpreted as indicating that success in suppressing the customary behavior is unattainable in such situations. The point is limited to the prediction that suppression of popular custom will require substantial amounts of enforcement activity, which may be difficult to generate.

Visibility of the Custom

Since enforcement of law is a significant part of the basis for predicting whether or not the legal threat will achieve high rates of compliance, the extent to which customary behavior is visible and therefore easier to bring to the attention of an enforcing authority can play a significant role in determining whether an attempt at changing custom through law will succeed. Some customs may be visible because the public nature of the behavior is part of the defining characteristic of the custom. Such is the case with demonstrations, refusals to pledge allegiance to the flag, and certain types of communications. The customary behavior may also achieve a high degree of visibility, without involving large numbers of people, if the practice often comes to the attention of a person who is out of sympathy with the custom. This type of visibility will often occur when a behavior can realistically be thought of as having a victim, as, for example, in the case of face-to-face racial discrimination. The fact that a custom is highly visible is no guarantee that a prohibition will be effectively enforced. And substantial enforcement efforts are, of course no guarantee that punishment on a mass scale will achieve social change. But it is certainly the case that visibility makes the task of enforcement easier if the will and ability to enforce the law exists, and it is clearly more probable that a law against social custom will succeed under conditions of widespread enforcement than under limited or nonexistent enforcement.

Will General Change Make the Custom Obsolete?

Sometimes the law can succeed in changing patterns of behavior because the change in law, if it reduces the gross rate of a custom or behavior, removes some of the reasons that individuals had previously supported the custom. To a certain extent this is true with all patterns of customary behavior, because a large part of the reason why any individual follows a particular custom will usually be that most of the people he knows follow that custom and expect him to do so as well. Any law that changes his expectation of other people's behavior and his notion of what other people expect from him will thus go part of the way toward restructuring the conditions that led to his initial compliance with the custom. In addition to this broad point about the interdependence of expectations, there are a number of other ways in which the abolition of a general expectation that other people will be adhering to a custom may undercut the incentive for an individual's doing so himself. Many people keep firearms in their homes, not because they think other people expect them to, but out of fear of guns in the hands of others. For this type of individual a change in law might provide a credible promise that others would not be armed and thus make it much easier for him to give up his gun. By the same token, the owner of a drugstore lunch counter in the South might be unwilling to desegregate his facility if it meant that his white customers would attribute the responsibility for this change to him, and if he faced the probability of losing his white clientele to other lunch counters that did not desegregate. Prohibition of the custom would, however, put him in the position where he could not be personally blamed for the change in policy, and his white patronage would be protected from raids by his competitors because of the generality of the change in practice. Under these circumstances, prohibiting the custom of discrimination might be an economic advantage to the individual entrepreneur by increasing the demand for his service, while a unilateral change in conduct might be to his economic disadvantage. Given this type of condition, change in custom can be more easily achieved if preceded by change in law.

Custom and Current Needs

It is more likely that the prohibition of customary behavior will attract enthusiastic enforcement and secure widespread compliance if there is a clear necessity which provides a socially acceptable reason for the change in custom. The best reasons yet devised for justifying change in legal relationships are external threat and internal emergency. It is thus much easier in times of war to explain to those affected why previously allowed behavior is being outlawed, e.g., featherbedding in the labor market, or the freedom to determine prices normally accorded to private producers. The drama of changing circumstance and needs can provide a basis for enthusiastic support among the general population for the enforcement of the new prohibition and give what is at least a powerful excuse for compliance to those who were following the old custom.

Because the reason for change is of some importance in predicting the consequences of a change in law, it should not be assumed that certain types of social change, adopted into law during periods of crisis, could be as successfully replicated in the absence of a similar crisis. This does not mean, however, that a change in custom facilitated through change in law may not often survive the crisis which initially gave rise to it. Though to some extent the end of a war or depression marks the end of the need for the change in custom, it cannot be seen as automatically heralding a return to the status quo. Intervening experience with the new way of doing things and the advantages of the change to some groups (perhaps at the expense of others) provide some reason for continuing the change beyond the duration of the conditions that accounted for its initial acceptance. Therefore the suggestion that many types of change in custom are not attainable in the absence of common crisis does not imply that the same changes are not maintainable in the absence of crisis. Indeed a history of emergency tax measures might suggest that some forms of change are very difficult to reverse.

Social Characteristics of the Threatened Audience

Different types of groups who have been used to adhering to customary behavior may come in conflict with a new law. Some groups are more cohesive than others, and cohesive group structure can militate for or against change in custom, depending upon whether group leadership chooses to urge compliance with or defiance of the new law. Perhaps the most important characteristic of groups adhering to custom, from the standpoint of predicting the response to prohibition, is the degree to which group members are integrated participants in the larger social system. The greater the degree of agreement among members of the group with the values of the larger society, the greater will be the pressure upon members of the group to comply with the command of the law. Similarly, incentive to comply with the new law will increase in proportion to the success that group members have experienced in participation in the larger society. Wealth and status provide a powerful motive for support of the legal system and the larger social system it usually represents. Poverty and discrimination, particularly if born of differentiations directly related to group membership, provide fertile ground for rebellion against the prohibition of custom, as well as a basis for generalizing that rebellion into a rejection of the entire value matrix of the legal system.

One complication in the relationship between group identification with the larger society and susceptibility to threat is that high status provides an incentive for compliance only if the threat of punishment for violation is credible. Even values in accordance with the larger society's values will usually require some assurance that the new law will be enforced before they provide a motive for complying. And it is precisely the high status and well-integrated groups in society against whom laws prohibiting customs are most difficult to enforce. But if the will to enforce is sufficient, the incentives that enforcement gives to a successful group to comply with the prohibition of custom will be substantial.

Variations in Law Enforcement

Any discussion of the variables involved in explaining why some attempts to legislate social change succeed while others fail must deal with the character of law enforcement as both a dependent and independent variable. The level of law enforcement must be seen as a dependent variable because many of the factors we have been discussing, such as the popularity of a custom and the characteristics of groups who adhere to it, may influence the kind of enforcement that an attempt to legislate change will produce. Yet the kind and degree of enforcement are not inevitably determined by situational factors of the type discussed above, the character of law enforcement deserves independent attention as a predictor of the effects of an attempt to change custom through law. The degree to which enforcement activities entail likelihood of detection, the extent of enforcement across class and group lines, and the severity of punishments meted out for offense—all are included among the significant variations in law enforcement that may condition rates of compliance.

Likelihood of Apprehension

The simplest statement one can make about the extent of enforcement is that the likelihood of achieving the aim of the law will increase as the perceived likelihood of apprehension for law violation increases. This axiom might deserve some qualification in the situation where a custom is viewed as morally imperative and conscientious objection occurs with a frequency that does not seem to be conditioned by the rate of apprehension or punishment. However, even in the case of a law that generates conscientious objection, increased probability of apprehension and punishment may still reduce the rate of deviation, if only because potential offenders with fewer scruples will respond to such increases.

Selective Enforcement

A second qualification of the general relationship between success in suppressing a custom and perceived likelihood of apprehension is that broader law enforcement means arresting greater numbers of high status people for violation. This increases the pressure on enforcement agencies to reduce and rechannel enforcement efforts and confronts the community with the full implications of what it means to punish deviation from the new law whenever it occurs. Under some circumstances, then, broad law enforcement can lead to an earlier crisis test of the law and perhaps ultimately to its demise. But if broad and nonselective enforcement is somewhat unpredictable in consequence, this in no way implies that the prospects for effective change in custom are any brighter when selective enforcement, focusing on low status groups, becomes the order of the day. Aside from its manifest injustice, the principal danger of highly selective enforcement is that groups who are spared will disobey the law because no real risks accompany their violations, while the target groups for enforcement efforts will perceive the enforcement as being directed against the group, rather than against the behavior. If such conditions persist, neither high nor low status groups are apt to show much respect for the specific law, and rates of noncompliance in the groups for whom the threat of enforcement is quite small will probably continue to be substantial.

If it is not exclusively based on caste or class factors, selective enforcement can have a profound deterrent effect on those with relatively little chance of being caught, since it is these high status groups in society that "scare easier" when confronted with the threat of social disapproval. Thus while one small businessman will doubtless be more impressed if he hears of another businessman of similar station in life being sent to jail for not reporting some of his income, even the incomplete analogy of a racketeer being jailed for this type of offense can teach the small businessman that people can and do get caught for this type of practice. Unless he can persuade himself that enforcement is based exclusively on class factors, this knowledge can produce the kind of anxiety associated with extensive general deterrence.

There is little doubt that enforcement plays a key role in determining whether an attempt to abolish a custom will succeed. We could go further and suggest that, with respect to customary behaviors that are not very important to a threatened audience, the risk of apprehension and punishment is the most important criterion of whether the new law will succeed. The policy value of knowledge about enforcement is less than it might seem, however, for two reasons previously mentioned. First, so many factors relating to the nature of the custom and the type of people against whom the law must be enforced have an effect on the rate of enforcement of a law that it might be wise to think of the risk of apprehension as merely a shorthand expression for a complex of variables. Second, because so many factors affect the rate of detection and punishment, it is difficult to estimate the parameters of practical variability in the enforcement of a particular law. Thus if unalterable conditions make Y the maximum achievable level of enforcement, it will be of little comfort to the law enforcer to tell him that a rate of detection of twice Y rather than Y will reduce the rate of crime by half. So the practical importance of enforcement may be far less than its predictive value.

Rate of Detection

One further question of importance is the degree of detection and punishment necessary to suppress customary behavior. If a custom is popular, the punishment for violating the new law prohibiting it must be severe enough to outweigh, for potential offenders, the advantages of continuing the custom even after the punishment is discounted by the chance of escaping detection. But the risks associated with escalating the level of punishment too far are substantial, because severe penalties may increase pressure on sympathetic jurors, judges, prosecutors, and police, thereby contributing to a breakdown in law enforcement and, ultimately, nullification of the law.

As to what rate of detection will suffice to suppress customary behavior, we would make one comment. The specific rate required will vary from case to case, of course, but the minimum level of apprehension sufficient to abolish customs may be lower than one would expect. While some early authors speak of "certainty" of punishment, rather than some less absolute term, as the key to deterrence, it is not inconceivable that for some customs a detection rate of one per several hundred offenses could lead to the general abandonment of a custom, or at least to substantial repudiation. It must also be added that such a detection rate would be a tribute to efficient enforcement in light of the present rates of one in many thousands that obtain for many victimless crimes in the United States.

Unfinished Business

We conclude this note with the list of significant variables hopelessly incomplete. It may be as well therefore to indicate briefly some of the more important lacunae.

One important omission is the failure to speculate on what differences between cultures make it easier for some legal systems to engineer change than others. The possibilities for discussion here are manifold, but we leave them for another time and more qualified discussants.

We have also failed to mention variations in the conditions of government that would influence the prospects of social change through law. Rather, we have assumed a government that has achieved legitimacy; occupation forces and other nonlegitimate governing bodies will operate under a set of further handicaps—and possibly also with some advantages—which we have not discussed.

A third gap in coverage, this one perhaps a deficiency of emphasis, is the absence of sustained speculation about how variations in social-change situations might affect the extent to which the law can succeed in prohibiting custom through its moral and educative effects. We have suggested that this is more difficult to achieve when the custom being prohibited has acquired positive moral value among its constituency, and we have hazarded a guess that selective enforcement based on caste or class and the lack of an adequate rationale for change might impede the moralizing potential of criminal law. But there are other, more basic, questions. Does the criminal law have the same moralizing and habit-building potential when it acts against the grain of custom? Under what circumstances will the prohibition of custom be counterproductive and act as a negative socialization force by turning parts of a threatened audience against the legal system in general because of the value the threatened individuals place on the prohibited custom? Our failure to treat these issues in detail is no indication that they lack importance but rather a tribute to their richness and complexity.

We have not discussed the many costs associated with regimes of threat and punishment. Thus, it does not follow from the fact that abolition of custom is possible that legal prohibitions will be worth their cost. Among the more interesting relevant questions is this: At what point will citizen loyalty snap under the pressure of coerced social change? Again, we must admit to being presently incapable of adequately discussing this question.

Finally, we have failed to examine, in detail, a single episode of attempted social change through legal threat in order to demonstrate the importance of some of the variables we have been discussing. We look forward to pursuing this path at some later date.

Notes

1. See Stjernquist (1963), at p. 158: "The above division into behaviour-changing and behaviour-stabilizing norms has proved to be practical in different social sciences. Means, in *The Structure of the American Economy* I (Washington: National Resources Committee, 1939), uses the terms 'administrative rules' and 'canalizing rules' respectively. . . . Homans, *The Human Group* (London, 1951), applies a similar division of norms but has a special terminology: 'norms apply to the maintenance of established behaviour, orders to future changes in behaviour.' Homans also points out that 'orders are always changing into law and custom.' "

References

Aubert, V. Some social functions of legislation. *Acta Sociologica*, 1966, 10, 98–110.
———. *Sociology of law.* Baltimore: Penguin Books, 1969.
Dicey, A. B. *Lectures on the relation between law and public opinion in England during the nineteenth century.* London: Macmillan, 1905.
Dror, Y. Law and Social Change. *Tulane Law Review*, 1959, 33, 787–802.
Gorecki, J. Divorce in Poland: A socio-legal study. *Acta Sociologica*, 1966, 10, 68–80.
Kechekyan, S. F. Social progress and law. *Transactions of the Third World Congress of Sociology*, 1956, 6, 42–51.
Massell, G. J. Law as an instrument of revolutionary change in a traditional milieu: The case of Soviet Central Asia. *Law and Society Review*, 1968, 2, 179–228.
Stjernquist, P. How are changes in social behaviour developed by means of legislation? In *Legal essays: A tribute to Frede Castberg on the occasion of his 70th birthday, 4 July 1963.* Oslo: Universitets-forlaget, 1963.
Sumner, W. G. *Folkways.* Boston: Ginn, 1906.

Five

Mental Illness and
the Criminal Law

7 The Brothel Boy
A Fragment of a Manuscript
Norval Morris (1982)

The piece is handwritten, in Eric Blair's characteristic, cramped, meticulous script. There are frequent crossings out and emendations. There are occasional spelling inversions, such as "gaurd" for "guard," which are surprising, considering the obvious overall attention the document has received.

As an essay it is uneven. Parts reveal Blair-Orwell at his most masterful—phrases and sentences that he will use again in his later writings; parts are verbose and pretentious, like the early efforts of one ambitious to be a writer but insecure in the craft, struggling too hard for effect.

The document also foreshadows many of the ideas its author later developed in depth and subtlety, themes that later supported novels and essays. That alone would assure its lasting importance. It is a major find.

I bought it for the equivalent of $185 while on a holiday pilgrimage, retracing Blair's travels during his period in Burma. The vendor was a Parsee; at least he was either a Parsee or a half-caste Anglo-Indian, but I think probably a Parsee since he did not affect an English accent. He bought the manuscript, he said, from some Dacoits who had boasted to him of their courage in breaking into a Government bungalow. He confessed to having purchased the few sticks of furniture and the few personal effects they had stolen. He had quickly got rid of everything other than these papers, which he now held in a crumpled, yellow, paper bag. All this was many years ago; he had turned to legitimate business long since of course—on that I could rely. He had heard of my interest in Eric Blair and thought I might like to see these papers.

It is true that Blair once wrote to his mother about a burglary of his quarters—"who should guard this guardian if he can't guard himself"—though he had not, possibly for reasons of embarrassment, reported it to his superiors in Mandalay; but he had made no mention to either of the loss of a manuscript, which is surprising.

So much for my find. The amount I paid for it, annas to the value of $185, still puzzles me; the sum is a tribute either to the vendor's ignorance or to the purchaser's gullibility.

"The Brothel Boy" appeared as number 18 of *Occasional Papers*, published by the University of Chicago. © 1982 by Norval Morris.

Here it is, gaps and all.

* * *

Moulmein
Upper
Burma
1927

I wonder does any other Old Etonian roll his own cigarettes? And I'm not sure why I do. They are cheaper, of course, but the taste is not very different and bits and pieces of tobacco do drift into one's mouth and require picking off the tongue or lips, which seems to disturb some who observe it. In the Club they make no secret of their disapproval—"A frightfully low-bred habit."

"Blair, *do* take one of mine, it's so much easier."

"No thanks, I prefer these," and I watch their foreheads wrinkle in revulsion.

I had carefully rolled a cigarette and was about to moisten the paper, my tongue protruding, mouth agape, when a native boy burst into my office shouting, "Come, come Sir. Hurry please. They are killing the brothel boy."

I knew, of course, of the local brothel, but not of any "brothel boy." A homosexual prostitute seemed most unlikely in Burma, quite out of character with local values and prevailing behaviour—but I had mistaken his role. At all events, I hurried to where I was led to find several village men standing over the unconscious youth but desisting now from further violence. They were, it seemed immediately obvious, the remainder of a mob of assailants, though how I knew remains unclear to me.

The boy was unconscious, bleeding from the head and face from wounds inflicted by repeated kicks. His shoulder was twisted, obviously broken. His clothes, when whole scarcely adequate, were now gaping, torn, and bloody, He lay in a fetal curve, clutching his groin. The expression on what was left of his features was of anguished surprise, the lips drawn back, mortal fear apparent. The smell of fear and violence, of sweat and vomit, was pervasive.

Resentfully they stood back to allow me to inspect him. Then, not concealing my reluctance, they helped me carry him to the police station, where I telephoned Dr. Veraswami at the nearby hospital. By the time Dr. Veraswami had arrived I knew the outline of the events that had led to the brothel boy's beating. Some villagers returning to the fields in the afternoon had heard a girl's screams from a heavily overgrown area near the river customarily used for washing, but not at this time of day. When they reached her the screaming had ceased; she lay, a young girl, naked in the brothel boy's arms. She had been raped. In her struggles she had apparently struck her head violently on a sharp rock. The boy had made no effort to flee.

The girl was taken to her home. More villagers arrived. The boy was attacked. He might or might not have been killed—my arrival may have saved him for the hangman. Or the villagers may have overcome their dislike of the Raj's justice sufficiently to bring him to me. It was, after all, a fairly clear case—a young girl, a virgin, raped and injured by the brothel boy.

And it became an even clearer case when, a few days later, she died from the combined effects of the head wound and septicaemia. A villainous mixture of local herbs which the villagers had applied to her head wound probably hastened her death. Dr. Veraswami had not been called.

The law began its processes. By this time I had been long enough in the service of the magistracy to know what must be done to prepare for and carry out a trial in a capital case. In such cases I usually acted only as judge and prosecutor, avoiding the further incongruous role of defense counsel I also assumed in less serious crimes. It was not required, but I had fallen into the practice of asking one or other of the three Burmese claiming some forensic skill to represent indigent natives accused in serious cases. But this time my requests were firmly rejected. There was nothing to be said. He had raped her and she had died. He had been caught immediately. He did not deny what he had done. The only question was whether the villagers would kill him or whether the Raj, with its quaint, imported formality and pretense of independence, would do so. They could see no reason in impeding the Raj. So I was judge, prosecutor, and defense counsel, equally untrained in all three roles, though with developing experience in minor disputes and lesser criminal matters. Certainly the boy could not do much for himself.

I interviewed him under close gaurd in the hospital. I tried to talk quietly to him; I didn't hurry, sitting silent for long periods. He would look down and away, immobile, never volunteering a word or gesture. The emanation was of one cloyingly anxious to please, but not knowing how to. Whenever I asked him what happened by the river, he would rush to sweaty verbosity, his head and shoulders bobbing forward with exaggerated sincerity, "Please, Sir, I paid, I'm sorry Sir. . . . Please Sir, I paid, I'm sorry Sir," the words running on with rising inflexion, flooding incoherently into one another, until he would begin to sob. When the crying stopped he would return to his motionless silence. And if I again even remotely probed the events by the riverside, the same miserable routine would be followed.

If I asked him to do something, to stand up or sit down, to open a window or a door, to bring me that chair, he would leap to obey, diligence gleaming in his eyes, ingratiatingly obedient, like a well-trained dog. But I could achieve no communication with him beyond his prompt obedience to simple order. I tried different tacks to relate to him, asking him about many things, always speaking clearly and slowly, but to little effect. Sometimes he would seem to understand and give a monosyllabic reply, accompanied always by a clipped "Sir," and sometimes would offer a shy and innocent smile, but words and smiles seemed quite random, having little to do with my question. And as soon as I approached the matter of the girl, or washing by the river, or even money, out would spill the "Please Sir, I paid, I'm sorry Sir" flowing to tears, sometimes preceded by the incongruous smile.

"A 'perseveration,' I believe it iss called," Dr. Veraswami told me. "Over and over and over he says the same things in the same words in hiss mind, believing them completely I think, but not an idea what they mean. Sometimes he will say it all, sometimes bits and pieces, you will find, but always in the same sequence, going round and round, exactly the same. You will get very little more from him. It iss all hiss silly mind will let him think about. Perhaps not silly, issn't it. Safer so. But I doubt he pretends; he does not malinger, I think. He tells you all he can tell himself."

So it proved. The boy was obviously stupid. And the meaningless repetition and cringing self-pity became increasingly distasteful.

I went to the brothel to try to learn more of the boy. He had, it seemed, been born there some twenty or so years ago. Who his mother had been was remembered—she had worked for the previous owners of the brothel but had died a few years after the boy's birth. His father was, of course, undiscoverable; any one of the older male population of this or neighbouring villages could be a candidate for that unsought honor. The present brothel keeper, a smarmy lady of large physique, expressed unqualified praise of her own virtue in having let the boy stay when she bought the brothel some years ago. He was, she said, until now an entirely reliable punkah puller, willing to keep the fans moving for the more prosperous clients who wanted them and would pay for them, while he faded into the background.

I could understand how unobtrusive he would have been. As interested in him as I was, I found it hard to see him as a person at all. On any subject apart from the crime, he said only what he thought he ought to say. Otherwise, immobile, slight, turned away, he seemed as present as the furniture.

"How did he keep himself?" I asked the proprietress of the brothel. She was lyrical in her praise of her generosity. She kept him without charge. Actually let him sleep inside. Clothed and fed him. And sometimes, she said, customers, anxious to show off, would give him a few annas. And she would, in her bountiful kindness, let him keep them. This was, I supposed, the source of his savings, which he tried to give to the girl he killed. "Did he help the girls if they were treated badly by a customer?" I further enquired. Indeed not; that was her job. And, archly, there were always men of the village to whom she could look for assistance if she needed. But that was very rare. The girls knew they should expect, even encourage, vigour in some customers. They were often the best customers. And the girls knew she would care for them if they were hurt. It would be most improper for the boy to intervene. He was enough trouble to her without that.

All he was expected to do, she explained, was to keep the punkah moving gently to begin with and perhaps later slightly more swiftly so that, by different methods, he and the girl could cool the customer. She laughed with betel-gummed delight at her own wit and then explained to me that the boy's job was very easy, that often he did it on his back, his arms pillowing his head, his heel in the loop of rattan which by regular pressures waved the overhead punkah. She developed this theme of his sloth and her generosity at some length.

"What of his schooling?" I asked. And this confirmed her view of the idiocy of the white servants of the Raj. Powerful eye-rolling laughter was her response, so that I had that often recurring sense of how alien and useless I was in this Burmese setting. A brothel boy at school would be more at home than this assistant police magistrate in Upper Burma. And about as useful, I suppose, in her view.

I asked the brothel keeper if she knew how the boy had met the girl he killed. Her already ample bosom rose, swelled, and trembled with indignation. He had met the girl when he helped her with her parents' laundry. Washing was men's work, but the girl's father was often unwell and the girl did it for him. It was, of course, the brothel boy's duty, in return for the brothel keeper's munificence towards him, to do the washing for the brothel, which took him daily to the river. The boy had, she thought, on occasion assisted the girl by helping her carry some of her parents' laundry to and from the river. She had, it appeared, most unwisely chatted with him in a friendly way when they met. The proprietress had on occasion made it her business, indeed gone out of her way, to warn the girl that the boy was a fool, a simpleton, not to be trusted, and that she should behave towards him like everyone else, not talk to the stupid boy except to tell him what to do or not to do or to reprimand him. But the girl would not listen. She was only a child of twelve or thirteen, but even so she should have known better, as the younger girls in the brothel all understood, certainly after the kindly but firm warnings so generously given.

I turned to Dr. Veraswami to try to understand the boy and his crime. As usual, Dr. Veraswami was pleased to talk to me about this or any other subject, it seemed. Both of us lacked friends and conversational partners in Moulmein. Dr. Veraswami's children by his first marriage were grown and departed, those by his second were old enough to love but not to talk with. And his present wife would run to hide in the kitchen when she saw me approaching their bungalow. She had, the Doctor told me with a gentle smile, "many fine qualities indeed, indeed, but the confidence in conversation of a particularly timid mouse."

Dr. Veraswami was the only person I enjoyed in Moulmein, certainly the only one I felt at all close to since, try as I would, I could never establish any reciprocal warmth of feeling with any of the natives, though I think some of them knew I respected them. My servants would not talk at all of the crime, looking anxiously resentful and falling silent if I mentioned the boy. By contrast, in the Club, it was a subject of unending, energetic, circumlocutiously salacious chatter, the details of which I spared myself by stressing that since the matter was *sub judice* I should not mention it or receive advice about it. This did no good, of course, but it did give me a further excuse to avoid the Club, and confirmed the prevalent view of me there as a posturing outsider, probably a coolie lover.

Dr. Veraswami had, after all, worked in a mental hospital, and he was closer to the Burmese, certainly in their illnesses, than anyone who was not Burmese. So I turned to him.

The evenings on the porch, the rattan armchairs, the foliage still hanging heavy from the regular late-afternoon rain-shower, the smells and sounds of the village and the nearby hospital and jail, the heat abating, and the bottles of Watney's beer with their wired glass stoppers clinking among the few tired lumps of ice in the oval bucket, made an oasis of mind talking to mind profoundly different from the relentless ritual phrases of the Club. And it was good to have the chance to learn from him about matters my reading had neglected.

"The boy iss, I think, quite retarded, but to what level iss hard to tell." Dr. Veraswami seemed perplexed. "Iss not easy to be sure. After all, my friend, he iss quite illiterate. Unlike you, he and books move in different circles, always have and will. Measuring such a mind iss beyond me, and others also issn't it. But he iss certainly far backward, far backward."

The villagers had made much of the girl's virginity; I wondered about the boy's sexual experience. Dr. Veraswami was again hesitant, but did not doubt my speculation that the violence by the river might have been the boy's first experience of intercourse. He had witnessed much, of course, but the brothel girls would certainly see themselves as superior to and distant from the boy. Chastity, in the sense of absence of congress with a woman, may well have been forced on the boy.

"Is he mad? Was he mad?" I asked the doctor.

"To be sure, I don't know at all. . . . He iss certainly not normal. But given hiss life, dear friend, how would you know what he thinks . . . if he does think, ass you mean it."

"Mad or not, dear doctor, is he likely to do something like this again, or has he learned his lesson?" Surely the swift and brutal punishment for his venery, then the arrest and everyone condemning him, had instructed even his dull mind.

Dr. Veraswami was not so sure. "One would think so, indeed one would. But I must tell you that there are cases like hiss where even after very severe punishment the act is repeated. You must not, dear friend, underestimate . . ." and here he grasped wildly in the air for an unembarrassing euphemism, and with triumph found it ". . . the power of the gonads! . . . Of course, if you hold him in prisson for twenty years there would then be little risk—these fires do with the years burn less intensely, believe me—but I doubt he would survive so long in prisson."

Dr. Veraswami's resignation in the matter began to annoy me. "Well, if you can't help with why he did it, or whether he's dangerous, what should be done about him?"

"He will be hanged, of course."

I protested that we both knew the boy meant no harm, no evil. The more I thought about him and his crime, the less wicked it seemed, though the injury to the girl and her family was obviously extreme; it was a tragedy, not a sin.

Dr. Veraswami was relentless. "You think him retarded, and he iss. You think him ignorant of what he should and should not do, and he iss. You think he meant no harm, just like an animal, a reaction to the girl. But don't you see, dear friend, all your English colleagues see him ass just the same ass other Burmese, indistinguishable from all other native boys. All look alike. All are stupid, ignorant, cunning, untrustworthy, dirty, smelly, sexually uncontrolled. All are the same. To excuse him because he iss just like the rest would in their minds be madness in you, not him."

I had no answer. "And," he continued, glancing toward the village, "so I fear iss the view of the Burmese. A brothel boy, yess, but in no other way different. They don't let mind speed worry them. You think he iss different and therefore innocent where others would be guilty; you may be right, probably so, but the villagers don't agree! You must do what your British friends at the Club and the villagers both expect you to do."

My testiness increased. "You seem so content in this, Doctor. The boy is surely *less* responsible than most killers; he meant no harm insofar as he understood what was happening; and you seem so swiftly to accept his hanging. Surely he is *less* worthy of being hanged than most murderers."

Dr. Veraswami was waving his head vigorously from side to side as I spoke. This, I had earlier discovered, was a frequent Indian gesture easily mistaken for dissent, but having the larger meaning of a qualified assent—in effect: you are nearly right but not quite. "The jail, the prisson, perhaps," he said, waving to the nearby dingy walls. "He could sit there on the other side of the wall with the others until he died perhaps. He will learn nothing there, ass you know. Have even less to do than in the brothel. If anything he will become even more idiot than now. And they will prey on him." Then, after a pause to acknowledge my troubled silence, "Or perhaps the place where we lock up the mad. Have you seen it? . . . Worse, I think, than the prisson. Have you been there?"

I had and it was. No psychiatrist could possibly wish to work in such circumstances and none did. It was indeed the least desirable service for any doctor, Burmese or Indian—and no English doctor had as yet ever drunk enough to find himself posted there.

"But iss it not much the same, . . . even in England?" Dr. Veraswami asked. It was not really a question. He knew. I did not know. What he implied was probably the truth.

"So what, dear police magistrate friend, would you have us do with the boy? Shall I take him home with me? Keep him here to serve us beer? Iss it not difficult enough for me to live in this dreadful place without taking him ass a son to my bosom? The villagers would indeed then reject me entirely quite. Or iss he to be a part of the police magistracy? You would be more doubted and even less respected—a most unwise move indeed, indeed. . . ." And he trailed off to vague head wavings.

"I wonder, Doctor, if one of us could have talked to the girl before she died, what would she have wanted me to do?"

"She would have been more scared of me than of you—Indian doctors, ass you know, bewitch village maidens and turn them into hyenas or other horrible animals; English policemen merely steal them! I doubt either of us could have made her understand very much about the boy. But what if we could? How could she forgive him? How tell him? Take the money from him, perhaps . . . ? It iss offensive. No, you will get no help from such thoughts, my friend. It could not in any way have been her problem. It iss yours."

Later, reflecting on the realities Dr. Veraswami had held up to me, I found myself dreaming the reformer's dreams, summoning resources of medicine, psychiatry, prisons without brutality, and a political caring ages removed from Burma under the Raj.

Did much change? I was not sure. Certainly, the boy would not be executed, since with the movement towards minimum social decencies the executioner is one of the first functionaries to be retired. But others tend to take his place. A larger self-caring often accompanies a larger caring for others. The boy might well be held until cured. And how would one ever know that? Only by letting him out. And one can't do that until he is cured. So he must be held. The false language of treatment and cure would replace the Burmese bluntness of condign punishment—and who could tell which is to be preferred? If the boy could choose he would choose to avoid the hangman, but there would be other whips and torments waiting for him even in my dream of the all-loving State.

My daydreams of the boy and I being elsewhere and at another time, rather than here and now in Moulmein, were understandable but gave me no comfort. My decision would have been cruelly lonely had not Dr. Veraswami seemed to enjoy our discussions and to wish to help me in my thrashings around to avoid hanging the boy. Sometimes, however, he struck home hurtfully. I was pressing him for his opinion of how the boy felt in killing—caring, cruel, lost, bewildered? I suggested confusion and a sense of isolation. Dr. Veraswami looked incredibly embarrassed. "Did you not tell me, dear friend, of some difficulties you and some of your distinguished young friends . . . ass it were . . . experienced at that fine English preparatory school you attended before Eton? St. Cyprian's, isn't it?" I had no idea what he was talking about and remained silent. He blushed. Indians do blush, though less obviously of course than Englishmen. "Enuresis, issn't it, I believe. . . . Flogged for what you did not know how to avoid, I think you said." And I knew that I too was suddenly blushing, the lobes of my ears scarlet, the guilt of my childhood bed-wetting still upon me. Dr. Veraswami was sure he had offended me; his agitation increased. He got up, fussing about with bottles of beer, now warming as the bits of ice he had somewhere found melted to fragments.

He was, of course, quite right. In a sense I had been where the brothel boy found himself. I had been beaten for my sins, sins which were clearly both wicked and outside my control, yet nevertheless sins, or so they seemed to me and to Bingo and to Sim, who wielded the cane and broke the riding crop on me.

It was possible, therefore, to commit a sin without knowing you committed it and without being able to avoid it. So it had seemed then, and the feeling of guilt undeniably remained, and strong. Sin was thus sometimes something that happened—to me as to the brothel boy. You did not properly speaking *do* the deed; you merely woke up in the morning to find in anguish that the sheets were wringing wet.

I tried to calm Dr. Veraswami, to assure him that he had not offended me, that I appreciated his directness, that I needed his help. This led me to an excessive confession, one I had made to no one else, and probably no one else knew about it, not even Sim. The last time Sim had flogged me for bed-wetting I remember with great pain a further loss of control of my bladder and a warm flow inside my short pants, down the inside of my left knee, onto my long socks and into my left shoe. Sim had me bent over a desk, posterior protruding; but I hoped most desperately and still in misery believe that the desk shielded his eyes from my pants and the pool which may have formed at my feet. The shame, had the puddle been seen and almost surely commented on, would have been beyond bearing. But I still don't know if it was.

Dr. Veraswami's hands were flying about in near frenzy. I tried hurriedly to make the link to the case of the brothel boy, straining thus to calm him. I thought he feared a breach in our friendship, but that is unfair; on reflection I think his only anxiety was that he was troubling me too deeply. Perhaps he was.

Were my feelings then, and the brothel boy's now, at all comparable? Had I become a ponderous, unfeeling mixture of Bingo and Sim, punishing the boy by death because of the harshness of the environment into which he had been flung, compared to which my trials at St. Cyprian's were trivial?

Dr. Veraswami would have none of it. "Dear friend, bed-wetting and rape which kills . . . how can you compare them at all? . . . misplaced guilt . . . childish fears and adversities loom ever large, but no, not at all, not in any way like the brothel boy's guilt."

Perhaps gallows humor would reassure the Doctor that he had not wounded me. "At all events, Dr. Veraswami, after that beating, when I wet my sock and shoe, I did not wet my bed again. I was cured. Sim cured me. The hangman will surely cure any lack of control our brothel boy may have over his burgeoning sexual instincts!"

But Dr. Veraswami was hardly listening. "No, no, no, dear Sir . . . enuresis while you sleep; sexual attack while awake; nothing similar."

So I pressed the analogy, suggesting that precautions might be taken to empty the bladder. One might arrange to be awakened during the night if others would help. What were the precautions the brothel boy should have taken against copying what he had seen, and seen as acceptable, to be purchased when the flesh engorged? The brothel boy could hardly be justly punished for the desire. Obviously he had nothing to do with it, less than I had with the springs of enuresis. And whence was he to find the wisdom and control, in unsought and unexpected heat, not to do what probably seemed to him an obvious and acceptable act. He had observed in the brothel apparent gratitude by both parties, simulation and true appreciation being indistinguishable by him. Where were the differences between him and me in sinning? The distinctions seemed to favour him.

Dr. Veraswami's intensity increased. "No, you are very wrong, forgive me contradicting you, but you are off a lot. The boy must have known he was hurting her, dull though he iss. The girls in the brothel fear and complain of violence, they talk to each other about it often, the boy must have known. Once he came close upon her, he knew, he knew, believe me my friend. The cases are quite different. You do yourself too much injustice. You did not sin, he did, and most grievously. Your comparison with your bed-wetting misses the essential difference, isn't it—he was conscious of what he wass doing, you were not. And being conscious, backward and confused though he iss, mistreated and bewildered though he wass, he must be held responsible. You must convict him, punish him, hang him! He iss a citizen of Burma, a subject of your Imperial Majesty, but you must treat him ass a responsible adult and punish him. That is what citizenship iss."

I had never before heard such a lengthy, passionately sibilant speech from Dr. Veraswami. It seemed to have calmed him. Again, it didn't help me.

It seemed to me that the discussion had tilted crazily against the brothel boy. Responsibility . . . citizenship . . . consciousness of what he was doing . . . were these sensible standards for a youth of his darkly clouded intelligence and blighted situation? And, if not, what standard should be applied, to what end, with what results?

An all-wise God could by definition draw these fine distinctions, but it was hard to think of the brothel boy and an omniscient God as in any way related, hardly an omnibenevolent God to be sure. And I knew that I was no plenipotentiary of such a divinity; a minor agent of the Raj was enough for me. My employers had never distinguished themselves in drawing delicately generous moral distinctions; indeed, they seemed to judge entirely by the results and not by the intentions, which surely must inhibit any fine gradations in attributing responsibility.

Did this mean that there was no room at all in my jurisdiction for mercy, for clemency? I decided to put the question to Dr. Veraswami.

Unlike my fellow members of the Club, Dr. Veraswami enjoyed my skill in rolling cigarettes. He rarely smoked but occasionally would accept one of my home-made cigarettes. He preferred to moisten the paper himself, I holding the enfolded tobacco out to him; but he also cheerfully accepted those the product of my own hands and tongue.

When talking to Dr. Veraswami, I found I sometimes rolled a cigarette to give me time to phrase a point of delicacy or difficulty, as many who smoke a pipe use the ritual of filling, lighting, and tamping as time for meditation. On this occasion, the cigarette rolling was a preamble to an effort to seek Dr. Veraswami's views on the moral aspects of the problem of the brothel boy. And, if he agreed that the boy was less culpable, to press him why he was so adamant about the hanging.

"Do you know a painting by Peter Paul Rubens of the Last Judgment?" I asked Dr. Veraswami. "It is a huge painting with lovely though overweight naked ladies and gentlemen going up to unclothed inactivity above the right hand of Christ. Just below His left hand there is an interesting Prince of Darkness in control of a lecherous team dragging the damned off to un-painted horrors, with a face at the bottom of the Devil's side of the painting screaming in agony."

Dr. Veraswami said he had seen a poor print of it once, he thought, but in any event he plunged ahead of my circumlocution to the heart of the question. "You ask, I suppose, my friend, where will the boy be if the admirable Mr. Rubens paints truth? Of course, I don't know. I am not a Christian but, if I were, I would guess he will not be among those damned."

"Well, then, how can you tell me to hang him? I asked, pressing Dr. Veraswami for reconciliation of what some would see as conflicting positions.

Dr. Veraswami yielded to no difficulty in the reconciliation. Mercy, a full and forgiving understanding of behaviour, was the prerogative of whoever was God, if there was one, and if he had so little to do that he interested himself in us after we died—which Dr. Veraswami doubted. Nor did he believe, as did some Hindus, that we came back in some other form; but if we did the boy was as likely to ascend as to descend in the hierarchy— whatever it was. All in all, if God had made the boy as he was, and put him where he was, it was hard to see that the boy had behaved any better or worse than God must have expected. But all that, he argued most vigor- ously, had nothing to do with Assistant Police Magistrate Blair, who, admirable though Dr. Veraswami knew he was, educated and wise beyond his years, could not now help the boy. "Justice, my friend, iss your job. Justice, not mercy." And his gesturing hand fell and was still, simulating the fall of the gallows.

"Surely, Doctor, mercy can be a part of justice. They are hardly in opposition. Cannot mercy infuse justice, shape it, direct it?"

"Sometimes, sometimes, but often it iss beyond our competence." And he launched again into a lengthy speech, his plump white-clad behind balanced against the veranda rail, his black thumb and forefinger nipping at the air as if to capture ideas as they floated by. The tenor of his argument was, so far as I followed it, Freudian. If we knew all we could about any murderer, including the brothel boy, all about his inherited capacities and all his life experiences, we would find more than sufficient explanation for all his actions, including the killing. Conduct was apparently "overdeter- mined," once you included the unconscious and the subconscious. And for most of these pressures which collectively and massively determine every- one's behaviour, it would seem unfair to hold anyone responsible. "But, my dear friend, fair or not, it iss essential to do so! Within justice there may be room for clemency, for mercy, for human understanding, providing only the essential purposes of punishment under law are not frustrated. Here they would be. He hass killed while deliberately doing what iss a very serious crime. There iss no room for mercy, no room at all." And then as if he thought it would clinch the matter: "Why even the good Viennese doctor himself, Sisigmund Freud, holds you responsible for your unconscious. There it iss!"

"But, dear Doctor, if we can assess differences of fault, or think we can, sufficiently to reduce or increase the punishment of the guilty, to be merciful or to be severe, why can't we, why can't I, by the same means reduce guilt itself? After all, sometimes we do that—when people kill accidently we call it manslaughter, if they have been very careless indeed; and if they have not been careless and yet have killed, it is usually no crime and never murder. We may not be very good at judging moral fault; but in a rough and ready way we can. And surely the boy is nearer innocence than guilt."

"No, no, my magistrate friend, you make the same mistake, forgive me please. We are talking only of intentional acts, not acts of carelessness—they are quite different. That iss what distinguishes the boy's act from your enuresis, issn't it. And for such acts . . ." and here Dr. Veraswami grabbed two handfuls of ideas from the air around him ". . . the boy is either to be treated ass a responsible man or he issn't. There are no half-men for guilt in the eyes of the law. If there were a choice of punishments for what he hass done, perhaps you could be merciful, because he hass been much abused and iss of weak mind. But there issn't, there issn't. It iss circular you see, dear friend."

I didn't see at all, but he pressed on, now almost skipping about with the released energy of uninhibited talk, which I suddenly realised was an even more cherished luxury for him than for me—"Man iss defined by hiss capacity for moral choice. That iss what man iss, nothing else, otherwise an animal." And then, chuckling at the cruel pointedness of the joke: "Dr. Freud and the law agree, you see. For his unconscious mind and for hiss conscious mind, such ass they are, the brothel boy iss twice responsible. Otherwise you would have to excuse everyone, certainly everyone you took the trouble to understand."

Though an elusive conclusion, the point was strong. Justice cannot excuse everyone, obviously. And if our judgment of moral guilt reflects mainly our degree of ignorance of the relevant moral facts, then all we would do in a mercy-controlled system of punishment would, in effect, be to excuse or be merciful towards those we knew a lot about or decided to find out about—and not the others. To my dismay it seemed to me, therefore, that if Justice stands in opposition to Mercy, we are damned (or, certainly, this Assistant Police Magistrate is); and if Mercy is to infuse Justice, to be a part of it, we probably claim beyond our competence.

Dr. Veraswami understood my difficulty in this whole matter, my search for some principle to guide me. "I think a lot about it, my friend, since it iss such a worry to you. And, if I may please, I hope you agree, here iss my conclusion": And after a pause, a thumb-and-forefinger, tweezer-like nip in the air to catch his words, "There iss no steady principle to guide you, none at all. You must be a man of principles, not of principle."

Dr. Veraswami seemed to be becoming more elliptic than before, and in annoyance I told him so. "No, you misunderstand me," he replied, "I mean there iss no moral principle to guide you, moral, moral. . . . There are, of coruse, other guides, other principles. The main one iss that you English should use the executioner ass little ass you can—rarely, if you use them at all. And how to know how little iss ass little ass you can?" Here he paused again, hands still, achieving impressive rhetorical effect. "I have it: if the British do not wish him killed, there iss no problem unless the natives want him killed very much, and the British think they should let them have their way. If it is a native to be executed they will not care too much. But if the British and the natives *both* want him killed, ass with the brothel boy, unless he iss so very mad ass to be obviously mad to all, natives and British, you can do nothing unless you also wish to leave the service of the Raj and be seen by all ass a treasonable fool."

Hesitantly, regretting the force of "treasonable fool," he added: "I would like to help you, but I can't. Perhaps you should leave here . . . I would miss you. You would be happier in England I think. But iss this the way? Iss this the way to go? And even if you do save the boy, what can we do with him? Ass I said, the jail? . . . the madhouse?"

It appalled me to realize that I was in Pilate's role, at least as Pilate may have seen it, though otherwise the comparison made no sense. Nor, increasingly it seemed to me, did I. Perhaps it was me for the madhouse that Dr. Veraswami saw as useless for the boy. No; I understood the issue all too well; it was now clear and I was not confused. Dr. Veraswami was right. As a moral issue, the boy was nearer to innocence than most of us; at the Last Judgment I would back his chances over most. But as a political matter, what a weak reed he had in me to sustain his life.

I recalled another occasion in Moulmein when I had failed to stand for the right against public pressures. Was it to become a habit? A recidivist Pilate indeed! A few months ago, very much against my better judgment and every inclination, I had shot a working elephant that had recovered from a period of "must" in which he had damaged some property and killed a native. As soon as I saw the elephant I knew with perfect certainty that I ought not to shoot him; but the natives expected it of me and I had to do it; I could feel their dark, sweaty wills pressing me forward, irresistibly. If I did nothing it was quite probable that some of them would laugh. So I shot the elephant.

I had to contend then only with native opinion; the Europeans would have divided on the question, some holding it to be a damn shame to shoot an elephant for killing a coolie, because an elephant was worth more than any damn Coringhee coolie. Now, with the brothel boy, the forces pressing on me were different and probably greater. No one would laugh if I did not hang the boy, but both European and native opinion was agreed and vehement: that is what I ought to do, what I must do.

Memories of St. Cyprian again swept in. I remembered how Latin was beaten into me and I still doubted that a classical education could be successfully carried on without corporal punishment. Bingo, Sim, and the boys all believed in its efficacy; as in Moulmein, public opinion was unanimous about the value of physical punishment. I recalled Beacham, a boy of dull mind, not as dull as the brothel boy but certainly not bright, whom Sim flogged towards their joint goal of a scholarship for Beacham, as the heartless might flog a floundered horse. And when Beacham was severely beaten yet again for his failure in the scholarship exam, his words of poignant regret came back to me: "I wish I'd had that caning before I went up for the exam."

[Here there are pages missing in the manuscript. It leaps to a few concluding paragraphs.]

As I walked with Dr. Veraswami into the jail yard I caught sight of him. Six gaurds were getting him ready for the gallows. He stood, surrounded by the gaurds, slim and muscular, with shaven head and vague liquid eyes. He seemed genuinely bewildered, puzzled, uncomprehending though deeply fearful. The gaurds crowded close to him, with their hands always on him in a careful, caressing grip, as though all the while feeling him to make sure he was there. He seemed hardly to notice what was happening. His eye caught mine and paused while it dawned on him that he knew me and that I had been gentle with him. The vague eyes developed a semblance of communication.

By the time he stood by the scaffold no marks remained of the beating. His body had repaired itself, but the intervening weeks had not helped my mind to repair its anguish.

I walked behind him to the gallows. Though his arms were bound, he walked quite steadily. And once, in spite of the men who gripped him by each shoulder, he stepped lightly aside to avoid a puddle on the path. The puddle—and I understood why—brought me back to the unreasoning St. Cyprian guilt. That I should be destroying a healthy conscious man, dull and dangerous though he might be. The unspeakable wrongness of cutting short a life in full tide. The struggle for rational judgment came as a minor anodyne. How can I refashion the world of the just and the unjust, of the forgiving and of the prejudiced, myself an uncertain observer rather than a shaper of justice, a player without influence on the rules. Only by my own death would I escape the pain of these cruel games. I must leave Burma.

So that when he was dead, and the Superintendent of the jail asked Dr. Veraswami and me and the rest of the little procession to join him in a drink—"I've got a bottle of whiskey in the car. We could do with it."—I found myself drinking and laughing, perhaps too loudly, with the rest of them, quite amicably, natives and Europeans alike.

Veraswami was right; I must leave Burma.

Six   Organized Crime

8   Organized Crime in Urban Society Chicago in The Twentieth Century

Mark H. Haller (1972)

Many journalists have written exciting accounts of organized crime in American cities and a handful of scholars have contributed analytical and perceptive studies.[1] Yet neither the excitement in the journalistic accounts nor the analysis in the scholarly studies fully captures the complex and intriguing role of organized criminal activities in American cities during the first third of the twentieth century. The paper that follows, although focusing on Chicago, advances hypotheses that are probably true for other cities as well. The paper examines three major, yet interrelated, aspects of the role of organized crime in the city: first, the social worlds within which the criminals operated and the importance of those worlds in providing social mobility from immigrant ghettos; second, the diverse patterns by which different ethnic groups became involved in organized criminal activities and were influenced by those activities; and third, the broad and pervasive economic impact of organized crime in urban neighborhoods and the resulting influence that organized crime did exert.

Crime and Mobility

During the period of heavy immigrant movement into the cities of the Northeast and Midwest, organized crime provided paths of upward mobility for many young men raised in ethnic slums. The gambling kings, vice lords, bootleggers and racketeers often began their careers in the ghetto neighborhoods; and frequently these neighborhoods continued to be the centers for their entrepreneurial activities. A careful study of the leaders of organized crime in Chicago in the late 1920s found that 31 percent were of Italian background, 29 percent of Irish background, 20 percent Jewish, and 12 percent black; none were native white of native white parents.[2] A recognition of the ethnic roots of organized crime, however, is only a starting point for understanding its place in American cities.

At a risk of oversimplification, it can be said that for young persons in the ethnic ghettos three paths lay open to them. The vast majority became, to

"Organized Crime in Urban Society" first appeared in *Journal of Social History* 5 (1971–72): 210–34.

use the Chicago argot, "poor working stiffs." They toiled in the factories, filled menial service and clerical jobs, or opened mom-and-pop stores. Their mobility to better jobs and to homeownership was, at best, incremental.[3] A second, considerably smaller group followed respectable paths to relative success. Some of this group went to college and entered the professions; others rose to management positions in the business or governmental hierarchies of the city.

There existed, however, a third group of interrelated occupations which, although not generally regarded as respectable, were open to uneducated and ambitious ethnic youths. Organized crime was one such occupational world, but there were others.

One was urban machine politics. Many scholars have, of course, recognized the function of politics in providing mobility for some members of ethnic groups.[4] In urban politics, a person's ethnic background was often an advantage rather than a liability. Neighborhood roots could be the basis for a career that might lead from poverty to great local power, considerable wealth, or both.

A second area consisted of those businesses that prospered through political friendships and contacts. Obviously, construction companies that built the city streets and buildings relied upon government contracts. But so also did banks in which government funds were deposited, insurance companies that insured government facilities, as well as garbage contractors, traction companies and utilities that sought city franchises. Because political contacts were important, local ethnic politicians and their friends were often the major backers of such enterprises.[5]

A third avenue of success was through leadership in the city's labor unions. The Irish in Chicago dominated the building trade unions and most of the other craft unions during the first 25 years of this century. But persons of other ethnic origins could also rise to leadership positions, especially in those unions in which their own ethnic group predominated.[6]

Another path of mobility was sports. Boxing, a peculiarly urban sport, rooted in the neighborhood gymnasiums, was the most obvious example of a sport in which Irish champions were succeeded by Jewish, Polish and black champions. Many a fighter, even if he did not reach national prominence, could achieve considerable local fame within his neighborhood or ethnic group. He might then translate this local fame into success by becoming a fight manager, saloon keeper, politician or racketeer.[7]

A fifth area often dominated by immigrants was the entertainment and night life of the city. In Chicago, immigrants—primarily Irish and Germans—ran the city's saloons by the turn of the century. During the 1920s, Greek businessmen operated most of the taxi-dance halls. Restaurants, cabarets and other night spots were similarly operated by persons from various ethnic groups. Night life also provided careers for entertainers, including B-girls, singers, comedians, vaudeville and jazz bands. Jewish comedians of the 1930s and black comedians of our own day are only examples of a larger phenomenon in which entertainment could lead to local and even national recognition.[8]

The organized underworld of the city, then, was not the only area of urban life that provided opportunities for ambitious young men from the ghettos. Rather, it was one of several such areas. Part of the pervasive impact of organized crime resulted from the fact that the various paths were interrelated, binding together the worlds of crime, politics, labor leadership, politically related businessmen, sports figures and the night life of the city. What was the nature of the interrelationships?

To begin with, organized crime often exerted important influences upon the other social worlds. For aspiring politicians, especially during the early years after an ethnic group's arrival in a city, organized crime was often the most important source of money and manpower. (By the turn of the century, an operator of a single policy wheel in Chicago could contribute not only thousands of dollars but also more than a hundred numbers writers to work the neighborhoods on election day.) On occasion, too, criminals supplied strongarm men to act as poll watchers, they organized repeat voters; and they provided other illegal but necessary campaign services. Like others engaged in ethnic politics, members of the organized underworld often acted from motives of friendship and common ethnic loyalties. But because of the very nature of their activities, criminal entrepreneurs required and therefore sought political protection. It would be difficult to exaggerate the importance of organized crime in the management of politics in many of the wards of the city.[9]

Furthermore, it should not be thought that the politics of large cities like Chicago was peculiarly influenced by organized crime. In a large and heterogeneous city, there were always wards within which the underworld exercised little influence and which could therefore elect politicians who would work for honest government and law enforcement. But in the ethnic and blue-collar industrial cities west or southwest of Chicago, the influence of organized crime sometimes operated without serious opposition. In Cicero, west of Chicago along major commuting lines, gambling ran wide open before the 1920s; and after 1923 Capone's bootlegging organization safely had its headquarters there. In other towns, like Stickney and Burnham, prostitution and other forms of entertainment often operated with greater openness than in Chicago. This symbiotic relationship, in which surrounding blue-collar communities provided protected vice and entertainment for the larger city, was not limited to Chicago. Covington, Kentucky, had a similar relationship to Cincinnati, while East St. Louis serviced St. Louis.[10]

The organized underworld was also deeply involved in other areas of immigrant mobility. Organized criminals worked closely with racketeering labor leaders and thus became involved in shakedowns, strike settlements and decisions concerning union leadership. They were participants in the night life, owned many of the night spots in the entertainment districts, and hired and promoted many of the entertainers. (The comedian Joe E. Lewis started his career in Chicago's South Side vice district as an associate and employee of the underworld; his case was not atypical.)[11] Members of the underworld were also sports fans and gamblers and therefore became managers of prize fighters, patrons at the race tracks and loyal fans at ball games. An observer who knew many of Chicago's pimps in the 1920s reported:

> The pimp is first, last and always a fight fan. He would be disgraced if he didn't go to every fight in town. . . .
> They hang around gymnasiums and talk fight. Many of them are baseball fans, and they usually get up just about in time to go to the game. They know all the players and their information about the game is colossal. Football is a little too highbrow for them, and they would be disgraced if they played tennis, but of late the high grade pimps have taken to golf, and some of them belong to swell golf clubs.[12]

However, criminals were not merely sports fans; some ran gambling syndicates and had professional interests in encouraging sports or predicting the outcome of sports events. Horse racing was a sport conducted primarily for the betting involved. By the turn of the century, leading gamblers and bookmakers invested in and controlled most of the race tracks near Chicago and in the rest of the nation. A number of successful gamblers had stables of horses and thus mixed business with pleasure while becoming leading figures in horse race circles. At a less important level, Capone's organization in the late 1920s owned highly profitable dog tracks in Chicago's suburbs.[13]

The fact that the world of crime exerted powerful influences upon urban politics, business, labor unions, sports and entertainment does not adequately describe the interrelations of these worlds. For many ambitious men, the worlds were tied together because in their own lifetimes they moved easily from one area to another or else held positions in two or more simultaneously. In some ways, for instance, organized crime and entertainment were barely distinguishable worlds. Those areas of the city set aside for prostitution and gambling were the major entertainment districts of the city. Many cabarets and other night spots provided gambling in backrooms or in rooms on upper floors. Many were places where prostitutes solicitied customers or where customers could find information concerning local houses of prostitution. During the 1920s, places of entertainment often served liquor and thus were retail outlets for bootleggers. In the world of entertainment, the distinction between legitimate and illegitimate was often blurred beyond recognition.[14]

Take, as another example, the career of William Skidmore. At age fourteen, Billie sold racing programs at a race track near Chicago. By the time he was twenty-one, in the 1890s, he owned a saloon and cigar store, and soon had joined with others to operate the major policy wheels in Chicago and the leading handbook syndicate on the West Side. With his growing wealth and influence, he had by 1903 also become ward committeeman in the thirteenth ward and was soon a leading political broker in the city. In 1912 he was Sergeant-at-Arms for the Democratic National Convention and, afterwards, aided Josephus Daniels in running the Democratic National Committee. Despite his success as gambler and politician, his saloon, until well into the 1920s, was a hangout for pickpockets and con men; and "Skid" provided bail and political protection for his criminal friends. In the twenties Skidmore branched into the junk business and made a fortune selling junk obtained through contracts with the county government. Not until the early 1940s did he finally go to prison, the victim of a federal charge of income tax evasion. In his life, it would be impossible to unravel the diverse careers to determine whether he was saloon keeper, gambler, politician or businessman.[15]

The various social worlds were united not simply by the influence of organized crime and by interlocking careers; the worlds also shared a common social life. At local saloons, those of merely local importance met and drank together. At other restaurants or bars, figures of wider importance had meeting places. Until his death in 1920, Big Jim Colossimo's restaurant in the South Side vice district brought together the successful from many worlds; the saloon of Michael (Hinky Dink) Kenna, first ward Alderman, provided a meeting place in the central business district. Political banquets, too, provided opportunities for criminals, police, sports figures and others to gather in honor of a common political friend. Weddings and funerals were occasions when friends met to mark the important passages through life. At the funeral of Colossimo—politician, vice lord and restauranteur—his pallbearers included a gambler, two keepers of vice resorts, and a bailbondsman. Honorary pallbearers were five judges (including the chief judge of the criminal courts), two congressmen, nine resort keepers or gamblers, several aldermen and three singers from the Chicago Opera. (His good friend, Enrico Caruso, was unable to be present.) Such ceremonial events symbolized the overlapping of the many worlds of which a man like Colossimo was a part.[16]

Thus far we have stressed the social structure that linked the criminal to the wider parts of the city within which he operated. That social world was held together by a system of values and beliefs widely shared by those who participated in crime, politics, sports and the night life of the city. Of central importance was the cynical—but not necessarily unrealistic—view that society operated through a process of deals, friendships and mutual favors.

Hence the man to be admired was the smart operator and dealer who handled himself well in such a world. Because there was seen to be little difference between a legal and an illegal business, there was a generally tolerant attitude that no one should interfere with the other guy's racket so long as it did not interfere with one's own.[17] This general outlook was, of course, widely shared, in whole or in part, by other groups within American society so that there was no clear boundary between the social world of the smart operators and the wider society.

In a social system held together by friendships and favors, the attitude toward law and legal institutions was complex. A basic attitude was a belief that criminal justice institutions were just another racket—a not unrealistic assessment considering the degree to which police, courts and prosecutor were in fact used by political factions and favored criminal groups. A second basic attitude was a belief that, if anyone cooperated with the law against someone with whom he was associated or to whom he owed favors, he was a stoolpigeon whose behavior was beneath contempt. This does not mean that criminal justice institutions were not used by members of organized crime. On a day-to-day basis, members of the underworld were tied to police, prosecutors and politicians through payments and mutual favors. Criminal groups often used the police and courts to harass rival gangs or to prevent the development of competition. But conflicts between rival groups were also resolved by threats or violence. Rival gambling syndicates bombed each others' places of business, rival union leaders engaged in bombing and slugging, and rival bootlegging gangs after 1923 turned to assassinations that left hundreds dead in the streets of Chicago.[18] The world of the rackets was a tough one in which a man was expected to take his knocks and stand up for himself. Friendship and loyalty were valued; but so also were toughness and ingenuity.

Gangsters, politicians, sports figures and entertainers prided themselves for being smart guys who recognized how the world operated. They felt disdain mixed with pity for the "poor working stiffs" who, ignorant of how the smart guys operated, toiled away at their menial jobs. But if they disdained the life of the working stiff, they also disdained the pretensions of those "respectable" groups who looked askance at the world within which they operated. Skeptical that anyone acted in accordance with abstract beliefs or universalistic principles, the operators believed that respectable persons were hypocrites. For instance, when Frank J. Loesch, the distinguished and elderly lawyer who headed the Chicago Crime Commission, attacked three criminal court judges for alleged political favoritism, one politician declared to his friends:

> Why pick on these three judges when every judge in the criminal court is doing the very same thing, and always have. Who is Frank Loesch that he should holler? He has done the same thing in his day.

. . . He has asked for plenty of favors and has always gotten them. Now that he is getting older and is all set and doesn't have to ask any more favors, he is out to holler about every one else. . . . There are a lot of these reformers who are regular racketeers, but it won't last a few years and it will die out.

In short, the world view of the operators allowed them to see their world as being little different from the world of the respectable persons who looked down upon them. The whole world was a racket.[19]

Ethnic Specialization

Some have suggested that each ethnic group, in its turn, took to crime as part of the early adjustment to urban life. While there is some truth to such a generalization, the generalization obscures more than it illuminates the ethnic experiences and the structure of crime. In important respects, each ethnic group was characterized by different patterns of adjustment; and the patterns of involvement in organized crime often reflected the particular broader patterns of each ethnic group. Some ethnic groups—Germans and Scandinavians, for instance—appear not to have made significant contributions to the development of organized crime. Among the ethnic groups that did contribute, there was specialization within crime that reflected broader aspects of ethnic life.

In Chicago by the turn of the century, for example, the Irish predominated in two areas of organized crime. One area was labor racketeering, which derived from the importance of the Irish as leaders of organized labor in general.[20]

The second area of Irish predominance was the operation of major gambling syndicates. Irish importance in gambling was related to a more general career pattern. The first step was often ownership of a saloon, from which the owner might move into both politics and gambling. Many Irish saloon keepers ran handbooks or encouraged other forms of gambling in rooms located behind or over the saloon. Those Irishmen who used their saloon as a basis for electoral politics continued the gambling activities in their saloons and had ties to larger gambling syndicates. Other saloon keepers, while sometimes taking important but backstage political positions such as ward committeeman, developed the gambling syndicates. Handbooks required up-to-the-minute information from race tracks across the country. By establishing poolrooms from which information was distributed to individual handbooks, a single individual could control and share in the profits of dozens or even hundreds of handbooks.

The Irish also predominated in other areas of gambling. At the turn of the century they were the major group in the syndicates that operated the policy games, each with hundreds of policy writers scattered in the slum neighborhoods to collect the nickels and dimes of the poor who dreamed of a lucky hit. They also outfitted many of the gambling houses in the Loop which offered roulette, faro, poker, blackjack, craps and other games of chance. Furthermore, many top police officers were Irish and rose through the ranks by attaching themselves to the various political factions of the city. Hence a complex system of Irish politicians, gamblers and police shared in the profits of gambling, protected gambling interests and built careers in the police department or city politics. Historians have long recognized the importance of the Irish in urban politics. In Chicago, at any rate, politics was only part of a larger Irish politics-gambling complex.[21]

The Irish politics-gambling complex remained intact until about World War I. By the 1920s, however, the developing black ghetto allowed black politicians and policy operators to build independent gambling and political organizations linked to the Republicans in the 1920s and the Democratic city machine in the 1930s. By the 1920s, in addition, Jewish gamblers became increasingly important, both in the control of gambling in Jewish neighborhoods and in operations elsewhere. Finally, by the mid-1920s, Italian bootleggers under Capone took over gambling in suburban Cicero and invested in Chicago gambling operations. Gambling had become a complex mixture of Irish, Negro, Jewish and Italian entrepreneurship.[22]

Although the Irish by the twentieth century played little direct role in managing prostitution, Italians by World War I had moved into important positions in the vice districts, especially in the notorious Levee district on the South Side. (Political protection, of course, often had to be arranged through Irish political leaders.) Just as the Irish blocked Italians in politics, so also they blocked Italians in gambling, which was both more respectable and more profitable than prostitution. Hence the importance of prohibition in the 1920s lay not in initiating organized crime (gambling continued both before and after prohibition to be the major enterprise of organized crime); rather, prohibition provided Italians with an opportunity to break into a major field of organized crime that was not already monopolized by the Irish.[23]

This generalization, to some extent, oversimplifies what was in fact a complex process. At first, prohibition opened up business opportunities for large numbers of individuals and groups, and the situation was chaotic. By 1924, however, shifting coalitions had emerged. Some bootlegging gangs were Irish, including one set of O'Donnell brothers on the far West Side and another set on the South Side. Southwest of the stockyards, there was an important organization, both Polish an Irish, coordinated by "Pollack" Joe Saltis. And on the Near North Side a major group—founded by burglars and hold-up men—was led by Irishmen like Dion O'Banion, Poles like Earl (Hymie) Weiss and George (Bugs) Moran, and Jews like Jack Zuta and the

Gusenberg brothers. There were, finally, the various Italian gangs, including the Gennas, the Aiellos, and, of course, the Capone organization.[24]

The major Italian bootlegging gang, that associated with the name of Al Capone, built upon roots already established in the South Side vice district. There John Torrio managed houses of prostitution for Big Jim Colossimo. With Colossimo's assassination in 1920, Torrio and his assistant, Capone, moved rapidly to establish a bootlegging syndicate in the Loop and in the suburbs south and west of the city. Many of their associates were persons whom they had known during humbler days in the South Side vice district and who now rose to wealth with them. Nor was their organization entirely Italian. Very early, they worked closely with Irishmen like Frankie Lake and Terry Druggan in the brewing of beer, while Jake Guzik, a Jew and former South Side pimp, became the chief business manager for the syndicate. In the bloody bootlegging wars of the 1920s, the members of the Capone organization gradually emerged as the most effective organizers and most deadly fighters. The success of the organization brought wealth and power to many ambitious Italians and provided them with the means in the late 1920s and early 1930s to move into gambling, racketeering and entertainment, as well as into a broad range of legitimate enterprises. Bootlegging allowed Italians, through entrepreneurial skills and by assassination of rivals, to gain a central position in the organized underworld of the city.[25]

Although Jewish immigrants in such cities as Cleveland and Philadelphia were major figures in bootlegging and thus showed patterns similar to Italians in Chicago, Jews in Chicago were somewhat peripheral figures. By World War I, Chicago Jews, like Italians, made important inroads into vice, especially in vice districts on the West Side. In the 1920s, with the dispersal of prostitution, several Jewish vice syndicates operated on the South and West Sides. Jews were also rapidly invading the world of gambling.[26] Although Jews took part in vice, gambling and bootlegging, they made a special contribution to the organized underworld by providing professional or expert services. Even before World War I, Jews were becoming a majority of the bailbondsmen in the city. By the 1920s, if not before, Jews constituted over half the fences who disposed of stole goods. (This was, of course, closely related to Jewish predominance as junk dealers and their importance in retail selling.) Jews were also heavily overrepresented among defense attorneys in the criminal courts. It is unnecessary to emphasize that the entrepreneurial and professional services of Jews reflected broader patterns of adaptation to American urban life.[27]

Even within relatively minor underworld positions, specialization by ethnicity was important. A study of three hundred Chicago pimps in the early 1920s, for instance, found that 109 (more than one-third) were black,

60 were Italian, 47 Jewish and 26 Greek.[28] The large proportion of black suggests that the high prestige of the pimp among some elements of the lower-class black community is not a recent development but has a relatively long tradition in the urban slum. There has, in fact, long been a close relationship of vice activities and Negro life in the cities. In all probability, the vice districts constituted the most integrated aspect of Chicago society. Black pimps and madams occasionally had white girls working for them, just as white pimps and madams sometimes had black girls working for them. In addition, blacks held many of the jobs in the vice districts, ranging from maids to entertainers. The location of major areas of vice and entertainment around the periphery and along the main business streets of the South Side black neighborhood gave such activities a pervasive influence within the neighborhood.[29]

Black achievements in ragtime and jazz had their roots, at least in part, in the vice and entertainment districts of the cities. Much of the early history of jazz lies among the talented musicians—black and white—who performed in the famous resorts in the Storyville district of New Orleans in the 1890s and early 1900s. With the dissolution of Storyville as a segregated vice district, many talented black musicians carried their styles to Chicago's South Side, to Harlem, and to the cabarets and dance halls of other major cities. In the 1920s, with black performers like King Oliver and Louis Armstrong and white performers like Bix Beiderbecke, Chicago was an important environment for development of jazz styles. Just as Harlem became a center for entertainment and jazz for New Yorkers during prohibition, so the black and tan cabarets and speakeasies of Chicago's South Side became a place where blacks and whites drank, danced and listened to jazz music—to the shock of many respectable citizens. Thus, in ways that were both destructive and productive, the black experience in the city was linked to the opportunities that lay in the vice resorts, cabarets and dance halls of the teeming slums.[30] In the operation of entertainment facilities and policy rackets, black entrepreneurs found their major outlet and black politicians found their chief support.

Until there has been more study of comparative ethnic patterns, only tentative hypotheses are possible to explain why various ethnic groups followed differing patterns. Because many persons involved in organized crime initiated their careers with customers from their own neighborhood or ethnic group, the degree to which a particular ethnic group sought a particular illegal service would influence opportunities for criminal activities. If members of an ethnic group did not gamble, for instance, then ambitious members of that ethnic group could not build gambling syndicates based upon local roots. The general attitude toward law and law enforcement, too, would affect opportunities for careers in illegal ventures. Those groups that became most heavily involved in organized crime migrated from regions in which they had developed deep suspicions of government authority—whether the Irish fleeing British rule in Ireland, Jews escaping from Eastern Europe, Italians migrating from southern Italy or Sicily, or blacks leaving the American South. Within a community suspicious of courts and government officials, a person in trouble with the law could retain roots and even respect in the community. Within a community more oriented toward upholding legal authority, on the other hand, those engaged in illegal activities risked ostracism and loss of community roots.

In other ways, too, ethnic life styles evolved differently. Among both Germans and Irish, for instance, friendly drinking was part of the pattern of relaxation. Although the Irish and Germans by 1900 were the major managers of Chicago's saloons, the meaning of the saloon was quite different from the two groups. German saloons and beer gardens were sometimes for family entertainment and generally excluded gambling or prostitution; Irish saloons, part of an exclusively male social life, often featured prostitution or gambling and fit more easily into the world of entertainment associated with organized crime. Finally, it appears that south Italians had the highest homicide rate in Europe. There was, in all probability, a relationship between the cultural factors that sanctioned violence and private revenge in Europe and the factors that sanctioned the violence with which Italian bootleggers worked their way into a central position in Chicago's organized crime.[31]

There were, at any rate, many ways that the immigrant background and the urban environment interacted to influence the ethnic experience with organized crime. For some ethnic groups, involvement in organized crime wa snot an important part of the adjustment to American urban life. For other groups, involvement in the organized underworld both reflected and influenced their relatively unique patterns of acculturation.

Economic Impact

The economic role of organized crime was an additional factor underlying the impact of organized crime upon ethnic communities and urban society. Organized crime was important because of the relatively great wealth of the most successful criminals, because of the large numbers of persons directly employed by organized crime, and because of the still larger numbers who supplemented their income through various parttime activities. And all of this does not count the multitude of customers who bought the goods and services offered by the bootleggers, gambling operators and vice lords of the city.

During the first thirty or forty years after an immigrant group's arrival, successful leaders in organized crime might constitute a disproportionate percentage of the most wealthy members of the community. (In the 1930s at least one-half of the blacks in Chicago worth more than $100,000 were policy kings; Italian bootleggers in the 1920s may have represented an even larger proportion of the very wealthy among immigrants from southern Italy.)[32] The wealth of the successful criminals was accompanied by extensive political and other contacts that gave them considerable leverage both within and outside the ethnic community. They had financial resources to engage in extensive charitable activities, and often did so lavishly. Projects for improvement of ethnic communities often needed their support and contacts in order to succeed. Criminals often invested in or managed legitimate business enterprises in their communities. Hence, despite ambiguous or even antagonistic relations that they had with "respectable" members of their ethnic communities, successful leaders in organized crime were men who had to be reckoned with in the ethnic community and who often represented the community to the outside world.[33]

In organized crime, as in other economic activities, the very successful were but a minority. To understand the economic impact of crime, it is necessary to study the many persons at the middle and lower levels of organization. In cities like Chicago the number of persons directly employed in the activities of organized crime was considerable. A modest estimate of the number of fulltime prostitutes in Chicago about 1910 would be 15,000—not counting madams, pimps, procurers and others in managerial positions. Or take the policy racket. In the early 1930s an average policy wheel in the black ghetto employed 300 writers; some employed as many as 600; and there were perhaps 6,000 policy writers in the ghetto. The policy wheels, in this period of heavy unemployment, may have been the major single source of employment in the black ghetto, a source of employment that did not need to lay off workers or reduce wages merely because the rest of the economy faced a major depression. Finally, during the 1920s, bootlegging in its various aspects was a major economic activity employing thousands in manufacture, transportation and retailing activities.[34]

Yet persons directly employed constituted only a small proportion of those whose income derived from organized crime. Many persons supplemented their income through occasional or parttime services. While some prostitutes walked the streets to advertise their wares, others relied upon intermediaries who would direct customers in return for a finder's fee. During certain periods, payments to taxi drivers were sufficiently lucrative so that some taxi drivers would pick up only those passengers seeking a house of prostitution. Bellboys, especially in the second-class hotels found the function of negotiating between guests and prostitutes a profitable part of their service. (Many of the worst hotels, of course, functioned partly or wholly as places of assignation.) Bartenders, newsboys and waiters were among the many helpful persons who provided information concerning places and prices.[35]

Various phases of bootlegging during the 1920s were even more important as income supplements. In the production end, many slum families prepared wine or became "alky cookers" for the bootlegging gangs—so much so that after the mid-1920s, explosions of stills and the resulting fires were a major hazard in Chicago's slum neighborhoods. As one observer reported:

> During prohibition times many respectable Sicilian men were employed as "alky cookers" for Capone's, the Aiello's or for personal use. Many of these people sold wine during prohibition and their children delivered it on foot or by streetcar without the least fear that they might be arrested. . . . During the years of 1927 to 1930 more wine was made than during any other years and even the "poorest people" were able to make ten or fifteen barrels each year—others making sixty, seventy, or more barrels.

Other persons, including policemen, moonlighted as truck drivers who delivered booze to the many retail outlets of the city. Finally numerous persons supplemented their income by retailing booze, including bellboys, janitors in apartment buildings and shoe shine boys.[36]

The many persons who mediated between the underworld and the law were another group that supplemented its income through underworld contacts. Large numbers of policemen, as well as bailiffs, judges and political fixers, received bribes or political contributions in return for illegal cooperation with the underworld. Defense attorneys, tax accountants and bailbondsmen, in return for salaries or fees, provided expert services that were generally legal.[37]

For many of the small businessmen of the city, retailing the goods or services of the underworld could supplement business income significantly. Saloons, as already mentioned, often provided gambling and prostitution as an additional service to customers. Large numbers of small businesses were outlets for handbooks, policy, baseball pools, slot machines and other forms of gambling. A substantial proportion of the cigar stores, for example, were primarily fronts for gambling; barber shops, pool halls, newsstands, and small hotels frequently sold policy or would take bets on the horses. Drug stores often served as outlets for cocaine and, during the 1920s, sometimes sold liquor.[38]

The organized underworld also influenced business activity through racketeering. A substantial minority of the city's labor unions were racketeer-controlled; those that were not often used the assistance of racketeer unions or of strongarm gangs during strikes. The leaders of organized crime, as a result, exercised control or influence in the world of organized labor. Not so well known was the extensive racketeering that characterized small business organizations. The small businesses of the city were generally marginal and intensely competitive. To avoid cutthroat competition, businessmen often formed associations to make and enforce regulations illegally limiting competition. The Master Barbers Association, for example, set minimum prices, forbad a shop to be open after 7:30 P.M., and ruled that no shop could be established within two blocks of another shop. Many other types of small businesses formed similar associations: dairies, auto parts dealers, garage owners, candy jobbers, butcher stores, fish wholesalers and retailers, cleaners and dyers, and junk dealers. Many of the associations were controlled, or even organized, by racketeers who levied dues upon association members and controlled the treasuries; they then used a system of fines and violence to insure that all businessmen in the trade joined the association and abided by the regulations. In return for control of the association's treasury, in short, racketeers performed illgal services for the association and thereby regulated much of the small business activity in the city.[39]

Discussion of the economic influence of organized crime would be incomplete without mentioning the largest group that was tied economically to the underworld, namely, the many customers for the illegal goods and services. Like other retailers in the city, some leaders of organized crime located their outlets near the center of the city or along major transportation lines and serviced customers from the entire region; others were essentially neighborhood businessmen with a local clientele. In either case, those providing illegal goods and services usually attempted to cultivate customer loyalty so that the same customers would return on an ongoing basis and advertise among their friends. Organized crime existed because of wide customer demand, and a large proportion of the adult population of the city was linked to organized crime on a regular basis for purchase of goods and services.

Heroism and Ambiguity

Because of the diverse ways that successful criminal entrepreneurs influenced the city and ethnic communities, many of them became heroes—especially within their own communities. There were a variety of reasons for the admiration that they received. Their numerous philanthropies, both large and small, won them reputations as regular guys who would help a person in need. Moreover, they were often seen as persons who fought for their ethnic communities. They aided politicians from their communities to win elections in the rough and often violent politics of the slums and thereby advanced their ethnic group toward political recognition. Sometimes they were seen as fighters for labor unions and thus as friends of labor. And, on occasion, they fought directly for their ethnic group. There was, for instance, the case of the three Miller brothers from Chicago's West Side Jewish ghetto. In typical ghetto pattern, one became a boxer, one a gangster and one a policeman. The boxer and gangster were heroes among Jews on the West Side, where for many years Jewish peddlers and junk dealers had been subjected to racial slurs and violent attacks by young hoodlums from other ethnic groups. "What I have done from the time I was a boy," Davy Miller told a reporter,

> was to fight for my people here in the Ghetto against Irish, Poles or any other nationality. It was sidewalk fighting at first. I could lick any five boys or men in a sidewalk free-for-all.

When the Miller brothers and their gang protected the Jews of the West Side, the attacks against them abated.[40]

Particularly for youngsters growing up in the ghettos, the gangsters were often heroes whose exploits were admired and copied. Davy Miller modestly recognized this when he said:

> Maybe I am a hero to the young folks among my people, but it's not because I'm a gangster. It's because I've always been ready to help all or any of them in a pinch.

An Italian student at the University of Chicago in the early 1930s remembered his earlier life in the Italian ghetto:

> For 26 years I lived in West Side "Little Italy," the community that has produced more underworld limelights than any other area in Chicago. . . .
>
> I remember these men in large cars, with boys and girls of the neighborhood standing on the running board. I saw them come into the neighborhood in splendor as heroes. Many times they showered handfuls of silver to youngsters who waited to get a glance at them—the new heroes—because they had just made headlines in the newspapers. Since then I have seen many of my playmates shoot their way to the top of gangdom and seen others taken for a ride.[41]

Nevertheless, despite the importance of gangsters and the world within which they moved, their relations to ethnic groups and the city were always ambiguous. Because many of their activities were illegal, they often faced the threat of arrest and, contrary to common belief, frequently found themselves behind bars. Furthermore, for those members of the ethnic community who pursued respectable paths to success, gangsters gave the ethnic group a bad name and remained a continuing source of embarrassment. St. Clair Drake and Horace R. Cayton, in their book on the Chicago black ghetto, describe the highly ambiguous and often antagonistic relations of the respectable black middle class and the policy kings. In his book on Italians in Chicago, Humbert S. Nelli explains that in the 1920s the Italian language press refused to print the name of Al Capone and covered the St.

Valentine's Day massacre without suggesting its connection with bootlegging wars.[42]

The respectable middle classes, however, were not the only ones unhappy
about the activities or notoriety of gangsters. Organized crime sometimes
contributed to the violence and fear of violence that pervaded many of the
ghetto neighborhoods. Often local residents feared to turn to the police and
lived with a stoical acceptance that gangs of toughs controlled elections,
extorted money from local businesses and generally lived outside the reach
of the law. Some immigrant parents, too, resented the numerous saloons,
the open prostitution and the many gambling dens—all of which created a
morally dangerous environment in which to raise children. Especially immigrant women, who watched their husbands squander the meager family
income on liquor or gambling, resented the activities of organized crime.
Within a number of neighborhoods, local churches and local leaders undertook sporadic campaigns for better law enforcement.[43]

Organized crime, then, was an important part of the complex social
structure of ethnic communities and urban society in the early twentieth
century. For certain ethnic groups, organized crime both influenced and
reflected the special patterns by which the groups adjusted to life in urban
America. Through organized crime, many member of those ethnic groups
could achieve mobility out of the ethnic ghettos and into the social world of
crime, politics, ethnic business, sports, and entertainment. Those who were
successful in organized crime possessed the wealth and contacts to exercise
broad influence within the ethnic communities and the city. The economic
activities of the underworld provided jobs or supplemental income for tens
of thousands. Despite the importance of organized crime, however, individual gangsters often found success to be ambiguous. They were not always
able to achieve secure positions or to translate their positions into respecta-
bility.

Notes

1. The following are probably the most useful scholarly studies analyzing the
relationship of organized crime to the social structure of the city: John Landesco,
Organized Crime in Chicago, 2nd ed. (Chicago, 1968); St. Clair Drake and Horace
R. Cayton, *Black Metropolis: A Study of Negro Life in a Northern City* (New York,
1945), II, especially ch. 17 and 19; William F. Whyte, *Street Corner Society: The
Social Structure of an Italian Slum*, 2nd ed. (Chicago, 1955), ch. 5 and 6; Daniel Bell,
"Crime as an American Way of Life: A Queer Ladder of Mobility," *The End of
Ideology*, rev. ed. (New York, 1961), ch. 7; Humbert S. Nelli, *The Italians in
Chicago, 1880–1930: A Study in Ethnic Mobility* (New York, 1970), ch. 5 and pp.
210–22; and John A. Gardiner, *The Politics of Corruption: Organized Crime in an
American City* (New York, 1970).

I use the term "organized crime" for those activities involving the sale of illegal goods and services. Prostitution, gambling and bootlegging were the major types during the early twentieth century ("juice" and heroin came later). Because labor racketeering and small business racketeering were closely tied to organized crime, I also discuss them in the paper.

2. William F. Ogburn and Clark Tibbitts, "A Memorandum on the Nativity of Certain Criminal Classes Engaged in Organized Crime, and of Certain Related Criminal and Non-Criminal Groups in Chicago," Unpublished manuscript, July 30, 1930, pp. 9–11, in Charles E. Merriam papers, Univ. of Chicago Library, Chicago, Ill.

3. For statistical discussions of immigrant mobility, see Stephan Thernstrom, *Poverty and Progress: Social Mobility in a Nineteenth Century City* (Cambridge, Mass., 1964); Stephan Thernstrom and Richard Sennett, eds., *Nineteenth-Century Cities: Essays in the New Urban History* (New Haven, 1969), pp. 49–208.

4. The literature on urban politics and ethnic mobility is voluminous. For general discussions, see Harold Zink, *Bosses in the United States: A Study of Twenty Municipal Bosses* (Durham, N.C., 1930); Robert K. Merton, *Social Theory and Social Structure* (Glencoe, Ill., 1957), especially pp. 71–2; Eric L. McKitrick, "The Study of Corruption," *Political Science Quarterly*, LXXII (Dec. 1957), 505–6. For specific discussion of Chicago, see Joel A. Tarr, "The Urban Politician as Entrepreur," *Mid-America*, XLIX (Jan. 1967), 55–67. For social background of machine politicians, see Harold F. Gosnell, *Machine Politics, Chicago Model*, 2nd ed. (Chicago, 1968), especially ch. 3; and John M. Allswang, *A House for All Peoples: Ethnic Politics in Chicago, 1890–1936* (Lexington, 1971), especially pp. 84–90 and ch. 8.

5. For example, see Joel A. Tarr, "J. R. Walsh of Chicago: A Case Study in Banking and Politics, 1881–1905," *The Business History Review*, XL (Winter 1966), 451–466.

6. Royal E. Montgomery, *Industrial Relations in the Chicago Building Trades* (Chicago, 1927), passim; Italian involvement in labor leadership discussed in Nelli, *Italians in Chicago*, pp. 78–85.

7. The importance of boxing in local ethnic communities gathered from various news stories appearing in Chicago newspapers. A colorful and useful history is Nat Fleischer, *The Heavyweight Championship: An Informal History of Heavyweight Boxing from 1719 to the Present Day* (New York, 1961). A study of sports as a path of mobility is much needed; for tentative discussions see David Riesman and Reuel Denney, "Football in America: A Study in Cultural Diffusion," *American Quarterly*, III (Winter 1951), 309–325; concerning pool hustlers, see Ned Polsky, *Hustlers, Beats, and Others* (New York, 1969), especially 76–77.

8. Ethnic background of selected saloon keepers from *History of Chicago and Souvenir of the Liquor Interest* (Chicago, 1892), pp. 136–254; concerning Greek ownership of taxi-dance halls, see Paul G. Cressey, "Report on Summer's Work with the Juvenile Protective Association of Chicago," typewritten paper, Oct. 1925, in Ernest W. Burgess papers, University of Chicago Library, II-A, Box 39. Jewish comedians of the 1930s included Bert Lahr, Fannie Brice (who married Nicky Arnstein, a gambler and con man), Eddie Cantor, George Jessel, Groucho Marx, Willie Howard and Jack Pearl; see book review in *New York Times Book Review* (Nov. 23, 1969), p. 1.

9. Discussions of the relationship of organized crime and politics in Chicago are numerous: Landesco, *Organized Crime*, ch. 8; Lloyd Wendt and Herman Kogan, *Lords of the Levee: The Story of Bathhouse John and Hinky Dink* (Indianapolis, 1943); Ovid Demaris, *Captive City* (New York, 1969); or the various issues of *Lightnin'*, an occasional newspaper published by the Rev. Elmer L. Williams in the 1920s and 1930s.

10. For studies of Cicero, Stickney or Burnham, see Paul M. Kinzie, "General Summary" of crime in Cicero, typewritten report, Dec. 1923, in Juvenile Protective Association papers, folder 92, in Library of University of Illinois at Chicago Circle; "Commercialized Prostitution," typewritten report, May 2–26, 1922, ibid., folder 97; K. B. Alwood and J. L. Munday, "Stickney," unpublished termpaper, March 1930, in Burgess papers, II-A, Box 39; investigators' reports, Committee of Fifteen files, vols. X and XI, University of Chicago Library; Daniel Russell, "The Road House: A Study of Commercialized Amusements in the Environs of Chicago," A.M. thesis in sociology, University of Chicago, 1931, pp. 13–49, 61–75, and 95 ff; Jack McPhaul, *Johnny Torrio, First of the Gang Lords* (New Rochelle, N.Y., 1971), especially pp. 116–18 and ch. 12; and John Kobler, *Capone: The Life and World of Al Capone* (New York, 1971), pp. 55–56 and ch. 8.

11. Art Cohn, "The Joker is Wild," in Albert Halper, ed., *The Chicago Crime Book* (New York, 1967), pp. 45–64.

12. Ben L. Reitman, *The Second Oldest Profession: A Study of the Prostitute's "Business Manager"* (New York, 1931), pp. 169–170.

13. Good social histories of horse racing and betting, like social histories of other sports, still need to be written. Perhaps the best general picture of the interrelations of betting and racing can be gotten from Hugh Bradley, *Such was Saratoga* (New York, 1940); see also Josiah Flynt, "The Pool-Room Vampire and Its Money-mad Victims," *Cosmopolitan Magazine*, XLII (Feb. 1907), 368–370. For information about Chicago, see Wendt and Kogan, *Lords of the Levee*, especially pp. 28–30 and 50–58; *New York World*, Oct. 6, 1901; Citizen's Association of Chicago, *Bulletin* No. 14 (May 24, 1905); and various stories in Chicago newspapers.

14. There are numerous descriptions of entertainment and vice areas of Chicago, by newspaper reports and by other investigators. See, for example, the investigators' reports in the Committee of Fifteen files and the many reports on commercialized entertainment commissioned by the Juvenile Protective Association and now deposited in the Association's files. For relations of the Capone organization to the North Side entertainment district in the early 1930s, see R.H. Sayler, 'Capone Faction," undated, typewritten research paper in Burgess papers, II-A, Box 14.

15. George Murray, *The Madhouse on Madison Street* (Chicago, 1965), pp. 366–374; *Chicago Record-Herald*, Nov. 4, 1903, April 1, 4, 21, 27, and 28, 1904; Informant E, typewritten "Special Report," Aug. 22, 1914; in Charles E. Merriam papers, University of Chicago Library, Box 87, folders 2 and 3; Chicago *Daily Tribune*, Jan. 8, 1918; *Lightnin'*, III (June, 1929), 3; Demaris, *Captive City*, p. 139.

16. For discussion of Colossimo's life, see McPhaul, *Johnny Torrio*, pp. 69–115; Kobler, *Capone*, ch. 3 and 4; and Charles Washburn, *Come into My Parlor: A Biography of the Aristocratic Everleigh Sisters of Chicago* (New York, 1936), especially ch. 11; his funeral is described in Landesco, *Organized Crime*, ch. 9. Some of the local political and criminal hangouts are described in investigator's reports,

Charles E. Merriam papers, Boxes 87 and 88. Political banquets are described in Landesco, *Organized Crime*, p. 176–78, and in *Lightnin'*, I, No. 3, p. 2, and No. 5, pp. 1 and 3–4.

17. The philosophy is best described in Landesco, *Organized Crime*, ch. 10, but the same philosophy is expressed whenever gangsters were asked about themselves; see, for example, [anon.], "A Good Hoodlum," typewritten termpaper, 1933, Burgess papers, II-A, Box 72. For reminiscences of a person raised on the periphery of the subculture, see Joseph Epstein, "Coming of Age in Chicago," *Commentary*, XLVIII (Dec. 1969), 61–68.

18. The use of violence described in Landesco, *Organized Crime*, ch. 5–7.

19. Quotation from confidential report in Chicago Crime Commission, File No. 11170, Chicago, Ill. Al Capone echoed the same view when he explained to a lady reporter: "They talk about me not being on the legitimate. Why, lady, nobody's on the legit. You know that and so do they. Your brother or your father gets in a jam. What do you do? Do you sit back and let him go over the road, without trying to help him? You'd be a yellow dog if you did. Nobody's really on the legit, when it comes down to cases, you know that." See Kobler, *Capone*, pp. 268–69.

20. For discussions of Chicago labor racketeerings, see Montgomery, *Industrial Relations*, passim; John Hutchinson, *The Imperfect Union: A History of Corruption in American Trade Unions* (New York, 1970), especially chs. 4 and 9; and the extensive correspondence and printed material in the Victor A. Olander papers, folders 115 and 266–68, in Library of University of Illinois at Chicago Circle.

21. Discussion of the Irish politics-gambling complex based primarily on Herman F. Schuettler, Scrapbook of Newspaper Clippings . . . 1904–1908, 2 vols., in Chicago Historical Society; see also Citizen's Association of Chicago, *Bulletin* No. 11 (July 31, 1903), and Landesco, *Organized Crime*, ch. 3.

22. The development of gambling can best be followed in the extensive files of the Chicago Crime Commission, especially File No. 65. Negro policy is discussed in Drake and Cayton, *Black Metropolis*, II, ch. 17; see also Harold F. Gosnell, *Negro Politicians: The Rise of Negro Politics in Chicago*, Phoenix ed. (Chicago, 1966), pp. 122–35.

23. For descriptions of Italian involvement in South Side vice, see McPhaul, *Johnny Torrio*, pp. 69–155; Kobler, *Capone*, chs. 3 and 4; and investigators' reports, Merriam papers, Boxes 87 and 88.

24. Most accounts of Chicago bootlegging concentrate upon Capone and slight the contributions of other groups. The development of the other groups can be followed, however, in the extensive files of the Chicago Crime Commission dealing with each of the leading bootlegging gangs.

25. Of the many accounts of the rise of the Capone organization, the best are Kobler, *Capone*, and McPhaul, *Johnny Torrio*; see also Fred D. Pasley, *Al Capone: The Biography of a Self-Made Man* (New York, 1930). The movement of the Capone organization into racketeering can be followed in the Olander papers, folders 266–68; a series of stories in *Chicago Tribune*, March 19–27, 1943; and Demaris, *Captive City*, pp. 22–29. Despite their success in crime, Italians did not displace the Irish from politics; in 1929, out of 99 ward committeemen in Chicago, 42 were Irish and only one was Italian; see Ogburn and Tibbitts, "Memorandum on Nativity," p. 45.

26. On the role of Mike de Pike Heitler and other Jews in West Side vice before World War I, see Murray, *Madhouse on Madison Street*, ch. 30; and investigators' reports in Merriam papers, especially Box 88, folders 1 and 6. On Jewish syndicates in the 1920s, see the following investigative reports in the Juvenile Protective Association papers: "Law Enforcement and the Police," Nov. 29, 1922, and Dec. 3, 1922, folder 94, and "Commercialized Prostitution," Dec. 10, 1922, folder 92. For Jewish gamblers, see Chicago Crime Commission File No. 65; also Demaris, *Captive City*, pp. 104–107.

27. Bradstreet reports on 30 major bailbondsmen are attached to letters of Assistant Corporation Counsel to Harry J. Olson, April 9 and 29, 1913, in Chicago Municipal Court papers, folder 24, Chicago Historical Society. Ethnicity could be established for eighteen, of whom nine were Jewish. Half of the thirty bailbondsmen were saloon keepers. By the later 1920s, Jews constituted 51 per cent of bailbondsmen (out of 158 studied); see Ogburn and Tibbitts, "Memorandum on Nativity," p. 48. Figures on Jewish fences and defense attorneys in ibid., pp. 15 and 47–48.

28. Reitman, *The Second Oldest Profession*, pp. 167–68.

29. The relationship of blacks and vice districts is discussed in Chicago Commission on Race Relations, *The Negro in Chicago* (Chicago, 1922), pp. 342–48; Reitman, *Second Oldest Profession*, ch. 11; Walter C. Reckless, *Vice in Chicago* (Chicago, 1933), passim; and the many investigators' reports in Committee of Fifteen papers.

30. For the migration of jazz to Chicago and its development there, see Nat Shapiro and Nat Hentoff, eds., *Hear Me Talkin' to Ya: The Story of Jazz as Told by the Men Who Made It* (New York, 1966), pp. 80–164; Eddie Condon, *We Called It Music: A Generation of Jazz* (New York, 1947); and Milton Mezzrow and Bernard Wolfe, *Really the Blues* (New York, 1946). An excellent general social history of jazz is Neil Leonard, *Jazz and the White Americans: The Acceptance of a New Art Form* (Chicago, 1962).

31. Italian homicide rate is mentioned in Rudolph J. Vecoli, "*Contadini* in Chicago: A Critique of *The Uprooted*," *Journal of American History*, LI (Dec. 1964), 406. For an interesting discussion of ways that Italian criminals in the United States reflected south Italian values, see Francis A. J. Ianni, "The Mafia and the Web of Kinship," *The Public Interest*, XXII (Winter 1971), 78–100. A thorough criticism of the literature which interprets American organized crime as a transfer of the Sicilian mafia is in Joseph L. Albini, *The American Mafia: Genesis of a Legend* (New York, 1971), especially chs. 5 and 6.

32. On blacks, this is my surmise from information in Drake and Cayton, *Black Metropolis*, II, pp. 514 and 546.

33. See Drake and Cayton, *Black Metropolis*, II, pp. 492–94 and passim; Nelli, *Italians in Chicago*, especially pp. 222–34, describes gangster influence on Italian political representation.

34. Estimate of number of prostitutes from City of Chicago Civil Service Commission, *Final Report, Police Investigation, 1911–1912* (Chicago, 1912), p. 12; for a lower estimate, see Vice Commission of Chicago, *The Social Evil in Chicago* (Chicago, 1911), p. 71. Figures on Negro policy from Gosnell, *Negro Politicians*, pp. 124–25, and Drake and Cayton *Black Metropolis*, II, pp. 478–81. For discussions of the organization of bootlegging, see references listed in footnote 23; a description of

his organization by an ex-bootlegger is Roger Tuchy, *The Stolen Years* (Cleveland, 1959).

35. Fred Cotnam, "Conversations with Bell-boys," student termpaper, Winter 1929; Stanley Jenkins, "Prostitution and the Prostitute in a Study Centered around Hotel Life," typewritten, undated termpaper; and Morris Carl Bergen, "The City, as Seen by the Cab Driver," typewritten termpaper, July 1932; all in Burgess papers, II-A. Also Investigators' reports, Nov. 1922, in Juvenile Protective Association papers, folder 94; and Report F-2 in "Commercialized Prostitution," July 1933, ibid., folder 98.

36. Quotation from Raymond Sayler, "A Study of Behavior Problems of Boys in the Lower North Community," typewritten research paper [1934], p. 50, in Burgess papers, II-A, Box 53. Explosions of stills in Chicago *Tribune*, Sept. 28, 1927. See also Cotnam, "Conversations with Bell-boys," and Cressey, "Reports on Summer's Work," pp. 28ff.

37. On relations of criminals to politics, see references in footnote 9. For relations to police, see especially the investigators' reports in Merriam papers, Boxes 87 and 88. Of many discussions of judges and criminals, see Judge M. L. McKinley, *Crime and the Civic Cancer-Graft*, Chicago Daily News Reprints, No. 6 (1923), in Juvenile Protective Association papers, Supplement 1, folder 58. An excellent general analysis of the bailbondsman in Arthur L. Beeley, *The Bail System in Chicago* (Chicago, 1927), especially pp. 39–46. A long description of defense attorneys for organized crime is in Sunday *Chicago Tribune*, April 8, 1934.

38. On newsstands and gambling, see typewritten memo by C. O. Rison, private detective, to Chicago Federation of Labor, July 4, 1910, in John Fitzpatrick papers, folder 4, Chicago Historical Society. For other businesses acting as fronts for gambling, see Rison's many investigative reports for June and July, 1910, in ibid. Also Nels Anderson, "Report of Visit to Ten Gambling Houses in Hobohemia," Jan. 1, 1923, Doc. 79, in Burgess papers; Paul Oien, typewritten research notes describing a large proportion of the gambling places in Chicago, Summer 1935, in Burgess papers. On sale of cocaine at drug stores, see especially Informant No. 100, typewritten but undated list of places for securing cocaine [1914], in Merriam papers, Box 88, folder 1.

39. Landesco, *Organized Crime*, ch. 7; Samuel Rubin, "Business Men's Associations," typewritten termpaper, Winter 1926, Burgess papers, II-D, Box 115; Philip Hauser and Saul Alinsky, "Some Aspects of the Cleaning and Dyeing Industry in Chicago—A Racket," unpublished research paper (1929), Burgess papers; also the various issues of Employers' Association of Chicago, *Employers' News*, during the 1920s, which reported business racketeering in detail; also journalistic accounts, such as Fred D. Palsey, *Muscling In* (Ives Washburn Publisher, 1931), and Gordon Hostetter, *It's a Racket* (Chicago, 1929).

40. Quotation from William G. Shepherd, "How to Make a Gangster," *Colliers* (Sept. 2, 1933), p. 12.

41. First quotation from ibid., p. 13; second quotation from anonymous, typewritten research paper entitled "Introduction" [approx. 1934], p. 10, Burgess papers, II-A, Box 71.

42. Drake and Cayton, *Black Metropolis*, II, pp. 490–94 and 546–50; Nelli, *Italians in Chicago*, p. 22.

43. On the attitude of immigrant mothers, see the many letters to Mayor Dever (1923–27) from immigrant women reporting speakeasies and begging the Mayor to have them closed; in William E. Dever papers, Chicago Historical Society, especially folders 25–26. For a long article on the Chinese Christian Union and its campaign to close Chinese gambling dens, see *Chicago News*, May 11, 1904. On activities of black and of Polish church organizations, see Herbert L. Wiltsee, "Religious Developments in Chicago, 1893–1915," M.A. thesis in history, University of Chicago, 1953, pp. 14 and 23.

9 God and the Mafia
   Gordon Hawkins (1969)

And if any more proof is needed, I possess invisible horns.

Ibsen, *Peer Gynt*

A perplexing and elusive problem confronts the student seeking information about organized crime. It concerns the concept "organized crime"
itself. For a curious feature characterizes almost all the literature on the
subject, up to and including the Task Force Report on this topic published in
1967 by the President's Commission on Law Enforcement and Administration of Justice. This is that a large proportion of what has been written seems
not to be dealing with an empirical matter at all. It is almost as though what is
referred to as organized crime belonged to the realm of metaphysics or
theology.

Indeed the analogy with theology is quite striking. Nor is it merely a
matter of occasional similarities or likenesses, but rather of a systematic
resemblance recurring in a wide variety of different sources. The parallelism
is so pervasive that it is difficult to dismiss it as altogether fortuitous. But
before considering its significance it may be well to illustrate it.

Take first the question of the existence of organized crime, a matter about
which, like the existence of God, doubts have been expressed. On this
subject Estes Kefauver, in his *Crime in America*, which is based on testimony taken at the hearings before, and upon reports of, the Senate Crime
Committee between 1950 and 1951, writes as follows:

> A nationwide crime syndicate does exist in the United States of
> America, despite the protestations of a strangely assorted company of
> criminals, self-serving politicians, plain blind fools, and others who
> may be honestly misguided, that there is no such combine. . . . The
> national crime syndicate as it exists today is an elusive and furtive but
> nonetheless tangible thing. Its organization and machinations are not
> always easy to pinpoint. . . . However, by patient digging and by put-
> ting together little pieces of a huge and widely scattered puzzle, the
> picture emerges. . . . Behind the local mobs which make up the

"God and the Mafia" is reprinted with permission of the author from *The Public
Interest* 14 (1969): 24–51. © 1969 by National Affairs, Inc.

national crime syndicate is a shadowy, international criminal organization known as the Mafia, so fantastic that most Americans find it hard to believe it really exists.

Now, apart from the bizarre nature of it content, one of the most remarkable facts about this quite categorical statement, which occurs in the first chapter of Kefauver's book, is that the evidence necessary to substantiate it is never produced. Indeed Daniel Bell in his *The End of Ideology* comments as follows:

> Unfortunately for a good story—and the existence of the Mafia would be a whale of a story—neither the Senate Crime Committee in its testimony, nor Kefauver in his book, presented any real evidence that the Mafia exists as a functioning organization. One finds public officials asserting before the Kefauver committee their *belief* in the Mafia; the Narcotic Bureau *thinks* that a world-wide dope ring allegedly run by Luciano is part of the Mafia: but the only other "evidence" presented—aside from the incredulous responses both of Senator Kefauver and Rudolph Halley when nearly all the Italian gangsters asserted that they didn't know about the Mafia—is that certain crimes bear "the earmarks of the Mafia." (author's italics.)

Others have been equally skeptical. Thus, Burton B. Turkus, in *Murder Incorporated*, writing at the time when the Senate Crime Investigating Committee was publishing its findings, said:

> If one such unit had all crime in this country under its power, is it not reasonable to assume that somewhere along the line, some law agency—federal, state, county or municipal—would have tripped it up long before this? No single man or group ever was so clever, so completely genius, as to foil all of them forever. . . . In fact, as a factor of power in national crime, Mafia has been virtually extinct for two decades.

Gus Tyler, editor of *Organized Crime in America*, prefaces the section devoted to the Mafia with an essay in which he says that the Mafia "whose existence is assumed by some government agencies" is "a still unproven fact." He adds, however, that "while the existence of the Mafia is still legally conjectural, theories of its existence cannot be ignored."

But the "theories of its existence" prove on examination to consist of little more than a series of dogmatic assertions. Thus, the Final Report of the California Special Crime Study Commission on Organized Crime (1953) speaks of The Mafia, which it says is "now known as L'Unione Siciliana," as "the most sinister and powerful criminal organization in the world (with) headquarters on at least two continents." But after giving a somewhat desultory account of a variety of "illegal enterprises," and making further reference to "a criminal organization extending all over the world," the report falls back on the argument that "The study of these crimes over the years shows a definite pattern, the repetition of which in case after case cannot be laid to coincidence." This incidentally bears an extraordinary resemblance to one of the best known arguments for the existence of God: that is "the argument from design" in the form in which it was used by the eighteenth- and nineteenth-century rationalist theologians. But it is neither probative nor particularly persuasive.

Divine Attributes

Another respect in which assertions about the existence of organized crime in general, and a Mafia in particular, resemble statements about the existence of God is that in neither case is it clear what would be regarded as constituting significant counterevidence. Thus, in the Third Interim Report of the Special Committee to Investigate Organized Crime in Interstate Commerce (i.e., the Senate Crime Committee, or the Kefauver Committee), it is said that "Almost all the witnesses who appeared before the committee and who were suspected of Mafia membership, either denied that they had ever heard of the Mafia, which is patently absurd, or denied membership in the Mafia."

The only exception to this which stood up under cross examination was a witness who said "that the Mafia was freely discussed in his home when he was a child." It is not at all clear what the significance of this childhood reminiscence is supposed to be. What is perfectly clear however is that *whatever* witnesses had said would have been construed as evidence for the existence of Mafia. Acknowledgment of membership in, or awareness of the existence of a Mafia would have been accepted at face value. Denials, on the other hand, merely demonstrate that the Mafia "is a rare 'secret' society whose existence is truly secret"; secrecy being enforced by "Mafia killings" that themselves "are surrounded with the secrecy that has proved to be most difficult to penetrate."

But even when organized crime is not identified with a Mafia it is still referred to in terms that imply divine attributes, such as invisibility, immateriality, eternity, omnipresence, and omnipotence. Thus, in the President's Commission Task Force Report on Organized Crime, it is said that "organized crime affects that lives of millions of Americans, but . . . preserves its *invisibility*." Again, organized crime is said to have its own discipline, but "the laws and regulations they obey, the procedures they use, are private and secret ones that they devise themselves, change when they see fit, and administer summarily and *invisibly*." Moreover, "Agents and employees . . . cannot implicate the highest level figures, since frequently they have neither spoken to *nor even seen them*." Another Task Force Report, "Assessment of Crime," states that "organized crime thrives on

invisibility. . . . No one knows whether it is getting bigger or smaller. . . ."
And F. J. Cook, in *The Secret Rulers*, speaks of "a secret organization, an *invisible* government of crime." (My italics.)

As for immateriality, we are also told by the President's Commission:

> But to discuss the impact of organized crime in terms of whatever direct, personal, everyday effect it has on individuals is to miss most of the point. Most individuals are not affected in this sense, very much. . . . Sometimes organized crime's activities do not directly affect individuals at all.

And one writer, "the former attorney for an illicit New York organization," is quoted as speaking in mystical terms of "a mysterious, all pervasive reality."

The Task Force Report also emphasizes the perpetually enduring nature of organized crime. "[O]rganized crime maintains a coherent, efficient organization with a *permanency of form that survives changes* in working and leadership personnel." And Gus Tyler, in an article on "The Roots of Organized Crime," speaks of ". . . its *eternal life* . . . an institutional longevity extending far beyond the natural life span of its more mortal leadership." (My italics in both cases.)

With regard to omnipresence and omnipotence, Robert F. Kennedy said that "The insidious influence of organized crime can reach into almost every facet of our life, corrupting and undermining our society." The Task Force Report goes further and states that "Organized criminal groups are known to operate in all sections of the Nation." Professor D. R. Cressey writing of "the American confederation of criminals," in his paper on "The Functions and Structure of Criminal Syndicates," which is printed as an appendix to the Task Force Report, says that "while organized criminals do not yet have control of all the legitimate economic and political activities in any metropolitan or other geographic area of America," they have started "to undermine basic economic and political traditions."

As with the Deity, moreover, direct knowledge of this phenomenon is apparently not vouchsafed to us. "While law-enforcement officials now have detailed information about the criminal activities of individual men," Professor Cressey writes, "knowledge of the structure of their confederation remains fragmentary and impressionistic." He goes on to say that "Our knowledge of the structure that makes 'organized crime' organized is somewhat comparable to the knowledge of Standard Oil that could be gleaned from interviews with gasoline station attendants." But there is nothing tentative about his explicit statement that "in the United States, criminals have managed to organize a nationwide illicit cartel and confederation." And in a lengthy chapter beginning, "The structure of the nationwide cartel and confederation which today operates the principal illicit businesses in

America, and which is now striking at the foundations of legitimate business and government as well came into being in 1931," sufficient baroque detail is provided to suggest that interviews with gasoline station attendants may not be totally uninformative for those with ears to hear.

The Code of the Underworld

Yet, as Professor Cressey acknowledges, "some officials, and some plain citizens, remain unconvinced." And, although he regards skepticism as "misplaced," he does not, like Senator Kefauver, define unbelievers as criminals, self-servers, blind fools, and so on. This is, in the circumstances, prudent. For when only "fragmentary and impressionistic" data about an "elusive and furtive" phenomenon are available for judgment, it is unwise to assume that doubt must be disingenuous or perverse.

Thus, as an instance of the sort of thing that might occasion doubt on the part of a plain citizen, consider the tenets of the code that Professor Cressey says "form the foundation of the legal order of the confederation." He states frankly that he was "unable to locate even a summary statement of the code" and that his statement of it is based only on "the snippets of information we have been able to obtain." Yet, on this presumably exiguous basis, he constructs a code that, in regard to form and content, compares favorably with more easily accessible examples of such systems of general rules regarding conduct.

The sinister underworld code that "gives the leaders exploitative authoritarian power over everyone in the organization," reads like the product of collaboration between Rudyard Kipling and Emily Post. Most of it would not appear incongruous if embroidered on a sampler. Organized criminals are enjoined to "be loyal members of the organization," to "be a member of the team," to "be independent," and yet not to "rock the boat." At the same time, they are told to "be a man of honor" and to "respect womanhood and your elders."

The organized criminal "is to be cool and calm at all times"; "is not to use narcotics . . . not to be drunk on duty . . . not to get into fights. . . ." "He does not whine or complain in the face of adversity." "The world seen by organized criminals is a world of graft, fraud, and corruption, and they are concerned with their own honesty and manliness as compared with the hypocrisy of corrupt policemen and corrupt political figures."

In a world of corrupt police and politicians, it must be difficult to preserve these standards. But Professor Cressey explains that, by a "process of recruitment and indoctrination," the leaders of organized crime "have some degree of success" in inculcating "a sense of decency and morality—a sense of honor—so deep that there will be absolute obedience." It is no surprise when we are told that Mr. Vito Genovese, who is said to have been, in 1957, leaders of the "All-American 'Commission'" which is "the highest ruling body in the confederation," was "invested with charismatic qualities by his followers. He was almost revered, while at the same time being feared, like an Old Testament divine. Even his name had a somewhat sacred quality. . . ."

The truth is that this sounds very much like what Gus Tyler calls "the fantasy of the Mafia," and Daniel Bell refers to as the "myth of an omnipotent Mafia," all over again. Indeed, Professor Bell, in a subsequent article entitled, "The Myth of Cosa Nostra" (*The New Leader*, 1963), seems to have been one of the few persons to have remained unpersuaded by the later evidence that we shall examine critically in some detail. For others, however, the same sparsity of data supports an equally grandiose inferential superstructure. "Since we know so little," Professor Cressey says, "it is easy to make the assumption that there is nothing to know anything about." But the scarcity of "hard facts" does not appear to constrict him unduly. And although some of what he says sounds plausible in a nonderogatory sense, when it comes to the question of the *existence* of "the American confederation of criminals" he uses a form of argument that comes close to what one might call logical legerdemain.

The argument is worth examining briefly. Under the heading, "The Structural Skeleton," Professor Cressey provides an outline of the "authority structure" or "'organizational chart' of the American confederation." Twenty-four criminal "families," each with its "boss," are said to operate under the "commission" that "serves as a combination board of business directors, legislature, supreme court and arbitration board." After giving some details of "the formal structure of the organization," Professor Cressey deals briefly with street-level operations and more informal functions. He then concludes briskly:

> [T]he skeleton has more bones than those we have described, as our discussion of informal positions and roles indicates. *The structure outlined is sufficient to demonstrate, however, that a confederation of "families" exists.* (My italics.)

It scarcely seems necessary to point out that if "to demonstrate" here means "to prove by reasoning" or "to establish as true," the existence of the confederation cannot be said to have been demonstrated.

It may be said here, parenthetically, that the details of criminal hierarchies given by Professor Cressey and others in the literature on organized crime are curiously reminiscent of the details of celestial hierarchies to be found in the literature of angelology. Both the "Lord of Hosts" and the "Boss of all Bosses" stand at the apex of a pyramidal structure. Just as the "Lord of Hosts" is attended by superior orders of angelic being like Archangels and Seraphim, so the "Boss of all Bosses" has his attendant

Counsellor (or Consigliere) and Underbosses (or Sottocapi). The Cherubim and ordinary angels are paralleled by the Lieutenants (Caporegime) and Soldiers, lower-echelon personnel who, like the lower orders of angels, may have particular missions as agents, messengers, guards, and enforcers. Possibly in the light of this analogy, Professor Cressey's description of Vito Genovese, sometime "Boss of all Bosses," as "like an Old Testament divine" may not seem altogether incongruous.

But we come now to what must in this context and in the present state of knowledge be crucial questions. The first of these concerns what may be called the mythopeic factor that operate in this field. For it is important to recognize that, quite apart from the evidence available, the notion that behind the diverse phenomena of crime there exists a single mysterious omnipotent organization that is responsible for much of it is one that has long exerted a powerful influence on the minds not only of journalists, but also of law enforcement agents and serious students of crime. The second question which we have to ask is, leaving aside nonevidential and irrational considerations, what kinds of evidence may be regarded as providing a means of ascertaining the truth in this matter; and further what sorts of argument may be adduced as, if not being fully probative, at least having a significant bearing on the question at issue.

Folklore and Myth

With regard to the first question, it is evident that there is a considerable *folklore* relating to organized crime. Much of the literature on the subject consists of myths and folktales. The point is made in Earl Johnson's article, "Organized Crime: Challenge to the American Legal System" that:

> America has a new folklore. This folklore has grown up around— organized crime. Next to Westerns, war and sex, it is probably the chief source of material for TV plots, books—both fiction and non-fiction—and newspaper exposés. The names of "Scarface" Al Capone, Frank "The Enforcer" Nitti, Tony Accardo, Frank Costello, and "Lucky" Luciano have become as familiar to most present-day Americans as Pocohantas, Jesse James, "Wild" Bill Hickock, Paul Bunyan, or Nathan Hale.

The significance of this development has nowhere been fully analyzed, but in the light of the functionalist interpretation of myth made by anthropologists, it would be unwise to dismiss it as of little account. Bronislaw Malinowski, for example, holds that "Myth fulfills in primitive culture an indispensable function: it expresses, enhances and codifies belief; it safeguards and enforces morality. . . ." Nor, is this something confined to primitive cultures, although the character of the myths will obviously be different in different cultures. In regard to our own society, Ruth Benedict has pointed out that

> the fundamental opposition of good and evil is a trait of occidental folklore that is expressed equally in Grimms' fairy tales and in the *Arabian Nights*. . . . It determines some of the most deeply seated world views of western religions and western civilizations. The opposition of God and the devil, of Christ and Antichrist, of heaven and hell, is part of the fundamental intellectual equipment of those who participate in these civilizations.

It is probable that a large part of the appeal of such television series as "The Untouchables," "Target: The Corrupters," and "The F.B.I.," to mention only three, is that they dramatize the struggle against organized crime in terms of this fundamental myth. In this too, it seems likely lies some of the appeal of televised and reported congressional investigations, newspaper accounts of "crusades" against organized crime, and a vast literature dealing with law enforcement efforts against it.

Another function of mythology, however, is that it provides an *explanation*, in that it helps to introduce some intelligible order into the bewildering diversity of phenomena surrounding us. Thus, Ruth Benedict says that "Man in all his mythologies has expressed his discomfort at a mechanistic universe and his pleasure in substituting a world that is humanly motivated and directed." But all myths are not of a cosmic character, and discomfort can be induced just as much by an apparently formless and unstructured field of experience as by the theory that all natural processes are mechanically determined. Whenever alarm and uneasiness are induced by an apparently chaotic upsurge of crime and lawlessness, or whenever explanation in terms of anonymous and intangible "social forces" is found unsatisfying, it is likely that the attribution of responsibility to a group of identifiable human agents for a large proportion of the disturbing happenings could be both intellectually and emotionally reassuring.

Yet, something more than a demand for simplicity and order is involved. In this connection, the way in which anger and distress lead to a demand for the identification of a responsible individual or group, which is brought out by Professor Allport in his discussion of the psychological process of "scapegoating," is directly relevant to our discussion. "The common use of the orphaned pronoun 'they,'" says Allport, "teaches us that people often want and need to designate out-groups—usually for the purpose of venting hostility. . . ." And Daniel Bell attributes part of the attractiveness of the

> theory of a Mafia and national crime syndicate to the fact that there is in the American temper, a feeling that "somewhere," "somebody" is pulling all the complicated strings to which this jumbled world dances. In politics the labor image is "Wall Street" or "Big Business"; while the business stereotype was the "New Dealers."

In the field of crime, the national crime syndicate provides a specific focus or target for fear and discontent.

There is, of course, nothing exclusively or peculiarly American about this process. The popularity of "conspiracy" theories throughout history reflects a general human tendency. The objectification and institutionalization of fear reactions is not a native American development. Yet, as Richard Hofstadter demonstrates in his brilliant essay on "The Paranoid Style in American Politics," American history is singularly rich in examples of "conspiratorial fantasy." It is true that Hofstadter says, "the paranoid style is an international phenomenon." But he also admits that "it can be argued . . . that certain features of our history have given the paranoid style more scope and force among us than it has had in many other countries of the Western world." It is relevant to note here that, in describing "the basic elements in the paranoid style," Hofstadter says that "the central image is that of a vast and sinister conspiracy, a gigantic and yet subtle machinery of influence set in motion to undermine and destroy a way of life."

Yet, so much having been said about irrational factors that may be regarded as conducive to the acceptance of the notion of an all-powerful syndicate that dominates American crime, it remains true that the validity of an idea and the reasons for its popularity may be quite independent of one another. And this brings us to the second step in this analysis which concerns the problem of defining an objective approach to the question whether an All-American criminal cartel and confederation exists.

What Is "Organized Crime"?

When the existence of some social phenomenon or complex of phenomena is asserted, it is reasonable to ask, "What difference does it make?" For, however elusive and invisible and impalpable a social phenomenon may be, the assertion that it exists must, if it is to be regarded as significant, imply the occurrence of some concrete conditions, some specific actions, events, or series of events present in our society that constitute evidence for it. Otherwise, one is entitled, in the present context, to ask a question, analogous to the sort of question posed by skeptics in theological discussions: How does this elusive, invisible, impalpable organization differ from an imaginary organization or from no organization at all? What would count as evidence *against* the assertion that an All-American crime syndicate exists? What would constitute disproof of, or be regarded as sufficient reason for withdrawing, that assertion? Is there anything that might conceivably count against it and, if so, what?

At this point, it is necessary to define the question at issue a little more precisely than has been done so far. In the first place, there is no doubt that small groups of criminals organized for carrying out particular kinds of crime have existed for centuries. In their textbook on criminology, Sutherland and Cressey point out that such groups operated in the Elizabethan period and "have been described in some detail." They also point out that "similar groups exist today for purposes of bank burglary, shoplifting, confidence games, picking pockets and stealing automobiles." Organized crime at this level, it is said,

> involves association of a small group of criminals for the execution of a certain type of crime, together with the development of plans by which detection may be avoided, and the development of a fund of money and political connections by means of which immunity or relative immunity may be secured in case of detection.

It is only necessary to say that, about the existence of organized crime in this sense, there is general agreement.

It should be clear, however, that the concept of organized crime with which we are dealing here relates to something of different character from that just described. We are here concerned with what Sutherland and Cressey call the "organization of the vices." In this connection, they say:

> The most widespread organization of lawlessness is in connection with the vices. Relatively few people demand that burglars, pickpockets and confidence men engage in crime, but many persons demand opportunities for illicit sexual intercourse, gambling and consumption of narcotics. . . . This provides a basis for extensive organization which involves the places of vice, the patrons, the real estate dealers, the manufacturers of commodities used in the vices, the police and courts, the politicians, and sometimes a much wider public.

Here, too, there would be little dispute. Moreover, in the field of what we may call "service" crime, involving the supply of consumer goods and services for which there is a widespread demand, it would be surprising if there did not develop, as in legitimate business, what Professor Schelling refers to as "large-scale continuing firms with the internal organization of a large enterprise, and with a conscious effort to control the market."

The question we are considering, however, is whether in addition to such "large-scale continuing firms" located in various parts of the country, there is a national syndicate that dominates organized crime throughout the country—one large nationwide criminal organization that controls the majority, if not all, of the local undertakings. For the concept of organized crime that was presented in the evidence given by Attorney General Robert F. Kennedy before the Permanent Subcommittee on Investigations of the Committee on Government Operations (McClellan Committee) in 1963 involves a private government of organized crime, a government with an annual income of billions—run by a commission (which) makes major policy decisions for the organization, settles disputes among the families and allocates territories of criminal operation within the organizations.

Enter Valachi

Clearly a crucial question in this context concerns the evidence on which the Attorney General based his contention that such a government and such an organization existed. The nature of that evidence became clear as the McClellan Committee Hearings proceeded. For, at those Hearings, as Senator McClellan himself put it: "For the first time a member of the secret underworld government, Cosa Nostra, testified under oath describing the operations of the criminal organization, and the misguided and dedicated loyalty of its members." The witness referred to was Joseph Valachi, a sixty-year-old man with a long criminal record, at the time serving a life sentence for murder and a twenty-year sentence for a narcotics offense.

Of the significance attached to Valachi's evidence there seems to be no doubt. The Attorney General described his disclosures as "the biggest intelligence breakthrough yet in combating organized crime and racketeering in the United States." William George Hundley, head of the Justice Department's Organized Crime Section, was even more revealing. He said:

Before Valachi came along *we had no tangible evidence that anything like this actually existed.* He's the first to talk openly and specifically about the organization. In the past we've heard that so-and-so was a "syndicate man" and that was all. Frankly I always thought it was a lot of hogwash. But Valachi named names. He showed us what the structure is and how it operates. . . . (My italics.)

It becomes necessary therefore to examine Valachi's testimony critically. In this connection, it has to be remembered that, prior to his giving evidence, Valachi, who had the year before (June 1962) murdered a fellow prisoner, was, according to his own statements, in fear of his life. He claimed that his former criminal associates intended to kill him. His feelings for them were no less inimical. When asked why he had decided to cooperate with the Department of Justice, he replied: "The main answer to that is very simple. Number one: It is to destroy them." With such an objective in view, the witness could not be regarded as totally disinterested. Moreover, on his own evidence, he clearly did not regard veracity as always obligatory when speaking to law enforcement agencies.

In the circumstances, it is understandable that Senator McClellan attached importance to securing some corroboration for Valachi's testimony. Thus, in opening the Hearings, he said: "We believe a substantial part of his testimony can and will be corroborated." And, in closing them, he said: "The corroboration furnished by law enforcement officers makes Valachi's testimony more credible and important."

We may ask therefore how far that verdict is borne out. For in such a case as this, the corroborative process assumes unusual significance.

Cosa Nostra or Mafia?

Let us take first a point of detail that has already attracted some comment. What was the name of the organization about which Valachi testified? According to Valachi, it was "Cosa Nostra." He was asked if the organization was "anything like the Mafia, or is it part of the Mafia, or is it the Mafia?" He replied:

> Senator, as long as I belong to this Cosa Nostra, all I can tell you is that they never express it as a Mafia. When I was speaking, I just spoke what I knew. . . . I know this thing existed a long time, but in my time I have been with this Cosa Nostra and that is the way it was called. . . .

On this, F. J. Cook, in his *The Secret Rulers*, comments that:

> there is a consensus among the nation's best investigators, men with the most intimate knowledge of the underworld and its rackets that they had never heard the name before Valachi used it. . . . this has cast some doubt upon the validity of Valachi's story.

It is not a doubt that troubles Mr. Cook however. "Regardless of name," he says, "the vital fact remains: the criminal organization exists. . . . The name itself is secondary. What matters is the reality of a secret organization, an invisible government of crime. . . ." Yet for those more skeptical than Mr. Cook, and concerned about the *corroboration* of Valachi's testimony, it is not a matter that can be passed over so lightly. For the fact is that on this point Valachi's evidence was *never* corroborated, although a large number of expert witnesses were examined on this subject. "It is a name I am not familiar with," said New York City Police Commissioner Michael J. Murphy. "I have never heard of such a name; no sir," said Rhode Island State Police Superintendent Col. Walter E. Stone. "Not by the name 'Cosa Nostra,'" said Boston Police Commissioner Edmund L. McNamara. ". . . We in Detroit apply the name 'Mafia,'" said George C. Edwards, Detroit City Police Commissioner. Nor were any of the Italian-speaking experts on organized crime who testified more forthcoming on this point.

Senator McClellan took the view that "whether he calls it Cosa Nostra or the Mafia makes no difference." Commissioner Edwards of Detroit said,

"The last thing I am interested in doing is debating nomenclature." Yet it is doubtful whether so cavalier an approach to the evidence can be justified in this case. For, apart from the state and local police forces, according to the Attorney General, "over 25 various investigative bodies of the Federal Government" were pooling their information "in the organized crime section." It seems a little surprising that out of all those who appeared before the commission not one person was found to confirm Valachi's evidence on this matter.

Initiation Rites

But if the question of nomenclature is regarded as of no great significance, there are what may be seen as more substantial matters about which the state of the evidence is equally unsatisfactory. Take, for example, the question of initiation rites, about which a great deal has been written in the literature. The Attorney General told the McClellan Commission: "They literally take an oath and they have the bloodletting. I think it will be described to you before the committee, but those who are members of this organization, take the oath."

When he testified on this, Valachi described a ceremony at which thirty-five or forty persons were present in the course of which he took an oath ("I repeated some words they told me, but I couldn't explain what he meant."); burnt a piece of paper ("Well then he gave me a piece of paper, and I was to burn it."); had his finger pricked ("With a needle and he makes a little blood come out."); and repeated some more words ("I never asked what it meant.").

Now the purpose of this meeting, according to Valachi, was "to make new members and *to meet all of them*." Yet later, when questioned, Valachi, although he claimed to have proposed others for membership, twice stated that he couldn't remember being "invited to participate at any other initiation ceremony." No member of the committee thought to ask him how it was that subsequently—from 1930 onward—no new member was ever to meet *him* at an initiation ceremony. They appeared to be satisfied with his statement: "Let me explain it this way. You are only made once; that is all. If you live a hundred years, it will be just that once." Yet, earlier he had stated that the purpose of these meetings was "to meet the others that were in that family." It remains only to add that, although Valachi stated: "That is the same ceremony today, what I described in 1930," on this matter, too, there was no corroboration. The nearest the committee came to securing corroboration was a statement from Detroit Police Commissioner Edwards: "We would not be in the slightest surprised at the form of initiation which was described here, but we, unfortunately, do not have in our possession someone who could testify directly."

The Genovese "Family"

We come now, however, to what is unquestionably a matter of substance, to that part of Valachi's testimony that dealt with the membership and organizational structure of the Vito Genovese "family" in New York to which he belonged. It was in this connection that his evidence was said to be most valuable and reliable. John F. Shanley, Deputy Chief Inspector in the Central Investigations Bureau, which is the intelligence unit concerned with organized crime in the New York City Police Department, stated, "His strength is in the Genovese chart, his greatest strength . . ."; the chart referred to being one prepared by the Central Investigations Bureau showing details of the Vito Genovese "family." It is important, therefore, to see how far Valachi's evidence was corroborated by the police. In this connection, the evidence given by Deputy Chief Shanley reveals that the information given by Valachi coincided with that put forward by the police in a number of respects. Yet an examination of the record reveals other facts which also make it clear that:

1. It would have been very surprising indeed if the police evidence had not agreed with that of Valachi, and,

2. To talk to the police evidence as *corroborating* Valachi's testimony is to totally misrepresent the situation.

In order to demonstrate this point, it is only necessary to reproduce two brief passages from Deputy Chief Inspector Shanley's testimony. The first passage is taken from the beginning of that testimony:

> THE CHAIRMAN: Have you gone over the information that the committee has obtained and conferred with the staff regarding it, and also with this witness, Joe Valachi?
>
> MR. SHANLEY: I haven't conferred with the witness.
>
> THE CHAIRMAN: You never conferred with the witness?
>
> MR. SHANLEY: No, Sir.
>
> THE CHAIRMAN: So, what you are going to testify here is not a result of any conference you have had with Valachi?
>
> MR. SHANLEY: No, sir.
>
> THE CHAIRMAN: Very well, you may proceed.

The second passage occurs toward the end of Deputy Chief Inspector Shanley's evidence, after he had produced the chart referred to above and testified about the Genovese "family." It runs as follows:

> THE CHAIRMAN: Senator Muskie, you have a question?
>
> SENATOR MUSKIE: You testified earlier, Inspector Shanley, that you had not personally talked to Mr. Valachi.
>
> MR. SHANLEY: That is right.
>
> SENATOR MUSKIE: Yet these charts are based heavily on his information, am I correct?

MR. SHANLEY: That is correct.

SENATOR MUSKIE: What was the source of your access to his information?

MR. SHANLEY: The Committee.

SENATOR MUSKIE: Yes, sir. We received the information prior to the hearings.

SENATOR MUSKIE: Would it have been possible for you to reconstruct these charts without his testimony?

MR. SHANLEY: No, sir.

SENATOR MUNDT: Mr. Chairman.

THE CHAIRMAN: Senator Mundt.

SENATOR MUNDT: While we are talking about the value of the charts, you have been in the hearing room, I think, Inspector, since the very beginning of the Valachi testimony. Is that right?

MR. SHANLEY: *Yes, sir.*

It is only necessary to add that sedulous reproduction is not the same thing as substantiation. Nor is it suffiicent merely to assert, as Mr. Shanley did, that Valachi's information possessed "an apparent authenticity that is hard to doubt." Mr. Stanley appears to have felt that the impossibility of verifying much of what Valachi said did not necessarily detract from its credibility or value.

[T]he specific information that he gave, this will be pursued. But even if this specific information does not pan out, it *would not necessarily detract from the effectiveness of the information*, because the lapse of time, as you well know, goes for the defendant and what happens in 10, 20, 30 years is that the witness is not available, memories fade, locales change. In New York, some of the things this man is talking about no longer exist as to locale. The buildings are torn down. Physical evidence has gone. (My italics.)

It never became clear exactly what he meant by "effectiveness" in this context.

The Case of Abe Reles

There is, however, one example in the transcript of the McClellan Committee Hearings which throws some light on the credibility of Valachi's evidence, and the reliability of the sources from which he derived his information. That is the case of Abe Reles. Early in the hearings, Valachi cited Reles' death as an example of the way in which "the organization" was able "to kill somebody when they are in prison if they want to." He testified as follows:

MR. VALACHI: There was another one, Abe Reles. He was also supposed to testify. He fell out of the window.

SENATOR BREWSTER: How did he fall out of the window, do you know?
MR. VALACHI: They threw him out.

Later in the hearings, the committee returned to this point. Senator Javits read out the passage quoted above and then asked:

SENATOR JAVITS: Who threw him out?
MR. VALACHI: That was the rumor that they threw him out.
SENATOR JAVITS: Who is "they"? You used the word.
MR. VALACHI: Let us put it this way, whoever was in charge.
SENATOR JAVITS: That is on the gang side; is that right: What was the rumor, as you knew it?
MR. VALACHI: That the police threw him out.
SENATOR JAVITS: That was the rumor as you knew it?
MR. VALACHI: Yes.
SENATOR JAVITS: Do you know any more about it?
MR. VALACHI: No; that is all.
SENATOR JAVITS: Did you hear that confirmed in prison or in any way?
MR. VALACHI: The boys talked about it; that is good enough for me.
SENATOR JAVITS: The boys in prison?
MR. VALACHI: No; the boys outside.
SENATOR JAVITS: The boys in your gang, is that right?
MR. VALACHI: Yes.
SENATOR JAVITS: Any particular boy?
MR. VALACHI: Well, now, I would say in general conversation here and there. When you have a conversation, it is pretty solid.
SENATOR JAVITS: You believed it?
MR. VALACHI: Yes, anything I hear.

Eight days later, the committee was to hear more about the death of Abe Reles. Picturesque stories about "the organization" were one thing; allegations against the police were a different matter. Deputy Chief Inspector Shanley, who had been so impressed by the "apparent authenticity" of Valachi's information, reappeared, speaking in a somewhat different vein.

THE CHAIRMAN: Very well. Is there anything further?
MR. ADLERMAN: I think that Inspector Shanley has something that he would like to put into the record, a statement he would like to make.
MR. SHANLEY: I have here a grand jury presentment in the matter of the investigation of the circumstances surrounding the death of Abe Reles on November 12, 1941. . . .

Shanley then read a statement to the effect that the grand jury, after examining 86 witnesses, viewing 127 exhibits, and hearing scientific reports from the FBI, had concluded:

That Abe Reles met his death while trying to escape, by means of a knotted sheet which was attached to a wire, which wire was in turn attached to the radiator in his room. He fell to his death, while suspended from or supporting himself in this sheet, when the wire parted as a result of the strain on his weight on it. We find that Reles did not meet with foul play and that he did not die by suicide.

Organizational Discipline

We turn now from "the corroboration furnished by law enforcement officers [that] make Valachi's testimony more credible and important," to what, in the circumstances, is the only other criterion of validity available, that is, the internal consistency of the evidence. Here there are a variety of matters that might be considered. In view, however, of the great emphasis that is always placed, in the literature, on the strictness of organizational discipline, and the obvious necessity for this if such an organization is to cohere and continue to exist, it is interesting to examine first the evidence on this topic.

In this connection, Senator McClellan spoke in his opening address of "the strict discipline imposed upon the members." He said: "This tightly knit association of professional criminals demands and gets *complete dedication and unquestioned obedience* by its members to orders, instructions and commands from the ruling authority or boss or bosses thereof." Subsequently, many witnesses were to refer to this. Thus, William H. Schneider, commissioner of police of Buffalo, spoke of the syndicate as "a multibillion dollar syndicate which depends on brutal assault and murder as its means of *cold, dispassionate discipline.*" (My italics.) Valachi was asked about this by Senator McClellan.

> THE CHAIRMAN: [T]hat (i.e., Cosa Nostra) is an organization, is it that requires *absolute obedience and conformity* to its policy as handed down by those in authority? (My italics again.)
> MR. VALACHI: Yes, sir.
>   . . .
> THE CHAIRMAN: Is that correct?
> MR. VALACHI: Yes, sir.

It is interesting to compare these statements with some passages in Valachi's later testimony. It appears that, because of "the heat of the naroctics prosecutions, and the investigations and the publicity" in 1957, "those in authority" decreed that there was to be no more dealing in narcotics among members of Cosa Nostra. As Valachi put it: "No narcotics. You are in serious trouble if you were arrested for narcotics. You had to prove to them—you have another trial after having a trial with the government." His examination on this topic ran as follows:

MR. VALACHI: After Anastasia died in 1957, all families were notified—no narcotics.

MR. ADLERMAN: Who laid down that rule?

MR. VALACHI: That was a rule that was discussed by the bosses themselves.

MR. ADLERMAN: Was that the consigliere and the bosses themselves made that rule?

MR. VALACHI: That is right; that covered all families.

It is instructive to read what came next:

MR. ADLERMAN: Was the narcotics trade one of the principal moneymakers for the members of the Cosa Nostra?

MR. VALACHI: Yes, it was.

MR. ADLERMAN: And was this rule disregarded to a large extent?

MR. VALACHI: You mean there were lots of people in business?

MR. ADLERMAN: That is right.

MR. VALACHI: Yes, sir.

Valachi went on to say that even some of "the bosses" violated the rule and he was then asked:

MR. ADLERMAN: What was the reason why the members, the soldiers and so forth, and even some of the bosses disregarded the rule?

MR. VALACHI: Because of the moneymaking, the profit in it.

MR. ADLERMAN: There was big money?

MR. VALACHI: They would chance their own lives.

MR. ADLERMAN: And there was a conflict between the desire to make money and the desire to obey the rules; is that right?

MR. VALACHI: Well, they just defied the rules.

MR. ADLERMAN: They defied the rules?

MR. VALACHI: That is the way I can explain it that way.

In the light of what had been said earlier about "complete dedication and unquestioned obedience," it was not an entirely satisfactory explanation. But then no explanation, however ingenious, could encompass the logically impossible task of reconciling the development described with the concept of a ruthless, unquestionable authority imposing "cold, dispassionate discipline" and securing "absolute obedience and conformity." Indeed, the evidence casts doubt also on the validity of the Attorney General's belief that "Cosa Nostra . . . establishes an allegiance for its members that is higher than family, country and religion. It becomes the primary allegiance of the member." Not quite the *primary* allegiance apparently. Yet, Senator McClellan was still talking a week later about "Cosa Nostra . . . and the misguided and dedicated loyalty of its members."

Mutual Aid?

It is, in fact, extremely difficult to understand what membership of the organization was supposed to entail either in the way of rights or duties. When Valachi was describing his initiation, he was asked:

SENATOR MUNDT: In executive session you said when you had your hands clasped together and repeated some words in Italian or Sicilian, that what it meant was "One for all and all for one."
MR. VALACHI: Yes; that is the way I explained it.
SENATOR MUNDT: One for all and all for one.
MR. VALACHI: That is right. But I didn't know the words, Senator. You remember, I did not know the words.
SENATOR MUNDT: That is right, but you said that is the reaction you got.
MR. VALACHI: That is correct.
SENATOR MUNDT: All right, then you became there a full-fledged member.
MR. VALACHI: Yes, sir.

It would seem reasonable to assume that the slogan, assuming that Valachi understood it correctly, implied some kind of mutual aid and protection. Certainly Senator McClellan had told the committee that "The benefits of membership . . . are a share in its illicit gains from criminal activities and protection from prosecution and the penalties of the law. . . ." Later Valachi was asked:

SENATOR MUNDT: I want to ask you a couple of questions dealing with the first part of your testimony. You belonged to Cosa Nostra for about 30 years?
MR. VALACHI: Since 1930.
SENATOR MUNDT: What was your average income from your criminal contacts during those 30 years, your average annual income?
MR. VALACHI: Senator, I wouldn't be able to tell you. Sometimes I was doing bad, sometimes I was doing good.
SENATOR MUNDT: What I am trying to establish is that you were working as a soldier in this family, I am trying to determine what your income was as a soldier working for Genovese.
MR. VALACHI: You don't get any salary, Senator.
SENATOR MUNDT: Well, you get a cut then.
MR. VALACHI: You get nothing, only what you earn yourself. Do you understand? . . .
SENATOR MUNDT: You say the only thing you got out of your membership and for carrying out your assignments that Genovese gave you was protection?
MR. VALACHI: Yes. . . .

So much then for Senator McClellan's "share in its illicit gains." What about "protection from prosecution and the penalties of the law"? Deputy Chief Inspector Shanley had told the Committee that "[T]he family will help with laywers, bail bondsmen, *et cetera*, if anything goes wrong."

The following passages are relevant here:

SENATOR JAVITS: Were you represented, for example, by lawyers in that time when you were picked up?

MR. VALACHI: When you are picked up, sometimes yes; sometimes no. Sometimes you don't even require a lawyer.

SENATOR JAVITS: How did you seek the help of your family when you were picked up?

MR. VALACHI: I used to get my own help. What family do you mean?

SENATOR JAVITS: The family to which you belonged, the Genovese family.

MR. VALACHI: I never bothered them. If I got picked up, I got myself out, I got my own lawyers.

SENATOR JAVITS: They did not furnish lawyers?

MR. VALACHI: Never.

SENATOR JAVITS: Or bondsmen?

MR. VALACHI: Never, I got my own bondsmen, my own lawyers.

. . .

SENATOR JAVITS: Do you attribute the fact that you were not convicted of a crime for 35 years to your membership in this family? Do you connect the two at all?

MR. VALACHI: No.

SENATOR JAVITS: You were just lucky?

MR. VALACHI: That is right.

SENATOR JAVITS: And you changed the nature of activities?

MR. VALACHI: Put it that way.

SENATOR JAVITS: So your membership in the family had nothing to do in your opinion . . .

MR. VALACHI: I was never is a position, if I was I would tell you, Senator, I was never in a position where the family helped me.

In his evidence before the McClellan Committee, the Attorney General spoke of the commission ("We know that Cosa Nostra is run by a commission . . .") as a body that "makes major policy decisions for the organization, settles disputes among families and allocates territories of criminal operation within the organizations." It sounds a very businesslike and efficient operation on the part of men about whom the committee were later told "frequently they don't make out in the legitimate business" because they are "not very smart businessmen." But it is hardly consistent with Valachi's testimony. He was asked:

SENATOR CURTIS: In that connection, did they divide up the territory? Even though you operated on your own, you knew where you
could operate?

MR. VALACHI: No, you see, Senator, you take Harlem, for instance.
We have about four families all mixed up there. *There isn't any territory.* You find Brooklyn gangs in New York and New York into
Brooklyn. They get along very well. If anything, you have in Brooklyn, in fact they help protect it for you. *I would not say it is territories.*
You take for instance in Harlem, we have about three families bump-
ing onto one another. You have the Gambino family, the Lucchese
family, and you have the Genovese family right in Harlem. . . . You
have three families right there. You have members there from all
different groups. (My italics.)

Precepts and Rules

We may deal briefly with one other matter and then leave the McClellan
Committee. Senator McClellan told members that "The penalty for disloyalty or any serious deviation from the precepts, rules and dictates of the
order is usually death." But what were the precepts and rules of the order?
We have already noted Professor Cressey's remarkable "code of good
thieves everywhere." What did Joseph Valachi have to say on the subject?
He stated that at the time of his initiation he was told that he must never
divulge the secrets of the initiation ceremony or of the organization. On this
point, he said:

As to what I am telling you now, I need go no further to say nothing else but this here, what I am telling you, what I am exposing to
you and the press and everybody. This is my doom. This is the promise I am breaking. Even if I talked, I should never talk about this,
and I am doing so. That is my best way to explain it.

His examination continued as follows:

THE CHAIRMAN: Were any of the rules explained to you there, or
were they explained to your later?

MR. VALACHI: Just two rules at this time.

THE CHAIRMAN: Just two at that time?

MR. VALACHI: At this time.

THE CHAIRMAN: What were they?

MR. VALACHI: One was the secret which I was just telling you about,
and the other rule was, for instance, a wife, if you violate the law of
another member's wife, or sister, or daughter, these two rules were
told; in other words, you had no defense.

THE CHAIRMAN: You have no defense?

MR. VALACHI: These two main rules. If you give away the secret or you violate—at this time that is all of the rules I was told.

THE CHAIRMAN: Those two.

MR. VALACHI: At this time.

THE CHAIRMAN: If you violate the family relationship of husband and his wife, and if they were members of Cosa Nostra; is that all?

MR. VALACHI: If they were members. If they were members of Cosa Nostra.

THE CHAIRMAN: You were prohibited from violating the rules of family relationship.

MR. VALACHI: That is right.

THE CHAIRMAN: Those two at that time.

MR. VALACHI: That is right.

But, although Valachi testified that later on he "learned the rules," the only other example he gave was, "For instance you can't hit another members with your fist." He admitted having broken this rule himself when he found his partner "was stealing most of the profit." Senator McClellan seems to have scented another rule at this point, for he asked: "Was that against your code, to steal from each other?" But Valachi's replay was somewhat equivocal "Well yes," he said, "against my code it was." And that was all the committee learnt about "the code" which, according to the President's Commission Task Force Report on Organized Crime "gives the leaders exploitative authoritarian power over everyone in the organization."

Of the three rules he mentioned, Valachi had avowedly broken two. Was he unusual in this? He was certainly not unique in becoming an informer. According to the Attorney General, the *main* thing that distinguished him was that he was willing to "come and testify in public." Over two years later, J. Edgar Hoover told a House of Representatives Appropriations Subcommittee that "*all the Valachi information* . . . had been obtained from informants of the Bureau" prior to the McClellan committee hearings. But, apart from this sort of disloyalty, did the chivalric code of "One for all and all for one" otherwise prevail? Almost everything in Valachi's testimony suggests the opposite. He spoke of vicious power struggles and murderous internecine conflicts like the Masseria-Maranzano war and the Gallo-Profaci feud. He spoke of "the bosses" as being "very bad to the soldiers and they have been thinking for themselves, all through the years." He portrayed Professor Cressey's "almost revered" Vito Genovese as mean, murderous, and megalomaniacal. If there existed anywhere amongst organized criminals that "sense of decency and morality—a sense of honor," which Professor Cressey remarks as charactertistic of them, it seems to have escaped Joseph Valachi's notice.

In sum then, what can be said about the Valachi evidence? In the first

place, the Attorney General's assertion that "For the first time an insider
. . . has broken the underworld's code of silence," was misleading. It was
contradicted later both by the Attorney General himself and by J. Edgar
Hoover. Apart from his willingness to testify in public, only one feature of
the Valachi testimony was unique. What that was is clear from the Attorney
General's statement:

> You look back on organized crime and people who are talking bout
> organized crime, somebody might talk about a particular criminal act.
> What we have always lacked is somebody who could come in and tell
> the whole picture. Now he tells it. . . .

In short, what Valachi added to the already available evidence about
particular crimes and criminals was the story of the syndicate, its organization, its operations, and its membership.

What was his evidence on the subject worth? A great deal of it was the
loosest kind of hearsay. Valachi believed and repeated on oath, as matters
of act, "anything" he heard in conversation "here and there" with his fellow
criminals. Despite what Senator McClellan said about his evidence being
corroborated, it was not corroborated on any points essential to the hypothesis we are considering. It was neither consistent with itself nor with other
evidence that was presented to the Committee. Valachi both contradicted
himself and was contradicted by others. Moreover, what the Attorney
General called "the biggest intelligence breakthrough yet" appears to have
produced nothing in the way of tangible results.

Two and a half years after Valachi testified, J. Edgar Hoover was asked
before the House of Representatives Appropriations Subcommittee mentioned earlier:

> MR. ROONEY (CHAIRMAN): Has Valachi been of any assistance to the
> Bureau in the prosecution of any criminal as a result of which there
> has been a conviction?
> MR. HOOVER: There has been no person convicted as a direct result of
> any information furnished by Valachi.

And four years later, the President's Commission Task Force Report on
Organized Crime described the situation regarding organized crime in precisely the same terms as those used by the Attorney General before the
McClellan Committee. Almost the only development reported is that "FBI
intelligence indicates that the organization as a whole has changed its name
from the Mafia to La Cosa Nostra." The report is not very clear on this point
but seems to suggest that the name was changed at some time between 1951
and 1966. So that even this contradicts Valachi who maintained that it had
been called Cosa Nostra ("they never express it as a Mafia"), when he
joined in 1930!

Apalachin

There is one other piece of "evidence" which should be mentioned here before we conclude. This relates to what J. Edgar Hoover called the "meeting of hoodlums at Apalachin, N.Y.," which has been referred to somewhat more grandly by others as the "Crime Convention at Apalachin" and the "historic rally of the Mafia at Apalachin." Senator McClellan says of it:

> The meeting gave to millions of Americans their first clear knowledge that we have in this country a criminal syndicate that is obviously tightly organized into a secret brotherhood which none of its members dare betray, and which has insinuated its tentacles into business and labor and public life at high levels. . . .

But whatever else can be derived from the mass of confused and contradictory evidence available regarding Apalachin, it is certainly not "clear knowledge."

There seems to be general agreement that on November 14, 1957, a number of individuals, most of whom "had criminal records relating to the kind of offense customarily called 'organized crime,' " gathered at the home of Joseph Barbara in Apalachin, N.Y., and that the gathering was interrupted by the police. But, beyond that point, the evidence becomes extraordinarily confused. Indeed, even such basic information as how many persons were present at the gathering is lacking. Thus, Senator McClellan states that: "*Fifty-eight* men were picked up on the Barbara estate or in the immediate surrounding countryside." *The Report of the State of New York Joint Legislative Committee on Government Operations* on "the Gangland Meeting in Apalachin, N.Y." states, "On November 14, 1957, *about 65* individuals gathered at the home of a man named Joseph Barbara, in Apalachin, N.Y. . . ." *The Task Force Report: Organized Crime* talks of "the meeting in Apalachin, N.Y., of *at least 75* criminal cartel leaders." Attorney General Robert Kennedy testified to the McClellan Committee that: "In 1957, *more than a hundred* top racketeers met at the now infamous crime convention at Apalachin, N.Y." (My italics in each case.)

Where such discrepancies exist about a matter that is, at least in principle, subject to quantitative measurement, it is not surprising that there is disagreement about less objective features. The following brief passages by authors, both of whom derived their information from, and cite as their authority, the Federal Bureau of Narcotics, give almost totally disparate accounts of such matters as the weather, the number, dress, demeanor, and spirits of the guests at Apalachin. Frederic Sondern, in *Brotherhood of Evil: The Mafia*, says that, of the "more than sixty" persons present, many were engaged in "conclaves" inside Barbara's house. Sondern continues:

Others were grouped around the huge stone barbecue pit. . . . The weather at Apalachin was unusually mild for November and most of the guests were dressed in immaculate light suits of Italian silk, white on white shirts, and highly polished shoes of soft leather. The majority were in their late fifties and early sixties—dignified, even pompous. All seemed to be in a decorous good humor.

Renée Buse, in *The Deadly Silence*, on the other hand says:

It was an odd day for a barbecue. The sky was gray. The November temperature hovered just above freezing. Cold, damp rain-winds swirled through the barren trees. The hundred-odd men who stood in uncomfortable clusters around the barbecue pit were quiet, even glum. Somehow, the party spirit had failed to penetrate. Dutifully the guests ate and drank . . . but their loud, Broadway type sports jackets, their thin, pointed shoes, and their pasty complexions bespoke their awkward discomfort.

It is true that this is not a matter of great significance. Such differences could easily be due to one informant having drunk from the "selection of choice wines," which Sondern says was available, more "dutifully" than another. But discrepancies regarding more substantial matters are less easy to discount.

Consider, for instance, the question of the nature of the gathering at Apalachin. John T. Cusack, District Supervisor for the Federal Bureau of Narcotics, testified before the New York State Legislative Committee that "the meeting at Apalachin, New York, should be considered a meeting of the Grand Council" of "the Mafia Society." Attorney General Robert Kennedy, in his evidence to the McClellan Committee, cited "the meeting at Apalachin" as an example of a meeting of the commission that runs Cosa Nostra and "makes major policy decisions for the organization." But he also testified that "membership" in the commission varies between 9 and 12 active members." He made no attempt to reconcile this evidence with his earlier statement that "more than a hundred top racketeers" were present at Apalachin. Senator McClellan allowed himself a rhetorical flourish. "The meeting of the delegates to the Apalachin convention," he said, "suggests a lawless and clandestine army . . . at war with the government and the people of the United States." He failed to mention, however, that not one of these lawless warriors was armed, and that only one (a parole violator from New Jersey who should not have left the state) was wanted anywhere by the police.

What business was conducted at Apalachin? Renée Buse, who says that Federal Bureau of Narcotics Commissioner H. L. Giordano's "desire to have the story told accurately" made his investigation possible, describes a hearing of an appeal to "the Bosses" by Carmine Lombardozzi, against conviction by "a kangaroo court of his peers . . . for having tied to muscle into another man's exclusive jukebox territory," as being the principal business in progress when the police closed in. Frederic Sondern, whose accuracy is vouched for by former Federal Bureau of Narcotics Commissioner, H. J. Anslinger, states:

> The business of the meeting at Barbara's—according to well placed informers who have pieced the picture together for the Treasury Department's agents—*concentrated on two questions* crucial to the future of big organized rackets, narcotics and gambling.

But, another well-placed informer, Joseph Valachi, testified to the McClellan Committee:

> The meeting *was held for two main reasons* that I know of. One was to talk about the justifying of the shooting of Albert Anastasia. The other one was that they were going to talk about eliminating some couple of hundred new members.

Valachi, incidentally, stated that Vito Genovese "called the meeting at Apalachin," whereas Sondern says that the McClellan Committee "had very reliable information" that "William Bufalino . . . was responsible for organizing—for his close friend and associate of many years, Don Giuseppe Barbara—the whole Apalachin meeting." Giuseppe, he says, "was a capo mafioso of the first order, of unusual experience, wisdom and authority."

It scarcely seems necessary to multiply examples. When, subsequently, twenty of those present at Apalachin were charged with "conspiring to obstruct justice and commit perjury," the government frankly admitted at the outset of the trial "that it would not be able to show what was going on at the meeting." Regarding this trial, the *Task Force Report: Organized Crime* says: "In 1957, twenty of organized crime's top leaders were convicted (later reversed on appeal) of a criminal charge arising from a meeting at Apalachin, N.Y." It is characteristic of the inconsequential way in which the whole subject is treated in both official and unofficial reports that the defendants are said to have been convicted in 1957 of charges on which they were not even indicted until May 1959. But the report is accurate in stating that all the convictions were reversed on appeal.

What remains after one penetrates the fog of senatorial fustian and journalistic rhetoric? Professor Cressey is unusually restrained on this question. "No one has been able to prove the nature of the conspiracy involved," he says. But he adds, reasonably enough, "no one believes that the men all just happened to drop in on the host at the same time." Professor Bell says: "The accidental police discovery of a conference of Italian figures, most of them with underworld and police records at Apalachin, New York, in

November, 1957, revived talk of a Mafia." But he says the " 'evidence' that
many gangsters congregate . . . by itself does not prove much; people "in
the trade' usually do. . . ." A reasonable explanation seems to be that it was
as suggested by *Time* magazine reporter, Serell Hillman who was assigned to
check the story over some weeks—a meeting "of criminals in various cities
and areas, who run their own shows in their own fields but have matters of
mutual interest to take up." One thing is certain: the information available
about Apalachin provides no serious evidence that "a single national crime
syndicate" dominates organized crime in America; nor does it make this
seem probable.

An Article of Faith

Yet if the evidence for the existence of an All-American crime confederation or syndicate is both suspect and tenuous to the point of nullity, it is clear
that for the believer there is nothing that could count decisively against the
assertion that it exists. Indeed, precisely those features that in ordinary
discourse about human affairs might be regarded as evidence in rebuttal are
instantly assimilated as further strengthening the case *for* the hypothesis.
The absence of direct evidence, apart from Valachi's uninhibited garrulity
(and other unspecified informants), merely demonstrates "the fear instilled
in them by the code of nondisclosure." Thus, denials of membership in, or
knowledge of, the syndicate can not only be dismissed as self-evidently false,
but also adduced as evidence of what they deny. If there is gang warfare, this
indicates that "an internal struggle for dominance over the entire organization" is going on; and also provides "a somber illustration of how cruel and
calculating the underworld continues to be." If peace prevails this may be
taken either as evidence of the power of the syndicate leadership and the
fear in which it is held; or alternatively as reflecting the development of "the
sophisticated and polished control of rackets that now characterize that
organization."

It is said that "practically all" the members of the organization "are of
Sicilian birth or ancestry." Professor Cressey, for example, speaks of "the
Italian-Sicilian apparatus [that] continues to dominate organized crime in
America." But counterevidence relating to the activities of those from other
ethnic backgrounds (e.g., Meyer Lansky, said by J. Edgar Hoover to be
"generally recognized as one of the most powerful racketeers in this country"), can easily be accommodated as illustrating the "characteristic Mafia
method of utilizing non-Sicilian associates where it serves its criminal objectives." In the end, it is difficult to resist the conclusion that one is not dealing
with an empirical phenomenon at all, but with an article of faith, transcend-
ing the contingent particularity of everyday experience and logically un-
assailable; one of those reassuring popular demonologies that, William

Buckley has remarked, the successful politician has to cherish and preserve and may, in the end, come to believe.

In conclusion, two things can be said. First, here as elsewhere, it may be salutary to bear in mind the principle expressed in the celebrated scholastic dictum that has become known as Occam's Razor: *entia non sunt multiplicanda praeter necessitatem* (entities ought not to be multiplied except out of necessity). For it seems likely that what Laplace found in the sphere of cosmology will also obtain in the more mundane field of criminology: there are hypotheses that we do not need. Second, it is inherently improbable that organized crime is for the most part in the hands of monolithic nationwide crime syndicate controlled by a single "commission." As Thomas C. Schelling says in his "Economic Analysis and Organized Crime," which is printed as an appendix to the President's Commission Task Force Report, "A large part of organized crime involves selling commodities and services contrary to law." But, "not all businesses lend themselves to centralized organization," and "the inducements to expansion and the advantages of large-scale over small are especially present in some markets rather than others." It is conceivable, of course, that the economy of the underworld is totally different from that of legitimate business. But it seems reasonable to assume that, as Professor Schelling says,

> a good many economic and business principles that operate in the "upperworld" must, with suitable modification for change in environment, operate in the underworld as well, just as a good many economic principles that operate in an advanced competitive economy operate as well in a Socialist or a primitive economy.

In other words, the assumption that, despite the diversity of the activities involved and the absence or presence of the market characteristics that would be likely to determine whether or not, or to what degree, organization would be likely to occur, one vast criminal monopoly has developed with the profits pouring into "the treasury of the Cosa Nostra"—this assumption seems extraordinarily fanciful. But it is true that we do not have the data that would enable us to reject it. What is needed—and here the Task Force Report is unexceptionable—is that the "relevant disciplines such as economics, political science, sociology and operations research" should "begin to study organized crime intensively," and preferably without too many preconceptions.

Seven   Police

10 The Historical Roots of Police Behavior Chicago, 1890–1925

Mark H. Haller (1976)

In order to understand patterns of police behavior in American cities at the turn of the century, it is important to grasp a crucial fact: the police, although they were formally engaged in *law* enforcement, were little oriented toward legal norms.[1] As late as 1900, when Chicago's police department numbered 3,225 men, there was no organized training. New policemen heard a brief speech from a high-ranking officer, received a hickory club, a whistle, and a key to the call box, and were sent out on the street to work with an experienced officer.[2] Not only were policemen untrained in law, but they operated within a criminal justice system that generally placed little emphasis upon legal procedure. Most of those arrested by the police were tried before local police justices, who rarely had legal training. Those arrested seldom had attorneys, so that no legal defense was made. Thus, there were few mechanisms for introducing legal norms into the street experiences and crime control activities of policemen.

If patterns of police behavior cannot be understood in terms of an orientation toward law, how can they be understood? Four interrelated orientations explain much of the day-to-day behavior of the police, as well as other criminal justice institutions, in their order maintenance functions during the late nineteenth and early twentieth centuries. First of all, police and courts were highly decentralized and often reflected, in important ways, the values of local communities. Democratic sensitivities rather than legal norms were expected to guide police behavior and check abuses.[3] Secondly, the police, part of a larger political system, were a significant resource at the command of local political organizations. Police, courts, and prosecutor provided political leaders with patronage jobs, were a source of favors for constituents, and were important agencies for collecting the money that lubricated

"The Historical Roots of Police Behavior" appeared first in *Law and Society Review* 10 (1976): 303–23.

I wish to thank the Center for Studies in Criminal Justice in the Law School of the University of Chicago for support that has made possible my research into the history of crime and criminal justice and to thank especially Norval Morris, Hans Mattick, and Franklin E. Zimring for their assistance and encouragement. A Number of scholars, particularly Perry Duis, David R. Johnson, and Wilbur R. Miller, strengthened this article by their comments and criticism.

political campaigns. Thirdly, criminal justice institutions operated as rackets—providing the means by which policemen and other officials earned extra income. Finally, policemen and other criminal justice personnal developed informal systems of operation that reflected their own subculture and organizational needs. These informal methods of operation bore, at best, only an indirect relationship to the formal legal system.

In short, the police perceived their responsibilities from a number of overlapping orientations. The purpose of this paper is to examine several aspects of police organization and behavior in Chicago from 1890 to 1925 in order to explore the ways in which various orientations shaped day-to-day police behavior.

Recruitment and Control

America's major cities developed modern, unified police departments in the 1840's and 1850's. Chicago, a burgeoning rail center and Great Lakes port, established its department in 1855. By the post–Civil War period, in Chicago as in other cities, the department had two major branches. Most policemen were in the patrol service. They wore uniforms and badges, carried handguns and hickory sticks, and patrolled assigned beats. Other policemen served as detectives. They often wore plain clothes and were responsible primarily for criminal investigations. A military model determined the department's organization, symbolized by the fact that supervisory officers had military titles of sergeant, lieutenant, and captain.[4] In more than a century from the Civil War to the present, city police have undergone little change in organization or function. Those changes that occurred have resulted primarily from technology. Most important were communications and transportation advances: the call box, telephone, motorcycle, automobile, and radio. Of much less importance were new investigative techniques such as photography, fingerprinting, chemical analysis of evidence, and, eventually, computer storage and retrieval of information. Despite technological change, policing has remained labor intensive, so that the basic orientations of patrolmen and detectives have continued to determine police activities.

Chicago policemen came to their jobs from a skilled or semi-skilled blue collar experience and from an ethnic, disproportionately Irish, background. In 1887, in a city that was 40 percent foreign born, some 54 percent of the force was foreign born. In a city in which the Irish-born and their children were less than 20 percent of the population, about half the force was Irish—fully 35 percent Irish-born and another 13 percent, at least, of Irish parentage. Only the German-born, with 10 percent of the force, constituted a rival ethnic group within the department.[5] Ethnic diversity continued into the twentieth century, as a 1908 news story made clear:

> Assistant Chief of Police [Herman] Schuettler's ambition to have every nationality represented on the Chicago Police force came one step nearer realization yesterday when Frank Z. Khubier . . . was sworn in as one of seventy-four probationary patrolmen. Khubier is a Persian, having been born at Teheran. . . . A Chinese patrolman is all that is lacking now, according to the assistant chief.

In 1913, at a time when the department numbered slightly more than 4,000, there were 83 black policemen.[6]

Biographical sketches of policemen in an 1887 history of the department listed such previous occupations as machinists and other skilled factory factory operatives, teamsters, construction workers, railroad men, and craftsmen of various sorts. Commenting on 84 new recruits in 1906, a newspaper noted: "Street car motormen, press feeders, teamsters, city firemen, clerks and patrol wagon drivers were the principal occupations." Police work, then, ranked as a high status blue collar occupation.[7]

The background of the force was intimately tied to its methods of operation. Because new recruits, many of whom were born abroad and most of whom had left school by the age of 13 or 14, were put on the streets without training, it is clear that no legal expertise was expected of them. Instead, it was through ethnic diversity that the department related to an ethnically diverse city in which substantial proportions of the population spoke no English and distrusted authority. Black detectives were assigned to pursue black felons hiding in black neighborhoods; Italian policemen before World War I were given special responsibility to control the "black hand" gangs that preyed on the city's Italians through extortion. When policemen were protectors or coordinators of crime, Jewish policemen were often the primary protectors of Jewish pickpockets and other Jewish thieves, while black patrolmen were assigned to the precincts of politically powerful black gamblers to help operate their gambling enterprises.[8]

During these years, little attention was given to formal training; when such training did appear, it had low priority and reflected the department's military conception of organization. Apparently beginning in the fall of 1910, a one-month school for recruits operated sporadically until it was abolished in 1919. Reestablished in the 1920's, the school became institutionalized, and all recruits were required to attend. In the month of training about one-quarter of the time was devoted to close-order drill, another quarter to revolver and other weapons training, another to departmental rules and to laws and ordinances (learned in alphabetical order), and a final quarter to tours of courts and specialized divisions of the department. A 1929 study of the recruit school found not only that the instruction was inadequate but, as has generally been the case with police training, no recruit had ever failed the course.[9]

The police department operated the pervasive influence of local ward organizations and the mayor's office. Until 1895 the Chicago police were not under civil service. Yet the introduction of civil service at that time, although altering the formal rules for recruitment and promotion, probably had little significant impact upon police behavior. Before civil service, a tradition had already grown up that, in general, a policeman had job security, so that little turnover occurred with a change in administration. But local ward leaders, both before and after the introduction of civil service, often influenced assignments and promotions. The police superintendent was generally chosen from among the captains and inspectors on the basis of his known loyalty to the party organization that won the last election; and, until the 1960's, his office was in city hall rather than police headquarters. Captains and inspectors were assigned to districts and precincts to work with locally powerful ward political leaders. Patrolmen and detectives, in turn, often linked themselves to political factions and, in any event carried out the political policies of local police captains. Those wishing to avoid punitive assignments far from home or ambitious to rise in the department had to be skillful in finding their way through the complicated maze of urban politics.[10]

As important cogs in political machines, policemen were expected to contribute a portion of their salaries to the dominant party. (Before the 1904 election, Mayor Carter H. Harrison had the police payday moved forward, so that the police would have an opportunity to make an extra contribution to the fund being raised for the mayor's supporters.) The police, in addition, sold tickets to party picnics, distributed campaign posters, and in some cases worked the precincts in the days before the election. Furthermore, powerful local politicians, especially in ethnic and slum neighborhoods, financed their organizations through levies upon businesses, and the police often assessed and collected such payments. This was true not only of illegal activities such as houses of prostitution and gambling dens but also of legal activities: saloons, pool halls, dance halls, and numerous retail stores. Finally, of course, police aided local politicians by ignoring or protecting those illegal activities carried on by local politicians and, sometimes, by harassing illegal activities of political rivals.[11] In many ways, then, police behavior was shaped by the organizational needs of political factions; control of the police department, because of its size and crucial role in the city, was a major prize that went with political success.

If police were tied to politics, they were also tied in important respects to the neighborhood. Patrolmen, because they walked their beats with only minimal supervision, spent much of their time in saloons, barbershops, and other neighborhood centers. In 1880, when the department proposed to install call boxes so that a policeman would have to report periodically to the station, the patrolmen resisted the innovation out of an unrealistic fear that they might have to patrol their beats. When an investigator studied the city's police for several months in 1903–4, however, he found only one patrolman in the city who walked his beat for as long as thirty minutes. Lax central supervision and police socializing on the job make it likely that policemen came to reflect the values of those members of the neighborhood with whom they had ongoing social contacts.[12]

In these formative years, then, the police had strong ties to local politics, neighborhood institutions, and ethnic communities. Neither their training nor the civil service system provided an alternative orientation toward a formal system of rules or laws.

Police and Courts

Police behavior was also shaped in part by the criminal court system. (Unfortunately, the criminal courts and prosecutor are the legal institutions that have probably received the least study by legal historians.) Until 1906 police justices handled the bulk of routine criminal cases in Chicago. This included ordinance violations, misdemeanors, and preliminary hearings in felony cases. Although justices in Cook County outside the city received fees according to the fines that they levied, police justices in Chicago received a salary from the city and remitted the fines to the city treasury. (If a police justice held court at night, however, he could retain a portion of the fees as a form of overtime payment.) Police justices were selected locally and were active in local politics—thus reinforcing neighborhood and political dominance of the criminal justice system. In police districts with high arrest rates, the police courts of Chicago operated like lower courts elsewhere: through the mass processing of persons arrested for minor offenses. Because few defendants had a specific charge made against them and few had defense attorneys, it seems clear that, when there was any hearing at all, inquiry was generally made not into legal guilt or innocence but rather into the status of the defendant in the community. Year after year, most defendants brought before the courts were discharged, so that the courts served as a clearing house where, following a lecture of warning, defendants were turned loose after several hours or several days in the police lockup.[13]

In 1906, after a reform crusade led by élite members of the local bar, Chicago became one of the first cities to replace the justice courts with a Municipal Court system for both criminal and civil matters. The municipal Court was a unified court, with a chief justice and associate justices who were required to be lawyers and were elected for terms of six years. Immediately after establishment of the Municipal Court, police arrests fell by one-third (from 91,554 in 1906 to 63,132 in 1907). According to the Chief Justice, the decline resulted because the new court imposed higher legal standards upon the police. But given the continuation of mass processing of most suspects, and the absence of defense attorneys for most defendants, the change in the lower courts did not result in more than a marginal introduction of legal standards into criminal justice.[14]

The new court, despite the optimistic hopes of its supporters, increasingly fell under the influence of local ward politicians. Judgeships were a reward for service to political factions, judges generally continued to serve as ward leaders after election to the bench, and political considerations and political favors often shaped judicial decisions. In the 1920's, in fact, judges often did not hold court on election day, for the entire staff—bailiffs, clerks, and the judges themselves—were busy working their precincts. Furthermore, assistant corporation counsels and assistant states's attorneys were often assigned to local courts at the behest of local political leaders.[15]

Both policemen and court officials often used the criminal justice system to supplement their incomes. Before 1906, in police districts adjoining the skidrows and redlight areas, the police sometimes made night raids for profit. One hundred or more persons would be rounded up. The bailbondsman charged $1.00 to $5.00 for a bond and the police justice received a fee of $1.00 from the defendant for agreeing to the bond. The money was, of course, shared with the arresting officers. After establishment of the Municipal Court, this particular racket ceased, but mutually beneficial relations continued between judges, bailiffs, bondsmen, police, and members of the underworld.[16]

Police and Crime Control

In order to understand the interrelationships of police and professional thieves, it is necessary to keep in mind a number of factors. To begin with, the main expertise of a detective was his knowledge of the underworld—his ability to recognize criminals and to keep informed concerning when and how they operated. For these purposes, detectives developed informers and maintained extensive informal relationships with the underworld. Often they exchanged freedom from arrest for information. Even conscientious detectives were so involved with the underworld that there was only a thin line between being guardians against crime and partners with criminals. In addition, relationships between detectives and thieves were often influenced by the fact that some thieves had ties with politicians made by performing services on election day or by hanging out in saloons operated by persons with political influence. As a result, there was often an uneasy alliance of professional thieves, police, and politicians.[17]

Pickpocket gangs, for instance, sometimes divided territories under the guidance of the police. Then, if an individual citizen lost his wallet and made a complaint, detectives would know which gang was working the area and could recover the stolen property. On other occasions, pickpocket gangs would take a patrolman into partnership. When a victim discovered a hand in his pocket, an obliging policeman would be at hand to hustle the pickpocket away (and later set him free). In the coordination of con games in 1914, the bunco squad insisted that a con man, newly arrived in the city, would be subject to arrest unless he sought out a member of the squad and made a payment of $20.00. This gave the con man the privilege of operating; but, if a victim made a complaint to the police, then the con man involved was expected to share ten percent of the take with the police—apparently as a penalty for operating so ineffectively that a complaint resulted. The system even allowed for credit arangements. A down-and-out con man could request permission to work until he had earned his $20.00 fee.[18]

Close relationships between detectives and criminals could also be a basis for harassment. One of the standard crime control measures used by detectives was to "vag" known criminals until they left town. That is, known criminals were arrested for vagrancy (having no visible means of support) and taken to court to be fined. Faced with repeated arrests, thieves, might well seek a more congenial city in which to practice their professions.[19]

Members of the professional underworld, because of their knowledge of the realities of the system, did not approach the police and courts as legal institutions but as rackets to be manipulated. If possible, of course, underworld figures established mutually profitable relationships with policemen or politicians to protect themselves against arrest. If arrested, their first move was to attempt to bribe the arresting officer or the police sergeant. If that failed, a number of strategies remained: pay a political fixer to bring pressure upon the police or court; visit the complaining witness and offer full or partial restitution in return for an agreement to drop charges; or jump bail until witnesses were no longer interested. Only as a last resort did a criminal turn to a legal defense. Even then, he would feel that conviction resulted from his failure to find the proper strings for manipulating the outcome rather than from a triumph of legal norms.[20]

Another common police tactic, used when a particularly notorious crime occurred or when newspapers complained of a crime wave, was for police officials to order dragnet arrests. In the early 1890's, for instance, when the police were attempting to reduce crime on the near South Side, a newspaper reported:

All Thursday afternoon and evening the Harrison Street wagon was kept busy rattling over the pavements bringing in colored and white men and women of evil reputation. Some were arrested in the streets and alleys, and others were taken from the most notorious brothels on Plymouth and Custom House places. About 200 men and women of vile character were captured.

Last night the raiding was kept up with unabated vigor and at least 200 more prisoners were landed at the station.

In the event of a "crime wave," the purpose was to drive the "lawless elements" underground and, no doubt, to present the appearance of police vigor. After a notorious crime, those arrested in dragnet raids were searched and interrogated. This standard police technique was so firmly entrenched that in 1906 the police chief explained:

> We can't do away with [the dragnet]. The detectives and patrolmen get their order to bring them all in. . . . And the chances are that nine times out of ten the persons picked up are not guilty of the crime. But if the tenth time we should get the guilty man we are well repaid, as is society.[21]

Finally, the police believed that, in the prevention of crime, the control of tramps and other rootless men was a central responsibility. As the major rail center and crossroads of the Midwest, as well as the most rapidly growing city in the nation, Chicago had a constant stream of persons flowing into and through the city. Skidrow areas west and south of the Loop housed thousands of men (and boys) who sought occasional work and often lived in the interstices of industrial society. In part, the police exercised control by their standard system of harassment through vagrancy and disorderly conduct laws. In 1876, the police Superintendent argued for a stronger vagrancy law "so that [strangers] could be sent out of the way of doing harm, without waiting until they commit some crime." For, he warned, "in the absence of any crime committed by them a good vagrancy law is the only safeguard, and the only way by which they can be effectually disposed of." Until at least the 1930's, vagrancy and disorderly conduct constituted between 40 and 66 percent of all arrests each year; those arrested were disproportionately young men, out of work, and often from out of town. Yet such statistics do not capture the complexity of police interaction with the homeless. Police stations, until the opening of a municipal lodging house in the early twentieth century, were regularly thrown open in the winter as sleeping quarters for the homeless. Indeed, arrests often functioned partly as a disguised room-for-the-night, since most of those arrested for vagrancy and disorderly conduct were released after a warning by the judge. In a variety of ways, then, the police managed and serviced a rootless population that they, and others, defined to be particularly prone to crime and disorder.[22]

Police and Public Morals

Throughout the nineteenth and early twentieth centuries, urban moralistic reformers were shocked by the drunkenness, gambling, and open prostitution that, from their point of view, corrupted the morals of youth and made cities dangerous and unpleasant places to live. They brought pressure upon politicians and criminal justice officials to secure enforcement of saloon closing laws and of laws forbidding gambling and prostitution. The policies of the police not only highlighted the distance that separated police values from those of moralistic reformers but also revealed much about the attitudes and forces that shaped police behavior.

In Chicago, although state law required that saloons be closed on Sundays and at a set hour each night, actual enforcement policies were mediated through the local political system. Despite their dedication and fervor, those citizens who favored temperance and strict enforcement of the liquor laws were a hopeless minority in the face of a strong support for "personal liberty." From 1873 until the coming of prohibition, no mayoral candidate stood a chance if he was suspected of favoring enforcement of saloon closing laws. Carter H. Harrison, III, the popular and respected mayor from 1897 to 1905, was clear in his statement of policy:

> I don't believe in closing saloons on Sunday. I do believe in lowering the blinds and closing the front doors . . . I don't believe in closing saloons at midnight. . . . Public sentiment is against enforcing them [saloon laws]. The man doesn't live who could shut up Chicago saloons on Sunday. I shall not try to do it.

Politicians, reacting to dominant opinion, determined that, behind the occasional semblance of a closed saloon, men might drink as they wished. The policy reflected police values, as well; for the police were recruited from among the Irish, Germans, and other groups that were the strongest friends of personal liberty.[23]

Within the context of an open city, there existed, nevertheless, considerable neighborhood diversity. Many neighborhoods, in fact, had prohibition ordinances or local option—either because they retained their local saloon laws when annexed to the city in the late 1880's or because of a state local option law passed in the early twentieth century. The densely populated inner city had a high concentration of saloons, while the peripheral regions of the city, containing most of the land area but a minority of the population, excluded or restricted saloon operations. In some peripheral areas, neighborhood associations, spurred on by Protestant religious leaders, were able to shape their neighborhoods to their own values. But, despite vigorous legal and political campaigns, they were unable, except in tangential and temporary ways, to secure strict and uniform law enforcement applicable to the entire city. State law yielded to political pressures representing neighborhood customs.[24]

The coming of prohibition in 1920 created a new legal situation, but not a new political situation. Chicago politicians vied with each other in condemning the news laws, Chicago citizens expressed their opposition through several referenda, and the police chiefs in the 1920's—with one possible exception—kept liquor in their offices to serve visitors. Against a background in which federal enforcement was at first minimal and corrupt and in which bootleggers enjoyed local political protection, the city's police quickly established friendly relationships with bootleggers, gladly accepted favors that ranged from money to free booze, escorted beer trucks through the city's streets, and peddled confiscated liquor in station houses. Then from 1923 until 1927 Mayor William E. Dever, despite his personal opposition to prohibition, insisted that the police enforce the law; and a reluctant police force closed many breweries and distilleries and raided speakeasies. But the established relationships of police and bootleggers, combined with police opposition to prohibition enforcement, were too tenacious for the mayor to break. When Dever failed to win re-election in 1927 because of his attempts to enforce the law, the police rapidly and openly resumed the patterns of cooperation with bootleggers that had been disrupted but not destroyed during his administration. Once more, the political system shielded the police from pressures to treat the liquor problem as one of law enforcement.[25]

Police displayed a variety of attitudes toward gambling and prostitution. Policemen, themselves sports fans and bettors, attended the races at the tracks around the city and hung out at gambling houses, where they might play a friendly game of poker or place bets on their favorite nags. They had little more inclination to enforce gambling laws than they had to enforce saloon closing laws. As for prostitution, the police thought that such activity was inevitable and could not be prevented; hence, the best policy was to permit redlight entertainment districts rather than pursue a policy of enforcement that would drive prostitutes into respectable residential neighborhoods. When the redlight districts flourished in the years before 1913 or 1914, serious police efforts were aimed primarily at regulation rather than strict law enforcement. The police sometimes arrested streetwalkers; periodically they raided sporting houses that robbed customers or held young girls against their wills; and, to avoid upsetting respectable citizens, they removed houses from streetcar lines and tried to prevent naked girls from leaning out of windows to advertise their charms. But the police seldom bothered well-run brothels or interfered with soliciting in bars or second-class hotels. In short, until pressured to change their policies in the period of 1912 to 1914, the police acted to provide a minimal regulation of illegal activity.[26]

Police policies toward prostitution and gambling reflected local opinion as well as the values of the police themselves. In neighborhoods where the men were interested in sports and gambling, gambling rooms, local bookmakers, and the policy wheels were accepted recreation activities. Within the segregated entertainment districts, customers and entrepreneurs wished the saloons, dancehalls, burlesque shows, and parlor houses to operate with minimal interference. Moreover, in tolerating gambling and prostitution, police acted in the service of powerful local politicians, some of whom collected substantial funds from entrepreneurs in the entertainment districts and many of whom were partners in gambling syndicates. Indeed, in some wards the political organization and gambling syndicates were so intertwined that they were virtually one and the same. In such wards local political leaders selected the police captain for the precinct chiefly on the basis of his sympathy with local gamblers, and some patrolmen in the neighborhood served virtually as employees of local gamblers.[27]

Finally, the tolerant attitude of policemen toward gambling and vice arose from a desire to supplement their incomes. Gamblers, despite their political influence, usually made goodwill contributions to the police, and assignment to the entertainment districts constituted a lucrative and interesting challenge for patrolmen and detectives. Toleration of neighborhood gambling and segregated red light districts, however, did not exist because of payoffs to police. Rather, the corrupt relationships institutionalized a policy of tolerance and regulation that the police would have followed anyway.[28]

Police Violence

The basic theme thus far has been that the police were not oriented primarily toward legality in their law enforcement activities. No such discussion would be complete without considering the patterns of police use of illegal violence. Leaving aside the police use of violence in controlling riots,[29] there were essentially three circumstances under which violence, *as an accepted norm*, became part of police procedure.

First of all, many policemen believed that they should themselves, at times, mete out punishment to wrongdoers. Policemen on patrol, particularly in high-crime areas, were often expected to be able to physically dominate their beats and to handle suspicious persons or minor crimes without resort to arrest. This was particularly true before the installation of call boxes in 1880. Arrests were difficult to make. A patrolman, unable to summon assistance, had to walk his prisoner as much as a mile to the station house. Drunks might be taken in a wheelbarrow. Reminiscing about his early days on the force in the 1880's, a Deputy Superintendent stated in 1906: "It was not customary for a policeman to arrest anyone for a small matter, then. The hickory had to be used pretty freely."[30]

Furthermore, in many neighborhoods it was understood that adults might punish rowdy teenagers. Policemen, as adult authority figures, sometimes whipped delinquent boys, believing that this was a more effective deterrent than an arrest and incarceration among adult criminals. One day, for instance, the parents of a Polish teenager told Gus, a Polish cop, that their son was at the station on a charge of theft. Gus explained in an interview:

I went down and said, "Mike, did you take those things from that garage?" And he knew I had the goods on him, so he admitted it. Then, bang, I socked him with my fist behind the ear. I just kept on beating the stuffins out of him, then I said "Mike, you know better than that. You got a good father and mother; good Polish people. Don't let me catch you taking anything again; if you do, what you got now will be nothing to what you'll get then." Then I took him to the captain and said, "This boy has learned a good lesson." The captain let him go. The boy is a good boy now, and every time he sees me, he says, "Gus, I want to thank you for that trimming you gave me. It made a man out of me." That's my motto, scare 'em to death and knock the hell out of them, and then let them go."

While summary punishment by the police sometimes aroused public outcry, it was sanctioned by the police subculture and was often supported by local opinion.[31]

A second type of police violence occurred as a tactic to persuade a recalcitrant defendant to confess his guilt or to reveal the names of accomplices. Indeed, standard interrogation in important cases, and many less important cases, was to place a suspect in the "sweat box," as it was called, for hours or days, until he broke down under continuous questioning. Newspapers often reported such events without comment, as the following example from 1906 demonstrates:

John L. Voss, accused by the police of the murder of his wife and the burning of his home to destroy the evidence of the crime, yesterday admitted to Assistant Chief of Police Schuettler and Inspector George M. Shippy that he had purchased a revolver and a box of cartridges some time prior to the crime on Sunday morning.

The admission, wrung from the prisoner after three days of cross examination, is regarded as important.

Such interrogations were publicly justified by police spokesmen and were regularly conducted by detectives and by high officials in the department. For, as the *Chicago Tribune* pointed out: "Every police department in this country has its 'sweaters' or inquisitors, and long practice has made them adepts at the art, if so it may be called."[32]

The detention of suspects for hours or days without charges or legal safeguards was the context within which physical violence—the third degree—was often practiced to speed up the process of interrogation. The point is not that one can easily collect numerous harrowing stories of beatings used to secure confessions. (After the murder of Bobbie Franks, for instance, the Chicago police forced a confession from an innocent school teacher before the evidence finally pointed to Nathan Leopold and Richard Loeb.) The point rather is that, although police officials did not publicly

admit the use of violence, the third degree was an accepted part of investigative work. Representatives of the State's Attorney, to say nothing of the
police chief or other high officers, were sometimes present while the third
degree was being administered. It was employed against juvenile as well as
adult suspects; and elite reformers often gained knowledge of the system
through their work with youthful offenders. By the 1920's, police terminology was that suspects were taken to the "gold fish room"—the "gold fish"
being a length of cable or rubber hose used to strike the suspect without
leaving marks. When a court in the early 1920's excluded the confession of a
defendant who had made a statement after being sweated (and beaten), one
police official claimed that, if the decision was allowed to stand, ninety-five
percent of the work of the department would be nullified. Another complained: "We are permitted to do less every day. Pretty soon there won't be
a police department."[33]

Finally, the police subculture often sanctioned violence to uphold the
personal dignity of the policeman. Such violence, given the absence of civil
liberties organizations to monitor police violations of individual rights, was
seldom recorded; and, when reported in newspapers, was difficult to distinguish from the random violence that some policemen occasionally visited
upon citizens."[34]

In the case of police use of violence, as in other violations of law by
policemen, there was little recourse for an aggrieved citizen, Very early, the
police developed a group loyalty that required policemen to rally to the
defense of an officer in trouble. Top officials of the department told new
recruits that, if they could not say something good about fellow officers, they
should remain silent. In 1906 a recruit showed that he had correctly learned
the lesson when he told a reporter: "I will not report any police officer for
neglect of duty, because I have been told not to. . . . If I reported some
policeman I would likely be transferred to an outlying station." When
charges were brought against a policeman, conviction was difficult for a
number of reasons. As one city hall official told a reporter in 1905, "It is well
nigh impossible to convict a favored policeman of any offense. . . . If ten
witnesses testify to a certain set of facts, and their testimony is unshaken, the
defendant puts twenty police witnesses on the stand to testify to an entirely
different set of facts." There were other strategies, as well. Witnesses
against policemen would be told the wrong date for a hearing so that they
would not appear. In many cases, other policemen harrassed, arrested or
even drove out of town unfriendly witnesses. Already, the police saw
themselves as a beleaguered and misunderstood group, dependent upon
each other for support, and fiercely loyal to a cop in need.[35]

It is important, in conclusion, to place these remarks in perspective.
Obviously, policemen did not spend their whole time taking bribes, solicit-

ing votes, harassing tramps, beating suspects, and assisting gamblers. Policemen on patrol, indeed, spent most of their time doing nothing at all—or in such routine activities as learning the beat or socializing with local people. Those assigned to outlying residential neighborhoods might go for days or weeks without making an arrest or engaging in law enforcement activities. Even when the police were active, they were often involved in functions only indirectly related to crime control. Police took injured persons to hospitals, mediated family quarrels, rounded up stray dogs for the city pound, returned lost children to parents, directed traffic on the downtown streets and at bridge crossings, removed dead horses from city streets, reported broken gas lamps, and performed the innumerable services that have always constituted most police work.

Furthermore, the police orientation toward values other than legal norms developed within a context in which the police mirrored what other groups within the society often defined as proper police behavior. The legislative intent in passing broad and vague statutes governing disorderly conduct and vagrancy was to provide tools by which local authorities could control those classes of the population that were, or seemed to be, threats to local social order. The use that police made of such statutes conformed to legislative intent. Although courts sometimes found that police acted illegally and the prosecutor sometimes criticized the police for inefficient handling of evidence, courts and prosecutors generally supported the non-legal orientations of the police. According to the value system accepted by most elected officials, politics was a matter of deals and favors; and most city agencies were as corrupt or as politically manipulated as the police. Hence, the orientation of the police was in keeping with the expectations of the officials elected to make policy and did not differ in kind from other municipal departments. Finally, although groups of élite reformers often attacked the police for corruption and sometimes insisted that certain laws—laws dealing with alcohol or prostitution, for instance—be more vigorously enforced, the same groups often approved of dragnet raids and other harassing tactics. The non-legal orientation of the police, in short, reflected not only the beliefs and background of the police but the expectations of the wider society relevant in defining the role of the police.

Besides, state laws and municipal ordinances directly and indirectly influenced the police in a number of ways. The laws against gambling and prostitution, for instance, were the basis for the police definition of such activities as their particular responsibility. The police became, therefore, the major regulating agency; and the laws provided the leverage used by the police to enforce the regulations. Furthermore, when reformers launched campaigns against gambling or prostitution, the police bore the brunt of the attack. Likewise, the laws against burglary and larceny conditioned the complex ways that police and thieves adapted to each other through systems of informers, bribes, regulation, and harassment. The legal system, too, determined that prosecutors and judges would review certain police decisions on an ongoing basis. To some extent, the prosecutors and courts were a channel for political influence; to some extent the mass processing of less serious crimes and plea bargaining of felonies muted the degree to which prosecutors and courts could convey legal values; but, especially after creation of the municipal court in 1906, the courts and defense attorneys sometimes introduced legal values into the criminal justice process. In a variety of ways, the police made use of or took account of the law and legal institutions in carrying out their crime control functions.

During the twentieth century, in fact, a variety of factors have brought legal norms to bear upon police behavior at a gradually accelerating pace. There has been a growing requirement that judges, even in the lowest criminal courts, be lawyers and that such courts be courts of record. Concurrently, through expanding systems of public defenders and other means, defendants even in the lower courts increasingly have had counsel. Appellate courts have not only extended the right to counsel and imposed exclusionary rules concerning confessions and other types of evidence but have also declared unconstitutional many of the vague laws, including disorderly conduct and vagrancy laws, which once constituted the majority of arrests and were the means by which police detained and regulated those whom they regarded as suspicious, deviant, or disturbing to the community. Finally, a number of civic organizations (often lawyer-dominated like the American Civil Liberties Union) have been founded and, in recent years, have more or less systematically monitored police behavior in large cities. As a result of a variety of pressures, police during the twentieth century, especially in major cities, have gradually, often grudgingly, brought their behavior more in keeping with legal norms. The trend has run counter to the historically entrenched police orientations and has been accompanied by bitterness on the part of both police and police critics.

Notes

1. See, for instance, Mark H. Haller, "Urban Crime and Criminal Justice: The Chicago Case," 57 *J. Am. Hist.* 619–635 (1970).

2. For size, see *Report of the General Superintendent of Police . . . for the Fiscal Year Ending December 31, 1900* (1901). Newspaper reports on induction of new policemen in *Chicago Daily News*, May 4, 1905; *Chicago Record-Herald*, March 20, 1906; and *Chicago Tribune*, November 3, 1906. Most newspaper stories in the period 1904 to 1908 are taken from the Herman F. Schuettler Scrapbooks (2 Vols.), Chicago Historical Society.

3. This has been argued by Wilbur R. Miller in an important article, "Police Authority in London and New York City, 1830–1870," 8 *J. Soc. Hist.* 81–95 (1975).

4. For founding of Chicago police, see John J. Flinn, *History of the Chicago Police* (1887; republ. Montclair, N.J., 1973), hereinafter Flinn, *Chicago Police*; also an excellent unpublished study by David R. Johnson, "Policing the Underworld, 1800–1885: An Experiment in Democratic Crime Control" (1975).

5. These are my computations based on nearly 1,100 biographical sketches in Flinn, *Chicago Police*, at chs. 19 and 23–28. Ethnic figures for Chicago from U.S. Bureau of the Census, *Compendium of the Eleventh Census: 1890*, Part III, 75, 83 (1897).

6. *Record-Herald*, April 3, 1908; Juvenile Protective Association, *The Colored People of Chicago* (1913).

7. Flinn, *Chicago Police; Record-Herald*, Oct. 27, 1906.

8. Humbert S. Nelli, *Italians in Chicago, 1880–1930: A Study in Ethnic Mobility*, ch. 5 (1970) and *Chicago Daily News*, Nov. 21, 1907. For Jewish detectives working with Jewish criminals, see various investigative reports in Charles E. Merriam papers, Univ. of Chicago Library, including Report of Investigator Friedner, Nov. 20, 1914, and Report of No. 100, Nov. 12, 1914, and other reports in Box 88, folder 6. During a city council committee investigation of corruption, headed by Mirriam, investigators were hired to hang out in the underworld and prepare daily reports. These reports are invaluable in providing a picture of police/criminal interaction.

9. For discussion of training, see Alexander R. Piper, *Report on Police Discipline and Administration* 13 (City Club of Chicago, Publ. No. 1, 1904); *Record-Herald*, March 20, 1906; Chicago Civil Service Commission, *Final Report: Police Investigation* 50 (1912); Police Department, City of Chicago, *Annual Report* 55 (1916); id. (1921–22), at 76; id. (1923) at 51; id. (1925) at 62; Citizens' Police Committee, *Chicago Police Problems* 79–84 (1931); and Mark H. Haller, "Civic Reformers and Police Leadership: Chicago, 1905–1935," in Harlan Hahn, ed., *Police in Urban Society*, esp. 49–50 (1971).

10. On job security before civil service, see David R. Johnson, "Law Enforcement in Chicago, 1875–1885," at 16 (unpublished research paper 1968). On introduction of Civil Service, Joseph Bush Kingsbury, "Municipal Personnel Policy in Chicago, 1895–1915" (Ph.D. dissertation in Political Science, Univ. of Chicago, 1923). On political influence in the department, see Lloyd Wendt and Herman Kogan, *Lords of the Levee: The Story of Bathhouse John and Hinky Dink* 165, 175, 181–82, & passim (1943); also *Senate Report* on the Chicago Police System (1898); and numerous stories in Chicago newspapers.

11. On 1904 election, see *Inter-Ocean*, April 30, 1904. For other accounts of political activities, see Report of Investigator Thompson, Dec. 22, 1914, and many other reports by investigators in Merriam papers, Box 88, folder 5; *Record-Herald*, March 26, 1905 & April 29, 1907; *Chicago Tribune*, June 21, 1905, & April 18, 1907.

12. On call boxes, see Flinn, *Chicago Police*, ch. 20. Police behavior on the beat is discussed in Piper, supra, note 9, esp. at 6–10, 44, and Appendix A and E. For follow-up news stories, see *Chicago Tribune*, March 21 & 22, 1904.

13. Sigmund Zeisler, "Report of the Committee on the Expediency of Calling a Constitutional Convention," in Illinois State Bar Association, *Proceedings of the Twenty-Sixth Annual Meeting*, Part II, 145–46 (1902); Robert McCurdy, "The Law Providing for a Municipal Court in Chicago," Illinois State Bar Association, *Pro-*

ceedings . . . of the Thirtieth Annual Meeting, Part II, 82–84 (1906); Albert Lepawsky, *The Judicial System of Metropolitan Chicago* 99–101, 144–155 (1932).

14. For founding of the Municipal Court, see Herman Kogan, *The First Century: The Chicago Bar Association 1874–1974*, 110–116 (1974); McCurdy, supra, note 13, at 81–99; Municipal Court of Chicago, *First Annual Report . . .* , Dec. 3, 1906, to Nov. 30, 1907 (1907). Arrest statistics from *Report* of the General Superintendent of Police for the years 1906 and 1907; analysis of the statistics in the correspondence of Chief Justice Harry Olson in Municipal Court papers, Chicago Historical Society.

On mass processing and non-legal orientation, see Raymond Moley, "The Municipal Court of Chicago," *Illinois Crime Survey*, esp. 404–10 (1929); Paul Livingstone Warnshuis, "Crime and Criminal Justice among the Mexicans of Illinois," esp. ch. 4 (M.A. thesis Univ. of Chicago, 1930); Herbert S. Futran, "The Morals Court of Chicago" (typewritten research paper dtd. March 1928), Burgess papers. Nels Anderson in 1922 described a visit to the Municipal Court presided over by Judge Joseph S. LaBuy. The judge ordered the the bull pen be emptied, and some 50 defendants crowded in front of the bench. After making a few jokes, the judge asked how many were working men. Nearly all hands were raised. So the judge asked, "Is there anybody here that is not a working man?" One Polish defendant, who had not understood the question, raised his hand. His case was dismissed for being an honest man. The clerk began to call the names that the defendants had given when arrested but got no answers. When one man finally responded, he was complimented by the judge for remembering his name and his case was dismissed. The judge asked anyone with a dollar to raise his hand—the implication being that they would be fined a dollar. About half the hands went up. The judge then tried one man and fined him $5.00, after which he asked. "How many of you men will go to work?" Every hand was raised. The judge warned, "If I catch any of you back here again I'll give you $200 and costs," and dismissed them. More than 50 cases were thus disposed of in less than 30 minutes. See Document 80, Report of Visit to Police Court, Aug. 29, 1922, in Burgess papers.

15. On the background of judges, see Lepawsky, supra note 13, at ch. 7; also Edward M. Martin, *The Role of the Bar in Electing the Bench in Chicago*, passim (1936); Judge M. L. McKinley, "Crime and the Civic Cancer—Graft," 6 *Chicago Daily News* Reprints, 4, 22–23 (1923) For general insight into management of the Municipal Court until 1930, see the extensive Municipal Court papers. On election day activity, see "Reports Concerning the Criminal Court," *Criminal Justice* 11 (1930); on assignment of prosecutors, see Samuel E. Pincus to Mayor William E. Dever, Nov. 18, 1924, in William E. Dever papers, Chicago Historical Society, folder 13.

16. *Senate Report*, supra note 10, at 21; Franklin Matthews, "Wide-Open Chicago," 42 *Harper's Weekly* 90 (1898); William Stead *If Christ Came to Chicago* 19–20 (1894).

17. See references in footnote 18.

18. On con men, see Informant B, Special Report, July 28, 1914, Merriam papers, Box 87, folder 4; Informant C, Special report, Aug. 1, 1914, Merriam papers, Box 87, folder 5. On pickpockets, see *Chicago Journal*, Oct. 30, 1907; Memorandum from Fletcher Dobyns, Oct. 2, 1914, in Merriam papers, Box 86,

folder 2; John Landesco, "The Criminal Underworld of Chicago in the '80's and '90's," *J. Crim. L. & Criminology* 341–57 (1934), and "Chicago's Criminal Underworld of the '80's and '90's," 25 *J. Crim. L. and Criminology* 928–40 (1935).

19. Langdon W. Moore, *His Own Story of His Eventful Life* 466 (1893); printed Report of Activities from January 29, 1918 to June 24, 1918, of Vagrancy Court in Chicago, Municipal Court papers, folder 35. In *Chicago Post*, Nov. 1, 1907, Chief George M. Shippy was quoted: "Recently we have arrested every known pickpocket and had them arraigned in the Municipal Court. The judges have made records of their names, and each has been given a certain number of days in which to find respectable employment or get out of town." Also *Daily News*, April 19, 1907.

20. The court game is described in Clifton R. Woolridge, *Hands Up! In the World of Crime, Or 12 Years a Detective*, 471–76 & passim (1901); also Special Report by Informant B, Aug. 31, 1914, Merriam papers, Box 87, folder 4; Landesco, supra note 18, "Criminal Underworld of Chicago," 341–346.

21. Quotations from 1892 newspaper clipping in Burgess papers and from *Chicago Tribune*, Feb. 18, 1906. In August 1905 Chief John M. Collins ordered a squad of 54 detectives: "You are the men who are to catch thieves and hold-up men. I am going to send you into each quarter of the city after suspiscious characters. There must be no partiality. Arrest every man you see loafing around with the look of a criminal. The streets will be safer with those fellows at Harrison street [station]." *Inter-Ocean*, Aug. 1, 1905; for follow-up, see *Inter-Ocean*, Aug. 3, 1905, and *Chicago Chronicle*, Aug. 6, 1905. See also Wooldridge, supra note 20, at 440; Frances Opal Brooks, "Crime in 1908," at 6, 11, 24 (typewritten termpaper dtd. Winter 1928), Burgess papers; stories in *Chicago Tribune*, Sept. 9, 1904; *Record-Herald*, July 23, 1905; and in Chicago newspapers for March 4, 1908.

22. Quotation from *Report of the General Superintendent . . . 1876* 12 (1877). Statistics on arrests are my calculations from figures in the annual police reports; see also Johnson, supra note 10, at 1012. On the role of the police among tramps, see annual police reports; Nels Anderson, *The Hobo: The Sociology of the Homeless Man* (1923); and early chapters of Ben L. Reitman, "Following the Monkey," (unpublished autobiography in Library of the Univ. of Illinois at Chicago Circle).

23. Quotation from Matthews, supra note 16, at 90. On the history of the saloon issue, see Arthur Burrage Farwell, "Sunday Closing in Chicago," printed history in Julius Rosenwald papers, Univ. of Chicago Library, Vol. 12; John E. George, "The Saloon Question in Chicago," 2 *Econ. Studies* 96–100 (1897); Victor S. Yarros, "The Sunday Question in Chicago," *Nat. Munic. Rev.* 75–80 (1910). For the general political background, see Alex Gottfried, *Boss Cermak of Chicago* (1962); Joel A. Tarr, *A Study in Boss Politics: William Lorrimer of Chicago* 18–23, 192, & passim (1971).

24. Chicago Commission on the Liquor Problem, *Preliminary Report* (December 1916); Hyde Park Protective Association papers, Chicago Historical Society; Tarr, supra note 23, at 184; Michael Perman, "Towards a Dry Chicago," undated, unpublished seminar paper.

25. Chicago bootlegging has been dealt with in numerous books and articles; for instance, John Kobler, *Capone: The Life and World of Al Capone* (1971). On drinking by police chiefs, Fred D. Palsey, *Al Capone: The Biography of a Self-Made Man*, 163 (1931). On enforcement under Dever, see the extensive Dever papers.

Much about local enforcement can be learned through Justice Department records; see Central Files of the Department of Justice, No. 23–23–0 through 626, in Washington National Records Center, Suitland, Md. For newspaper clipping and other records, see Chicago Crime Commission Files No. 600–9, 3485, and others. On the prohibition referenda, see John M. Allswang, *A House for All Peoples: Ethnic Politics in Chicago, 1890–1936*, 119–121 (1971).

26. The structure of Chicago prostitution has been extensively dealt with: Walter C. Reckless, *Vice in Chicago* (1933); The Vice Commission of Chicago, *The Social Evil in Chicago* (1911); Charles Washburn, *Come into My Parlor: A Biography of the Aristocratic Everleigh Sisters of Chicago* (1936); Herbert Asbury, *Gem of the Prairie: An Informal History of the Chicago Underworld*, chs. 4, 8, 9 (1940). Relations of the police to the vice districts are revealed in the investigative reports, Merriam papers, Boxes 87 & 88. With regard to gambling, see Mark H. Haller, "The Rise of Gambling Syndicates," unpublished chapter for a book on the history of Chicago crime; also John Landesco, *Organized Crime in Chicago*, chap. 3 (new ed. 1968); *Senate Report*, supra note 10, at 13–14, 18–20.

27. See references in footnote 24. For the general impact of prostitution and gambling on politics, see Wendt and Kogan, supra note 10; for the specific impact of gamblers, see Harold F. Gosnell, *Negro Politicians: The Rise of Negro Politics in Chicago*, 122–135 (Phoenix ed. 1966); and Chicago Crime Commission, File No. 65.

28. See references in footnotes 24 & 25. For additional information about relations between police and prostitutes, see extensive investigative reports in Committee of Fifteen Files, University of Chicago Library; also Investigator's Reports, "Law Enforcement and Police," Nov. 29, 1922, in Juvenile Protective Association papers, Library of the University of Illinois at Chicago Circle, folder 94, and other investigative reports in the J.P.A. papers.

29. For extensive discussion of police use of violence during riots, see Flinn, *Chicago Police*; Howard B. Myers, "The Policing of Labor Disputes in Chicago, A Case Study (Ph.D. Dissertation, Univ. of Chicago, 1929); William M. Tuttle, Jr., *Race Riot: Chicago in the Red Summer of 1919* (1920); and news clippings in Schuettler scrapbooks.

30. *Chicago American*, June 17, 1906.

31. Quotation from Everett C. Hughes, "The Policeman as a Person," (typewritten research paper dtd. 1925), Burgess papers; there are other similar stories in this paper. See also H. Lowenthal, "Juvenile Officer Kasarewyski," (handwritten termpaper [1920's]), Burgess papers. An interesting discussion concerning a more recent period can be found in Gerald D. Suttles, *The Social Order of the Slum: Ethnicity and Territory in the Inner City* 204 (1968).

32. Quotations from *Inter-Ocean*, Aug. 1, 1906; *Chicago Tribune*, Feb. 18, 1906. For a long feature story describing Assistant Superintendent Schuettler's methods of sweating, see *Chicago American*, March 25, 1906. Other stories in *Inter-Ocean*, Aug. 1 & Nov. 6, 1906; *Chicago American*, Nov. 24, 1933.

33. Quotation from news story cited in typewritten "Extract from Decision of Illinois Supreme Court, 1922," in John Howard Association papers, Chicago Historical Society, Box 4. For information about beatings of juveniles, see "The Gold Fish or Third Degree" [undated], a typewritten paper of a neighborhood boy; and "The Squealer" [undated], a statement by a delinquent, both in Burgess papers; also "The

Treatment of the Juvenile Offender" (a handwritten speech in Evelina Belden Paulson papers dtd. March 1914) in Library of the University of Illinois at Chicago Circle. For adults, see Zechariah Chafee, Jr., et al., *The Third Degree: Report to the National Commission on Law Observance and Enforcement*, 123–137 (republished 1969); George Murray, *The Madhouse on Madison Street*, 259 (1965); and copy of letter of John B. Skinner to Morgan Collins, Sept. 16, 1925, in Chicago Crime Commission, File No. 600–9.

34. During late 1906, Chicago papers reported a number of cases of police brutality; see, for instance, *Record-Herald* and *Examiner*, Dec. 14, 1906, *Chicago Tribune*, Dec. 14 & 15, 1906.

35. Quotations from *Chicago Chronicle*, Dec. 21, 1906, and *Chicago Record-Herald*, March 26, 1905. See also *Record-Herald*, Sept. 24, 1907; *Chicago Tribune*, Jan. 3, 1907; and Citizen's Association of Chicago, *Bulletin* No. 12 (Jan. 20, 1904).

Eight   Politics of Change

11 The Pessimistic Hypothesis
An Immodest Proposal
Hans W. Mattick (1973)

The pessimistic hypothesis asserts that, in at least one sub-set of social relations, the minimum equals the optimum. If, in the interaction of social forces (i.e., population, economic resources, social classes, political organization, value systems and institutional arrangements), a set of social relations or an interaction result remains constant, or exhibits a high degree of stability, that interactional result is socially determined. It represents what the forces at play in a society want. The pessimistic hypothesis is not a conspiratorial theory of history, nor does it ascribe conspiratorial motives to historical actors as a mode of social analysis. It accepts what appears to be a historical and contemporary judgment.

In general, the pessimistic hypothesis has some application to those institutional arrangements that allocate our economic resources to different social classes through our political organization as a reflection of our value system. It seems to apply with particular force to those areas of governmental administration allegedly designed to address themselves to the social welfare and legal problems of the poor and the offensive. It helps to explain the situation of incarcerated "inmates" of all kinds and of many kinds of "clients" of publicly financed services. Inmates include not only prisoners, but also mental patients, orphans, adult charity wards, the indigent ill and injured in public hospitals, and the like. Clients include persons on public welfare or social security, the indigent physically handicapped, alcoholics, drug addicts and, to a lesser degree, inner city public school children. They are all "offenders" in some sense of the word in that they offend against the abstract notions of justice we all entertain when it is convenient for us to do so. We all feel there "should not be" any poor or pariah classes, and it offends our sensibilities to have their existence affirmed in an undeniable way. So we label them in an offensive way and deny them their humanity: "dirty, lazy, stupid, crazy bums, beggars, lunatics and criminals," and act toward them in such a way that they will fulfill our expectations and make it difficult to escape the consequences of our so labeling them. These socially

"The Pessimistic Hypothesis" is reprinted with permission of the American Public Welfare Association from the Spring 1973 issue of *Public Welfare*, vol. 31, no. 2. Copyright 1973 by the American Public Welfare Association.

defined categories of inmate and client are not mutually exclusive; they overlap and there is an easy transition from one status to the other, e.g., from alcoholic to prisoner.

In its simplest form the pessimistic hypothesis asserts that nobody "really gives a damn" about any of these persons except their immediate families and, to some degree, the more conscientious public functionaries to whose charge or custody they have been relegated. When the rhetoric and political opportunism are subtracted, and the system of values and priorities of the larger society is examined to see where it invests its energies and treasure, inmates and clients, collectively dehumanized as "cases," are seen as the "natural victims" of that society. But a society that, in effect, creates victims that must subsist in social situations where the minimum is the optimum, must also create control measures to maintain the minimum-optimum situation. In the process a whole hierarchy of potential victims is created, with the society itself being the ultimate victim.

The pessimistic hypothesis points out that those public functionaries who have been made immediately responsible for the lowest level victim, the inmate or client, serve not only the control functions, but are the second-level victim of opportunity when the inevitable crisis in such socially determined minimum-optimum situations occur from time to time. Department heads, directors, wardens, supervisors, teachers, principals, superintendents, or whatever their titles may be, serve the second-level victim function quite apart from the question of their competence or responsibility. There is no necessary relationship between incumbency and competency; all permutations are possible. But when the crisis comes they are incumbents and will be sacrificed, if necessary, in order to continue to maintain the minimum-optimum situation.

The jailer and the prisoner are a good illustration of the implications of the pessimistic hypothesis. The institutional setting, the jail, for the lowest level victim, the inmate, is normally so neglected and deprived, and consequently so poorly administered, that it is constantly vulnerable to criticism, exposure and crisis. Therefore, the control functions exercised by the jailer are directed not only toward the inmates in the interest of "maintaining security," but also against the potential critic, the political opportunist and an uninformed public at large. In minimum-optimum situations "no news is good news." Nevertheless, from time to time, a naive but well-motivated citizen, or a political opportunist, or less frequently, a former inmate, "exposes" the conditions that exist as a matter of course in such institutions; and is able to do it in such a way as to find a public platform from which to escalate the normal level of crisis. When that happens, the routine response of the larger society, through its political representatives and their agents, is to enact a ritual known as "fixing the responsibility." Ad hoc investigative bodies are organized, a series of public and private persons make statements for the benefit of the mass-media, and a number of second-level victims are "suspended," "transferred," allowed to resign or, apparently, "fired." That is, if it is absolutely necessary, the next level in the hierarchy of victims, in this case the jailer, is sacrificed to help create "the illusion of constructive change." In the process, higher level officials have gained some favorable publicity for expressing appropriate sentiments, threats and promises addressed to the future have been made. There is a rapid circulation of middle range employees in a new allocation of public jobs. A moratorium on criticism is demanded "to give the new team a chance" to deal with the situation and make improvements. Sometimes a bewildered grand jury is convened and presented with such over-simplified atrocity stories that they are readily persuaded to vote indictments. In the end, more frequently than not, the entire ritual has served a whole range of tangential or irrelevant purposes, considering the original problem ostensibly addressed. The main purpose that the whole charade has served is to buy the time necessary to mollify a transiently aroused public interest. The tumult and the shouting dies. Few, if any, convictions follow upon the indictments, for they have reached the wrong persons. The real captains and the kings do not depart. The more things seem to change, the more they remain the same. The minimum-optimum situation has been maintained and the stage is set for a later repetition of the same cycle.

Viewed in historical perspective, progress on the jail problem has been glacial; at best it has been biological. As the generations pass we seem to gather more resolve that "something ought to be done by someone." The older order changeth, but the new is unable to act. In the last third of the twentieth century that is not good enough. A realistic appraisal of our past performance, however, would tend to indicate that the poet was more clear-sighted than the artless social reformer:

> . . . for the world which seems
> To lie before us like a land of dreams
> So variable, so beautiful, so new,
> Hath really neither joy, nor love, nor light,
> Nor certitude, nor peace, nor help for pain;
> And we are here as on a darkling plain
> Swept with confused alarms of struggle and flight,
> Where ignorant armies clash by night.
>
> M. Arnold, "Dover Beach."

After twenty years of working in the field that, with some reservations, we sometimes call criminal justice, I really should know better than to indulge my diminishing capacity for optimism; but I really was hoping that a few more saving graces could be found among the ways in which we treat offender-victims or victim-offenders. They are, for the most part, young, and the young, after all, are our only real national treasure, for they represent the future. Even those who have offended against us are a part of that future. But, as the Illinois Jails Survey, at the latest in a series of such surveys in this State and others, makes evident, all we seem to be capable of doing, for the most part, is to substitute official neglect and abuse for private vulnerability and crime. Moreover, except for the persons immediately involved, nobody really seems to care. It is a melancholy picture.

One cannot help but wonder, after repeated investigations have found the same conditions; after national, state and local commissions have made the same kinds of recommendations for more than a century; just what does it take to capture the interest of "the establishment" and more "the power structure" in our society? Are the bulk of the politicians, the businessmen, the industrialists, the militarists, the scientists, the clergy, the professionals and the craft unions so ethnocentric and so blind to the future? How can their self-interest be enlisted toward the solution of what amounts to a national scandal? How can we combine a positive mental attitude with the profit motive and the silent majority to deal with this ancient evil? Surely, a nation with a national product in excess of $900 billion can find the needle of justice in this haystack of dollars. Since the traditional problem does not yield to the usual recommendations put forward for a solution, let me offer an immodest proposal that may win the necessary public support.

Dean Swift in his "Modest Proposal" pointed out that the way to deal with the offensive young of his era was to make them palatable enough for human consumption. He had the disadvantage, of course, of writing in a pre-industrial age, and thus had to content himself with setting forth simple recipes for the cooking, broiling and stewing of children to enrich the gourmet diets of a jaded aristocracy. While this primitive method of dealing with offender-victims still has some utility and may be resorted to in our backward rural areas, in our advanced state of space age knowledge and technology we can improve on this piecework and cottage-industry method suggested by Swift.

Our main trouble, in our more modern, mass production and institutional approach to offender-victims, is that we have been satisfied with half-measures. We have been content to destroy the accused and the convicted, but we have not yet learned how to achieve maximum feasible utility with them. The Nazi German regime and the Russian Stalinist bureaucrats did some crude pioneering in this field with industrial era efficiency methods, but an objective evaluation of these methods would tend to indicate that they did not progress very much beyond the human destruction already implicit in the suggestions of Swift. Surely, the combined ingenuity that has produced our military-industrial complex, our space programs, our equitable tax laws with their farm subsidies and oil depletion allowances, and that ultimate expression of civilized rationality, the war in Vietnam; surely all that brain power and money can help avoid the useless destruction of offender-victims in malfunctioning jails that process more than a million persons a year. The methods of the space station, the weapons development laboratory and computer technology should be able to do much better than the resources of an impoverished and misdirected criminal justice system.

It would be too much to expect of our scientific community, I suppose, to devise a chemistry whereby offender-victims, or victim-offenders, could be transformed directly into napalm, or at least mace. It has been well said that the only difference between throwing people into the fire and throwing fire into the people is an altitude of some thousands of feet. Perhaps our organ-transplanting medical specialists, whose doctor colleagues can hardly be induced to come to a jail, can transfuse the bloodstreams of inmates with nitroglycerin. We could then drop them from bombers in Vietnam and transform that unhappy conflict into a popular People's Crusade worthy of the blessings of an ambivalent clergy. But this is a temporary expedient, for we cannot always count on a war whose end has been predicted for years to help us solve annoying social problems.

A more productive suggestion is to remand the indigent accused and convicted offender to those socialistic, i.e., government financed, C.C.C. camps for the technically competent that we call our space program. Just think how full you could stuff that "rat hole in the sky" with offenders and victims. Considering the barrenness of the moon, with very little additional investment we can embark on a moon fertilization program, sending of moonshot after moonshot full of inmates and clients to serve as Aborigines of Luna. Ambrose Bierce defined aborigines as "persons of little worth found cumbering the soil of a newly discovered country," and added, "they soon cease to cumber; they fertilize." Since the sterile moon has no aborigines, modern social policy can supply them and, after the moon, an infinite universe in need of fertilization lies beyond to be conquered by our space program. Our ancestors, despite their profligacy of resources and energy were at least limited to building their cathedrals and royal palaces on earth, where they might later be turned to some useful social purpose; we shoot our cathedrals into the air.

Terrestrial and domestic needs, however, should not be neglected. We can utilize some of our offender-victims to supplement our farm subsidy program. Why should we spend millions of dollars to insure that farmland should lie idle and fallow when we can increase its fertility for later non-use with thousands of surplus victim-offenders. We might even be able to stop up a few prematurely productive oil wells with inmates to help support an impoverished industry that must resort to a depletion tax allowance to prevent it from dying of excess risk capital and profit.

A short-term capital gain tax loop-hole could be created by organizing a temporary, revolving, dependent allocation program for the wealthy, to be implemented every year around April 15th. At that time all the institutions could be emptied of their inmates and all the public bureaucracies could refer all their clients to the temporary custody of wealthy individuals and corporations for tax exemption purposes, somewhat on the model of the way money and other assets are transferred from banks to safety deposit boxes around that time. The onerous burden of supporting these "cases" for a few days will surely be more than offset by the tax advantage they can bring before they are relegated to one of the technological programs that are available. Such a program would require a few changes in tax law, but a conscientious Congress or State Legislature and a tax-wise legal profession should be equal to the task.

A more mundane suggestion for the more efficient processing of offenders and victims is to relate them to the need for housing and highways in such a way that supply and demand, or both, meet and cancel each other. In this age of junk autos and compressed garbage disposal there must be devised a technological way to press offensive people into the highway and building materials business. Union labor working hand in hand with building contractors and political contract-letters, will find a way; and that way will comport well with the ethics of neighborhood removal, high-rise public housing projects and public stadia building. Just think of the public ceremonies at ribbon-cutting time, when the governors of our states and the mayors of our cities, basking in the reflected lights of capital, labor and the mass-media, dedicate another all-season sports stadium built with the people's cement and another super-expressway paved with organic asphalt. The raw materials aspects of offenders and victims are almost limitless. A Presidential Commission should be appointed at once and, instead of concerning themselves with a bothersome form of "preventive detention," they should study the possibility of combining inmates and clients with increased water and air pollution. Maybe they can be pulverized or dissolved—it dazzles the imagination and accords with the principles of free enterprise.

These few hints must suffice to show our poverty of imagination in dealing with inmates and clients, offender-victims or victim-offenders. Surely, a good public relations program can convert a national scandal into an asset in our struggle for the hearts and minds of men. We wouldn't want the Communists to get ahead of us here. Excelsior!

12

The Popular Myth of the Victimless Crime

Dallin H. Oaks (1974)

My topic is decriminalization—the increasingly successful efforts to obtain the repeal of criminal laws on many forms of behavior that traditionally have been treated as crimes. Current proposals would decriminalize all forms of sexual behavior involving consenting adults, including adultery, fornication, prostitution, homosexuality, and other forms of deviate sexual behavior. The more extreme proposals would even decriminalize commercialized sex, such as procuring for prostitution. Most decriminalization proposals would repeal criminal penalties on the possession of marijuana, LSD, and comparable drugs. Some would repeal the laws against possession of heroin, and a few would even decriminalize the sale of hard drugs. Other crimes usually included in decriminalization proposals are pornography, abortion, gambling, public drunkenness, and vagrancy.[1]

We should not underestimate the importance of these proposals. The publicity and political power gathering behind various decriminalization proposals is impressive indeed. The long list of organizations currently involved includes the President's Crime Commission, the National Council on Crime and Delinquency, the American Assembly, and even the American Bar Association.

Criminal law revision already adopted or under favorable consideration leave no doubt that we are witnessing revolutionary changes in the function and content of criminal law. The effects are likely to be as far-reaching as the eighteenth-century reform movement that made the punishment fit the crime (thus abolishing capital punishment for several hundred minor crimes) and the nineteenth-century reforms that made the punishment fit the offender (thus introducing probation and indeterminate sentences). The decriminalization movement could appreciably change the business of the courts and the functions of the police. It could also bring about significant changes in our standards of morality.

Mr. Oaks delivered "The Popular Myth of the Victimless Crime" as part of Brigham Young University's Commissioner's Lecture Series. The paper was published by Brigham Young University Press in 1974 and is reprinted by permission of the author.

I will identify the principal arguments for and against decriminalization, emphasize an important but neglected consideration, discuss the relationship between law and morality, and, finally, offer my recommendations on several of the specific proposals for decriminalization.

One of the principal arguments in favor of decriminalization is that the inevitable effect of criminal penalties on many of these acts is to increase other crimes. Proponents suggest three ways this increase occurs. First, when we pass a law criminalizing particular goods or services, we drive out legal competition and leave the business to criminals. This underground trade will encourage organized crime, which will charge high prices as compensation for the risk of illegal behavior and then use its high profits to promote other criminal activities, just as the bootlegger's profits from prohibition days provided the capital for later investments in gambling, prostitution, and the drug traffic. Second, the high prices that patrons, such as drug addicts, must pay to the criminal proprietors will force these patrons to commit other crimes like robbery or theft to support their addiction. Third, criminal penalties on certain conduct will drive its participants to associate with other criminals, thus strengthening a subversive criminal subculture.[3]

Such arguments have considerable force in support of proposals to decriminalize offenses of a commercial nature like the drug traffic, gambling, and prostitution. They have little persuasive force for proposals to decriminalize crimes like public drunkenness, vagrancy, and most sex crimes.

A second argument relies on the obvious overloading of our police resources and the overcrowding of our courts and prisons. The crimes proposed for decriminalization are said to be less important to the public than many of the so-called serious crimes that we already lack sufficient resources to enforce properly. Decriminalization would therefore permit improved enforcement of criminal laws of greatest concern to the public.[4]

As with the first argument, this point has considerable force as to some decriminalization proposals and little or none as to others. For example, the amount of law enforcement resources currently committed to the enforcement of laws pertaining to drug offenses and public drunkenness is considerable. In contrast, the resources involved in enforcing laws against adultery or other private sexual offenses are negligible. A New York judge recently observed that so far as he was aware there had never been a criminal prosecution for adultery in New York State, although, as he observed dryly, "the opportunity has surely been presented."[5]

This argument for reallocating law enforcement resources has some vital flaws even as to those crimes that currently involve significant resources. Would the resources really shift, and would the increased efforts be effective if they did? Moreover, can we be so sure, as this argument glibly assumes, that it is the will of the people or in the best interest of society to close out our enforcement efforts on one crime in favor of some increase in effort on another? For example, on what objective criteria or system of values do we conclude that we should abandon enforcement of drug laws or drunkenness in order to shift public resources and increase the enforcement of laws against robbery or theft?

In terms of its prominence in popular discussion, the third argument in favor of decriminalization seems to be the most persuasive. Unlike the first two arguments, which apply only to some of the proposed crimes, this third argument unites the whole group of crimes under one theory and one label. The label is "victimless crime." The theory is that, if a person's conduct will not injure anyone other than himself—in other words, if the crime is "victimless"—it shouldn't be a crime. The intellectual scripture for this position is John Stuart Mill's classic essay *On Liberty*, which argues that "the only purpose for which power can be rightfully exercised over any member of a civilized community, against his will, is to prevent harm to others."[6] A modern characterization of Mill's argument is the following:

> [M]an has an inalienable right to go to hell in his own fashion, pro-
> vided he does not directly injure the person or property of another on
> the way.[7]

Along with the label "victimless crime," this argument has an apparently irresistible drawing power. More and more persons seem to be catching hold of the argument and label and climbing aboard the decriminalization band-wagon.

My objection to the victimless crime argument is twofold. First, I will discuss my contention that Mill's principle is misapplied in many of the proposals for decriminalization because these acts do involve harms and victims. Second, I will contend that Mill's argument is unsound in any case because the criminal law has an important function in addition to the protection of an identifiable victim.

I will discuss my first contention under the somewhat overstated subtitle "There is no such thing as a victimless crime." Some so-called victimless crimes have readily identifiable personal victims other than the criminal himself. Take the drug traffic, for example. The press has recently carried accounts of newborn babies suffering drug withdrawal symptoms because of their mothers' addiction during pregnancy. Another press account de-scribed addict mothers nursing infants who became addicted and wailed endlessly if the mothers were long deprived of their drug.[8] Not long ago a University of Utah Medical Center scientist announced the discovery of "a significant amount of chromosome breakage in most users" of marijuana, even among those who only smoked the drug less than once a week. Users had three times the rate of chromosome breakage as nonusers, a fact that could later be related to birth defects and even to cancer in their future offspring.[9] Other directly identifiable victims of so-called victimless crimes are the innocent children whose family life is destroyed by the sexual irregularities of a parent or whose parents are pauperized by gambling or twisted by alcohol or drugs.

In other instances it is not possible to identify persons who are the direct victims of a particular crime. In some so-called victimless crimes, all society is the victim. In a close-knit, predominantly urban society such as ours, and in a country that is presently committed to an extensive program of welfare assistance for disadvantaged persons of many types, our lives are so interwoven that one person cannot rationally contend that what he does to or with himself is of no concern to anyone but himself. Each person steers his ship of life through a very narrow passage. The wreckage of one person in that passage becomes a serious navigational hazard for many others. Thus, in John Stuart Mill's time it may have been possible to make a rational argument that society had no interest in restraining an individual who chose to destroy himself, such as by alcohol or drugs. But whatever the merit of that argument in nineteenth-century England, which had a relatively limited system of employing tax revenues to care for the sick and disabled, it is without persuasive force today.

Whether we like it or not, we live in a welfare state, where one or another agency of government is the ultimate provider for the aged, sick, disabled, and unemployed. If men or women wreck their health or destroy their capacity to labor, they and their natural dependents are almost certain to become a burden to some tax-supported agency of the local or national government. Taxpayers—all society—are the victims. The cost of rehabilitating a narcotic addict runs from $1,300 to $3,000 per year.[10] If a hunter shoots a hole in a $200 road sign, he can be arrested and put in jail. Vandalism is not a victimless crime. But if he shoots himself in the arm with heroin and becomes addicted, it may cost the state as much as $3,000 to rehabilitate him or more thousands to hospitalize him and care for his family. Yet some persons argue that a narcotics offense involving a consenting adult is a victimless crime.

Some would argue that the appropriate response is to withdraw welfare assistance from those who have deliberately destroyed their capacity to labor. But even if it were practical to enforce that rule against the guilty parties, which I doubt, our society would not penalize their families. Whether on moral or on practical grounds, our current charitable impulses and our welfare programs should be taken as an established fact for purposes of this argument. The potential financial burden gives society a keen interest in personally destructive behavior that once may have appeared of concern to no one but the person himself. A society that is committed to support has a basis to control.

Although the evidence is admittedly less well focused, I content that we can also identify some personal and societal victims of crimes like pornography and sex-related offenses.

Hard empirical evidence that pornography is damaging to society is scarce or nonexistent. But common sense is sufficient evidence for some. I believe it would be acknowledged as common experience that the pictures and literature of the gutter produce the thoughts of the gutter and that the thought is parent to the act. Those who would reject this reasoning should consider the premise they are rejecting. Society and our school systems foster ennobling literature and educational material on the assumption that this material will affect behavior for good. If wholesome literature has a wholesome effect, how can the proponents of pornography be so sure that what is ugly and vicious will not encourage ugly and vicious behavior?

The most readily measurable social cost of irregular sexual behavior is the tax burden imposed on our society by illegitimacy. The annual number of illegitimate births in the United States is more than 300,000, with over half being born to women under twenty years of age.[11] Without the emotional and financial support of a normal family relationship, most of these illegitimate children are handicapped in their emotional development and need to be supported by tax revenues.

Recently the American Bar Association passed a resolution urging the states to "repeal all laws which classified as criminal conduct any form of non-commercial sexual conduct between consenting adults in private. . . ."[12] This would wipe out laws against adultery, fornication, homosexuality, and other irregular sexual behavior. Such laws are frequently used as prototype illustrations of "victimless crimes." In contrast, I contend that society is the victim of these crimes because they pose a threat to the integrity of the family structure, which is the basic supportive institution in our society.

There is no social institution in which society has greater interest than the family. The survival of our society depends upon our having a predominance of citizens whose social interactions are secured by the adhesive of common moral values. The family is the indispensable agency for educating or socializing children in the values of the society.[13] The basic attitudes, characteristics, and values that guide us throughout our entire lives are acquired in our family surroundings at a very early age. There is no substitute for the family. "[T]he organized community has not developed methods of discipline and training which are equal in efficiency to those of the adequate home."[14] Thus, a prestigious federal commission suggesting goals for criminal reduction and prevention recommended the "highest attention" to preventing juvenile delinquency. The report observed that "society has long depended on the authority of the family as a major instrument of social control and thus of crime prevention."[15] There is also abundant evidence on the vital importance of the family as the most effective institution to provide the basic emotional nutriment and support necessary if infants are to become adequately functioning human beings.[16] Adequate performance of this function may be more important in today's impersonal mass society than ever before.[17]

Though I know of no empirical evidence on the proposition, I believe that decriminalization of conduct involving sexual relations outside the bonds of marriage would weaken the ideal and practice of family life in this country. Sexual behavior is more than procreative. It is a great force that solidifies the relationship of the father and mother in a family.[18] Or it may tear the relationship asunder. Any sexual behavior outside the bonds of marriage can be a threat to family life in our society because our moral standards forbid it and because our laws make it a basis for divorce. If such behavior does not weaken or destroy family organization and functioning, it at least carries an unacceptable risk of such results. Adultery and fornication, if they do not produce illegitimate and unwanted children, may at least disrupt the tranquility of homes that should be devoted to raising well-balanced, stable children. The importance that society must attach to the stability of the family structure and the effectiveness of its function gives society a sufficient interest in the sexual behavior of persons who may affect families.

When a family is weakened, the children are affected and all society is the victim. As Commissioner Neal A. Maxwell has cautioned, "The unloved individual can be as dangerous as untreated sewage, and the sewage of sin is so devastating downstream in life" that it deserves as much time in the priorities of our planning as the other environmental concerns that are so often urged upon us in these times. "The consequences of unchastity may be less visible than those of drugs, but can be just as destructive. Both may be rooted in loneliness, or thrill seeking, and both produce tragic human debris with which we must deal."[19] In this manner the consequences of sexual relations outside the bonds of marriage extend beyond the participants to the detriment of members of their families, born and unborn, and to the public at large.

One of the most striking illustrations of the inappropriateness of the label "victimless crimes" in many of these situations I have been discussing is the fact that even John Stuart Mill, the patron saint of the decriminalization movement, recognized a legitimate social interest in criminal penalties on individual conduct that imposed "a definite damage, or a definite risk of damage, either to an individual or to the public. . . ."[20] Thus, Mill's celebrated essay *On Liberty* concedes that a person could be punished for idleness where the person was receiving support from the public.[21] A person could be punished for drunkenness where past experience had shown that drunkenness made him dangerous to those around him.[22] Although Mill advocated doing away with criminal punishment of persons indulging in gambling and fornication, he conceded that it might be appropriate to have criminal penalties on those who kept gambling houses or procured for prostitution because of the general social interest in discouraging such conduct.[23]

Mill also argued that the general social interest in an educated citizenry justified the state in forcing everyone to be educated up to a minimum standard. He said that parents who brought children into existence without providing instruction and training for their minds were guilty of "a moral crime, both against the unfortunate offspring, and against society. . . ."[24] Mill even carried this theory to the extent of arguing that, in a country either over-peopled, or threatened with being so," parents who produced more than a small number of children had committed a serious wrong against all laboring people whose wages would be reduced by the excessive competition produced by overpopulation, as well as against all other persons affected by the "wretchedness and depravity" of the offspring.[25] In this respect John Stuart Mill was obviously more willing than most of us to see social injury in individual conduct and even to affix criminal penalties to that conduct. It is therefore ironic that his essay *On Liberty* is so often cited in support of decriminalization of crimes in which there is no identifiable personal victim but for which there is demonstrable "damage or a definite risk of damage . . . to the public."[26]

By now you may be concluding that the whole concept of "victimless crimes" is artificial and unhelpful. I agree. The late Professor Herbert Packer, one of the principal proponents of decriminalization, conceded that Mill's formula "solves very little" because "it is usually possible to make a more or less plausible argument that any given form of conduct" involves some damage or risk of damage to the interests of others.[27] By conceding that the absence of an identifiable victim should not preclude criminal liability, Packer rejected Mill's test of "harm to others" as a criterion for criminal liability, but he contended that the victimless characterization should still serve as a limitation on the imposition of criminal sanctions in two ways. First, Packer contended that the absence of an identifiable victim should force an inquiry into the advantages and disadvantages of trying to suppress particular conduct by the criminal law. I agree with the appropriateness of that inquiry and will undertake it myself before I conclude. However, I cannot agree with Packer's other point—that the "victimless crime" characterization should help us assure "that a given form of conduct is not being subjected to the criminal sanction purely or even primarily because it is thought to be immoral."[28] To the contrary, the entire process of identifying the victims of crime is heavily dependent upon our basic assumptions about morality.[29] For example, our opinion on whether abortion is a victimless crime is a function of whether we recognize any protectable interest in the embryo or fetus, and this decision is itself dictated by moral assumptions about the nature and origin of life.

Thus far I have decribed and evaluated various arguments in favor of decriminalization, assigning significance to some arguments but concluding with an attempt to discredit the rhetoric of the so-called victimless crime. I now proceed to my second main topic, an argument against decriminalization, in which I contend, contrary to John Stuart Mill and Herbert Packer, that the criminal law has an important function other than the protection of an identifiable victim. That function is to reinforce certain moral values or standards. Speaking in headlines, I assert that there are times when the law can and does and should legislate morality.

I begin by highlighting the important standard-setting and teaching function of the criminal law. The point needs emphasis because it is often omitted by persons whose "victimless crimes" orientation causes them to focus exclusively on the question of measurable harm to identifiable victims. The criminal law also exists for the protection of society at large. The standard-setting function of law can also be overlooked by those who are preoccupied with whether a particular law can be effectively enforced. Enforcement is an important consideration but not a dispositive one. Because of its teaching and standard-setting role, the law may serve society's interest by authoritatively condemning what it cannot begin to control directly by criminal penalties. This standard-setting function of law is of ever-increasing importance to society in a time when the moral teachings and social controls of our nation's families, schools, and churches seem to be progressively less effective.

It is easy to give examples of the enormous educative influence of the law. Law focuses our attention on a particular problem, enacts a solution, and sometimes even provides and persuades us with reasons for the solution. By these means, laws sometimes resolve and put a mark of official finality on bitterly contested social issues. This has been the case with entitlement to social security, the legality of labor unions and the right to strike, the progressive income tax, and the right to be free from racial discrimination in government, common carriers, and places of public accommodation.

This last example is recent and persuasive. You will recall the prolonged debate over the Civil Rights Act of 1964, especially the section forbidding racial discrimination in public accommodations. The issue was whether a proprietor on an interstate highway should be compelled to provide service to blacks or any other group with whom he preferred not to deal. The country was bitterly divided over that issue, and only Senator Everett

Dirksen's last-minute change of mind (an important decision by an influential conservative Republican) obtained passage of the Civil Rights Act by a very narrow margin. Today, just ten years later, the controversy seems as if it had come from another century. With the passage of the Civil Rights Act we not only changed our law, but we also changed our minds. Today the proposition adopted in that legislation is well accepted from coast to coast and from north to south.

The *repeal* of laws can also have an educative effect. If certain activities are classified as crimes, this is understood as a public declaration that the conduct is immoral, bad, unwise, and unacceptable for society and the individual. Consequently, if an elected legislative body removes criminal penalties, many citizens will understand this repeal as an official judgment that the decriminalized behavior is not harmful to the individual or to society. Indeed, some may even understand decriminalization as a mark of public approval of the conduct in question. In these reactions lies a great danger for some decriminalization proposals.

The law is an effective teacher, and it can teach for good or for ill. Laws can affect the attitudes of our citizens about what is right and wrong, fair and unfair, proper or improper, advisable or inadvisable. The criminal law is a moral force, and that force is exerted without regard to whether or not there is an identifiable victim and, to a certain extent, without regard to whether or not the particular law is enforced. As Dr. Richard J. Neuhaus recently reminded us:

> Through laws a community tries to reinforce what it considers right and good, and to restrain or suppress what it considers wrong and bad. . . . Law-making never has been and never can be value-free, objective, computerized. . . .
> The debate, then, about what ought and what ought not to be a crime is a debate about morality. Legal discourse—at least reflective legal discourse—is moral discourse.[30]

Neuhaus' comment explains why it is shortsighted and simplistic to say that we cannot legislate morality. As Yale Law School Dean Eugene Rostow declared, "We legislate hardly anything else."[31]

But whose morality or values is the law to teach? Here we meet an old controversy over the relationship between the criminal law and the principles of morality or right and wrong. A hundred years ago Sir James Fitzjames Stephen confronted John Stuart Mill on this issue.[32] In our own day the most prominent protagonists are Sir Patrick Devlin and Professor H. L. A. Hart.[33]

My support belongs to Lord Devlin, who argued that society has the right to "legislate against immorality" because without a "common morality,"

which he defined as the moral judgment of the "reasonable man," society
would disintegrate.[34] Devlin's adversary, Professor Hart, who classified
himself with "John Stuart Mill and other latter-day liberals," rejected this as
"an unjustifiable extension of the scope of the criminal law."[35] By this view,
the only "common morality" the law could enforce would be principles
"essential to the existence" of a society of human beings, like rules against
violence or other harm to an identifiable victim.[36]

In common with Lord Devlin, I contend for the desirability of legislating
on a broader moral front. I would not, however, agree to Lord Devlin's
assertion that "the law must base itself on Christian morals and to the limit
of its ability enforce them."[37] In past centuries most criminal laws were
almost direct codifications of religious principles. Historic abuses such as the
Salem witch trials and official penalties for religious heresy have forced the
direct religious source of law to yield to our constitutional separation between church and state. Today no thoughtful American would advocate
using the criminal law to enforce that portion of the religious-moral law
pertaining to religious belief or practice. But religious principles of right and
wrong or good and evil in matters of individual behavior continue to wield
an important moral influence on the content of the criminal law through
their effect on the opinions and action of individual citizens in the lawmaking process.

In his illuminating John Randolph Tucker Lecture at Washington and Lee
University, Professor Edward H. Levi improves Lord Devlin's position and
makes it acceptable to American secularism. Here is how he describes it:

> In matters of morality, the law-maker's function, as Lord Devlin saw
> it, was to enforce those ideas about right and wrong which are already
> accepted by the society for which he was legislating and which were
> necessary to preserve its integrity. . . . In so doing they were reflect-
> ing and changing the collective morality which was the substitute in a
> democratic society for any other authority outside of the law.[38]

Whether finding its origin in religious belief, ethical system, or rational
process, this "collective morality" is a legitimate source of criminal law in
our society. By this means our criminal laws teach and compel the observance of standards of behavior not demonstrably related to harm to others or
the survival of society but nevertheless important to our individual or
collective well-being. Our laws forbidding obscenity, indecent exposure, or
lewdness are of this type, protecting our traditional moral sensibilities rather
than our physical welfare. Other examples could be cited.[39]

Most of our laws—particularly our criminal laws—are, in fact, an expression of what our lawmakers deem good for society. Their reasons are usually
unstated or inarticulate, but that is inherent in the complexity of the task.
Lawmakers who pass zoning and land-use laws on the basis of their perceptions of aesthetics can just as validly pass criminal laws on the basis of their

judgments of morality.[40] Any democratic lawmaking proceeds from a composite of factual findings based on empirical evidence or assumptions, combined with moral values attributable to religious belief or other ethical systems. It is therefore inevitable that the law will codify and teach moral values, including moral values not shared by some portion of the society— usually a minority. I find that circumstance both understandable and desirable because it maintains an essential relationship between the moral values of citizens and the requirements and teachings of law in a democratic society.

This formulation of the relationship between moral values and the criminal law obviously contemplates that the law can change to accommodate what Chief Justice Warren called "the evolving standard of decency that marks the progress of a maturing society."[41] Thus, in constitutional interpretation our Eighth Amendment limitation on "cruel and unusual punishment" is not forever bound to a 1793 interpretation that would apparently have permitted criminals to be punished by "cropping ears and branding."[42]

But the law must not depart too far from the collective morality, either to lead or to lag, or it will lose its force as a prescriber of behavior and its persuasiveness as a teacher and setter of standards. Here is the true significance of the slogan "You can't legislate morality." The law will be ineffective if it attempts to *criminalize* conduct that is not condemned by collective morality. Thus, as Professor Levi notes in his lecture, "the test of the community's intolerance, , indignation and disgust . . . is a continuing one which has to be met if the law is to be maintained."[43] That is the lesson of the unsuccessful attempt at prohibition of alcoholic beverages.

Similarly, I contend that the law will be discredited if it attempts to *decriminalize* conduct condemned under collective morality. A Missouri judge recently applied that principle in explaining why he supported the proposed Missouri Criminal Code in retaining criminal penalties on gambling, marijuana, prostitution, obscenity, and deviate sexual relations. For example, here is what he said about homosexuality:

> Rightly or wrongly, most Missourians today regard homosexuality as immoral; if the law fails to support that notion, disrespect for law and a general loosening of the bonds of society must follow. . . .
> [A] majority of the people in Missouri still regard homosexuality as disgusting, degrading, degenerate, and a threat to society. Whether this is rational or not, so long as the feeling persists the majority will insist that its condemnation be reflected in a positive manner in the criminal code even if it is unenforceable.[44]

The popularity of current efforts to restore the death penalty identifies this as another area where the lawmakers (in this case the United States Supreme Court) may have led out too far in advance of the collective morality.

Differences of opinion over the appropriate relationship between law and morality are also involved in the resolution of important legal issues other than decriminalization. For example, the principal thrust of Professor Levi's lecture was to explain how the United States Supreme Court had used ideas of "community standards" or "attitudes" as a basis of constitutional decisions adjudicating obscenity cases and upsetting criminal laws on abortion and capital punishment. Siding with Justice Lewis Powell's contention that "the assessment of popular opinion is essentially a legislative, not a judicial, function,"[45] Levi criticizes the Supreme Court—properly, in my view—for judicial decisions and techniques that have impaired the process by which collective morality is created and used, thus widening the gap between the people and the law.[46] By this view, the law-and-morality issue is a key consideration in the current debate over judicial activism. But that is a matter for another time.

For present purposes, the principal implication of this description of the relationship between collective morality and law is that no one need make apology for attempting to implement commonly accepted positions on moral behavior by giving them the force of law. The majority should surely exercise restraint, and the Bill of Rights will occasionally compel restraint, but society can properly promote collective morality by legislation. The law is a schoolmaster as well as a policeman, and its curriculum includes morality.

I will conclude by applying the principles I have discussed above to an evaluation of proposals for decriminalization of three categories of criminal conduct: sexual crimes, drug offenses, and public drunkenness and vagrancy.

First, I believe in retaining criminal penalties on sex crimes such as adultery, fornication, prostitution, homosexuality, and other forms of deviate sexual behavior. I concede the abuses and risks of invasion of privacy that are involved in the enforcement of such crimes[47] and therefore concede the need for extraordinary supervision of the enforcement process. I am even willing to accept a strategy of extremely restrained enforcement of private, noncommercial sexual offenses. I favor retaining these criminal penalties primarily because of the standard-setting and teaching function of these laws on sexual morality and their support of society's exceptional interest in the integrity of the family. The decision on decriminalization of these crimes depends on one's attitude toward legislation in support of moral principles. The other arguments have relatively less persuasive force.

In the case of drug offenses, it will come as no surprise that I believe in retaining criminal penalties on the possession and sale of currently illegal drugs. I reach this decision despite the undoubted force of the first two arguments for decriminalization. We are undoubtedly committing significant law enforcement resources in this area—resources that could be used elsewhere. I am also persuaded that our current criminal penalties on drugs, as presently enforced, probably have the effect of increasing the overall level of crime. Yet I am unwilling to adopt the conclusion of those who urge these arguments. According to one capable scholar, "decriminalizing heroin should drastically reduce the rate of serious crime since narcotics could then be provided to addicts at very low prices and they would not need to be committing crimes in order to support their habit."[48] Proponents further claim that this would remove the profit from the drug traffic and thus weaken the powers of organized crime. Though all of us would desire that result and hope it would occur as predicted, we should also look carefully at the price we would pay for the promised result.

I urge retention of criminal penalties on drug offenses because of the measurable harm drug use inflicts on identifiable victims and on society as a whole and also because criminal penalties are necessary if the law is to perform its function of teaching against and discouraging the use of drugs. Heroin and other hard drugs stand convicted of so much human misery and such staggering social costs[49] that there can be no doubt of the propriety of extensive government efforts to discourage their use. The retention of criminal penalties is part of those efforts. What would happen if the disribution of heroin and other hard drugs were decriminalized, making drugs readily available for all who wished to indulge? Experience suggests the high risk of an epidemic increase in the level of narcotics addiction. A Swedish psychiatrist who made an extensive study of the problem of drug addiction concluded that "the one factor that correlates most highly with the epidemic spread of addiction is availability of the drug in question."[50] According to this scientist, the only persons who advocate heroin maintenance are those "who don't know anything about addiction. . . ."[51]

Evidence on the effects of marijuana is far less compelling than that on heroin, at least partly because the history of experience is shorter. Yet there is accumulating evidence of disabling physical and mental deterioration from use of this drug.[52] I find it significant that the proponents of decriminalization of marijuana have chosen to associate their case with the record on alcohol. Thus, a Stanford law professor recently made this argument:

> When one adds together the physical, psychological, and social dangers of the drug . . . it is impossible for any reasonable person to conclude that marijuana is more dangerous than alcohol. . . . A very powerful argument can be made for licensing the sale of marijuana as we do the sale of alcohol.[53]

This is the same kind of reasoning employed by a personal finance company whose Chicago billboards used to invite people to come in and borrow enough money to get completely out of debt. Both arguments ignore the added costs of the remedy they advocate.

A former cabinet-level official in the Department of Health, Education, and Welfare has labeled alcoholism the most serious public health problem in the country. There are 9 million alcoholics or serious problem drinkers in the United States. Their life expectancies are shortened ten to fifteen years. Each year more than 85,000 people die of alcohol-related problems. The excessive use of alcohol has been linked to at least half of our 56,000 annual motor vehicle fatalities. The annual economic loss from alcohol-related problems, including medical costs, welfare services, and lost productivity, has been estimated at from $10 to $15 billion annually.[54]

These costs support the logic of imposing criminal penalties on the sale of alcohol. That proposal is persuasive but impractical. Our experience with prohibition shows the futility of using the criminal law against alcohol. The middle-class citizens who defied prohibition demonstrated that this law had exceeded and could not alter our collective morality.

The supposed widespread use of marijuana has been cited as a reason for decriminalizing this drug as well. But so far the collective morality seems to stand against marijuana. The National Commission on Marijuana and Drug Abuse found that 64 percent of the adult public agreed that "using marijuana is morally offensive," compared with only 40 percent for alcohol. It is also significant that 71 percent of the adults and 80 percent of the youth had never used marijuana,[55] the figures on the proportion of the population using alcohol are much higher.[56]

Logic would dictate similar treatment of alcohol and marijuana, either to criminalize both or to decriminalize both. But, as Justice Holmes observed, the life of the law has not been logic but experience, and in this case the teachings of experience oppose the criminalization of alcohol, and the dictates of collective morality oppose the decriminalization of marijuana. In that circumstance we should stay with the status quo.

There are other reasons for not decriminalizing drugs. If we increased the availability of drugs, we would be supporting addicts in their efforts to encourage others to join them in their addiction. Decriminalization of the drug traffic would only remove the drug problem from the public view. As with alcoholism, the problem would continue and grow. We would have to learn how to live with the abuse of drugs in the same calloused fashion that we have been taught to live with the staggering expense and shocking social cost of alcoholism.

Despite my opposition to decriminalization of drug offenses, I am persuaded that current criminal penalties for possession of marijuana, and even our penalties for the sale or distribution of small quantities of this drug, are too severe. For example, in New York a person who provides an adult with one marijuana cigarette can be imprisoned for up to twenty-five years; if the cigarette goes to a minor, the offense carries the same penalty as first-degree manslaughter and first-degree rape.[57] Experience teaches that, when the severity of penalties outruns our public appraisal of the seriousness of the offense, juries will refuse to convict, prosecutors will refuse to charge, and police and witnesses will neglect to enforce. I see that happening with the administration of the criminal laws against marijuana.[58] I believe we would lose little in the law's teaching effort against marijuana and perhaps gain considerable effectiveness in enforcement if we substantially reduced the severest penalties on possession and distribution of small quantities, at the same time continuing existing penalties and vigorous enforcement efforts on the sale or possession of wholesale quantities.

Although opposing decriminalization of sex and drug offenses, I favor decriminalization of the laws against public drunkenness, vagrancy, and similar crimes. I am brought to this conclusion for two reasons. First, the standard-setting function of law has little or no force in respect to public drunkenness and vagrancy. The criminal penalty has already shown itself ineffective against alcohol, and it will be even less effective against the skid-row derelect who is arrested for public drunkenness or vagrancy than it was against the middle-class citizen during prohibition. Second, the enforcement of criminal laws on drunkenness and vagrancy requires significant law enforcement, judicial, and penal resources that could be more usefully employed in the enforcement of crimes in which society has a greater interest. Thus, studies show that drunkenness and vagrancy offenses account for about two million arrests annually, about 40 percent of the total arrests for all crimes in this country.[59] Most of these arrests involve skid-row men who are arrested, jailed, convicted, released, and rearrested in a meaningless revolving door that accomplishes nothing except to impose a burden on police, courts, and jails and inflict a temporary inconvenience or convenience (bed and board and a brief period of forced sobriety) on the arrested person. The criminal process does have the effect of "cleaning the streets" of derelicts. This is a legitimate social interest, but one that ought to be pursued by some civil remedy that is subject neither to the abuses involved in the vague criminal statutes that seek to punish drunks and vagabonds nor to the expenses entailed in arrest, booking, jail, and court appearance to achieve the simple expedient of transporting a person out of a situation where he is a threat to himself or others.

The current movement for decriminalization involves vital matters of social policy and requires our most careful attention. We should examine the proposals crime by crime since the principal arguments apply to some crimes but not to others. The popular label of the "victimless crime" is misleading, if not meaningless; so is the popular slogan "You can't legislate morality." Preservation of the public health, safety, *and morals* is a traditional concern of legislation. This does not justify laws in furtherance of the special morality of a particular group, but it does justify legislation in support of standards of right and wrong of sufficient general acceptance that they can qualify as "collective morality." In the exercise of its important but underestimated standard-setting function, the law should teach observance of that collective morality, thus preserving the essential relationship between the moral values of citizens and the requirements and teachings of law in a democratic society.

Notes

1. E.g., Morris & Hawkins, *The Honest Politicians's Guide to Crime Control* (1970); Schur, *Crimes without Victims* (1965); Olivieri & Finkelstein, 18 *N.Y.L. Forum* 77 (1972); Boruchowitz, "Victimless Crimes: A Proposal to Free the Courts," *Judicature* 69 (Aug./Sept. 1973).
2. I am indebted to Edward L. Kimball, professor of law, and Darwin L. Thomas, associate professor of CDFR and sociology and director of the Family Research Center, for valuable suggestions and to Mark Zobrist for research assistance. Eric Andersen, Scott Jenkins, Bryce McEuen, and Nicholai Sorensen provided research assistance for an earlier draft.
3. Morris & Hawkins, note 1 supra at 5.
4. Id. at 6.
5. Wachtler, "The High Cost of Victimless Crimes," 28 *Record of the Ass'n of the Bar of the City of New York* 357, 360 (1973).
6. Mill, *On Liberty* 23 (7th ed. 1871).
7. Morris & Hawkins, note 1 supra at 2.
8. Markham, "What's All This Talk of Heroin Maintenance," *N.Y. Times Magazine* 6 (July 2, 1972).
9. *University of Utah Medical Center Report* 3 (Sept. 1973).
10. Bureau of Narcotics and Dangerous Drugs, "Fact Sheet" 13 (Washington, D.C., 1970).
11. Dept. of Health, Education & Welfare, Public Health Service, "Natality," 1 *Vital Statistics of U.S.* 1–22 (1968).
12. 59 *American Bar Ass'n Journal* 1131 (October 1973).
13. Murdock, *Social Structures* 10–11 (1949).
14. Sutherland & Cressey, *Principles of Criminology* 178 (6th ed. 1960).
15. National Advisory Commission on Criminal Justice Standards and Goals, *A National Strategy to Reduce Crime* 25, 33–34 (1973). The Commission lamented the "declines in traditional family stability" (p. 25) foretold in rising rates of illegitimate births and divorces, but, surprisingly, its recommendations for action to combat crime included no proposals for strengthening the family. It is apparently easier and more acceptable to propose structural changes in the criminal justice system.
16. Evidence is reported in Monroe, *Schools of Psychoanalytic Thought* 185–86 (1955); Walters & Stinnert, "Parent-Child Relationships: A Decade Review," *A Decade of Family Research and Action* 99, 100–101 (Broderick, ed. 1971); Reiss,

"The University of the Family: A Conceptual Analysis," 27 *Journal of Marriage and the Family* 443 (1965).

17. Nimkoff, *Comparative Family Systems* 361 (1965).

18. Murdock, note 13 supra at 4–5.

19. Maxwell, *A Time to Choose* 14 (1972).

20. Mill, *On Liberty* 158 (7th ed. 1871).

21. Id. at 189.

22. Id.

23. Id. at 191.

24. Id. at 204.

25. Id. at 209–10.

26. Id. at 23. In light of Mill's reputation as an advocate of liberty it is also ironic that he applied his principle of liberty only to members of a "civilized community" (p. 23). In his view even despotism was "a legitimate mode of government in dealing with barbarians, provided the end be their improvement," because in that instance the end justifies the means (p. 24). We still have aristocrats who will cut the corners of liberty in order to improve the lot of the barbarians.

27. Packer, *The Limits of the Criminal Sanction* 266 (1968).

28. Id. at 267.

29. Quinney, "Who Is the Victim," 10 *Criminology, An Interdisciplinary Journal* 314 (Nov. 1972).

30. Neuhaus, "We Can't Legislate Morality: True or False?" *The National Observer* 24 (June 16, 1973).

31. Rostow, "The Enforcement of Morals," 18 *Camb. L. J.* 174, 197 (1960).

32. Stephen, *Liberty, Equality, Fraternity* (White ed. 1967).

33. Devlin, *The Enforcement of Morals* (1959); Hart, *Law, Liberty and Morality* (1963).

34. Devlin, "The Enforcement of Morals," The Maccabaen Lecture in Jurisprudence, 14 *Proceedings of the British Academy* 129, 138–41 (1959).

35. Hart, "Social Solidarity and the Enforcement of Morality," 35 *Univ. Chi. L. Rev.* 1, 2 (1967).

36. Id. at 9. A recent application of the "individual harm" standard is found in the use of the Surgeon General's findings on the harmful effects of tobacco as a basis for laws restricting cigarette advertising. To return briefly to my thesis about the standard-setting function of the law, I would suggest that in the long run the immediate effect of this law in ending advertising may be less significant than its impact as an official teacher of the semi-moralistic proposition that smoking is harmful and inadvisable.

37. Devlin, note 34 supra at 151.

38. Levi, "The Collective Morality of a Maturing Society," 30 *Wash. & Lee L. Rev.* 399, 426 (1973).

39. See Henkin, "Morals and the Constitution: The Sin of Obscenity," 63 *Colum. L. Rev.* 391 (1963); Schwartz, "Morals Offenses and the Model Penal Code," 63 *Col. L. Rev.* 669 (1963).

40. This argument comes from Neuhaus, note 30 supra.

41. Trop v. Dulles, 356 U.S. 86, 101 (1958).

42. "Address of Governor John Hancock," in Powers, *Crime and Punishment in Early Massachusetts, 1620–1692: A Documentary History* 192–93 (1966).

43. Levi, note 38 supra at 424.

44. Richardson, "Sexual Offenses under the Proposed Missouri Criminal Code," 38 *Mo. L. Rev.* 371, 387–88 (1973).

45. Furman v. Georgia, 408 U.S. 238, 443 (1972), quoted in Levi, note 38 supra at 420.

46. Levi, note 38 supra at 428–30.

47. Morris & Hawkins, note 1 supra at 19–23.

48. Packer, "Decriminalizing Heroin," *The New Republic* 12 (June 3, 1972).

49. U.S. House Committee on Foreign Affairs, House Res. 109 (92d Congress, 1st Session, Committee Report, 1971).

50. Markham, note 8 supra at 30.

51. Id.

52. E.g., Nahas, *Marihuana—Deceptive Weed* (1973); note 9 supra. But compare "First Report of the National Commission on Marihuana and Drug Abuse," *Marihuana: A Signal of Misunderstanding* 83–91 (1972).

53. Kaplan, "Official Views on Marijuana," *Science* 167 (Jan. 12, 1973).

54. Sources cited in Olivieri & Finkelstein, note 1 supra at 93; 117 *Congressional Record* 42344–45 (92d Congress, 1st Session).

55. "The National Commission Report," note 52 supra at 81, 133.

56. "The National Commission Report," note 52 supra at 81, 137.

57. Olivieri & Finkelstein, note 1 supra at 101.

58. "The National Commission Report," note 52 supra at 109–25, contains some evidence of this.

59. Nimmer, *Two Million Unnecessary Arrests* 1, 155 (1971); President's Commission on Law Enforcement and Administration of Justice, *Task Force Report: Drunkenness* 3–4 (1967). In general, see Bahr, *Skid Row* ch. 7 (1973).

13   In Defense of Decriminalization
        A Reply to Dallin Oaks

Gordon Hawkins (1976)

My attention has been drawn to Dallin H. Oaks's article, "The Popular Myth of the Victimless Crime," in the last issue of this Journal. That sounds pompous, but it's true. The former Chairman of the Editorial Board not only did the attention-drawing but also invited a response. And it seems to me that someone ought to respond to Mr. Oaks' provocative but courteous and scholarly animadversions.

As Mr. Oaks disclaims speaking for Brigham Young University or its sponsoring church, perhaps I should also enter a disclaimer. For my part, I can't claim to speak for the impressive gathering of political power that Mr. Oaks discerns ranged behind various discriminalization proposals. In fact, although the book I co-authored with Norval Morris (to which Mr. Oaks kindly refers a number of times) was addressed to "The Honest Politician," the response from politicians, when not downright hostile, could best be described as wary. Neither at the time of publication nor since has there been, as Mr. Oaks suggests, any feverish "climbing aboard the decriminalization bandwagon." However, things may be different in Utah.

Elsewhere, despite the increasing urgency of the need for effective crime control, politicians are still finding that they can give the appearance of responding to the crime problem by declaring war on drug addicts, prostitutes and pornographers. Such posturing is of course irrelevant to the continued alarming increase in violent and predatory crime, which has so extensively eroded the quality of life in America. It is because Dallin Oaks' article might be interpreted as providing some justification for that kind of wearisome irrelevance that, quite apart from considerations of polemic politesse, a reply to Mr. Oaks is called for.

The first thing to be said about "the popular myth of the victimless crime" is that, in addition to its not being notably popular, it is not mythical. In *The Honest Politician's Guide to Crime Control* we defined victimless crime as "crimes (which) lack victims, in the sense of complainants asking for the protection of the criminal law."[1] This definition may not be entirely satisfactory, but there can surely be no doubt that such crimes exist. To this Mr.

"In Defense of Decriminalization" appeared first in *University of Chicago Law Alumni Journal* 2, no. 1 (1976): 3–11.

Oaks' objection is two-fold. First, he says that some so-called victimless crimes have readily identifiable personal victims other than the criminal himself, such as "the innocent children whose family life is destroyed by the sexual irregularities of a parent or whose parents are pauperized by gambling or twisted by alcohol or drugs." Second, he maintains that in the case of some so-called victimless crimes, all society is the victim. Thus the rehabilitation of narcotics addicts is expensive, and taxpayers—all society—are the victims; pornography may ("hard empirical evidence . . . is scarce or nonexistent") be damaging to society; adultery, fornication, homosexuality and other irregular sexual behavior may ("I know of no empirical evidence") weaken the ideal and practice of family life in this country.

But what do these objections amount to? Of course it has to be admitted that there is a wide variety of parental behavior, by no means confined to sexual irregularity, gambling or the consumption of alchohol or drugs, and some of it no doubt benevolently motivated, which may harm innocent children. It is undeniable also that some narcotics addicts become a burden to tax-supported agencies; and although Mr. Oaks' inferences from the nonexistent evidence relating to the effects of pornography, adultery, fornication, etc., could be mistaken, he does not appear to represent them as more than contingent or possible. But does Mr. Oaks demonstrate any more than the point made by the late Professor Herbert Packer, that it is usually possible to make a more or less plausible argument that any given form of conduct involves some damage or risk of damage to the interests of others?[2]

This may be an effective rhetorical response to what Mr. Oaks calls "the rhetoric of so-called victimless crime" but it is hardly any more than that. The characterization of certain crimes as "victimless" is not intended to imply that there are kinds of criminal behavior, or for that matter kinds of human behavior, about which it can be stated categorically that they could not conceivably in any circumstances harm anyone other than the agent himself. It is intended merely to distinguish crimes in which the victimization is remote or uncertain and where no one *identifies* himself as the victim from those in which there are direct, identifiable victims. The distinction is not absolute, and no doubt most crimes could be theoretically ranged on a continuum, distinguished from one another only by imprecise and indefinite variations in the degree of harm occasioned to others. But although there would inevitably be disagreement about the appropriate placement on the continuum of many offenses, there would surely, *pace* Mr. Oaks, be little dispute about such polar extremes as violent predatory crimes on the one hand and noncommercial sexual conduct between consenting adults in private on the other. The distinction is in fact, as Packer said,

> a prudential criterion rather than a hard and fast distinction of principle . . . which brings into play a host of secular inquiries about the effects of subjecting the conduct in question to the criminal sanction.[3]

In short, it is the practical implications of drawing this distinction which are important. If we ask what are the practical implications of Mr. Oaks' failure to recognize it, we are compelled to the conclusion not merely that we should eschew decriminalization but that what society needs is a massive criminalization program. For there is a large range of widely disapproved behaviors, especially on the part of young people, which on the basis of unsubstantiated assertion ("common sense is sufficient evidence") could be assessed as detrimental to society and proper subjects for criminal sanctions. Of course Oaks does not advocate anything of the kind; indeed, he says quite specifically that he favors the decriminalization of some conduct which currently attracts criminal penalties. Yet, having rejected the "victimless" criterion, it is very hard to understand on what basis he discriminates between offenses.

Thus it is interesting to examine his varying attitudes to the types of behavior which he cites as destroying the family life of innocent children. In the case of sexual irregularities such as adultery he favors retaining criminal penalties, although many readers (especially any police officers amongst them, and possibly some congressmen) will have been relieved to find that he is "willing to accept a strategy of extremely restrained enforcement." Nevertheless, he favors the retention of the penalties primarily because of "the standard-setting and teaching functions of these laws on sexual morality. . . ." In the case of gambling, however, he says nothing about restrained enforcement, and presumably believes that the law should be enforced as fully as possible, although that is unlikely to alarm operators in this field.

In the case of alcohol consumption he says that "the teachings of experience oppose the criminalization of alcohol" and furthermore that he favors the "decriminalization of the laws against public drunkenness." In this connection he says that the criminal law has shown itself ineffective against alcohol; will be even less effective against public drunkenness; and requires significant law enforcement, judicial and penal resources that could be more usefully employed elsewhere. In the case of drugs he says, to take marijuana as an example, that while "logic would dictate similar treatment of alcohol and marijuana . . . the dictates of collective morality oppose the decriminalization of marijuana." (The dictates of collective morality, incidentally, were derived from an opinion poll which found that 64 percent of the adult public agreed that "using marijuana is morally offensive" compared to only 40 percent in the case of alcohol.)

The puzzling thing about this confusing congeries of attitudes is that in relation to the victims no consistent underlying principle can be discerned. "The innocent children whose family life is destroyed by the sexual irregularities of a parent" are entitled only to the modified protection of "extremely restrained" criminal law enforcement. "The innocent children . . .

whose parents are pauperized by gambling" are entitled to the protection of the criminal law only if the form of gambling happens to be illegal, although parents can as easily, if not more easily, be pauperized by legal gambling and the children will be no less innocent. "The innocent children . . . whose parents are . . . twisted by alcohol or drugs" will receive no protection at all if their parents indulge in a legal but lethal drug like alcohol, which kills 85,000 people per year, but will be protected by the criminal law if their parents use marijuana, which has never killed anyone.

"The law is an effective teacher," says Mr. Oaks, "and it can teach for good or for ill. Laws can affect the attitudes of our citizens about what is right and wrong, fair and unfair, proper and improper, advisable or inadvisable. The criminal law is a moral force. . . ." No one would dispute that the law can have an educative influence, but one wonders precisely what lessons the operations of the law in the areas mentioned in the last paragraph will inculcate into those who, because "the moral teachings and social controls of our nation's families, schools and churches seem to be progressively less effective," are bereft of guidance. They will certainly learn nothing about logic, although that won't worry Mr. Oaks unduly for he quotes approvingly Justice Holmes's observation that the life of the law has not been logic but experience. But can it be seriously maintained that they will learn anything about morality?

"The law is a schoolmaster," says Mr. Oaks, "as well as a policeman, and its curriculum includes morality." But he seems to forget a vital pedagogic principle: pupils learn as much from what is practiced as from what is preached. The law's educational role is not played out in a school for the blind. So it is relevant to ask what lesson is learned from the promulgation of a code of sexual behavior unrelated to reality (according to Kinsey, 95% of the male population is criminal by statutory standards) and its enforcement on an "extremely restrained" scale, in an arbitrary fashion? We are entitled to ask also in what way the law's pupils are edified by the selective prohibition of various forms of gambling and the spasmodic and discriminatory enforcement of these prohibitions, which are so widely disregarded that gambling provides the greatest source of revenue for organized crime. It is no less pertinent to inquire what moral principle is inculcated by the policy evinced in the decriminalization of alcohol, which gives rise to the most serious public health problem in the country and is responsible for some 28,000 motor vehicle fatalities each year, and the contemporaneous pursuit and prosecution (with a scale of penalties that causes even Mr. Oaks to blench) of the users of marijuana, about the harmful effects of which even a "not proven" verdict would grossly misrepresent the general tendency of the available evidence? Can it really be the case that morality will be the product of these examples? Or would hypocrisy be a likelier outcome?

Speaking of "the enormous educative influence of the law," Mr. Oaks says that "law focuses our attention on a particular problem, enacts a solution, and sometimes even provides and persuades us with reasons for the solution." But it is notable that the examples he gives—entitlement to social security, the legality of labor unions and the right to strike, the progressive income tax, and the right to be free from racial discrimination in government, common carriers and places of public accommodation—are somewhat remote from what would ordinarily be regarded by society as part of "the crime problem." In regard to that problem it can hardly be maintained that the law enacts a satisfactory solution, and even the most avid and devoted student must have difficulty in understanding, let alone being persuaded by, the reasons underlying the operations of the criminal law.

What is there to be learned from a situation in which, while citizens suffer helplessly from the ravages and incursions of violent and predatory criminals, we annually set our police to arresting four million assorted drunks, addicts, loiterers, vagrants, prostitutes and gamblers? What is there to be learned from the fact that, in a country which has more violent crime than any other nation, half of all arrests are for crimes without direct victims, crimes which bring no complainant to the station house, no call to the police switchboard? What is to be learned from the fact that the law's attempt to prevent people from obtaining goods and services they have clearly demonstrated they do not intended to forgo has led to the development of organized crime on a scale unparalleled anywhere else in the world and an equally unsurpassed degree of corruption amongst law enforcement agents and public officials?

Mr. Oaks is well aware of, and of course disputes, the conclusions which Norval Morris and I arrived at after careful consideration not only to the facts referred to above but also of many other features of the crime problem. But as there may conceivably be readers who are not familiar with those conclusions, I may perhaps be forgiven for reproducing them here:

> . . . [W]e must strip off the moralistic excrescences on our criminal justice system so that it may concentrate on the essential. The prime function of the criminal law is to protect our persons and our property; these purposes are now engulfed in a mass of other distracting, inefficiently performed, legislative duties. When the criminal law invades the spheres of private morality and social welfare, it exceeds its proper limits at the cost of neglecting its primary tasks. This unwarranted extension is expensive, ineffective, and criminogenic.
>
> . . . We think it improper, impolitic, and usually socially harmful for the law to intervene or attempt to regulate the private moral conduct of the citizen. In this country we have a highly moralistic criminal law and a long tradition of using it as an instrument for coercing

men toward virtue. It is a singularly inept instrument for that purpose. It is also an unduly costly one, both in terms of harm done and in terms of the neglect of the proper tasks of law enforcement.

Most of our legislation concerning drunkenness, narcotics, gambling, and sexual behavior and a good deal of it concerning juvenile delinquency is wholly misguided. It is based on an exaggerated conception of the capacity of the criminal law to influence men. We incur enormous collateral disadvantage costs for that exaggeration and we overload our criminal justice system to a degree which renders it grossly defective as a means of protection in the areas where we really need protection—from violence, incursions into our homes, and depredations of our property.[4]

In *The Honest Politician's Guide to Crime Control* we then go on to detail the ways in which the "overreach" of the criminal law contributes to the crime problem. But there is no need to go into that here, for Mr. Oaks in his article provides a very fair and succinct summary of our argument in this connection and even acknowledges that it has "considerable force" at least in regard to offenses like those relating to the drug traffic, gambling and prostitution. This brings us, however, to what is surely the crucial question in the decriminalization debate.

That question is: what is the criminal law good for? It is of course a question with which Dallin Oaks is concerned, for he quotes and rejects Lord Devlin's assertion that "the law must base itself on Christian morals and to the limit of its ability to enforce them."[5] By contrast he believes, if I read him aright, that the law must base itself on what he refers to as "collective morality" and to the limits of its ability enforce that. Our criminal laws, he says, "teach and compel the observance of standards of behavior not demonstrably related to harm to others or the survival of society but nevertheless important to our individual or collective well-being." And by way of example he cites such laws as those forbidding obscenity which protect "our traditional and moral sensibilities rather than our physical welfare."

The example is an interesting one, for the history of law enforcement in the field of obscenity in recent years raises not only the question of how effectively "traditional moral sensibilities" have been protected but also the more fundamental question whether, in a society with increasingly manifold moralities and various aesthetic standards, the law has any business, beyond preventing affronts to public decency, in determining what individual citizens may be permitted to hear, view or read. Individual susceptibilities to pleasurable or painful experiences are extremely diverse in our society, and there is no universal conformity with "traditional moral sensibilities." Nor is there any reason to believe that our individual or collective well-being would be enhanced if such conformity could be brought about by means of criminal sanctions. Incidentally, Mr. Oaks' curious categorical assertion that it is "common experience that the pictures and literature of the gutter produce thoughts of the gutter and the thought is parent to the act" seems to imply the existence of an unusual uniformity of response of a rather different character.

The essential point though is that, just as Dallin Oaks has *his* reasons for rejecting Lord Devlin's view that the law must be based on "Christian morals" and must try to enforce them, so in a pluralistic, secular society there will be those who have *their* reasons for rejecting Dallin Oaks' views that the law must be based on "collective morality" and must try to enforce that. Nor is this at all surprising. Certainly what he tells us about collective morality is, to say the least, uninspiring. Thus it appears to be in favor of the death penalty: "The popularity of current efforts to restore the death penalty identifies this as another area where the lawmakers . . . may have led out too far in advance to the collective morality." It appears to be opposed to the prohibition of alcoholic beverages: "The middle-class citizens who defied prohibition demonstrated that this law had exceeded and could not alter our collective morality." It appears to disapprove of marijuana; as noted earlier, "64 percent of the adult public agreed that 'using marijuana is morally offensive.'" It appears, in Missouri at any rate, to regard homosexuality as immoral: "A majority of the people in Missouri still regard homosexuality as disgusting, degrading, degenerate and a threat to society." In fact, it appears generally to be against "any sexual behavior outside the bonds of marriage . . . our moral standards forbid it."

Moreover, whatever the content of collective morality, it is by no means clear what Mr. Oaks means by his contention that "the law will be discredited if it attempts to decriminalize conduct condemned under collective morality." In what sense, for instance, would the law be discredited if adultery, now punishable in some states by up to five years' imprisonment (and Mr. Oaks believes in retaining the criminal penalties on adultery), were to be declared no longer subject to the criminal law? No doubt there would be those who were annoyed by the change just as there are many people who are annoyed by the failure to decriminalize adultery. But even among those most annoyed it is hard to believe that *the law*, including all the other rules proscribing crimes against the person and against property, would thereafter be viewed as invalid or illegitimate.

Ironically, it used to be argued by those urging the decriminalization of adultery, that the law was "discredited" by the retention on the statute book of laws which were virtually unenforceable. It wasn't a very good argument then, and it isn't improved by being stood on its head. In its earlier usage what seems to have been suggested was that resentment of the unfairness in operation or impropriety of a particular prohibition would lead to disapproval of all other prohibitions in the criminal law. In Mr. Oaks's usage what seems to be suggested is that resentment of the impropriety of the repeal of a particular prohibition would lead to contempt for, or dissatisfaction with, the rest of the criminal code. In neither formulation does it appear particularly plausible. There are few people who could not think both of some legal prohibitions of which they disapprove and of some types of conduct not prohibited which might profitably be prohibited; but in neither case does this cause them to refuse to accept the criminal law in general or regard it as discredited.

What is at issue, *au fond*, is surely the question posed above: what is the criminal law good for? Or to make it a little more concrete: are there good reasons for using the criminal law against this type of conduct? To which the beginning of an answer was given nearly sixty years ago by the late Ernst Freund when he said: "Not every standard of conduct that is fit to be observed is also fit to be enforced."[6] And not even the most rigorous moralist would be likely to disagree with that and argue that all morally wrong or undesirable actions should be proscribed by the criminal law. At the same time it is obvious that when we come to consider which standards of conduct fit to be observed are also fit to be enforced, no meaningful answers can be given which are not related to a particular political and social context. What was an acceptable answer in sixteenth-century Geneva under John Calvin would not be acceptable in Geneva today. What would be acceptable in a culturally homogeneous society under an authoritarian patriarchal form of government would not be acceptable in a culturally heterogeneous society under a democratic form of government.

That, of course, is what underlies the answer suggested as a possible one by H. L. A. Hart, to which Dallin Oaks refers so briefly that all that emerges is that he rejects it. That answer is that the criminal law should enforce only that part of social morality which contains those restraints and prohibitions essential to the existence of a society of human beings. This moral minimum essential for social life "includes rules restraining the free use of violence and minimal forms of rules regarding honesty, promise-keeping, fair dealing, and property."[7]

In every society discriminations are made between those aspects of social morality or society's moral code which are suitable for legal enforcement, and are required to be enforced by the criminal law, and those which are not. Hart's suggestion is that in a society where there is no single moral code, beyond recognition of the restraints necessary for social cohesion, plural moralities may co-exist in a condition of mutual toleration. Indeed, he suggests that, in fact, "over wide areas of modern life, sometimes hiding behind lip-service to an older common morality, there actually are divergent moralities living in peace."[8]

The decriminalization movement and the enormous growth of public discussions of the relationship between law and morality in the last two decades can be viewed in fact as the reflection of a condition of moral plurality. Indeed, if one were to accept Dallin Oaks' description of the contemporary scene—with a "decriminalization bandwagon" attracting adherents, amassing power and gathering momentum; with a substantial aggregation of publicity and political power gathering behind various de-criminalization proposals; and with criminal law revisions already adopted or under favorable consideration amounting to "revolutionary changes in the function and content of criminal law"—one might conclude that any attempt to stem the tide and legally enforce standards reflecting "traditional moral sensibilities" must be hopelessly anachronous.

But the decriminalization movement insofar as it can be identified does not necessarily involve the rejection of traditional moral standards or the values reflected in "collective morality" insofar as that can be identified. Support for decriminalization does not involve the advocacy of general permissiveness in the field of morals. What Ernst Freund was concerned about was our over-reliance upon the criminal law to such an extent that, as he said, we submit to public regulation and control "in ways that would appear inconceivable to the spirit of oriental despotism."[9] Francis Allen had a similar concern when he wrote that "the system of criminal justice may be viewed as a weary Atlas upon whose shoulders we have heaped a crushing burden of responsibilities. . . ."[10] In other words, the argument is about the extent to which the criminal law, rather than other means of social control, is the appropriate vehicle for dealing with undesirable behavior and motivating compliance with social rules. Disagreement about what types of conduct should be prohibited by the criminal law is not necessarily connected with disagreement about what forms of conduct are undesirable or deserve moral censure.

Moreover, not only does support for decriminalization not imply support for general moral permissiveness, neither does it imply support for wholesale legalization and the total deregulation of conduct. As the President's Commission *Task Force Report: The Courts* put it:[11]

> The criminal law is not the sole or even the primary method relied upon by society to motivate compliance with its rules. The community depends on a broad spectrum of sanctions to control conduct. Civil liability, administrative regulations, licensing, and noncriminal penalties carry the brunt of the regulatory job in many very important fields, with little additional force contributed by such infrequently used criminal provisions as may appear in the statute books.

What is required is better regulation. One of the crucial points to be made in this context is that *it is impossible to regulate behavior that you prohibit.* The proper role of the law in many of the areas under discussion is to back up rational regulatory efforts with criminal sanctions. The fundamental objection to the Volstead Act is not that it "exceeded and could not alter our collective morality," as Dallin Oaks would have it, but that it was prohibitory, not regulatory. Repeal of the Act led to a reasonably enforceable regulatory system, with admitted defects but inflicting nothing like the societal damage caused by Prohibition. Oaks of course is aware that the choice is not between the use of the criminal law and complete decontrol. For in advocating the decriminalization of the laws against public drunkenness, vagrancy and similar crimes, he says that the legitimate social interest which the criminal law seeks to protect in this area ("cleaning the streets of derelicts") is "one that ought to be pursued by some civil remedy that is subject neither to the abuses involved in the vague criminal statutes that seek to punish drunks and vagabonds nor to the expenses entailed in arrest, booking, jail, and court appearance to achieve the simple expedient of transporting a person out of a situation where he is a threat to himself or others."

What is required is that we should substitute for our present absolute prohibitions multiple and diverse strategies of regulatory intervention which effectively control that which we ineffectively attempt to abolish. In the case of drugs, for example, quite a complex regulatory system would be necessary. The rational control of dangerous drugs might involve (1) the *prohibition* of nonmedical importation, manufacture and sale of opium derivatives like heroin, (2) the *regulation* of the prescription and distribution of some other drugs like the barbiturates, and (3) the *decriminalization* of the medically controlled consumption of some drugs by addicts and of the consumption of some other drugs like marijuana by any adult.

The important point about drugs such as heroin is not whether crimes like the acquisition, purchase or possession of it should properly be described as "victimless" because of the burden imposed on taxpayers when addicts wreck their health and destroy their capacity to work. The important point is whether the invocation of the criminal process so that the addict lives in almost perpetual violation of one or several criminal laws is the most effective, economical and least collaterally damaging way of exercising social control. Mr. Oaks is well aware of the problem of collateral disadvantage costs and admirably summarizes the way in which the effect of criminal penalties "is to increase other crimes." He does not, however, mention the fact that the use of criminal penalties in the case of drug addiction also stimulates the recruitment of addicts.

Thus he notes that the high prices that criminal organizations engaged in the narcotics trade force addicts to pay cause addicts to commit other crimes like robbery and theft in order to support their addiction. He does not mention that one of the most common methods of obtaining money to support addiction is that of becoming a narcotics salesman or "pusher." So that the addict engages in proselyting, seeking to promote the sale of the drug by influencing or inducing others to experiment with it, so that they in turn may become addicts and regular customers. In this way the prohibition of the addicts' access to drugs spreads the contagion and helps to attract newcomers to the market.

Clearly the way to reduce that market, reduce addiction-supportive crime, and reduce the incentive for organized criminals to engage in the narcotics traffic is to make narcotics available to addicts through controlled outlets. Recently law-enforcement efforts to intercept drugs at the source have enjoyed increased success and this suggests that the problem of cutting off the supply to non-addicted users would be manageable if the addicts' demand were otherwise supplied. The recommendation of the Consumers Union report on *Licit and Illicit Drugs* that "policies and practices be promptly revised to insure that no narcotics addict need get his drugs from the black market"[12] is based on a sound analysis of the nature of the problem. And until that is recognized, all efforts at control and treatment are doomed to impotence. Dallin Oaks appears to suggest that the only alternative to retaining our current criminal penalties on drugs is "making drugs readily available for all who wish(ed) to indulge"; but, as far as I know, no one has ever advocated the withdrawal of all regulation and the making available of heroin or any other dangerous drug for unrestricted purchase.

Few would question Dallin Oaks' statement that "Heroin and other hard drugs stand convicted of so much human misery and such staggering social costs that there can be no doubt of the propriety of extensive government efforts to discourage their use." But it is reasonable to question the wisdom of the retention of the criminal penalties on the possession of currently illegal drugs as a feature of those government efforts, when the considerable law enforcement resources committed in this area operate so ineffectively (and could be more profitably used elsewhere) and, as Oaks acknowledges, those penalties as currently enforced have the effect of increasing the overall level of crime and moreover also have the effect of stimulating the recruitment of drug addicts. To say that the "criminal penalties are necessary if the law is to perform its function of teaching against and discouraging the use of drugs" not only ignores the enormous social costs of this particular mode of social education but rests on the extremely dubious assumption that the use of criminal penalties is an effective educational technique in relation to drug abuse.

It is necessary, in conclusion, to say something about another of Dallin Oaks' assertions about the function of the criminal law in relation to behaviors condemned by "collective morality." "The law," he says, "must not depart too far from the collective morality, either to lead or to lag, or it will lose its force as a prescriber of behavior and its persuasiveness as a teacher and setter of standards." And it is clear that he believes that the decriminalization of drug offenses would be opposed to "the dictates of collective morality." Yet it is questionable whether in matters of this kind legislators should regard themselves as bound to do no more than reflect in their decisions what an often ill-informed constituency happens to feel about an issue.

There are occasions when legislators are called upon to act in accordance with the conception of the proper role of a representative set out in Burke's classic "Speech to the Electors of Bristol" in 1774; in essence they should vote according to their own judgment and informed consideration of the facts.[13] When legislators act in that way, they may by their own actions produce a change in public opinion. Indeed, Dallin Oaks gives a striking example of this himself when, in relation to the educative influence of the law, he cites the effect of the passage of the Civil Rights Act of 1964. "With the passage of the Civil Rights Act," he says, "we not only changed our law but we also changed our minds. Today the proposition adopted in that legislation is well accepted from coast to coast and from north to south."

In relation to criminal law reform and penal reform, where public opinion is frequently apathetic if not hostile and sometimes influenced by facile demogoguery, the acceptance of "the dictates of collective morality" should never be unquestioning. As Gresham Sykes has said:[14]

> There is a great temptation to treat society as if it were a person—to speak of society doing this or that, the reactions of society, the morals of society, and so on. The usage is convenient, for it avoids a cumbersome phrasing; but it carries the danger of viewing society as much more homogeneous than it is in actuality. Society is a diversity, a collection of individuals with varied patterns of sentiments and behavior. And this variation is particularly marked in the area of crime and punishment. How and why the criminal should be penalized is subject to sharp dispute.

And in relation to the death penalty, where Dallin Oaks says that the lawmakers "may have led out too far in advance of the collective morality," it is arguable that such a lead was desirable. Thus, R. J. Buxton in a 1973 article on "The Politics of Criminal Law Reform," in *The American Journal of Comparative Law*, notes that although in England, in the case of capital punishment the legislators "still lead from the front," as a result "the tone of the debate has moved on to a markedly more rational level."[15] Both responsible lawmaking and what Dallin Oaks calls "preserving the essential relationship between the moral values of citizens and the requirements and teachings of law in a democratic society" require more than assiduous attention to public opinion polls.

Notes

1. N. Morris & G. Hawkins, *The Honest Politician's Guide to Crime Control* 6 (1970).

2. H. Packer, *The Limits of the Criminal Sanction* 266 (1968).

3. Id. at 266–67.

4. N. Morris & G. Hawkins, n. 1 supra, at 1–3.

5. Devlin, "The Enforcement of Morals," 14 *Proceedings of the British Academy* 151 (1954).

6. E. Freund, *Standards of American Legislation* 106 (1917).

7. Hart, "Social Solidarity and the Enforcement of Morality," 35 *U. Chi. L. Rev.* 9–10 (1967).

8. Id. at 13.

9. E. Freund, n. 6 supra, at 21.

10. F. Allen, *The Borderland of Criminal Justice* 4 (1964).

11. President's Commission on Law Enforcement and Administration of Justice, *Task Force Report: The Courts* 98 (1967).

12. Brecher, *Licit and Illicit Drugs* 530 (1972).

13. E. Burke, *Works*, Vol. II, 89–98 (1865).

14. G. Sykes, *Crime and Society* 81 (1956).

15. Buxton, "The Politics of Criminal Law Reform: England," 21 *Am. J. Comp. Law* 244 (1973).

Nine   Sentencing

14 Sentencing Reform in America

Michael H. Tonry and Norval Morris (1978)

In *Criminal Law—The General Part* Glanville Williams subjected the principles of substantive criminal law to sustained analysis. His success is manifest, requiring neither elaboration nor documentation. In the United
States, the American Law Institute embarked on a similar and contemporaneous enterprise to develop a Model Penal Code—a project in which
Glanville Williams also played an important role.[1] *The General Part* and the
Model Penal Code are now classics, the starting points for serious analysis of
questions of substantive criminal law in both England and the United States.

Efforts to bring system and principle to American criminal law administration have shifted in recent years from substance to procedure, and from
procedure to sentencing. In this paper, we describe that shift and attempt to
identify some of the problems and perceptions which underlie current
efforts at sentencing reform in the federal system of justice. Most recent
sentencing reform proposals in the United States urge the adoption of
determinate sentencing systems intended to reduce unwarranted sentencing
disparities and to establish more principled and predictable sentencing
practices. We will discuss two recent federal sentencing reform proposals—
the Kennedy-McClellan[2] and Hart-Javits[3] Bills in the United States Senate.
The Kennedy-McClellan Bill proposes the establishment of a federal sentencing commission—a politically insulated independent government commission—which would promulgate presumptive sentencing guidelines for
judicial sentencing decisions, though the court would retain authority to
disregard the guidelines in appropriate cases and to impose any other lawful
sentence. The Hart-Javits proposal would also establish a sentencing commission, but under this Bill the commission's sentencing standards would be
prescriptive, fixing the sentence to be imposed. The Kennedy-McClellan
Bill offers the greater promise for achievement of the goals of sentencing
reform. Sentencing proposals whch too severely constrain the sentencing
court tend in the United States to result in an unfortunate transfer of
dispositive sentencing power from the judge and the parole release author-

"Sentencing Reform in America" is reprinted with permission from *Reshaping the
Criminal Law: A Festschrift in Honour of Glanville Williams*, edited by P. R.
Glazebrook (London: Sweet and Maxwell, Ltd., 1978).

ities (who together now determine the duration of most prison sentences) to the prosecutor.

In this essay we will discuss several practical and jurisprudential questions which these sentencing reform proposals raise, particularly the systemic difficulties confronting any attempt to re-order sentencing discretions, and we will consider the proposition, implicit in many determinate sentencing proposals, that unequal sentences are necessarily unjust. We will conclude by offering our immodestly dogmatic views on sentencing reform in the United States.

I

Substance to Procedure to Sentencing

Criminal law codification movements flowered in the nineteenth century, with the work of Macaulay and others on the Indian Penal Code, of the Criminal Law Commissioners and Stephen in England, and of Livingston and Field in the United States. In the United States, criminal law codification thereafter lay dormant until the 1950s when the American Law Institute's draftsmen began their work on the Model Penal Code. Piecemeal legislation and dogmatically diverse case law had multiplied anomalies and undermined principles. The American Law Institute sought to influence legislative reform both in the states and in the federal system by drafting a model criminal code to bring order and principle not only to the substantive criminal law but also to its system of sanctions.

Any morally acceptable criminal law system, not based on determinist premises, requires a coherent set of substantive rules which define proscribed conduct with clarity, which differentiate on reasonable grounds between serious and minor offences, which comport with notions of moral and legal responsibility, and which recognise mitigating, excusing and justifying explanations for otherwise culpable conduct by otherwise responsible persons.

The Model Penal Code provided such a basis for a morally acceptable criminal law system and inspired the movement for criminal law codification which swept the United States during the 1960s and seventies. New state criminal codes were enacted, many influenced by the provisions of the Model Penal Code;[4] all to a degree reflect the work of Glanville Williams. The proposed new federal criminal code of the influential United States National Commission on Reform of Federal Criminal Laws[5] bears the vivid imprint of these influences as does the Kennedy-McClellan Bill, the pending proposal for a federal criminal code.

Hindsight demonstrates that the Model Penal Code was only part of the answer. A principled substantive criminal law is a necessary but not a sufficient precondition to decent and efficient criminal law administration. A criminal code cannot achieve just results unless it is administered fairly, impartially and efficiently. This is an area neglected in legislative reform but which has been the focus of judicial concern in the United States.

During the late 1950s and the sixties, the United States Supreme Court attempted substantial reform of the criminal justice system by recognising and amplifying constitutional procedural standards applicable to police, prosecutorial and judicial processing of criminal cases. Relying upon the due process and equal protection clauses of the Fourteenth Amendment to the Constitution, the Supreme Court, in a series of celebrated cases, prescribed *inter alia*, minimum constitutional standards guaranteeing the rights to counsel and jury trial and regulating the use of search warrants, arrest warrants, identification lineups and informers. *Mapp* v. *Ohio* (1961)[6] and *Miranda* v. *Arizona* (1966)[7] held that the state courts must enforce exclusionary rules forbidding use of unlawfully obtained evidence against criminal defendants. Recently that movement has been slowed, perhaps stopped or turned back; the struggle for procedural fairness continues, albeit no longer led by the Supreme Court.[8]

The search for a fair and just system of criminal law in the United States has now taken yet another turn. The objectives of current reform efforts are the judicial and administrative sentencing processes. Substantive laws can define criminal offences, the commission of which authorises the state to assert penal authority over its citizens. Equable criminal procedures can increase the likelihood that determinations of criminal guilt will be made impartially and dispassionately. But these will not suffice, certainly in the United States. A procedurally perfect administration of the Model Penal Code would, without more, be perceived by many to produce, and would in fact produce, unfair and uneven results.

Compelling evidence exists that, seen as a system, the disposition of convicted criminal offenders in America is capricious and inconsistent. Decisions as to the nature and duration of punishment flow from a complex network of legislatively authorised sentences and even more complex divisions of sentencing power between the police, prosecutors, defense counsel, judges, parole authorities and correctional administrators.

At the time of writing, four states—California, Indiana, Maine and Oregon—have adopted determinate sentencing laws and many other states are considering doing so. Several developments of the past decade have focused attention on sentencing reform. Before describing and commenting on the federal sentencing reform proposals, we will describe several of those developments: disillusionment with the rehabilitative ideal; increased concern over sentencing disparities; recognition of discretion as a proper object of study and focus for reform; and a renascence of retribution as a respectable justification of punishment.

Rejection of Rehabilitation as a Purpose of Punishment

Recent exhaustive surveys of correctional research evaluations by Robert Martinson in the United States[9] and R. S. Brody[10] in England counsel that our demonstrated capacity constructively to change prisoners does not justify imposing punishment for that purpose.

The consensus among American scholars and reformist politicians in 1977 is that penal rehabilitation can no longer justify taking power over offenders or the extension of the duration of punishment otherwise imposed. Rehabilitation has been rejected by many as a proper consideration in decisions to punish or extend the duration of punishment, to be replaced by various conceptions (and mixtures) of desert and deterrence.

The problem is not that we cannot affect criminal behaviour. In many cases we know how coerce, cure and prevent future criminal (at least violent) conduct. We choose not to do so. We can kill offenders; chemical surgical and psychological devices can change personalities and behaviour; protracted, secure imprisonment will "cure" all but the most exceptional proclivity to violent crime. Fundamental views of the importance of the individual, historical evidence of the misuse of power, moral and ethical self-doubt, prevent us from so doing. Coerced cure within ethical limits does not appear to work. We may be able to facilitate self-change by providing opportunities for those so motivated, but no more.

Scepticism about the efficacy and morality of rehabilitative measures may be too fashionable. Although rehabilitative programs in prisons have been characterised more by false rhetoric than by solid achievements, it does not follow that rehabilitative ideals and programs should be discarded. Though "rehabilitation" must cease to be a purpose of the criminal sanction, this does not mean that the various developed treatment programs within prisons should be abandoned. To the contrary: they need expansion. But it does mean that they must not be seen as purposive in the sense that criminals are to be sent to prison for treatment. We must rehabilitate the rehabilitative ideal by liberating it from the corrupting effects of coercive participation and connection with the duration of imprisonment.[11]

Rediscovery of Sentencing Discretion

The American system of sentencing has long produced grossly dissimilar sentences for like offenders convicted of like offences, and sentences disproportionate—on any rational punitive hierarchy—to the gravity of offences or the cupability of offenders. Unjustifiable sentencing disparities has long been recognised as a problem in America, but it has recently received renewed attention. Chief Justice Warren Burger observed in his 1976 address on "The State of the Judiciary": "some form of review procedure is needed to deal with this dilemma [of sentencing disparity]." Forty-five years ago, for example, Messrs. Gaudet, Harris and St. John reported the results of a study of all sentences imposed by six New Jersey judges for 19 different criminal offences, randomly assigned to them over a nine-year period. One judge (1,489 cases) imposed prison sentences in 57.7 per cent. of cases and suspended sentences or probation in 39.2 per cent. of cases. Another (1,693 cases) ordered imprisonment in only 33.6 per cent. of cases and imposed probation or suspended sentences in 64.2 per cent. The imprisonment rates for all six judges were 33.6 per cent.—35.6 per cent.—45.0 per cent.—50.0 per cent.—53.3 per cent.—57.7 per cent.[12]

Nor is modern evidence of sentencing disparity lacking. In a recent experiment in the Federal Second Circuit, all 43 active trial judges and seven senior trial judges rendered sentences in 20 identical cases described in pre-sentence reports (which contained information regarding criminal charges, plea or trial, prior record, age, narcotic history, family background, etc.). Sentences varied enormously. In one case the sentence varied from three to 20 years. In another the range was probation to seven and a half years. Substantial variation persisted even when extreme sentences were disregarded. The norm was the absence of a norm. The average disparity from the mean was 48 per cent.[13]

In a recent study of sentences in federal courts throughout the country, Tiffany, Avichai and Peters found substantial variation in sentences that related to such apparently unprincipled factors as type of trial: bench or jury; type of counsel: retained or appointed (but only in bench trials); race of defendant (but only where defendant had no prison record).[14]

The empirical literature on sentencing disparities is enormous, growing and unanswerable.[15]

The Discovery of Other Discretions

Kenneth Culp Davis' *Discretionary Justice* (1969) focused attention on the unregulated discretion which percolates the entire criminal justice system. Concern for identification and regulation of these discretions became a growth industry.[16]

Many actors and institutions affect whether any sentence is imposed and, if so, of what type and duration. Legislatures define criminal offences and establish sentencing choices. Police decide (or decide not) to process a complaint, to file an arrest report, in some jurisdictions to file a criminal complaint. Prosecutors decide whether to file a complaint, and for what charges (or whether to prosecute a police-filed complaint), whether to accept a plea bargain, and on what terms, whether to recommend or not oppose a specific sentence to the court. Defence counsel play a role in plea, charge and sentence bargaining. Courts can dismiss charges. Courts (and juries) determine guilt and often can limit sentence maxima by convicting a defendant of one offence rather than another. After conviction, the prosecutor can offer sentence recommendations. Judges impose sentences: whether imprisonment, probation or fine and of what duration or amount. Judges can also vary sentences by imposing concurrent or consecutive sentences on defendants convicted of multiple offences. Correctional authorities affect prison release dates and eligibility by awarding, not awarding or revoking good behaviour credits towards sentence length. Correctional authorities influence release decisions by endorsing or opposing convicted offenders' parole petitions and can provide extended and terminal furloughs. Parole authorities can release a convicted offender at any time after he has become eligible for parole release—typically after serving the greater of one year or one-third of his sentence. Executive officials have legal authority to pardon or grant clemency.

Having rediscovered sentencing discretion, we have identified some of its properties: like quicksilver, when obstructed, discretion flows somewhere else; unlike quicksilver, it cannot be contained. If legislative fixed sentences do not permit judges to decide sentence length, prosecutors become the primary sentencers and they decide what charges to file, what plea bargains to accept, what sentences to recommend or not oppose. When indeterminate sentencing deprives the prosecutor and the judge of much of their sentencing power, parole release authorities determine sentence. If determinate sentencing deprives the parole release authorities of their sentencing power, the prosecutor and the judge will play the dispositive roles. Someone must do it.

The Renascence of Retribution

Retribution, or deserts, has replaced rehabilitation as the conventional justification for the amount of punishment. The renascence of retribution as a respectable justification for punishment in America can fairly be attributed to *Struggle for Justice* (1971), a report on American prisons prepared by a Working Party for the American Friends Service Committee. The Quaker Working Party proposed a system of determinate sentencing which others have since attempted to justify.

Writing in California where the rehabilitative ideal produced the most conspicuously indeterminate and individualised prison sentences in the United States, the Working Party was troubled by immense disparity in sentences imposed and time served by prisoners in California and proposed the adoption of a system in which:

> Whatever sanction or short sentence is imposed is to be fixed by law. There is to be no discretion in setting sentences, no indeterminate sentences, and unsupervised street release is to replace parole.[17]

Definitions of offences should specify relevant aggravating or mitigating circumstances to justify variations in the normal sentence. Other circumstances of the offender and the offence should be irrelevant:

> A necessary corollary of our principle of punishing for the act is the specific punishment be assigned to the act. All persons found guilty of the same criminal act under the same circumstances are dealt with uniformly.[18]

The Working Party proposals were essentially negative. The rehabilitative ideal was inherently flawed and functionaries cannot be trusted to make discretionary decisions without bias or caprice. Others provided the positive justification for retributive punishment. Andrew von Hirsch's *Doing Justice* (1976) and Norval Morris' *The Future of Imprisonment* (1974) undertook principled analyses of punishment to justify, respectively, ostensibly retributive and utilitarian systems of punishment designed to achieve many of the Quakers' goals. David Fogel's *We Are the Living Proof . . .* (1975) traversed much the same territory as *Struggle for Justice* and proposed an influential "flat-time" system of sentencing.

Two influential private commissions proposed adoption of frankly retributive sentencing regimes. Andrew von Hirsch's *Doing Justice* (1976), the report of the Committee for the Study of Incarceration, proposed a system of determinate sentencing in which the trial court would be required to impose a specific sentence, subject only to authorised variations, to reflect defined aggravating and mitigating circumstances. *Fair and Certain Punishment* (1976), a report of the Twentieth Century Fund Task Force on Criminal Sentencing, refined and developed the *Doing Justice* proposals and offered a more sophisticated system of presumptive sentencing in which the trial court could impose an applicable sentence from within a narrow "presumptive range" or impose any other lawful sentence on condition that reasons be given for the sentence imposed and subject to a right of sentence appeal. Bills were introduced in the United States Senate by Senator Lloyd Bentsen to establish a sentencing system based on the *Fair and Certain Punishment* proposals[19] and by Senators Gary Hart and Jacob Javits to establish a *Doing Justice* approach to federal sentencing.[20]

The new retributivism has influence most modern proposals for sentencing reform, including those discussed in this essay. The sentencing schemes which have been built on the ruins of the rehabilitative ideal and the foundations of desert and utility attempt to establish tariffs for crime.

II

The headlong leap towards determinate sentencing has resulted from the developments just described and no doubt others as well. The real and indefensible phenomenon of unjustified and unjustifiable sentencing disparities and modern doubts about rehabilitation and unguided sentencing discretions provide persuasive support for determinate sentencing proposals. In our view most determinate sentencing proposals fail to recognise the complexity of the sentencing process in the United States and the central importance of prosecutorial sentencing power. To the extent that determinate sentencing proposals legislate specific sentences for specific offences committed by defined categories of offenders, the judge's sentencing power will be displaced by the prosecutor, not by the legislature. In 1976, 85 per cent. of federal criminal convictions resulted from guilty pleas. Many of those pleas were induced by prosecutorial undertakings to dismiss, or not file, certain charges, or to recommend or not oppose a specific sentence. There is little reason to believe, and much reason to doubt, that unreviewable and often invisible prosecutorial undertakings to dismiss, or not file, certain charges, or to recommend or not oppose a specific sentence. There is little reason to believe, and much reason to doubt, that unreviewable and often invisible prosecutorial sentencing practices will be fairer, more predictable or more just than judicial sentencing practices.

Illustrative Reform Proposals

Three critical aspects of sentencing reform proposals are (i) what sorts of guidance the new system would offer to the sentencing judge, (ii) where formal sentencing authority would be placed and how that would relate to the *locus* of real sentencing power, and (iii) what mechanisms would be created to control discretionary sentencing decisions.

In our view, both the Hart-Javits and Kennedy-McClellan Bills offer promise as means to the achievement of a more predictable and principled system of criminal sanctions. Both Bills envisage a sentencing commission which would develop known, knowable and principled standards to guide judicial sentencing decisions. The greatest deficiency of the Hart-Javits Bill is that it would apparently authorise a sentencing commission to develop sentencing policy, but—by removing most overt sentencing discretion from the court—would place real sentencing power in the hands of the prosecutor. The Kennedy-McClellan Bill does not suffer from the defect (subject always to the prosecutor's general influence on sentences through plea bargaining practices) but contains inadequate checking mechanisms to control judicial sentencing decisions.

Prescriptive Sentencing—the Hart-Javits Bill

The Hart-Javits Bill would establish an independent sentencing commission which would be appointed by the President by and with the consent of the Senate. The sentencing discretions of the sentencing commission and the sentencing judge would be rigidly structured. The commission would be charged to establish prescriptive guidelines for sentencing consistent with the principle that the severity of a sentence "shall be commensurate with the gravity of the criminal offence to which such presumptive sentence is assigned." The commission would establish schedules setting forth gradations of gravity for each criminal offence and prescribing a "presumptive" sentence for each gradation of severity.

The commission would establish schedules and rules prescribing variations from presumptive sentences to reflect aggravating and mitigating circumstances, specifying what types of circumstances should be considered in mitigation and aggravation, and for each type of mitigating or aggravating circumstance, specifying a particular amount or maximum amount or maximum amount of variation from the presumptive sentence. Aggravating circumstances could not be invoked to justify an increase of the presumptive sentence by more than 50 per cent. Except for designated violent offences, no presumptive sentence would exceed five years.

Under the Hart-Javits Bill, the sentencing judge would be required to impose the prescribed presumptive sentence varied only as authorised by rule to recognise aggravating and mitigating circumstances. The only basis for an appeal against sentence would be that "the sentencing judge imposed such sentence in violation of a rule established by the Commission under this Act or a provision of this Act." Sentences not authorised by applicable guidelines would constitute reversible error.

The Hart-Javits Bill illustrates two basic shortcomings of many determinate sentencing proposals. First, the prosecutor would in most cases control sentence length. Assume that sentencing guidelines specified that a defined category of offenders (*e.g.* adults with two prior convictions for violent offences) convicted of theft, robbery and armed robbery be sentenced, respectively, to prison terms of 2.2, 3.2 and 4.5 years. Because the court would possess only limited authority to adjust sentences for aggravating and mitigating circumstances (and for an offender in a given case these adjustments would presumably be comparable regardless of the offence charged), the prison sentence received by a defendant who could have been charged with armed robbery will depend on what charge the prosecutor elects to press. That ability in most cases to determine sentence by charging (or withdrawing or not proving) specific sentence-determining offences will give prosecutors valuable chips for use in charge, plea and sentence bargaining negotiations. And, given that, the likelihood will not be great that like offenders convicted of like offences will receive like sentences.

Some state sentencing reform proposals would give the prosecutor even greater sentencing power. California's Uniform Determinate Sentencing Act 1976[21] requires imposition of significant prison sentence increases for defined aggravating circumstances. (*e.g.* use of a weapon, use of a firearm, infliction of great bodily injury, prior incarcerations, substantial property loss or damage) which have been charged and proven. Prosecutorial decisions to charge and prove aggravating circumstances requiring imposition of additional years of imprisonment could in many cases determine whether a convicted defendant will receive a prison sentence of two years or 10 or something in between. The sentencing court can refuse to impose additional years imprisonment for aggravating circumstances if it determines that there are circumstances in mitigation and states reasons for that decision on the record. There is no reason to expect that widely disparate sentences will not result when hundreds of prosecutors interact with hundreds of trial judges in determining sentences.

A second significant problem with the Hart-Javits Bill is that it would either forbid the use of non-incarcerative sentences for all persons convicted of specified offences or would establish an anomalous gap effect for offences for which probation could be ordered: courts must sentence convicted offenders to either probation or a prison term of considerable length, with nothing in between.

Any legislative sentencing reform which would severely limit the sentencing discretion of the criminal court judge will tend to produce a system of either prosecutorial or parole sentencing. The Hart-Javits Bill seems to us fundamentally flawed for that reason. The Kennedy-McClellan Bill avoids that trap but has other shortcomings.

Presumptive Sentencing—the Kennedy-McClellan Bill

The Kennedy-McClellan Bill would establish a United States Sentencing Commission which would be charged to promulgate policy statements and guidelines for judicial sentencing decisions. The guidelines would recommend sentencing ranges within statutory limits for specific categories of offenders convicted of specific categories of offence. The Bill identifies purposes of sentencing which the sentencing commission and sentencing judges should attempt to further in the establishment and application of sentencing policy. All criminal offences would be classified into nine categories, each authorising a maximum sentence of imprisonment, probation or fine. Following a conviction, the court could impose any lawful sentence but should first consider applicable guidelines and policy statements, statutory purposes of sentencing and the circumstances of the offence and the offender. The sentencing court would be required to state the reasons for its sentence, and, if the sentence it decided to impose was not authorised by the applicable sentencing guidelines, the specific reason for the choice of sentence outside the guideline range. Finally, the Bill would establish, for the first time in the federal courts, a limited system of appellate review of sentences. The sentence could be modified, or vacated and remanded, if the appellate court determined that a sentence imposed outside the range recommended by applicable sentencing guidelines was "clearly unreasonable."

We believe that the Kennedy-McClellan Bill offers greater promise for the achievement of just and efficient sentencing than the Hart-Javits Bill or any of the prescriptive sentencing proposals. Its proposal for the classification of offences is a necessary, albeit not sufficient, first step. Existing federal criminal penalty ranges are arbitrary and perverse—having resulted from 200 years of piecemeal codification. Too many offences of seemingly comparable social injury and indicative of comparable personal culpability bear widely disparate authorised sentences. Armed robbery of a United States postal officer is punishable by a 25 year prison term.[22] Armed robbery of a bank chartered by the United States is punishable by a fine, probation or up to 25 year's imprisonment.[23] Sensible sentencing will not obtain until such indefensible anomalies are eliminated.

The Kennedy-McClellan Bill's proposal for a sentencing commission to recommend sentencing ranges within statutory maxima is preferable to systems like California's Uniform Determinate Sentencing Act of 1976, in which the legislature attempts the fine tuning of punishment. Better insulated from political pressures, passions and posturing than a legislature, the sentencing commission may be better positioned to make principled and dispassionate decisions about sentencing policy, and it will certainly be better situated to refine and develop policy, for legislatures both lack special expertise and are beset by myriad competing demands for legislative consideration of matters of politics and policy.

A final major advantage of the Kennedy-McClellan Bill is that it would formally, and to some extent actually, make the trial judge the key sentencing figure (although in any foreseeable federal sentencing system the prosecutor—because of that 85 per cent. guilty plea rate—would retain a major sentencing role). The judge is the inexorably appropriate sentencing figure in the drama of crime and punishment. The judge would be required to consider sentencing guidelines and policy statements, but the sentencing decision would be his, subject to appellate review. The existence of published sentencing guidelines and a requirement that courts give specific reasons for sentences not authorised by the guidelines may tend to produce more consistent sentencing practices. In any case, sentencing practices would become more visible and unusual sentences would be recognised as such.

Although earlier versions of the Bill[24] provided for rigorous appellate review to police judicial sentencing, the Kennedy-McClellan Bill's weak review standard—only "clearly unreasonable" sentences can be remedied—is a significant shortcoming.

Under the "clearly unreasonable" standard the effective sentencing range will consist of sentences authorised by guidelines plus "unreasonable" sentences outside the guideline range. Only the genuinely aberrant sentence will be remediable—as it often is, for constitutional reasons, under existing law.[25]

In the committee stage of this Bill in the Senate Judiciary Committee the problem of the appropriate range of appellate review received close attention. The tension is between, on the one hand, overloaded courts in arrears in their dockets and a consequent disinclination further to defer final decision in criminal cases, and on the other the desire for a relatively free appellate process to help to bring order and principle to the present anarchy of sentences in federal criminal cases. These conflicting pressures will continue to be discussed as the Bill receives further Congressional attention during 1978.

III

Equality and Proportionality[26]

Much of the rhetoric of sentencing reform invokes equality as a paramount priority in sentencing. *Struggle for Justice* proposed:

> All persons found guilty of the same criminal act under the same circumstances [should be] dealt with uniformly.[27]

Section 1170 (*a*) (1) of California's Uniform Determinate Sentencing Act 1976 declares:

> The Legislature finds and declares that the purpose of imprisonment for crime is punishment. This purpose is best served by terms proportionate to the seriousness of the offence with provision for uniformity in the sentences of offenders committing the same offence under similar circumstances.[28]

We think it important that a case of just but unequal sentences should be recognised. The developments earlier described—scepticism about the rehabilitative ideal, increased awareness of discretion and the existence of sentencing disparities, arguments for retributive conceptions of punishment—should not lead to a system in which all offenders receive like sentences. Such a system would be both unwise and impracticable. Equality in punishment is not an absolute principle. It is a value to be weighed and considered among others. There can be just sentences in which the offenders are not treated alike, either as to who goes to prison or for how long.

Our reasons for thinking that principled sentencing disparity is justifiable are both practical and moral. First, there is our conception of punishment. Secondly, there are many instances of exemplary punishment which demonstrate that disparate sentencing is not generally perceived to be unjust. Thirdly, there is an argument which derives from the practical consideration that equality in sentencing is not realisable.

A Conception of Punishment

H. L. A. Hart asserts in his *Prolegomenon to the Philosophy of Punishment*[29] that an adequate philosophy of punishment must separately address questions of general justifying aim and distribution (the latter divided into subsidiary questions of liability: whom do we punish? and amount: how much?). The justifying aim of our conception of punishment is utilitarian, including deterrence, the community educative effects of condign punishment, and the reaffirmation of the moral and ethical values of the community. Liability must of course be determined retributively: conviction by jury or bench trial or following an acceptable plea of guilty to an offence for which punishment is legislatively prescribed must be a pre-condition to the imposition of punishment.

No simple answer can be given to the question of amount and it is here that concern for equality and proportionality is apposite. Questions of amount should be limited by a principle of parsimony—the least afflictive sanction necessary to achieve defined social purposes should be imposed. Desert is a factor: no sanction should be imposed greater than that which is "deserved" by the last crime, or series of crimes, for which the offender is being sentenced. Nor should a sanction be imposed which is so lenient as to unduly depreciate the seriousness of the offence.

Equality and proportionality are important values. We will argue that the limiting principle of parsimony (which is a principle of justice with which persons in Rawl's original position could be expected to agree)[30] is inconsistent with and should sometimes override the values of equality and proportionality. Not to so conclude would produce gratuitous, socially unnecessary, imposition of penal suffering.

Exemplary Punishments

An argument against equality in sentencing derives intuitive support from several illustrations of generally approved instances of exemplary punishment. Exemplary punishment is surely discordant to the principle that like cases should be treated alike, if that principle is regarded as either limiting or defining the amount of just punishment.

During a period of racial strife in the Notting Hill district of London in 1958, sentences of four years' imprisonment were imposed on each of nine young white men who had participated in attacks on blacks.[31] The sentences were at least double the sentence normally imposed for that offence and were stated by the judge to be in excess of the normal sentence for such offences. They were imposed expressly as exemplary punishments, to capture public attention and to deter such behaviour by a dramatic punishment. No refined analysis is required to demonstrate that these nine offenders were selected for *unequal* treatment before the law. If the increased penalty is within the legislatively prescribed range, concern for equality should not prevent such a sentence from being in the appropriate case a just punishment. There are many such examples. They occur in all countries and times and are generally viewed as necessary and legitimate.

Let us consider another hard case for that principle, this time a law teacher's hypothetical. Imagine that each of six Dover doctors last year understated his income by £ 10,000. As advisers to the Inland Revenue, we discuss what should be done. Clearly, each of the six must pay tax on the income he failed to declare, interest at appropriately high rates on that tax and substantial penalties. All this can be arranged without criminal prosecution. Must all six be prosecuted? Must all six be sent to prison? We submit not. Our purpose is utilitarian. We wish, as Voltaire said of the English practice of killing an occasional admiral to encourage the others to be brave, publicly to punish by sending to prison an occasional medical practitioner "to encourage the others" to integrity in their tax returns. We do not need to send all six to prison. The extra increment of deterrence would be bought at too high a cost. It would be wasteful of our resources, wasteful of the court's time and, what is perhaps also in point, it would inflict unnecessary suffering on those doctors whose punishment did not substantially increase the deterrent impact we would gain by the imprisonment of, say, two of their number.

How should we select those to be imprisoned? Perhaps we should struggle for some distinguishing characteristics of deserved severity or some opportunity of extra deterrent utility in the punishment of some amongst the six. What must be recognised is that we are involved in a conscious breach of a principle that like cases should be equally punished.

Would it be unjust? It cannot be treating like cases alike if any reasonable concepts of the quality of guilt and deserved suffering are to be applied. In our view, such a system is both unequal and just, and it is precisely that apparent paradox we seek to defend.

An Argument in Justification of Principled Inequality

Equality can be no more than a subsidiary principle in any jurisprudence of punishment. No realisable conventional jurisprudence of punishment *requires* equality in sentencing in all events. We can only imagine defining principles of punishment which would specify the precise penalty to impose on any offender for any offence. With perfect knowledge a hypothetical utility-maximising deterrent penalty could be calculated. With a perfect moral sense we could specify precisely calibrated deserved punishments. Utility or desert could thus operate as principles which define an appropriate amount of punishment. Unfortunately, we lack defining principles. We lack perfect knowledge. Few claim (and fewer possess) a perfect moral sense.

We believe that there are no realisable defining principles of punishment and that the limiting principles of punishment should be desert and parsimony. Desert sets the maximum and minimum of the sentence that may be imposed for any offence (and helps achieve proportionality by establishing the punishment relationships between offences). It does not give more fine tuning to the appropriate sentence than that. The fine tuning must be done on other principles. Parsimony forbids imposition of punishment in excess of that required to achieve defined social purposes.

Others argue that reform and incapacitation are appropriate tuning devices and that a principled system of sentencing could encompass them. We will not here enter into that debate although Norval Morris has done so elsewhere.[32]

We recognise that moral philosophers may object to exemplary and unequal punishments based on a utilitarian justification. To punish some more severely than others for reasons of deterrence may be using human beings only as a means. One could argue that enhancing punishment for deterrent reasons is equivalent to punishing the innocent for deterrent purposes. If the community believed the innocent to be guilty, punishment would have the same deterrent efficacy as if the defendant were guilty, yet to punish the innocent would be unjust. Argument could be made, for similar reasons, that offenders should not receive additional increments of punishment for deterrent purposes. Deterrence would then have to depend on the effects of imposition of "deserved" uniform sanctions.

Our response is that desert can give only rough guidance in setting the amount of punishment. Some penalties would be unjust because too harsh and others inappropriate because too lenient. Within that range, choices must be made according to criteria which are known, rational and principled. We have argued that some utilitarian considerations are socially appropriate for that purpose, but that punishment of all, when punishment of some would suffice, is unjust because it would violate a limiting principle of parsimony and would impose socially unnecessary suffering.

We agree with H. L. A. Hart, when he noted that just punishment:

> not only insists on the restriction of punishment to an offender, but also on the general retention of the doctrine of *mens rea*, and allows some place, though a subordinate one, to ideas of equality and proportion in the gradation of the severity of punishment.[33]

As you will gather, we have difficulty with these problems and by no means pretend to their solutions; but we do strenuously argue that we have demonstrated situations of exemplary punishment in which justice and the principle of equality (and by necessary implication, proportionality) do not appear to be coterminous.

IV

Toward a Common Law of Sentencing

Principled sentencing lies at the heart of an effective criminal justice system. Sentencing involves a heavy responsibility and raises difficult issues; it thus requires reasons given, critical public consideration of those reasons, critical appellate review of those reasons, and a system of precedent leading to principled justice under law.

The Kennedy-McClellan Bill offers promise for the development of a rational and principled sentencing system in the federal criminal courts. It offers a coherent division of power between legislature and judge which may provide a rational frame of reference for the judge in his difficult task of selecting an appropriate punishment for the convicted criminal. By reducing the number of offence categories and providing for the development of general sentencing standards to guide the judge in deciding whether imprisonment is an appropriate sanction and, if so, for what duration, the Bill may foster more regular and predictable sentencing practices. To continue this evolution towards a common law of sentencing, the Bill would require the judge to give reasons for this choice of a sentence. His sentences and thus his reasons should be subject, as in other countries, to effective appellate review.

What can sentencing reform achieve? The journey will not be short nor the results easy of achievement but, in our view, we can reasonably expect perceptible progress towards the emergence of a principled, evenhanded, effective yet merciful Common Law of Sentencing, consistent with human rights and just freedoms, competent to the deterrence of crime, the adumbration of minimum behavioural standards, and the better protection of society from its human predators.

Notes

1. Model Penal Code (American Law Institute) (P.O.D. Philadelphia 1962). Glanville Williams was a Special Consultant to the Reportorial Staff of the Institute.
2. S. 1437, 95th Cong., 1st Sess. (1977). The sentencing reform provisions of S. 1437 were previously proposed by Senator Kennedy, in somewhat more radical form, as S. 2269, 94th Con., 1st Sess. (1975), and S. 181, 95th Cong., 1st Sess. (1977). S. 1437 is a complete proposed federal code into which the substance of Senator Kennedy's sentencing reforms was inserted. This essay discusses the legislation pending on 1 October 1977.

3. S. 204, 95th Cong., 1st Sess. (1977).

4. For a general description of the codification movement, see Wechsler, "Codification of Criminal Law in the United States: The Model Penal Code," 68 *Colum. L. Rev.* 1425 (1968), and Wechsler, "Sentencing, Corrections and the Model Penal Code," 109 *U. Pa. L. Rev.* 465 (1961).

5. U.S. National Commission on Reform of Federal Criminal Laws, *A Proposed New Federal Criminal Code* (Final Report 1971).

6. 367 U.S. 643.

7. 384 U.S. 436.

8. See, e.g., American Law Institute *A Model Penal Code of Pre-Arraignment Procedure* (P.O.D. Philadelphia 1975).

9. Martinson, "What Works? Questions and Answers about Prison Reform," 35 *Pub. Interest* 22 (1974); and Lipton, D., Martinson and Wilks, *The Effectiveness of Correctional Treatment: A Survey of Treatment Evaluation Studies* (New York 1975).

10. Brody, R. S., *The Effectiveness of Sentencing* (1976).

11. Norval Morris has developed these arguments in *The Future of Imprisonment* (Chicago 1974).

12. Gaudet, Harris and St. John, "Individual Differences in the Sentencing Tendencies of Judges," 23 *J. Crim. L. and Criminology* 811 (1933).

13. *The Second Circuit Sentencing Study: A Report to the Judges of the Second Circuit* (eds. Partridge and Eldridge) (1974).

14. Tiffany, Avichai and Peters, "A Statistical Analysis of Sentencing in Federal Courts: Defendants Convicted after Trial, 1967–68," 4 *J. Legal Stud.* 369 (1975).

15. See Clarke and Koch, "The Influence of Income and Other Factors on Whether Criminal Defendants Go to Prison," 11 *L. and Soc'y Rev.* 57 (1976); Nagel and Neef, "Racial Disparities That Supposedly Do Not Exist," 52 *N.D. Law* 87 (1976). See generally authorities cited in Twentieth Century Fund Task Force on Criminal Sentencing, *Fair and Certain Punishment* (1976), pp. 101–106.

16. See, e.g., Davis, K. C., *Discretionary Justice in Europe and America* (Illinois 1976); ibid., *Police Discretion* (Illinois 1975); Kadish, M. R., and Kadish, S. H., *Discretion to Disobey: A Study of Lawful Departures from Legal Rules* (Stanford 1973).

17. American Friends Service Committee, *Struggle for Justice* (1971), p. 144 [hereinafter cited as *Struggle*].

18. Ibid., p. 148.

19. S. 3752, 94th Cong., 2nd Sess. (1976).

20. S. 204, 95th Cong., 1st Sess. (1977).

21. 1976 Cal. Legis. Serv. Ch. 1139, effective, as amended by A.B. 476 (1977 Cal. Legis. Serv.), 1 July 1977.

22. 18 U.S.C. §2114 (1970).

23. 18 U.S.C. §2113(d) (1970).

24. S. 2269, 94th Cong., 1st Sess. (1975); S. 181, 95th Cong., 1st Sess. (1977).

25. For a general review of evolving constitutional sentence review standards, see Berger, "Equal Protection and Criminal Sentencing: Legal and Policy Considerations," 71 *Nw. L. Rv.* 29 (1976).

26. Norval Morris has developed this argument in greater length in "Punishment, Desert and Rehabilitation," in United States Department of Justice, *Equal Justice under Law: Department of Justice Bicentennial Lecture Series* 136 (1977).

27. *Struggle* (above, n. 17) p. 148.
28. 1976 Cal. Legis. Serv. Ch. 1139 §1170(a)(1).
29. Hart, H. L. A., *Punishment and Responsibility* (Oxford 1968), Chap. 1.
30. Rawls, J., *A Theory of Justice* (Cambridge, Mass. 1971).
31. The Notting Hill case is described and discussed in Walker, N., *Sentencing in a Rational Society* (London 1971), pp. 69, 70.
32. *The Future of Imprisonment* (Chicago 1974).
33. Op. cit. (n. 29, above) p. 233.

15 Making the Punishment Fit the Crime: A Consumer's Guide to Sentencing Reform

Franklin E. Zimring (1977)

In its current crisis the American system of criminal justice has no friends. Overcrowded, unprincipled and ill-coordinated, the institutions in our society that determine whether and to what extent a criminal defendant should be punished are detested in equal measure by prison wardens and prisoners, cab drivers and college professors. What is more surprising (and perhaps more dangerous), a consensus seems to be emerging on the shape of desirable reform—reducing discretion and the widespread disparity that is its shadow, abolishing parole decisions based on whether a prisoner can convince a parole board he has been "reformed," and creating a system in which punishment depends much more importantly than at present on the seriousness of the particular offense.

A number of books and committee reports that have endorsed these goals and proposed various structural reforms to achieve them are the stimulus for this essay. While diverse in style, vocabulary and emphasis, at least six books in the past two years have proposed eroding the arenas of discretion in the system.[1] Some authors, such as James Q. Wilson and Ernst van den Haag, see reform as a path to enhancing crime control. Others, such as Andrew von Hirsch, the Twentieth Century Fund Committee and David Fogel, advocate reform for less utilitarian reasons, with titles or subtitles such as "Doing Justice," "A Justice Model of Corrections," and "Fair and Certain Punishment."

This note cannot comprehensively review such a rich collection of literature, nor is it politic for me to oppose justice, fairness or certainty. Rather, I propose to summarize the present allocation of sentencing power in the criminal justice system and discuss some of the implications of the "structural reforms" advocated in some current literature.

Multiple Discretions in Sentencing

The best single phrase to describe the allocation of sentencing power in state and federal criminal justice is multiple discretion. Putting aside the enor-

"Making the Punishment Fit the Crime" appeared as number 12 of *Occasional Papers*, published by the Law School of the University of Chicago (1977).

mous power of the police to decide whether to arrest, and to select initial charges, there are four separate institutions that have the power to determine criminal sentences—the legislature, the prosecutor, the judge, and the parole board or its equivalent.

The *legislature* sets the range of sentences legally authorized after conviction for a particular criminal charge. Criminal law in the United States is noted for extremely wide ranges of sentencing power, delegated by legislation to discretionary agents, with extremely high maximum penalties and very few limits on how much less than the maximum can be imposed. In practice, then, most legislatures delegate their sentencing powers to other institutions. For example, second degree murder in Pennsylvania, prior to 1973, was punishable by "not more than 20 years" in the state penitentiary.[2] Any sentence above 20 years could not be imposed; any sentence below 20 years—including probation—was within the power of the sentencing judge.

The *prosecutor* is not normally thought of as an official who has, or exercises, the power to determine punishment. In practice, however, the prosecutor is the most important institutional determinant of a criminal sentence. He has the legal authority to drop criminal charges, thus ending the possibility of punishment. He has the legal authority in most systems to determine the specific offense for which a person is to be prosecuted, and this ability to select a charge can also broaden or narrow the range of sentences that can be imposed upon conviction. In congested urban court systems (and elsewhere) he has the absolute power to reduce charges in exchange for guilty pleas and to recommend particular sentences to the court as part of a "plea bargain"; rarely will his recommendation for a lenient sentence be refused in an adversary system in which he is supposed to represent the punitive interests of the state.

The *judge* has the power to select a sentence from the wide range made available by the legislature for any charge that produces a conviction. His powers are discretionary—within this range of legally authorized sanctions his selection cannot be appealed, and is not reviewed. Thus, under the Pennsylvania system we studied, a defendant convicted of second degree murder can be sentenced to probation, one year in the penitentiary or 20 years. On occasion, the legislature will provide a mandatory minimum sentence, such as life imprisonment for first degree murder, that reduces the judge's options once a defendant has been convicted of that particular offense. In such cases the prosecutor and judge retain the option to charge or convict a defendant for a lesser offense in order to retain their discretionary power.[3] More often the judge has a wide range of sentencing choices and, influenced by the prosecutor's recommendation, will select either a single sentence (e.g., two years) or a minimum and maximum sentence (e.g., not less than two nor more than five years) for a particular offender.

The *parole* or *correctional authority* normally has the power to modify judicial sentences to a considerable degree. When the judge pronounces a single sentence, such as two years, usually legislation authorizes release from prison to parole after a specified proportion of the sentence has been served. When the judge has provided for a minimum and maximum sentence, such as two to five years, the relative power of the correctional or parole authority is increased, because it has the responsibility to determine at what point in a prison sentence the offender is to be released. The parole board's decision is a discretionary one, traditionally made without guidelines or principles of decision.

This outline of our present sentencing system necessarily misses the range of variation among jurisdictions in the fifty states and the federal system, and oversimplifies the complex interplay among institutions in each system. It is useful, however, as a context in which to consider specific proposed reforms; it also helps to explain why the labyrinthine status quo has few articulate defenders. With all our emphasis on due process in the determination of guilt, our machinery for setting punishment lacks any principle except unguided discretion. Plea bargaining, disparity of treatment and uncertainty are all symptoms of a larger malaise—the absence of rules or even guidelines in determining the distribution of punishments. Other societies, less committed to the rule of law, or less infested with crime, might suffer such a system. Powerful voices are beginning to tell us we cannot.

Parole under Attack

Off all the institutions that comprise the present system, parole is the most vulnerable—a practice that appears to be based on a now-discredited theoretical foundation of rehabilitation and individual predictability. The theory was that penal facilities rehabilitate prisoners and that parole authorities could select which inmates were ready, and when they were ready, to reenter the community. The high-water mark of such thinking is the indeterminate sentence—a term of one-year-to-life at the discretion of the correctional authority for any adult imprisoned after conviction for a felony. Ironically, while this theory was under sustained (and ultimately successful) attack in California, New York was passing a set of drug laws that used the one-year-to-life sentence as its primary dispositive device. Yet we know (or think we know) that prison rehabilitation programs "don't work," and our capacities to make individual predictions of future behavior are minimal.

So why not abolish parole in favor of a system where the sentence pronounced by the judge is that which is served by the offender? The cost of post-imprisonment sentence adjustments are many: they turn our prisons into "acting schools," promote disparity, enrage inmates, and undermine both justice and certainty.[4]

There are, however, a number of functions performed by parole that have little to do with the theory of rehabilitation or individual predictability. A parole system allows us to advertise heavy criminal sanctions loudly at the time of sentencing and later reduce sentences quietly. This "discounting" function is evidently of some practical importance, because David Fogel's plan to substitute "flat time" sentences for parole is designed so that the advertised "determinate sentences" for each offense are twice as long as the time the offender will actually serve (since each prisoner gets a month off his sentence for every month he serves without a major disciplinary infraction). In a system that seems addicted to barking louder than it really wants to bite, parole (and "good time" as well) can help protect us from harsh sentences while allowing the legislature and judiciary the posture of law and order.

It is also useful to view the abolition of parole in terms of its impact on the distribution of sentencing power in the system. Reducing the power of the parole board increases the power of the legislature, prosecutor and judge. If the abolition of parole is not coupled with more concrete legislative directions on sentencing, the amount of discretion in a system will not decrease; instead, discretionary power will be concentrated in two institutions (judge and prosecutor) rather than three. The impact of this reallocation is hard to predict. Yet parole is usually a statewide function, while judges and prosecutors are local officials in most states. One function of parole may be to even out disparities in sentencing behavior among different localities. Abolishing parole, by decentralizing discretion, may increase sentencing disparity, at least as to prison sentences, because the same crime is treated differently by different judges and prosecutors. Three discretions may be better than two!

There are two methods available to avoid these problems. Norval Morris argues for retaining a parole function but divorcing it from rehabilitation and individual prediction by providing that a release date be set in the early stages of an offender's prison career. This would continue the parole functions of "discounting" and disparity reduction, while reducing uncertainty and the incentive for prisoners to "act reformed." It is a modest, sensible proposal, but it is not meant to address the larger problems of discretion and disparity in the rest of the system.[5]

Fixed Price Sentencing

A more heroic reform is to reallocate most of the powers now held by judges and parole authorities back to the legislature. Crimes would be defined with precision and specific offenses would carry specified sentences, along with lists of aggravating and mitigating circumstances that could modify the penalty. The three books with "justice" or "fairness" in their titles advocate this "price list" approach, albeit for different reasons and with different degrees of sophistication. The Twentieth Century Fund study goes beyond advocating this approach and sets out sections of a sample penal code, although all members of the committee do not agree on the specific "presumptive sentences" provided in the draft.

There is much appeal in the simple notion that a democratically elected legislature should be capable of fixing sentences for crimes against the community. Yet this is precisely what American criminal justice has failed to do, and the barriers to a fair and just system of fixed sentences are imposing. The Twentieth Century Fund scheme of "presumptive sentences," because it is the most sophisticated attempt to date, will serve as an illustration of the formidable collection of problems that confront a system of "Fair and Certain" legislatively determined punishments. In brief, the proposal outlines a scale of punishments for those first convicted that ranges (excluding murder) from six years in prison (aggravated assault) to probation (shoplifting). Premeditated murder is punished with ten years' imprisonment. Burglary of an empty house by an unarmed offender has a presumptive sentence of six months; burglary of an abandoned dwelling yields a presumptive sentence of six months' probation. The sample code clearly aims at singling out violent crimes such as armed robbery for heavier penalties, while the scale for nonviolent offenders led two of the eleven Task Force members to argue that the "range . . . appears to be unrealistically low in terms of obtaining public or legislative support."[6] Repeat offenders receive higher presumptive sentences, under specific guidelines.

The Task Force proposal produces in me an unhappily schizophrenic response. I agree with the aims and priorities of the report, at the same time that I suspect the introduction of this (or many other) reform proposals into the legislative process might do more harm than good.

Why so skeptical? Consider a few of the obstacles to making the punishment fit the crime:

1. *The incoherence of the criminal law.*[7] Any system of punishment that attaches a single sanction to a particular offense must define offenses with a morally persuasive precision that present laws do not possess. In my home state of Illinois, burglary is defined so that an armed housebreaker is guilty of the same offense as an 18-year-old who opens the locked glove compartment of my unlocked stationwagon. Obviously, no single punishment can be assigned to crime defined in such sweeping terms. But can we be precise? The Task Force tried, providing illustrative definitions of five different kinds of night-time housebreaking with presumptive sentences from two years (for armed burglary, where the defendant menaces an occupant) through six months' probation. The Task Force did not attempt to deal with daylight or nonresidential burglary.

The problem is not simply that any such penal code will make our present statutes look like Reader's Digest Condensed Books; we lack the capacity to define into formal law the nuances of situation, intent and social harm that condition the seriousness of particular criminal acts. For example, the sample code provides six years in prison for "premeditated assault" in which serious harm was intended by the offender, and one-third that sentence where "serious harm was not intended." While there may be some conceptual distinction between these two mental states, one cannot confidently divide hundreds of thousands of gun and knife attacks into these categories to determine whether a "Fair and Certain Punishment" is six years or two.

Rape, an offense that encompasses a huge variety of behaviors, is graded into three punishments: six years (when accompanied by an assault that causes bodily injury); three years (when there is no additional bodily harm); and six months (when committed on a previous sex partner, with no additional bodily harm). Two further aggravating conditions are also specified.[8] Put aside for a moment the fact the prior consensual sex reduces the punishment by a factor of six and the problem that rape with bodily harm has a "presumptive sentence" one year longer than intentional killing. Have we really defined the offense into its penologically significant categories? Can we rigorously patrol the border between forcible rape without additional bodily harm and that with further harm—when that distinction can mean the difference between six months and six years in the penitentiary?

I am not suggesting that these are problems of sloppy drafting. Rather, we may simply lack the ability to comprehensively define in advance those elements of an offense that should be considered in fixing a criminal sentence.

2. *The paradox of prosecutorial power.* A system of determinate sentences reallocates the sentencing power shared by the judge and parole authorities to the legislature and the prosecutor. While the judge can no longer select from a wide variety of sanctions after conviction, the prosecutor's powers to select charges and to plea-bargain remain. Indeed, a criminal code like that proposed by the Twentieth Century Fund Task Force will enhance the relative power of the prosecutor by removing parole and restricting the power of judges. The long list of different offenses proposed in the report provides the basis for the exercise of prosecutorial discretion: the selection of initial charges and the offer to reduce charges (charge-bargaining) are more important in a fixed-price system precisely because the charge at conviction determines the sentence. The prosecutor files a charge of "premeditated" killing (10 years) and offers to reduce the charge to "intentional" killing (5 years) in exchange for a guilty plea. In most of the major crimes defined by the Task Force—homicide, rape, burglary, larceny and robbery—a factual nuance separates two grades of the offense where the presumptive sentence for the higher grade is twice that of the lower grade.[9]

This means that the disparity between sentences following a guilty plea and those following jury trial is almost certain to remain. Similarly, disparity between different areas and different prosecutors will remain, because one man's "premeditation" can always be another's "intention." It is unclear whether total disparity will decrease, remain stable, or increase under a regime of determinate sentences. It is certain that disparities will remain.

The paradox of prosecutorial power under determinate sentencing is that exorcising discretion from two of the three discretionary agencies in criminal sentencing does not necessarily reduce either the role of discretion in sentence determination or the total amount of sentence disparity. Logically, three discretions may be better than one. The practical lesson is that no serious program to create a rule of law in determining punishment can ignore the pivotal role of the American prosecutor.

3. *The legislative law-and-order syndrome.* Two members of the Twentieth Century Fund Task Force express doubts that a legislature will endorse six-month sentences for burglary, even if it could be shown that six months is above or equal to the present sentence served. I share their skepticism. When the legislature determines sentencing ranges, it is operating at a level of abstraction far removed from individual case dispositions, or even the allocation of resources to courts and correctional agencies. At that level of abstraction the symbolic quality of the criminal sanction is of great importance. The penalty provisions in most of our criminal codes are symbolic denunciations of particular behavior patterns, rather than decisions about just sentences. This practice has been supported by the multiple ameliorating discretions in the present system.

It is the hope of most of the advocates of determinate sentencing that the responsibilities thrust on the legislature by their reforms will educate democratically elected officials to view their function with realism and responsibility—to recognize the need for priorities and moderation in fixing punishment. This is a hope, not firmly supported by the history of penal policy and not encouraged by a close look at the operation and personnel of state legislatures.

Yet reallocating power to the legislature means gambling on our ability to make major changes in the way elected officials think, talk and act about crime. Once a determinate sentencing bill is before a legislative body, it takes no more than an eraser to make a one-year "presumptive sentence" into a six-year sentence for the same offense. The delicate scheme of priorities in any well-conceived sentencing proposal can be torpedoed by amendment with ease and political appeal. In recent history, those who have followed the moral career of the sentencing scheme proposed by Governor Brown's Commission on Law Reform through the Senate Subcommittee on Crime can testify to the enormous impact of apparently minor structural changes on the relative bite of the sentencing system.[10]

If the legislative response to determinate sentencing proposals is penal inflation, this will not necessarily lead to a reign of terror. The same powerful prosecutorial discretions that limit the legislature's ability to work reform also prevent the legislature from doing too much harm. High fixed-sentences could be reduced; discretion and disparity could remain.

4. *The lack of consensus and principle.* But what if we could trade disparity for high mandatory sentences beyond those merited by utilitarian or retributive demands of justice? Would it be a fair trade? It could be argued that a system which treats some offenders unjustly is preferable to one in which all are treated unjustly. Equality is only one, not the exclusive, criterion for fairness.

This last point leads to a more fundamental concern about the link between structural reform and achieving justice. The Task Force asks the question with eloquent simplicity: "How long is too long? How short is too short?[11] The question is never answered in absolute terms; indeed, it is unanswerable. We lack coherent principles on which to base judgments of relative social harm. Current titles of respectable books on this subject range from "Punishing Criminals" to "The End of Imprisonment," and the reader can rest assured that the contents vary as much as the labels. Yet how can we mete out fair punishment without agreeing on what is fair? How can we do justice before we define it?

Determinate sentencing may do more good than harm; the same can be said for sharp curtailment of judicial and parole discretion. Such reforms will, however, be difficult to implement, measure and judge. Predicting the impact of any of the current crop of reform proposals with any degree of certainty is a hazardous if not foolhardy occupation.

Not the least of the vices of our present lawless structures of criminal sentencing is that they mask a deeper moral and intellectual bankruptcy in the criminal law and the society it is supposed to serve. The paramount value of these books and reform proposals is not the "structural reforms" that each proposes or opposes. It is the challenge implicit in all current debate: no matter what the problems with particular reforms, the present system is intolerable. The problems are deeper than overcrowding or lack of coordination, more profound than the structure of the sentencing system. These problems are as closely tied to our culture as to our criminal law. They are problems of principle that have been obscured by the tactical inadequacies of the present system.

Notes

1. Norval Morris, *The Future of Imprisonment* (University of Chicago Press, 1974); James Q. Wilson, *Thinking about Crime* (Basic Books, 1975); Ernst van den

Haag, *Punishing Criminals* (Basic Books, 1975); Andrew von Hirsch, *Doing Justice—The Choice of Punishments, the Report of the Committee for the Study of Incarceration* (Hill and Wang, 1976); David Fogel, *We Are the Living Proof: The Justice Model of Corrections* (W. H. Anderson, 1975); *Task Force on Criminal Sentencing, Fair and Certain Punishment—Report of the Twentieth Century Task Force on Criminal Sentencing* (McGraw-Hill, 1976).

2. The old Pennsylvania statute is used as an example because we have recently studied the old distribution of punishment for criminal homicide in Philadelphia. See Zimring, Eigen and O'Malley, "Punishing Homicide in Philadelphia: Perspectives on the Death Penalty," 43 *University of Chicago Law Review* 227 (1976).

3. See Zimring, et al., supra note 2, at pp. 229–41.

4. Fogel, supra note 1, at pp. 196–99.

5. Morris, supra note 1, at pp. 47–50.

6. Task Force Report, supra note 1, at 55–56.

7. The phrase is borrowed from my colleague, James White, who is preparing a book with this title.

8. The aggravating factors are (1) "the victim was under 15 or over 70 years of age" and (2) the victim was held captive for over two hours. Task Force Report at p. 59.

9. The presumptive sentence for rape doubles with an assault causing bodily injury. The penality for armed robbery where the offender discharges a firearm is three years if the offender did not intend to injure and five years if intent can be established. The presumptive sentence is two years if the weapon is discharged but the prosecutor cannot or does not establish that "the likelihood of personal injury is high." The penalty for armed burglary doubles when the dwelling is occupied. An armed burglar who "brandishes a weapon" in an occupied dwelling receives 24 months while a nonbrandishing armed burglar receives 18. Assault is punished with 6 years when "premeditated" and committed with intent to cause harm. Without intent, the presumptive sentence is two years. See *Fair and Certain Punishment* at pp. 38–39, 56–59. Threat of force in larceny means the difference between six and twenty-four months. As I read the robbery and larceny statutes, armed taking of property by threat to use force is punished with a presumptive sentence of six months on page 40 of the report while the same behavior receives 24 months on pages 60–61.

10. Compare the *Final Report of the National Commission on Reforms of Federal Criminal Laws* (Government Printing Office, 1971) with Senate Bill 1, 94th Cong., 1st Session (1975). Among other things, the Senate Bill changes a presumption in favor of probation to a presumption against probation, increases the number of felonies in the proposed code and increases the length of authorized sentences by a considerable margin. See Schwartz, "The Proposed Federal Criminal Code," *Criminal Law Reporter*, Vol. 17, p. 3203 (1975).

11. Task Force Report, supra note 1, at p. 4.

Ten   Violence

16 Black Crime, Black Victims

Norval Morris and Michael H. Tonry (1980)

1. Blacks, Crime Rates, and Prisons

Race relations remain the American dilemma—and nowhere more than in the prisons. The prison population of the United States is at a record high: 314,083 on Dec. 31, 1979. And more than half were black. If the figures for juveniles in detention and for jail populations are included, the black disproportion increases. In short, America cages a larger proportion of its black citizens than any other country—including South Africa.

Blacks are genetically neither more nor less inclined to crime than whites. Yet blacks, disproportionately to whites, are both the perpetrators and the victims of those types of crime which in our society attract imprisonment as a punishment.

For three years as editors of "Crime and Justice: An Annual Review of Research," we have unsuccessfully tried to lure leading scholars to write on this topic, to explain its causes and explore its cures. Probably wisely, in the light of the calumny the essay would attract, after reflection they all declined.

To write on race and crime is to invite certain castigation from right and left. From the right, for letting the side down, by alleging racial prejudice by police, prosecutors, judges, jailers, and wardens on insufficient and ambiguous violence. From the left, for being racist.

Yet the topic cannot be buried. Here are some blunt and far from comforting facts:

Homicide is the leading cause of death of black men and women aged 25 to 34. Among men aged 25 to 44, the risk of homicide for blacks is 11 times the risk for whites.

One of every nine Americans is black, yet one of every two male murder victims is black, as is one of every two people arrested for homicide.

Blacks are disproportionately the victims of violent crime; they are two and one half times more likely than whites to be victims of rape or robbery.

More American blacks [5,734] were killed by other blacks in 1977 than were killed in the entire Viet Nam War [5,711].

"Black Crime, Black Victims" appeared as a series of articles under the title "Blacks, Crime Rates, and Prisons" in the *Chicago Tribune*, 18–21 August 1980.

More than half of the people executed in the United States since 1930 were black.

The rate of imprisonment of blacks in 1979 was 8½ times the rate of imprisonment of whites.

De facto segregation already exists within the larger jails and prisons. Racial tensions inside the walls are bitter, pervasive, and explosive.

If secret votes were taken among prison administrators, prison staff, all prisoners, and each minority group of prisoners, overall and within each category, they would vote overwhelmingly for racially segregated institutions.

Paradoxically, many thoughtful black leaders press for more effective protection of black victims through the more ample detection, conviction, and condign punishment of those—mostly black criminals—who prey upon them. This would increase the disparity in the statistics between black and white rates of arrest, jailing, conviction, and imprisonment.

The list could continue. One might inquire into the killing of blacks and whites by police, or into other racial and minority imbalances in juvenile courts, juvenile detention institutions, and reformatories.

Why are blacks so often arrested for serious crimes and so numerous in the jails, the dockets, the prisons, and on death row?

The left prefers to stress racial bias in the control mechanisms of police, prosecutors, courts, and corrections. The right asserts that blacks are criminous by pointing to the differential incidence and frequency of black crime.

The problem is more severe, the challenge to all of us more profound, if the viewpoint of the left is wrong and those on the right speak the larger truth. If racism in the criminal justice system is the problem, it is reasonably readily remediable. Something can be done—and much is being done—to minimize racial prejudice among police, courts, and correctional personnel. The problem is more intractable if there is more to it than that—and there certainly is.

People shy away from this topic. It is emotionally upsetting for both blacks and whites. Discussion is too swiftly conclusionary, the lines of contention are swiftly drawn. Complexities are avoided. Allegations defeat analyses. We doubt that we can avoid these errors, but we will try.

2. The Crime Statistics

Blacks are disproportionately selected out by the American criminal justice system for imprisonment. The first question is why?

To some commentators, a nine-fold overrepresentation of blacks in prison compels an obvious conclusion: the criminal law and its institutions are racist to the core; the law disproportionately criminalizes socially threatening behavior that blacks commit while condoning or ignoring white behavior that causes greater social damage. [Compare ghetto burglary, for instance, to the corporate behavior that built the Corvair or befouled Lake Superior or the Hudson River.]

These commentators say that police arrest black suspects while whites are released with a warning. And throughout the system, they argue, similar discretionary choices favor whites, disfavor blacks: whom to prosecute and for what; whom to convict and of what; whom to imprison, for how long, and where [squalid century-old maximum security prisons for blacks; minimum security campus-like facilities for whites]; whom to release on parole and after how long. To such commentators blacks are disproportionately clasped in the arms of the law because whites prefer it that way.

From another perspective, the statistics of crime and imprisonment reveal a system surprisingly uncontaminated by racial discrimination. Black imprisonment patterns closely reflect black arrest rates. If imprisonment rates exactly reflected arrest rates, blacks would constitute about 4 percent less than they do of the prison population—and even this minor difference reflects the probability that the crimes for which blacks are arrested, in general, represent a more "imprisonable" collection of crimes than do the mass of white arrests. In other words, from arrest on, the criminal justice system does not appear to deal with blacks with discriminatory severity.

This claim is not Pollyanna's that there is no discrimination. All that is claimed is that the number of blacks in our prisons and jails more or less accurately reflects the disproportionate black involvement in serious crimes as shown by arrests.

This pushes us to look at arrest rates as a measure of serious crime, of crimes that attract imprisonment. If arrests are unfairly skewed against blacks, the case for stressing racial discrimination as contrasted with black criminality is to that extent strengthened.

Arrest rates, it is said, give an unfair picture of black criminality, since they do not include a mass of crimes that whites disproportionately commit. Very many business, white-collar, and financial crimes do not result in reported offenses or arrests. And those offenses are predominantly committed by whites. The real but hidden incidence of securities law, income tax, and fraud criminality must be staggering. A measure of crime in the United States that disregards those offenses overstates the black contribution to the totality of crime in a most unfair way. All this is true but not very compelling because of the problem we face. White-collar crimes well may cause more social damage than do the common law offenses like homicide, robbery, assault, rape, burglary, and theft. But it is the latter that do, and should, provoke imprisonment as a sanction. We may too often use imprisonment in relation to crime in the streets, but the knee-jerk rection to advocate a much greater use of imprisonment in relation to white-collar crime is no solution at all.

Only a miserable social policy would pursue equality by increasing the amount of suffering. We don't disagree that white-collar criminals who injure the economic and social structure should receive more severe punishments, often including imprisonment. But it would be no solution at all to hope that we could achieve equality between the races in imprisonment by the massive imprisonment of white-collar criminals.

Nor does it follow that crime in the streets should be seen as less of a problem simply because of the existence of crime in the suites. There breathe few men and women of any race who do not fear physical attacks, incursions into their homes, and theft of their personal belongings. Rape and robbery, murder and mayhem, burglary and battery are serious crimes of concern to most people in most places at most times. And it is for those crimes that blacks are overrepresented in America. That there are other important crimes in which they are underrepresented is hardly germane.

Indeed, we look forward with anticipation to the day when middle class blacks will be proportionately represented in the calendars of white-collar crime. More black embezzlers and income tax evaders and securities law violators will signify that more blacks are gaining entry to the social and economic positions that make these crimes possible.

All of these points are true, but they support only the weak claim that the details of arrest data are unreliable, not the stronger and more important claim that arrests are not meaningfully related to crimes committed.

One way to explore the relation between arrest rates and "real" crime is to ask the victims of crime what happened to them and who did it. The federal government has conducted massive victimization surveys since the mid-'60s and the results are generally consistent with arrest rates. Moreover, there is compelling evidence that black victims are *less* likely than whites to report crimes. Thus arrest rates almost certainly *underestimate* black involvement in serious street crime.

In talking with the police in Chicago one comes to the realization that, in a practical sense, the law against burglary is hardly enforced at all in the ghettos of the poor. Even knife woundings are pursued only when the victim or a complaining witness is willing to take the considerable risks of standing up as an informant and witness in the protracted processes of the criminal courts.

So arrest figures for certain types of serious crimes, in particular those crimes which attract jailing and imprisonment, do not seem to overstate black commission of those offenses.

3. Racial Patterns

We do not for a moment doubt that there are very many instances of individual racial discrimination in the criminal justice system. Race relations in this country remain strained and befouled by the application of stereotypes. Many arrest and punishment decisions no doubt result from those stereotypes. But racial bias cannot explain why blacks are so disproportionately arrested, jailed, and imprisoned for serious crimes.

Racially biased decisions appear to be the exception and do not create a situation skewed systematically toward more severe treatment of blacks. There have been countless studies of racial patterns in the criminal justice system, and most in recent years have concluded that blacks do not have significantly worse experiences than do similarly situated whites.

It could be fairly argued that so far we have not really been comparing similarly situated people. We have been comparing blacks and whites as if they were equally spread over the continuum from social privilege to social adversity—and they clearly are not.

Few will doubt the fact of racial inequity in our society. The question is whether the criminal justice system merely rests upon and reflects that social inequity or whether it makes it worse.

Proportionately more blacks go to jail than whites. Racial bias? So it would appear, if we only look at skin color. But perhaps not if we compare people accused of comparable offenses [say, armed robbery] who had comparable criminal records [say, two prior felony convictions]. And if further we compare only those accused persons who have family, employment, and community ties that make them unlikely to flee before trial, we may find that blacks are no more likely than whites to be jailed after arrest rather than bailed.

The critical reader may well suggest that we have missed the point. To say that, other things being equal, blacks and whites receive comparable treatment is to drift off the point. Other things are not equal.

Take the jail or bail example. The bail decision is crucial. Jailed defendants are more likely to be convicted and imprisoned than bailed defendants. If bail is more likely for the man with a home, an education, a stable work record, and marketable skills, and if those assets are—because of the legacy of slavery—more commonly the lot of whites than blacks, then there is discrimination. To lock people up for reasons that are thus infused with the inheritance of racism is profoundly troubling.

Little in life is more comforting than to find that your friends face the same problems that you do. So it is a relief to look at this problem as it occurs in the United Kingdom. There, as here, blacks are disproportionately represented in arrest rates and prison populations. In "Race, Crime, and Arrests," the British Home Office research unit tried to determine the extent to which socio-economic characteristics and demographic patterns accounted for the difference.

Their conclusions matched the broad thrust of similar studies in this country. The variables other than race accounted in large part—but not entirely—for the statistical differences.

These are not easy studies to carry out or to interpret. It is not easy to find inner-city areas populated other than by blacks which represent the same agglomeration of social disadvantages that beset the black areas. And even taking out all other variables, there remain measurably higher arrest and imprisonment rates among blacks than whites. Considering the long history of cultural adversity and its impact on the black family, it would be surprising if this were not so.

Where, then, does the argument lead us? Assume, as we believe, that disproportionate black criminality and poverty and unemployment and so on have nothing to do with biology but rather result from the social history of blacks in America. Blacks do disproportionately commit serious personal crime and disproportionately amass serious criminal records. And the problem does not grow less severe over time.

In the past 20 years more blacks, and in an increasing proportion, have moved into the middle class. But those blacks who have been left behind seem to have been left further behind and seem to be even more locked into a culture of despair and crime.

William Julius Wilson, a prominent black sociologist, has argued that class rather than race is the primary impediment to black progress in modern America. Yet, tragically, he observes that while talented and educated blacks experience opportunities comparable to those of whites, "the black underclass is in a hopeless state of economic stagnation, falling further and further behind the rest of society."

Unemployed, residentially-unstable individuals, whether black, white, or green, who have just committed an armed robbery, and who have previously been convicted of several violent felonies, both appear to be and are dangerous. There is little choice but to lock them up. We think that most Americans, whatever the pigmentation of their skin, would agree. And a discouragingly large number of blacks fit that or a comparable profile and should be imprisoned.

That one is left with a sense of social inequity is both clear and proper. But the choice to punish is not easily avoidable.

4. What Can Be Done

What is to be done to minimize black involvement in street crime and to reduce the number of blacks behind prison walls? In the areas of education, employment, housing, health, welfare, child-care, and public transportation it may well be necessary for political leadership to be color conscious as distinct from color blind in trying to minimize the inheritance of racial adversity. And that minimization will carry with it a reduction of the disproportionate number of blacks involved in street crime.

But there are some other steps to be taken within the criminal justice system itself. We see as a first duty the task of minimizing unjust racial discrimination at the police, prosecutorial, court, and correctional levels.

It is surely desirable that black and white accused persons be treated by the color-blind, including those who are color-blind as to the pigmentation of the victim of the crime. It is objectionable to find, as we do, that those who commit crimes against whites are treated more severely than those who commit crimes against blacks. This is certainly not to argue for a mindless increase of severity of punishment for those who prey upon blacks. Quite the contrary. A much more sensible path may well be an effort to increase the efficiency of our system in catching and convicting criminals and to reduce the severity of its punishments, but certainly on a basis of equality of treatment of the victims of crime.

That reduction of severity will come, we believe, from a great enrichment of the range of punishments available to the courts, from systems of community service and restitution, and an increasing arsenal of sanctions that is gradually emerging to supplement our simplistic punitive package of fine, probation, or prison.

We quickly agree that there is a long way to go to achieve racial justice in the operation of the criminal justice system, but we would also argue that there has been substantial progress in this direction over recent decades and that there is widespread agreement on the road to take.

This is not so with respect to prison conditions. We have made our large prisons hotbeds of racial hostility and racially motivated brutality. The record of violence and riot is clear. Blacks, Hispanics, and whites are separated and in unqualified conflict. There are basic questions of human rights which have to be confronted here. A country that preaches human rights to others cannot without hypocrisy continue to run the megaprisons of racial violence that we do.

It is not as if the remedies were not well known. They are. We know how to run small, safe prisons. There are several such, federal and state, in this country. All that is lacking is the political will. Surely whites and blacks of good will can combine in vigorous opposition to a situation where those in our jails and prisons move in fear of brutality, rape, and death, fueled by the cruel fires of ignorant racial animosities.

At the same time, something needs to be done for the black victim of crime. Street crime—homicide, robbery, burglary, rape, and assault—has a grossly disproportionate impact on black victims. At present we do not take their plight seriously. We tend to respond to it as if they were an alien group born to suffering. In the ghettos of our larger cities burglary has become, in effect, an unenforced crime. Woundings short of death will be prosecuted if the victim is prepared to take the very considerable risks of collaborating with police and prosecutors in catching and convicting the criminal—and they, frequently and understandably, will not. The weak in the ghetto move in fear and so, for that matter, do the strong unless they move in groups.

Perhaps all this could be changed. Certainly it would be worth the effort if it could. Suppose we assisted and protected the victim of crime in the inner-city areas as we would one of our friends or relatives. It may thus be possible over time to bring efficiency and decency to the treatment of street crime in the cities of America. The plague of handguns and their entourage of death, fear, and grievous injury would, of course, not thus be diminished, but much else might be changed. At least the thought is worth entertaining.

Let us establish a Victim and Witness Assistance Program in a store front in a black inner-city depressed area. The program will mobilize—though not necessarily have available on the premises—extra police, prosecutorial, legal advice, and social assistance resources to lend prompt and efficient assistance to any victim of a serious crime of personal violence or property predation.

It would aim to guarantee to the victim or complaining witness whatever protection was necessary to insure their safety. This would certainly require extra police protection beyond what is now available in such areas, and it should be supplied. The program would also seek to expedite the prosecution of cases involving those victims and complaining witnesses who became its concern. And it would insure their obtaining whatever compensation or restitution they were entitled to.

If extra court services were necessary to prevent an accumulation of any backlog that would flow from the substantial increase of prosecutions coming from such a program, they should be provided. In short, we should test the consequences of taking seriously the situation of the inner-city black victim of crime. They bear the major impact of the scourge of crime in this country. It is time that a disproportionate state effort was made to assist them.

Through such a program we would be dealing with the disheartening paradox of black crime. It would for a time increase the number of black incarcerated offenders, but one hopes for a longer term tradeoff of reduced severity of sanction, shorter prison terms, and shorter terms in jails, compensating for the increased efficiency of the system.

Regardless whether it did have those consequential and possibly remote advantages, it would at least be a principled response to a serious human plight. We have too long neglected the black victim of predatory crime. The case for eliminating this form of racial discrimination is compelling.

Eleven   Youth Crime

17 The Chicago Youth Development Project

Hans W. Mattick (1969)

There is nothing so frightful as ignorance in action.

—Goethe

The experience and practice reflected in this manual is that of the Chicago Youth Development Project (CYDP), the largest privately financed delinquency prevention and control project ever conducted in the City of Chicago. During its six-year life span, from July 1, 1960, to June 30, 1966, some eighty persons staffed its action and research programs, and more than 5,000 persons, youth and adult, were affected, in one way or another, by its multifarious activities. Although thus located in space and time, its methods and experience have a wide range of applicability to a large variety of public and private agencies located in towns, cities or suburbs across the nation. Any agency that is engaged in "out-reach work with youth," or plans to develop such a program, will find this recorded experience of its predecessors a useful source of information and training materials as it seeks to come to grips with the burgeoning youth problem of our era. Those who will not learn from history are doomed to repeat it. This experience and practice manual was written in order to enable our successors to profit from our knowledge so that they may surpass us in their efforts.

The CYDP was a joint project of the Chicago Boys' Clubs and the Institute for Social Research of The University of Michigan. It was financed by grants from the Ford Foundation ($1,225,000) and the W. Clement and Jessie V. Stone Foundation ($174,000), with about two-thirds of the money going to the action program and the remaining third being spent on research and evaluation. Although many persons in Chicago and Ann Arbor played an active role in the conduct of this project, the experience and practice reflected in the text is mainly that of the street-club workers and community organizers who carried out the out-reach action program that is the heart of the project.

"The Chicago Youth Development Project" appeared as the introduction to *Action on the Streets* by Frank J. Carney, Hans W. Mattick, and John D. Galloway. It is reprinted by permission of the Young Men's Christian Association of the United States of America.

Although there was a good deal of joint planning and interaction between the action and research teams of the CYDP, there was a definite division of labor between them. The action out-reach program was organized and implemented by the Chicago Boys' Clubs and, more particularly, by the CYDP staffs of the two boys clubs units (the Henry Horner Chicago Boys' Club and the Oldtown Chicago Boys' Club) located in the inner city areas where the project was conducted. The research design and evaluative program was planned and carried out by the Institute for Social Research and, more particularly, by a special research team based in Chicago.

The action out-reach program of the CYDP consisted of a three-fold attack on the problem of delinquency: (1) street-club work with young people, (2) community organization work with local adults, and (3) the use of informal facilities. The first was called the Extension Work program and consisted, essentially, of having street-club workers come into contact with young people wherever they might congregate in the action area, bringing them under the influence and supervision of the workers and attempting to deal constructively with the significant problems in their lives that might be amenable to intervention. We found that youth were not "hard-to-reach," they were only hard to work with after they *had* been reached. The second was the Community Organization program and consisted, essentially, of organizing local adults, agencies and resources around problem youngsters or local conditions with a view to resolving the problematic situation concerned. We found many persons in the local community who were willing to help if the problem involved could be clearly communicated. The third was the Outpost program and consisted, essentially, of providing informal facilities like store fronts, garages or basement rooms of public housing buildings, where the CYDP staff and the youngsters with whom they were working could be brought together under continuous and optimum counseling conditions. We found that the youngsters, and especially the older teen-agers, preferred such facilities to the more formal atmosphere of a boys' club or the traditional youth-serving agency. And it must be remembered, from the standpoint of providing informal facilities, a car or a station wagon is simply a mobile counseling room with a great attraction for young people.[1]

The five general areas of theoretical and practical interest which shaped the methods and goals of the CYDP were: (1) the inadequate conventional socialization of the young; (2) the lack of legitimate opportunity for the young, especially minority group members; (3) the alienation of youth from adults and the lack of consensus about conventional values; (4) the disorganization of family and community life under the impact of urbanization in the inner city; and (5) the latent negative effects of handling youthful offenders through formal legal channels and institutions. The action program of the CYDP was designed to effect some positive changes in those aspects of these five problem areas that expressed themselves in the form of antisocial behavior and juvenile delinquency.

The action out-reach goals of the CYDP were:

1. To reduce the absolute amount of illegal and antisocial behavior attributable to the target population in the experimental areas.

2. To change the behavior of individuals and groups in the contacted part of the target population, where necessary, from the more seriously antisocial to the less seriously, and from the less seriously antisocial to the conventional, within the class and cultural norms of the local population.

3. To help individuals and groups in the contacted part of the target population meet their emotional needs for association, friendship and status by providing conventional, organized and supervised activities for them, with a view to increasing their capacity for participation and autonomy.

4. To increase the objective opportunities for youth in the external environment, in the field of education, employment and cultural experiences.

5. To help youth prepare themselves for conventional adult roles by providing guidance in the fields of education, work, family life and citizenship through direct intervention in their life processes, especially at times of crisis.

6. To relate the target population to local adults and institutions in positive ways so that communication channels between youth and adults may be developed through which a shared, conventional system of values may be transmitted.

7. To develop in parents and local adults a concern for local problems affecting youth welfare, and to organize them with a view to having them assume responsibility for the resolution of local problems.

8. To create a positive change in attitude, in both youth and adults, about the possibility of local self-help efforts to improve the local community through active and cooperative intervention in community processes, and thus create a more positive attitude toward the local community itself.

The CYDP staff that conducted the action out-reach program designed to achieve these goals, and the research team that evaluated this effort, were organized into the following structure:

Chicago Boys Club   *Institute for Social Research*

CYDP Director, ISR & CBC

Associate Director—Street Work, CBC
Associate Director—Community Organization, CBC
Associate Director—Research, ISR
(Secretarial and Clerical Staff)

Area I-X	Area II-X	Research
(Horner), CBC	(Oldtown), CBC	Team, ISR
Club Director	Club Director	Program Director
Program Director	Program Director	Asst. Program Dir.
4 Street-Club Workers	2 Street-Club Workers	3 Research Asst., Chgo.
2 Community Organizers	1 Community Organizer	Sampling Consultant
1 Secretary-Clerk	1 Secretary-Clerk	Sec'y-Clerical support

Action area I-X (Horner) consisted of ten census tracts comprising a one-mile-square area. It was bounded by streets located 400 north, 400 south, 1600 west and 2400 west in Chicago's street-numbering grid pattern. According to the 1960 census, this area had a total population of 30,269 persons, 81.5% of whom were non-white and 7.2% of whom were males aged 10 to 19—the target population of the CYDP. Area II-X (Oldtown) consisted of six census tracts and was slightly more than one-half-mile square in area. It was bounded by streets located at 500 south, 1200 south, 1000 west and 1600 west. It had a total population of 20,524 persons, 17.3% of whom were non-white and 8.6% of whom were males aged 10 to 19. Combined, these areas had a total population of 50,793 persons, 3,926 of whom were males aged 10 to 19, whose behavior and life-chances the CYDP action out-reach staff and program hoped to affect in a positive manner.

At any one time, once the project was fully staffed and organized, in an average month, the action staff of the CYDP had some form of contact or association with about 1,500 youngsters and 1,200 local adults in the regular course of their work. In terms of organized groups, however, with whom the CYDP were in almost daily interaction, there were, on the average, about forty street gangs and the same number of adult community organizations and agencies. These organized gangs had a total core membership of 470 individuals (approximately 20% were female groups or hangers-on), and the adult organizations had about 780 active members (approximately 50% were males).

The organization and planning of the CYDP provided for extensive and frequent record-keeping procedures in order to gain the benefits of written records and to reduce the human distortions of fallible memories. Contact cards were made out for every youngster and adult contacted by the workers. Every street-club worker and community organizer wrote a Daily Activity Report of his day's experience as a regular part of his work. The Program Directors of the two participating boys' clubs submitted bimonthly summary reports on CYDP workers and their activities. Both Club Directors and all three Associate Directors of the CYDP wrote monthly summary reports. The three Research Assistants wrote Daily Activity Reports the first two years of the project, before they got involved in extensive survey and evaluative research activities. By special agreement with the Chicago Police Department Youth Division, every youngster arrested and not detained in custody, who lived in the action areas, was referred to the CYDP for a follow-up home visit.

The result of all this record-keeping was the systematic accumulation of: 7,000 contact cards, 12,000 daily activities reports, 350 supervisory and research reports, and 2,250 arrest cards on juveniles. Altogether, these records constituted an excellent running history of CYDP staff and client activities, a description of gross and minor changes in the action areas, a reflection of the changes in the nature of the population contacted by the staff, and a complete history of the incidence of arrest and recidivism among juveniles resident in the action areas during the last three years of the project. Although the research team was able to make use of these records, their main function was largely that of administrative and supervisory control over the action program. The research team devised its own separate research instruments, questionnaires and archival records relating to arrests, school drop-out rates, youth employment, gang membership and action staff relations with youngsters.

The foregoing would not have been detailed at such length if it were not the introduction to a point of central importance in out-reach work with youth. This stress on record-keeping is intended to convey the seriousness of purpose, the high degree of administrative and supervisory control, and the deep need of accurate and systematic knowledge that dominated the CYDP action staff and program. Most of the traditional youth-serving agencies, both public and private, maintain only the most elementary and transient records related to narrowly conceived functional needs. The result is that they have only the vaguest notions about the nature of their own work and its effects, if any, on the youngsters who are their client population. The main danger in the failure to keep systematic records is that of being led astray by individual and dramatic cases of success or failure that form the basis of poor generalizations. Thus the social reality of youth out-reach work is easily lost and the groundwork is laid for manufacturing a mythology that complicates and aggravates the very problem with which it is seeking to come to grips. More frequently than not, these myths serve public relations and fund-raising purposes rather than promoting an understanding of the reality situation of inner city youth.

No youth-serving agency, public or private, can afford to engage in myth-making operations by putting forward exaggerated claims or images, positive or negative, without alienating their youthful clients and making their own work more difficult in the long run. The traditional youth-serving agencies, or other bureaucracies, public and private, that relate themselves to youth, have to make up their minds whether they want to live off of the fact that youth have problems, or whether they want to deal with these problems in a constructive way. If, for purposes of fund-raising, empire-building or public-relations imagery, a public or private youth-serving agency portrays youth as a dangerous, slavering beast—a knife-wielding, chain-swinging, over-sexed, drug-using monster—from whom the community can best be protected by that agency's special expertise and mystique, then the youth problem has been compounded. This is the imagery of the short-sighted public-relations department that has its eye on the dollar rather than on the real task of the agency, which is to help train and assimilate youngsters into the conventional social structure. It is easy to frighten middle-class donors, or taxpayers, or to appeal to their sense of guilt, in the course of a fund-raising campaign; but when the campaign is over, very few of these middle-class types can be persuaded to teach, employ or otherwise associate with such "beasts." Yet, what the youth-serving agency really needs is the ability to provide educational and employment opportunities to youth, and to bring youth into fruitful association with adults whom they can respect. No amount of "conscience and fright money" can create such a conventional opportunities for youth. It is really much better for the youth-serving agency to portray their work with youth in a realistic and honest fashion; to simply tell the truth, the good with the bad and vice versa.

Many, if not most, of the claims and assertions made by the specialized bureaucratic hierarchies that relate themselves to, and report upon the activities of, inner city youth strike the experienced out-reach worker at the street level as being simply ludicrous.[2] This is true whether the assertions being made are the stereotypes of the mass media, the occupationally-structured perceptions of the school, welfare or police authorities, or the selective and dramatic cases so beloved of the traditional youth-serving agency engaged in public relations. It is not that these bureaucracies and occupational groups are dishonest; they are simply the "victims" of inadequate and structurally-biased reporting practices—a very human failing. The kind of thing that happens is this: (1) the worker at the lowest level (the street-club worker, the schoolteacher, the case-welfare worker, the patrolman or the news reporter) reports the "mess of reality" as it is reflected in his street-level perception of the situations he is obliged to deal with; (2) his supervisor (the club director, the school principal, the supervising social worker, the police captain or the copy editor), however, either cannot use, or does not want to hear about, this "mess of reality." He has problems of his own—too much work, not enough manpower, the exigencies of a busy life—which require a different view of reality. He wants to be helpful, but there are limitations on his time and energy that he communicates to the levels above and below him. thus, at this second level, a "clean-up" process of selection, rationalization and ordering of priorities begins. (3) When the first-level supervisor reports on his work to his supervisor (the executive director of several youth-serving agency units, the district school superintendent, the head of the branch welfare office, the police commissioner or the city editor), the selective process of communication has, again, refined the "cleaned-up mess of reality"; it is now simpler, more general, and beginning to take on the logical, conceptual form of processed information structured by the internal needs of a bureaucratic hierarchy. (4) By the time that the top level of the organization (the board of trustees of the youth-serving agency, the board of education, the city welfare board, the mayor's office or the newspaper publisher) receives what is left of the original street-level perception of the "mess of reality," it has undergone a remarkable transformation: the youth-serving agency has had a "high degree of success," the school system has been "educating" the youth, the welfare system has been "adequately serving" its clients, the city administration has been "coping" with crime and disorder, and the mass media have reported "accurately" on the nature of reality. Unfortunately, these refined versions of reality are not reflected in the work and experience of the lowest-level worker, who is obliged to confront the same old "mess of reality" and do what he can to bring order out of chaos while seeking the support and help of those above him who have their own version of reality.

How one avoids, or corrects for, the shortcomings of such a selective communication process that tends to mislead us all, is a difficult question. At least two suggestions can be made from the experience of the CYDP: (1) the reduction of day-to-day experience to writing and the maintenance of systematically kept records is not only a great corrective for a faulty memory and the mythology that grows out of individual, selected, dramatic cases (good or bad), but it tends toward the prevention of making poor generalizations and the construction of false stereotypes; (2) supervision procedures must be devised and practiced that link the top and the bottom levels of a bureaucratic hierarchy so that the top level is not "victimized" by the selective communication process that has been described. The image of Plato's philosopher-king descending into the cave again, or Mayor Lindsay of New York walking the streets of Harlem and talking to the people, comes readily to mind. The supervision processes of the CYDP "short-circuited" its own bureaucratic and hierarchical structure in the interest of gaining the fullest understanding possible of the youth situation in the areas where the project was conducted. Both the Associate Director of Street Work and the Associate Director of Community Organization were in the field every day, from 2:00 P.M. to 10:00 P.M., and the Project Director spent two or three evenings of every week in the field talking to all the workers and many of the young people with whom they were working. There was very little that went on in the action areas of the CYDP that was not known, personally and directly, by all levels of the field staff and their supervisors. The CYDP was far from a perfect project, but it suffered from far fewer delusions of reality than the traditional youth-serving agency or many of the bureaucracies that deal with youth.

In the end, the question must be faced: did the CYDP "succeed" in preventing juvenile delinquency, or in achieving its other goals? This is not a simple question with a simple answer, for much depends upon what is meant by "success." From one point of view it would be simple to produce a positive, but partial, answer that would give the appearance of success. For example, during its six-year life span the CYDP staff succeeded in finding 750 jobs for 490 young people; similarly, 950 school drop-outs were returned to school 1,400 times. CYDP out-reach workers made 1,250 appearances at police stations and courts on behalf of 800 youngsters and, in part because of their intervention, the police and courts were willing to dispose of such cases by station adjustments or probation. Finally, CYDP workers made 2,700 follow-up visits to the homes of 2,000 juveniles who were arrested during the last thirty months of the project, in an effort to get them involved in one aspect or another of the project's programs. All of these figures reveal a deeply committed, well-related and task-oriented staff that was doing its job and doing it well. Insofar as youth employment, school attendance, community supervision over offenders and contact with youth known to the police are indices of success, the CYDP succeeded to a remarkable degree. There is no doubt that most of the young people indicated by these statistics were helped in a constructive way through the efforts of the CYDP. In addition, hundreds of others were helped and influenced in a variety of ways through the counseling and guidance extended by the CYDP out-reach workers in their day-to-day association with young people. There is just no way to measure the longer range, "sleeper" effects of out-reach work, *i.e.*, the sense in which an older worker has a constructive influence on a young boy that does not become manifest until that younger boy begins to mature.

There is another way, however, of raising the question of the meaning of "success" in out-reach work, and that is to ask whether the CYDP had any effects on the *rate* of youth employment, on the school drop-out *rate*, or on the *rates* of arrest and conviction of young people who got into trouble. At first blush it would appear to be "obvious" that such a busy project as the CYDP must have had some positive effects on these rates; but the fact is that it did not. Despite the successful efforts of the staff in finding jobs, returning school drop-outs and intervening in formal legal processes, the youth unemployment rate remained at about the same level, the school drop-out rate increased slightly and the arrest rates of youngsters in the CYDP areas increased over time, with a lesser proportion of them being disposed of as station adjustments.

Here we have what seems to be a strange contradiction: the CYDP helped many individual youngsters, but the project failed to achieve its goals. How could that be? The explanation seemed to be that CYDP out-reach workers were very good at achieving "most-favored client" relations for the youngsters with whom they happened to be working. Thus, for example, a worker could bring a drop-out to a school counselor and convince the school authorities that they should re-admit this student. The authorities would agree on condition that the worker would support the motivation of the student and help him with his homework and other problems. More frequently than not, this procedure would work and the school drop-out would have been successfully returned to school. At the same time, however, some other youngster, not known or related to any part of the CYDP project, would have dropped out of school or gotten himself expelled and the school drop-out rate would remain static. Thus, despite the expenditure of time, effort and money, the basic situation remained largely the same.

No matter how the research team measured it, there were "no significant differences," as the social scientists put it, in the basic forces that tended to produce delinquency. Although CYDP workers could find work for a series of individuals, they could not expand the absolute number of jobs available in the job market; although they could return drop-outs to school, they could not influence the behavior of youngsters and school administrators in such a way as to increase the rate of school attendance; and, although they could intervene between the youngsters and the police and courts, they could not prevent the rate of arrest from increasing. Apparently, the development of a whole series of "most-favored client" relationships with employers, the schools and the police on behalf of youngsters was not sufficient to overcome the systemic production of delinquency and its symptomatic correlates. On balance, and in the final analysis, the "experimental" population resident in the action areas of the CYDP seemed to be slightly worse off than the "control" population resident in a similar area selected for comparative purposes. This is *not* an unusual result in projects that are *adequately* researched *on their merits*.[3] But if the "successes" detailed above could only be claimed in a qualified way by the CYDP, neither could the "failures" be attributed to the project in an unqualified way. The relationship between the CYDP, its clients, its successes and failures, are complex, and still in the process of being sorted out by members of the research team at the Institute for Social Research at The University of Michigan, but we already know the central thrust of the evaluation.

Apparently, the expenditure of $1,399,000 over a six-year period, the organization of a street-work and community organization project with a well-qualified and dedicated staff, operating in a mile-and-a-half-square area of an inner city, with a population base of 50,000 persons, including nearly 4,000 males aged 10 to 19 whose behavior is to be influenced in constructive ways, and a sustained and sophisticated effort to achieve this objective, can do a lot of good for many individuals who are touched by the project. If that is your main objective, out-reach work has the potential for achieving it. But, if you are mainly interested in dealing with the *problems* that contribute to delinquency: family disorganization, job opportunities, education, housing, discrimination, political representation and the negative impact of urbanization and large institutions on the lives of young people, then something more fundamental is required. Out-reach work has an important role to play, either as a stop-gap measure or as an essential element in a more fundamental program of social reform, but its strengths and weaknesses must be well understood. This experience and practice manual of out-reach work with youth is a contribution toward such understanding.

Notes

1. For a fuller description see: Hans W. Mattick and Nathan S. Caplan, *The Chicago Youth Development Project: A Descriptive Account of Its Action Program and Research Design*, Institute for Social Research, The University of Michigan, Ann Arbor, 1964.

2. See Walter B. Miller, "Violent Crimes in City Gangs," *The Annals of the American Academy of Political and Social Science*, Vol. 364, March, 1966.

3. See Edwin Powers and Helen Witmer, *An Experiment in the Prevention of Juvenile Delinquency: The Cambridge-Somerville Youth Study*, Columbia University Press, New York, 1951; Walter B. Miller, "The Impact of a 'Total Community' Delinquency Control Project," *Social Problems*, Vol. 10, No. 2, Fall 1962; and James C. Hackler, "Boys, Blisters and Behavior: The Impact of a Work Program in an Urban Central Area," *Journal of Research in Crime and Delinquency*, July, 1966.

18 Kids, Groups and Crime: Some Implications of a Well-Known Secret

Franklin E. Zimring (1981)

Social and policy sciences, reflecting human nature, are rich in contradiction and are occasionally perverse. It is sometimes possible both to know something important and to ignore that knowledge. To do this is to generate the phenomenon of the well-known secret, an obvious fact we ignore. When Edgar Allen Poe suggested that the best location to hide something is the most obvious place, he was teaching applied law and social science.

This article is about youth crime and sentencing policy. The "well-known secret" is this: adolescents commit crimes, as they live their lives, in groups. While the empirical evidence for this hypothesis is at least fifty years old, the consequences of this simple and important finding are frequently ignored when we measure crime, pass laws, and postulate theories of criminal activity. The problems associated with ignoring the obvious have grown more serious in recent years, as the study of criminal behavior has shifted from its sociological origins into a wide spectrum of social, behavioral, economic, and policy science disciplinary sub-specialties. We have failed to ask the right questions and have risked answering the questions we ask in the wrong way because we did not appreciate what we already know.

The sentiments expressed in this article are strong: the burden of proof is mine. I shall attempt to meet that burden in two stages. Part I discusses some evidence on adolescent crime as group behavior that emerged from the pioneering studies of the Chicago School in the 1920s, and supplements this rich information with more recent crime specific estimates of group crimi-

"Kids, Groups, and Crime" is reprinted by special permission from the *Journal of Criminal Law and Criminology* 72, no. 3 (Fall 1981): 867–85. © 1981 by Northwestern University School of Law.

The research reported in these pages was supported by Grant DJ/LEAA 79NI-AX-0072, National Institute of Justice. The data for analysis were provided by Wesley Skogan, Northwestern University; the Rand Corporation, Santa Monica, California; the Vera Institute of Justice, New York City; and Philip Cook, Duke University. My primary intellectual creditors in this venture include Peter Greenwood and Joan Petersilia, Rand Corporation; Gordon Hawkins, University of Sydney; Alfred Blumstein, Carnegie-Mellon University; Albert Reiss, Yale University, and Norval Morris, University of Chicago.

nality. Part II catalogues some of the things we do not know as a consequence of ignoring the obvious.

I. Kids, Groups and Crime: Then and Now

Clifford Shaw and Henry McKay wrote a major study for the first National Commission on Crime. The year was 1931. The title was *Male Juvenile Delinquency as Group Behavior*.[1] The essay was based on an analysis of all boys who appeared in the Cook County, Illinois Juvenile Court charged with delinquency during 1928. The analysis justified the title of their essay, as shown in their original Figure 9, now labeled Figure 1. Eight out of ten boys accused of delinquency were alleged to have committed their offenses in the company of one or more companions. Shaw and McKay extended this analysis by specifying the number of participants alleged in the 1928 petition sample as shown in Figure 2, their original Figure 10.

While these findings were dramatic, they were not surprising. A 1923 study of theft offenders in the same court had found that nine out of ten males charged with theft were believed to have committed their offenses in groups.[2]

More recent data on the relationship between groups and adolescent criminality are needed for two reasons. First, 1928 was quite a while ago. Second, the petty thieves depicted by Shaw and McKay hardly fit the contemporary image of serious delinquency in the American city. The authors of one textbook on criminology observed how "quaint" the Shaw and McKay "delinquents seem to us today, in their knickerbockers and cloth caps and pre-Atomic innocence."[3] Furthermore, while group activity is associated with most juvenile delinquency, there is a tendency to revert to individualistic models when discussing serious crime.

Modern evidence is available on the predominance of groups as a distinc-

FIGURE 1

Percentage of Lone and Group Offenders Among Offenders Brought to the Juvenile Court

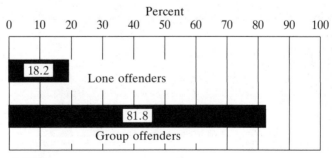

Source: Shaw & McKay.

FIGURE 2
Percentage Distribution of Offenders Brought to Court by Number of Participants

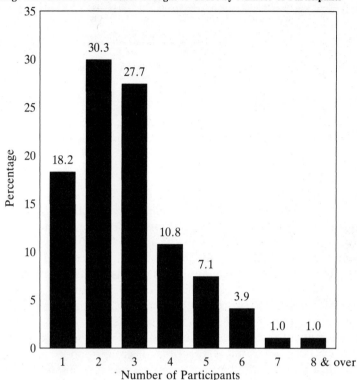

Source: Shaw & McKay.

tive aspect of adolescent criminality, including the serious offenses that are the focus of recent concern about youth crime policy. Table 1 shows data collected from a sample of robbery victims in the National Crime Panel in 1973. For present purposes, the National Crime Panel data are deficient in two aspects. Since the method of the survey was to ask victims to guess the ages of offenders, it was necessary to use crude age categories. Robberies committed by offenders "under 21" are hardly homogeneous events. The second shortcoming of the National Crime Panel data is that when victims are asked to guess ages, a substantial number of incorrect guesses may produce a random error factor that would mute any difference in pattern between younger and older offenders because of improper classification.

Despite its drawbacks, the National Crime Panel data show that the relationship between the offender's age and group robbery is striking. Slightly more than a third of the robberies committed by offenders under 21 are committed by a single assailant compared with 61 percent of those

TABLE 1
Robbery Incidents by Number of Offenders and Age Groups*

Number of Offenders	Under 21 percent	21 and Over percent
1	36%	61%
2	29	25
3	16	10
4 or more	19	4
Total	100%	100%

*Cases in which offenders were identified as mixed age groups deleted.

Source: National Crime Panel Data, provided by Wesley Skogan, Northwestern University.

robberies where the victim believes the offender was over 21. At the other end of the distribution, younger offenders commit five times as many victimizations in groups of four or more than do older offenders.

More precise data on youth criminality are available from the recent Vera Institute of Justice analysis of the delinquency jurisdiction of New York's Family Court. Figure 3 is an analysis of a sample of cases leading to court referral of offenders under age 16 and thus eligible for Family Court processing in New York City. This figure is comparable to the information presented in the first Shaw and McKay analysis. The Vera sample counts each alleged delinquent as a separate case. Thus, if two juveniles are referred for one robbery, this will result in two cases of group robbery while a single 15-year-old arrested for robbery counts as only one case. For this reason, the New York data overstate the number of offenses that are the product of group participation, but the method allows direct comparison with the Shaw and McKay figures which were compiled using the same approach.[4] With the exception of assault and rape (n = 8), the bar charts bear what can only be called a striking resemblance to each other and to the theft estimates that emerged from the Chicago area studies.

The predominance of group crime in this sample of young adolescent offenders (under 16) is similar to the earlier studies of juvenile theft, but occurs across a wide variety of offenses. For these age groups, the youthfulness of the offender appears to predict group participation more effectively than the nature of the offense.

The New York data were not coded in a way that could replicate the pre-computer precision of Shaw and McKay's distribution of theft offenses by number of offenders.[5] However, a sample of armed robbery arrests referred to Juvenile Court in Los Angeles collected by the Rand Corporation does permit this further detail, as shown in Figure 4.

In the Rand sample, 18 out of 103 robbery incidents attributable to juveniles involved lone offenders. The 97 robbery incidents for which the

FIGURE 3
**Multiple Offender Cases as a Percent of Total
Juveniles Charged, by Crime, New York City**

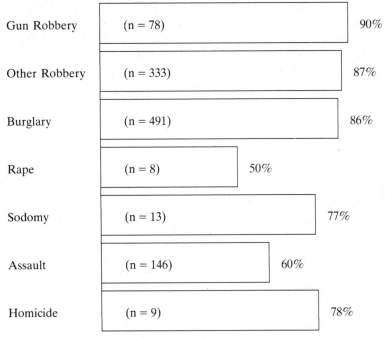

Source: Vera Wide Sample, Family Court Disposition Study.

number of offenders was coded provide a potential pool of over 225 robbery
arrests, and about a third of the incidents involved three or more offenders.
The Los Angeles robbery data supplement the broader New York sample in
several respects. First, the way in which the data were coded permits us to
move closer to "offender to offense" ratios. Each robbery event was reported only once, eliminating the systematic overestimation of group crime
that occurs when each offender charged is counted as a separate case.
Second, Los Angeles operates a juvenile justice system that defines the
eighteenth birthday as the end of juvenile court jurisdiction, while New
York cuts off jurisdiction at the sixteenth birthday. This two-year interval is
important: over half of the Los Angeles robberies (56%) involve defendants
of age sixteen or seventeen. The cases would not result in family court
processing of the sample defendants in New York. The proportion of all
robberies committed by these sixteen- and seventeen-year-olds in groups is
as substantial as that found among younger adolescents. Because the rate of
robbery and other serious violent offenses is much greater among older

FIGURE 4
Percent Distribution of Armed Robbery Offenses Involving
Juvenile Suspects by Number of Offenders, Los Angeles*

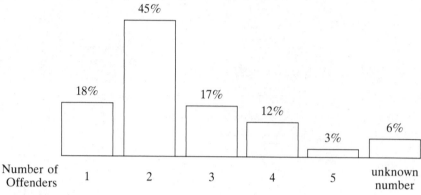

Source: Rand Corp./Juvenile Record Study, 1979.
*Percentages rounded.

adolescents, the Los Angeles findings suggest the impact of multiple offender adolescent crime and multiple arrests on aggregate statistics will be
much greater.

II. So What?

This essay is intended neither as a comprehensive survey of the evidence on
group criminality during adolescence, nor as an assessment of the importance of this data to criminological theories about delinquent behavior.
Empirical studies documenting adolescent crime abound.[6] The criminological literature discussing the implications of "dyadic," "triadic," and "other
group" conformations is extensive. Whatever else may be said of modern
criminology, the role of "male juvenile delinquency as group behavior" is
acknowledged as fundamental, and the extent to which different types of
criminality exhibit similar characteristics is well-known, although the New
York and Los Angeles data presented earlier provide us with larger numbers of serious offenses than many modern delinquency studies.[7]

This well-known pattern has important implications for contemporary
research dealing with crime statistics, general deterrence, incapacitation,
the construction of models of criminal behavior, the study of criminal
careers, and efforts to reform sentencing practices in juvenile and criminal
courts. These relatively recent research subspecialties are the intellectual
next-door neighbors to traditional studies of crime and delinquency. Lately,
however, the neighbors have not been speaking to each other.

1. Estimating the Proportion and Volume of Serious Youth Crime

No one doubts that young offenders account for a disproportionate share of most serious crimes. But the question is, how large a share? This cannot be answered with current data. The evidence for this assertion goes beyond fashionable doubts about a "dark figure" of crime or of offenders. The current state of the art for estimating the youth share of serious crime is:

    a. to establish the percentage of persons under 18 or 21 arrested for particular offense; and

    b. to assume, explicitly or implicitly, that the percentage distribution of arrests accurately reflects the percentage distribution of crimes.

In the process of passing the Juvenile Justice and Delinquency Prevention Act of 1974,[8] the very first thing that the United States Congress found was that juveniles account for almost half the arrests for serious crimes in the United States today.[9] One problem with inferring that juveniles account for half of all serious crime from these statistics is that the crude heterogeneous categories used in crime and arrest reporting lump serious and relatively minor offenses under single rubrics, such as robbery or assault.[10] A second problem is that younger offenders who are arrested in groups are counted two, three or even four times in single offense data far more commonly than are older offenders. The compound effect of treating minor and major offenses with equal statistical dignity in multiple offender counts is illustrated by Figure 5, adapted from the previously discussed National Crime Panel data based on robbery victim reports. Offenders under 21 comprise slightly over 60 percent of all the sample's "robbers," slightly over half of all "robberies," and less than a third of robberies committed with firearms.

Figure 5 is only the beginning. The estimates contained there use the twenty-first birthday as a cut-line, while juvenile court jurisdiction typically ends on or before the offender's eighteenth birthday. The statistics used to compile the congressional findings of fact are FBI estimates of arrests under age 18.[11] Since the rate of robbery arrests increases with age and the proportion of robberies committed with firearms also increases as a function of age, the proportion of firearm robbery events attributable to "juveniles" could plausibly range as low as 10 percent.

In dealing with currently available statistics, using hedge phrases like "could plausibly range" is well-advised. We simply do not know the youth share of particular forms of criminal activity, and we *cannot* use arrest statistics to derive estimates with acceptable margins of error.

2. Measuring Arrest and Punishment Risks in The Study of General Deterrence

The past decade has witnessed a resurgence of interest in the general deterrent effect of the threat of criminal sanctions, and a variety of efforts to

FIGURE 5
Percentage of Robbers, Robberies and Gun Robbers by Abe*

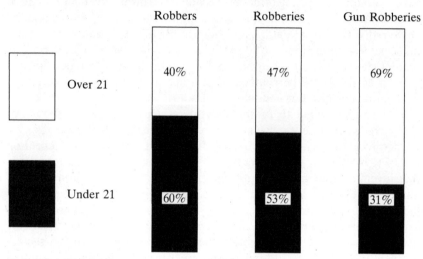

Source: National Crime Panel.
*mixed group cases (N = 106) deleted.

study deterrence by comparing crime rates and punishment levels over time or between jurisdictions.[12] Attempts to use existing aggregate data on offenses, arrests, and punishments are confounded by the overlapping jurisdictions of juvenile and criminal courts, and it is unlikely that researchers can use arrest statistics to "unconfound" matters.

The problem can be illustrated by examining common methods of estimating the risks of punishment and apprehension that are used to measure the credibility of threats in deterrence studies. The "risk of punishment" reported in Figure 6 is often used and fundamentally flawed.[13] By expressing adult prison admissions as a proportion of total reported offenses, "risk of punishment" measures no one's actual risk of punishment and will systematically be reduced as the proportion of juvenile offenses to total offenses increases. If juveniles are responsible for a large number of marginally serious offenses that either may or may not end up classified as a particular index offense, variations in police reporting and classification practices, as well as variations in the ratio of juvenile to adult offenses, will produce negative correlations between crime rates and the risk of punishment that have nothing to do with general deterrence.[14]

Measuring the risk of apprehension by comparing total gross arrests to total gross offenses in any particular crime category generates similar problems. The measure is of two separate risks of arrest that cannot be segre-

FIGURE 6
Conventional Methods of Estimating Risk
in Deterrence Research

$$\text{Risk of Punishment} = \frac{\text{Number of Prison Commitments (Adults)}}{\text{Number of Crimes (Juvenile and Adult)}}$$

$$\text{Risk of Apprehension} = \frac{\text{Number of Arrests (Juvenile and Adult)}}{\text{Number of Crimes (Juvenile and Adult)}}$$

gated and a pool of offenses that represents an unknown admixture of juvenile and adult offenses with varying degrees of severity. Unless the mixture of adult and juvenile crimes and risks does not vary over time or from city to city, the result of this mixing will confound attempts to measure deterrent effects.

Under such circumstances, variations in the age distribution of crime or in police policy can successfully masquerade as variations in sentencing policy until we can separately estimate juvenile and adult offense rates. But the lesson of Figure 5 is that using the age distribution of arrests to attempt this segregation will not succeed. For this reason, it seems unlikely that comparative studies using aggregate data can measure true risks.[15]

3. Measuring the Incapacitation Impact of Incarceration

The logic of incapacitation is straightforward: lock up people who would otherwise commit crimes and the general community will experience a lower crime rate.[16] But selecting the appropriate candidates for incapacitation and estimating the number of crimes saved proves to be a tricky business. Efforts to estimate "crimes saved" have proceeded from individualistic models of criminal behavior to what may be inaccurate conclusions. Those studies that found high offense rates in early adolescent target populations have failed to account for the problem of group involvement.[17] Simply stated, if one of three offenders is taken out of circulation for one year, we have no current basis for estimating whether, or to what extent, the crime rate is affected. If all three offenders are incapacitated, it is possible to estimate "crime saved" as a joint function of the crimes these offenders would have committed alone and with each other, but not in other groups. Using current methods of incapacitative accounting, however, assigning *each* member of *each* group *every* crime they would have committed together or in other groups creates a form of double and triple counting that overestimates "crime saved" in the group-prone adolescent years. The published studies that purport to measure incapacitation effects have not made serious efforts to correct for this bias.

4. Modeling Patterns of Criminal Behavior

Frequently, attempts to impose simplifying models to explain variations in particular offenses cannot succeed because of the diversity of behaviors subsumed in a single crime category. Robbery is a case in point, and an illustrative example concerns the determinants of whether firearms are used in robbery events. Working from a sample of robberies in Boston, John Conklin concluded "robbing with accomplices reduces the need to carry a weapon for self-protection, since the group itself acts as a functional equivalent of a weapon."[18] His data evidently did not control for age when relating weapon use to the number of offenders involved. Analyzing National Crime Panel data, Philip J. Cook found the opposite to be true: "Guns are *less* likely to be used by single offenders than by multiple offenders and . . . this pattern holds for subgroups of offenders . . . as well as for the entire sample . . . ! While it is plausible that a team of offenders has less 'need of a gun' than a single offender for a certain type of victim, the data suggest that teams of offenders tend to choose stronger victims."[19]

It may not be necessary to referee this particular dispute, because *both* Conklin and Cook are correctly describing the behavior of different subsets of robbery offenders—Professor Cook's analysis applies with force to unpremeditated robberies by young offenders. These patterns cannot be detected, however, by cross-tabulating weapon use and number of offenders for the total sample of robberies, as shown in Figure 7.

It turns out, however, that this flat pattern is misleading. Looking at these data without controlling for age is precisely the wrong way to examine the National Crime Panel data because of the greater likelihood that younger offenders (a) will rob in groups and (b) will use guns less often *whether or not*

FIGURE 7
Percentage Gun Use in Robberies by Number of Offenders

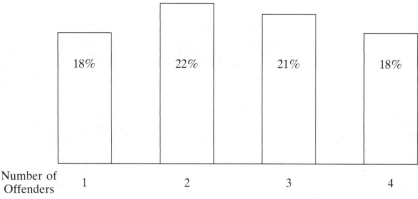

Source: National Crime Panel.

TABLE 2
Percentage Gun Use in Robbery By Age of Offender and Number of Offenders*

Number of Offenders	Under 21	Over 21
1	8	24
2	13	33
3	13	36
4 or more	12	40

*For total robbery event numbers, *see* Table 1   Source: National Crime Panel Data
supra.

they rob in groups.[20] Table 2 displays the results of separate analysis patterns of gun use and number of offenders by age. For reported victimizations where all of the offenders were thought to be over 21, there is a modest increase in gun use as the size of the group increases. For offenders under 21, their youth is a much more powerful predictor of gun use than the number of robberies. Consistently, gun use is about a third of adult levels across all categories of offender group size. Thus, it may be true that young offenders find "courage in numbers" when a pre-existing group spontaneously decides to commit a robbery. This is consistent with the low rate of gun use and the low rate of single offender robberies among young offenders. Older offenders engage in more planning and exhibit different target selection and accomplice selection patterns. For planned offenses, the target of the robbery has a substantial impact on the size of the group and the weapon used. In spontaneous robberies, the group and armaments have been determined before the target is selected, but failure to control for age of offender completely obscures these patterns.

5. Comprehending Criminal "Careers"

Almost all American adolescents commit crimes at some point in the transition to adulthood. Many of these offenses are trival; most of the time, adolescent criminality does not represent the beginning of a pattern of habitual criminality that will extend through adulthood. It is, however, also true that the majority of those who persist in patterns of predatory crime through early adulthood have started young.[21]

In recent years the study of criminal careers has been the subject of renewed interest and changing focus. For decades, criminologists have been interested in factors associated with desisting from or continuing to commit criminal offenses.[22] Recently, such studies have been undertaken with ambitions to contribute to policy: Finding characteristics that predict continued criminality is now seen as a path to sentencing policy, particularly sentencing policies that emphasize the incapacitative effects of incarcerative sanctions.[23] Similarly, if social scientists can find characteristics of adolescent-offending that are associated with a lack of recidivism, this information can be used to allocate scarce penal resources more efficiently and avoid unnecessary social control.

All of this, of course, depends upon the development of accurate discriminant indicators of future behavior. The Wolfgang *et al.* cohort study of Philadelphia boys who turned eighteen during 1963 has provided some promising preliminary cues but stopped far short of predicting adult criminal careers.[24] The follow-up study of that Philadelphia sample may provide further information.[25] More recent retrospective study of individuals imprisoned as adults provides a list of characteristics associated with persisting criminality in the adult years but cannot, by the nature of the sample, provide data on what factors are associated with nonpersistence of criminal activity.[26]

The distinctive group character of adolescent criminality may provide a perspective that can increase the capacity of research to empirically test the degree to which prior behavior predicts future offenses. At some point in adolescence or early adult development, most of those who have committed offenses in groups either cease to be offenders or continue to violate the law, but for different reasons and in different configurations. Either of these paths is a significant change from prior behavior. The transition from group criminality to noncriminal individual behavior is obviously worthy of sustained study. The equally important transition from adolescent to adult patterns of criminal behavior should also be a particularly important period in the analysis of criminal careers.

At the outset it is important to identify *when* transitions from juvenile to adult criminality and from adolescent criminality to desistance occur. This is not to suggest that the search is for a particular day when crime is abandoned or when patterns of criminality change; rather, both transitions should be expected to be processes that occur over substantial periods of time, and occur at different stages in the life history of different individuals. But identification and study of these transitional periods, in individual cases and cohorts, could enhance our understanding of criminality as a developmental event and sharpen the empirical focus of the questions to be asked in predicting future criminality.

One critical contribution of this focus would be to discriminate between predictive attributes or events that occur early in an adolescent career and those predictive events that occur more proximately to the transition out of crime or into different patterns of crime. A complete accounting scheme should separately consider:

1. Characteristics of the individual, such as age, location, and family structure that antedate or accompany the early adolescent years;

2. Aspects of the individual's involvement in early adolescent crime, including the kind of crime, age at first arrest, the type of group participating in crime, and the nature of the individual's role—dominant or passive—in adolescent group activities; and

3. Events or influences that occur later in adolescence that predict the nature of the change in the individual behavior.

Aggregate statistics on the distribution of arrests suggest that the transition out of criminality is not a random event spread over the late teens and through the mid-twenties, but rather clusters in late adolescence. However, my previous remarks suggest that aggregate arrest statistics are an insufficient foundation for studying this phenomenon. Those years where gross arrest rates decline are also periods when arrest statistics underestimate the extent of criminal participation when arrest rates of older age groups are compared to those of younger groups.[27]

When looking for the transition to "adult style" individual or planned group crime, there is no reason to select *a priori* any single one or two year period when we expect such a transition to occur. Case history studies and cohort samples can collect data on the nature of each individual offense coming to the attention of the police,[28] and other supplemental methods, such as self-report studies, can be used to determine the period of transition, its duration, and its significant concomitants.

6. Determining Appropriate Sanctions for Youth Crime

Statistics on the sanctions administered to young offenders in juvenile or family courts strike many observers as a classic instance of social non-control. The most impressive numbers come from New York City, a criminogenically congested urban area where only offenders under sixteen are referred to the Family Court. One study of nearly 4,000 juvenile robbery arrests found that more than half of these charges were dismissed without formal referral to the Family Court, and over three-quarters of all charges are eventually dismissed.[29] Barbara Boland and James Q. Wilson cite the end result of this study with evident disapproval, "In short, only three percent of the juveniles arrested for robbery and only seven percent of the juveniles actually tried in Family Court received any form of custodial care, whether with a relative, in a Juvenile Home or training school, or in an adult prison."[30] In Los Angeles, another study estimated the chances of a formal determination of delinquency at 17 for every 100 arrests.[31] This kind of statistical portrait lends itself nicely to fears of an army of young violent offenders roaming the streets unchecked. The observer may also be tempted to conclude that the philosophy and youth welfare policies of the juvenile court are the explanation for such epidemic leniency.

Serious study of the relationship between age, crime, and punishment has only recently been undertaken. But the early returns suggest that the forces that produce such apparently alarming examples of "case mortality" are at once more complicated and less dependent on juvenile court philosophy than many had supposed.[32]

The animating philosophy of child protection in the juvenile court undoubtedly reduces the number of arrests that result in formal adjudications of delinquency and post-adjudication commitment in secure facilities. However, a number of juvenile court policies *not* clearly related to leniency toward the young also contribute to high rates of informal disposition. In marginal cases, police might arrest juvenile offenders expecting the case to be "adjusted" at intake buy relying on the arrest as a sanction and an opportunity for compiling a dossier.[33] The juvenile court's well documented use of detention after arrest as a substitute for formal adjudication represents a troublesome social control device that is not visible when only the post-trial sanctions are examined. This is important because nationwide detention is about seven times as frequent as post-adjudication commitment to secure facilities.[34] It is difficult to view detention practices as part of a sentimental general theory of youth protection.

Aggregate statistics on juvenile arrests reflect more than the distinctive policies and style of the contemporary juvenile court. The offenders processed in juvenile justice systems are different from other criminal defendants—they are younger, and their youth is an important influence on sentencing policy in criminal as well as juvenile courts.[35] Furthermore, and of central importance for present purposes, the offenses committed in early and middle adolescence also differ qualitatively from the criminal activity characteristic of older offender populations. The propensity of adolescent robbers to commit less serious forms of the offense than their elders must be taken into account in providing an explanation for the New York and Los Angeles statistics discussed earlier.[36] It is far from clear what the most just or efficient social response should be to adolescent garage burglaries, fist fights, and school-yard extortions.

The pervasive problem of the adolescent accessory aggravates the difficulty of determining appropriate sanctions for youth crime. One useful example occurs early in the cohort study volume, when its authors are discussing the proper assessment of "seriousness scores":

> Let us suppose that three boys have committed a burglary. They range in age from 12 to 16 years. The oldest is the instigator and leader who actively committed the offense with one of the others: the youngest is an unwilling partner who was ignorant of the plan but was present because he happened to be with the others at the start of what began as an idle saunter through the streets of the neighborhood. Suppose the event is given a score of 4. Does this score, when

applied to each participant, accurately measure the involvement of each? Should the oldest boy and his active partner be assessed this score, but the younger given a lower one?[37]

In any system of justice that considers the magnitude of the harm done and the degree of the individual offender's involvement, the attempt to determine an appropriate sanction will confront the same difficulties as the researcher attempting to determine an appropriate score.

In discussing this case, Wolfgang and his colleagues state that all three offenders are equally guilty "from a legal point of view."[38] This statement is correct but potentially misleading. Assuming a trier of fact determines that the youngest was a reluctant but voluntary partner who aided and abetted the offense, all three adolescents can be found delinquent in a juvenile court.[39] This kind of group crime would also generate criminal liability for the appropriate degree of burglary in a criminal court through the magic of the doctrine of accessorial liability.[40] But prosecutorial discretion in selecting cases for prosecution, determining charges, and pressing for punishment combined with judicial discretion in determining sentences in both juvenile and criminal courts creates ample opportunity for differences in punishment policy that are not reflected in the formal substantive law of either crime or delinquency.

When sentencing policy is dispensed by a series of low visibility discretions, a system can have a policy toward accomplice problems in adolescence without announcing it, and not infrequently without knowing it. In the Rand study of the Los Angeles juvenile court, lone offenders arrested for armed robbery experienced a three-in-ten chance of commitment to the state's youth authority, while only thirteen percent of those who acted in groups received the most serious disposition available to the court. It seems plausible to suppose that much of this difference can be attributed to prosecutorial and judicial leniency toward individuals at the periphery of spontaneous adolescent crimes. But the discretionary decisions characteristic of juvenile justice hide rather than announce the real reasons they are made.

This article's ambitions fall short of resolving the complicated set of problems generated by the juvenile accomplice; instead, it is sufficient for present purposes to note the novelty and importance of these issues in the study of dispositional policy toward youth crime and realistic efforts to reform the law. To study dispositional patterns in juvenile court without paying careful attention to policies toward group offenses seems foolhardy. To assign to each of the three youths arrested in the hypothetical burglary discussed above the same seriousness score, and to use that score to predict the level of sanctions, will create the impression that serious crimes go unpunished if any of the group is excused because his participation was relatively minor.[41] This kind of research procedure will also continue our ignorance about how participants in group crime are sanctioned.

Attempts to reform sentencing practices in the juvenile court, expecially efforts to lead sanctioning models away from the jurisprudence of treatment and toward concepts of making the punishment fit the crime, will find the myriad problems of sanctioning the adolescent accomplice very close to the top of any sensible priority list for deliberation. These issues are important because they confront whatever set of institutions will process young offenders in a majority of all cases. The issues are novel because the nature of group criminality in adolescence bears scant resemblance to the classic image of the criminal conspiracy or the conceptual foundations of the common law of accessorial liability. The intelligent law reformer thus must take a short course in criminology as a preliminary to setting his agenda. My own review of recent literature and debate suggests that this sequence of events is infrequent.[42]

Conclusion

The path of progress in social science proceeds more frequently from the general to the specific than the other way around. A survey of some of the difficulties generated by inattention to the special character of adolescent criminality bears an uncanny resemblance to a revised research agenda. Much that needs to be done can be done in the near future, using relatively straightforward methods of measurement on less than staggering budgets.

The criminological excursion reported in these pages illustrates a broader point: Those who regulate particular forms of human behavior, or study the effects of regulation, abstract themselves from the knowledge base of other social and behavioral sciences only at great cost. In an era when the study of public policy has become a discipline of its own, at a time when the study of law and legal institutions has developed prescriptive ambitions, the well-known secret is an occupational hazard of no small significance.

Notes

1. C. Shaw & H. McKay, "Male Juvenile Delinquency as Group Behavior" in "Report on the Causes of Crime," 191–99 [*II Wickersham Comm'n Rep., No. 13* (1931)], reprinted as Chapter 17 in *The Social Fabric of the Metropolis* (J. Short, ed. 1971). [hereinafter cited as *The Social Fabric*].

2. See id., *The Social Fabric*, at 256, no. 2.

3. D. Taft & R. England, *Criminology* 180 (4th ed. 1964).

4. Vera Institute of Justice, Family Court Disposition Study (1981) (unpublished draft).

5. The Vera study dichotomized juvenile court cases into individual and group events. A case represented an individual charged. Id.

6. For general reviews of the literature on this subject see: R. Hood & R. Sparks, "Subcultural and Gang Delinquency," in *Key Issues in Criminology* 80–109 (1970) (includes data on British and Scandinavian group behavior by age); K. Sveri, "Group Activity," in 1 *Scandinavian Studies in Criminology* 173–85 (C. Christiansen, ed. 1965); *President's Comm. on Juvenile Delinquency and Youth Crime, Juvenile Gangs* (Report of G. Geis, 1965).

7. The number of unambiguously serious, particularly violent, offenses in the typical self report study is quite small. The Philadelphia cohort data apparently include larger numbers of homicide arrests, and rape arrests (14 and 44 respectively). See M. Wolfgang, R. Figlio & T. Sellin, *Delinquency in a Birth Cohort* 68–99 (1972). As the authors note, the method of scoring used in this study does not provide information on how many events these arrests represent. Id. at 23–24. A separate accounting of armed robbery or assault with deadly weapons was not published. The 193 robbery arrests in the Philadelphia cohort were not classified by event or seriousness, other than in seriousness scores. By contrast, the Rand juvenile court study reported 253 armed robbery arrests that resulted in the 104 case sample which is the basis for Figure 4.

8. Juvenile Justice and Delinquency Prevention Act of 1974, Pub. L. No. 93–415, 88 Stat. 1109 (codified at scattered sections of 5, 18, 42 U.S.C.) [hereinafter cited as Juvenile Justice Act].

9. Id.

10. See, e.g., Zimring, "American Youth Violence: Issues and Trends," 1 *Crime & Just. Annual Rev. Research* 67 (1979).

11. Juvenile Justice Act, supra note 8, *Uniform Crime Reports* (1974).

12. See, e.g., *National Academy of Science, Panel on Research in Deterrence and Incapacitation* (*Final Report* 1978), for a summary of deterrence literature and methods.

13. See id. at 99–103 for a list of more than a dozen studies that use risk variable displayed in Figure 6.

14. A particular fear with respect to statistics that generate "artificial deterrence" is that "junk crimes" and "junk arrests," defined as crimes and arrests that are not likely to receive serious sanctions in the adult system, are the major share of variations between cities and over time. If this is the case, variations in juvenile arrest rates could thoroughly confound efforts to assess the general deterrent impact of criminal sanctions over time or in comparative studies.

15. The alternative to this approach, however, is attractive. Given the difference between juvenile and adult criminal sanctions for similar behavior, deterrence theory is needed that can explain wide variations in the age of jurisdiction, and variations in patterns for similar crime to discover whether individuals respond to differences in risks when they cross over the borderline between juvenile and criminal justice at varying points in their criminal careers.

16. See, e.g., Shinnar & Shinnar, "The Effects of the Criminal Justice System on the Control of Crime: A Quantitative Approach," 9 *Law and Soc'y Rev.* 581 (1975). See also J. Q. Wilson, *Thinking about Crime* 198–291 (1975).

17. See, e.g., Shinnar & Shinnar, supra note 16; J. Petersilia & P. Greenwood,

Criminal Careers of Habitual Felons (1979). The only mention of the problem of incapacitating one of the group is found in the *Panel on Research*, supra note 12, at 65 (see especially n. 63 and the text accompanying n. 64). In contrast, Albert Reiss has recently demonstrated the impact of group offending on incapacitation effects. Reiss, "Understanding Changes in Crime Rates," in *Crime Rates and Victimization* 13–14 (A. Reiss & A. Biderman, eds. 1980).

18. J. Conklin, *Robbery and the Criminal Justice System* 108 (1972); see also the table at 106.

19. Cook, "A Strategic Choice Analysis of Robbery," in *Sample Surveys of the Victims of Crime* 180 (W. Skogan, ed. 1976).

20. The comparison between gun robbers and other robbers charged, see Figure 3 (90% versus 87% multiple offenders), lends further support to this interpretation.

21. See F. E. Zimring, *Confronting Youth Crime: A Report of the Twentieth Century Task Force on Sentencing Policy toward Young Offenders* (1978).

22. See, e.g., S. Glueck & E. T. Glueck, *Five Hundred Criminal Careers* (193); S.Glueck & E. T. Glueck, *Later Criminal Careers* (1937); S. Glueck & E. T. Glueck, *Criminal Careers in Retrospect* (1943) (Three volumes of follow-up studies on the post-release careers of 510 inmates of the Massachusetts State Reformatory released in 1921–22.)

23. See, e.g., Boland & Wilson, "Age, Crime and Punishment," *Public Interest*, Spring 1978, at 22; J. Q. Wilson, supra note 16.

24. For this discussion of the implications of the Wolfgang data on the concentration and predictability of youth violence, see Zimring, supra note 10, at 94–98.

25. For a preliminary report on the Philadelphia follow-up study see Wolfgang, "From Boy to Man," in *The Serious Juvenile Offender* 101 (Hudson & Mack, eds. 1978) (proceedings of a National Symposium, Government Printing Office). A book length report on this research is forthcoming.

26. J. Petersilia & P. Greenwood, supra note 17; a second Rand report, *Doing Crime*, utilizes a weighted sample of all prison inmates to retrospectively study pre-prison careers for currently incarcerated inmates. Rand Corp., *Doing Crime* (Apr. 1980).

27. For age specific arrest estimates (with insufficient warnings about this difficulty), see F. E. Zimring, supra note 21, Table I-2, at 37.

28. See M. Wolfgang, R. Figlio & T. Sellin, supra note 7.

29. Office of Children's Services, N.Y. Division of Criminal Justice Services, cited in Boland & Wilson, supra note 23, at 28.

30. Id. at 27–28.

31. This estimate was derived by Peter W. Greenwood, in P. Greenwood, J. Petersilia & F. E. Zimring, *Age, Crime, and Sanctions: The Transition from Juvenile to Adult Court* (1980), from K. S. Teilmann & M. W. Klein, "Assessment of the Impact of California's 1977 Juvenile Justice Legislation" (1977) (Draft, Social Science Research Institute, University of Southern California).

32. See P. Greenwood, J. Petersilia & F. E. Zimring, supra note 31.

33. See Coffee, "Privacy versus Parens Patriae: The Role of Police Records in the Sentencing and Surveillance of Juveniles," 57 *Cornell L. Rev.* 571, 579–94 (1972), for a discussion of arrests as a means of building a dossier on juveniles and for discussion of analogous procedures in New York City.

34. F. E. Zimring, supra note 21, at 65–82.

35. Id. at 35–44, 65–82.

36. A first effort to control for offense seriousness by age in Los Angeles is discussed in P. Greenwood, J. Petersilia, & F. E. Zimring, supra note 31.

37. M. Wolfgang, R. Figlio, & T. Sellin, supra note 7, at 23–24.

38. Id. at 24.

39. My discussion in the text assumes a "modern" definition of delinquency, that is, a status conferred when a minor is found to have committed an act that would have been criminal if performed by an adult. Broader definitions of delinquency, including standards such as "in danger of leading an immoral life," or "associating with bad companions," would obviate the necessity for determining the nature of our twelve year olds' participation. See Institute of Judicial Administration/American Bar Ass'n, *Standards Relating to Juvenile Delinquency and Sanctions* (tentative draft 1977) [hereinafter cited as *Juvenile Delinquency and Sanctions*].

40. See, e.g., Criminal Code of 1961, *Ill. Rev. Stat.*, ch. 38, §5-2 (1980); see also Sayre, "Criminal Responsibility for the Acts of Another," 43 *Harv. L. Rev.* 689 (1930).

41. This weakness characterizes any research procedure that converts events into seriousness scores and gives the total score to each offender as well as studies that use offense and arrest. See, e.g., M. Wolfgang, R. Figlio & T. Sellin, supra note 7; Strasburg, *Violent Delinquents* (1978) (A Report to the Ford Foundation from the Vera Institute of Justice).

42. For example, two of the Juvenile Justice Standards volumes are closely related to juvenile court policy toward youth crime, but they contain no substantive analysis of the appropriate role of doctrines of accessorial liability, or conspiracy. *Juvenile Delinquency and Sanctions*, supra note 39, Institute of Judicial Administration/American Bar Ass'n, *Standards Relating to Disposition* (tentative draft 1977). While the role of peer pressure is not discussed, standard 3.4 argues against delinquency jurisdiction if a parent or guardian coerced a juvenile's participation in a criminal act, *Juvenile Delinquency and Sanctions*, supra note 39 at 33, commentary. Further, the commentaries in these volumes contain no analysis of patterns of youth crime, the magnitude of the problem, or typologies of youth crime.

Appendix

In Memoriam: Hans Mattick, 1920–1978

Gordon Hawkins

It is particularly appropriate that this volume should be dedicated to the memory of Hans Mattick. Between the criminological work done in the University of Chicago's Department of Sociology in the 1920s and in the Law School from 1965 onward there was no formal connection. There was, however, a remarkable, informal connection in the person of Hans W. Mattick, who was first associate director and later codirector with Norval Morris of the Center for Studies in Criminal Justice. It is also appropriate that something should be said here about that connection and about the man himself. Mattick exemplified in a striking fashion the concept of the marginal worker between academia and the world of action referred to in the Introduction.

It was a supervising sociologist for the Chicago Area Project by the name of Joseph Lohman (later to become the first dean of the School of Criminology at the University of California in Berkeley) who played a crucial role in shaping the career which ultimately led to Mattick's becoming one of America's leading criminologists. Lohman first encountered Mattick in the near-northside area of Chicago in the mid-1930s when Lohman was engaged in delinquency prevention activity and Mattick was pursuing an unruly adolescence. Looking back over his career, Mattick described the meeting as a crucial event in his life, which led eventually to his going into criminology. At that time, however, neither of them would have predicted Mattick's future accurately. According to Mattick, "He viewed me as a 'client'—one who was of interest because of my background and because I had hoboed around the country so much."[1]

Mattick's education was sporadic, including six different grade schools and three high schools, as well as welfare institutions and reform schools. He left home and "went on the road" for the first time at the age of fourteen, and thereafter at frequent intervals. During those years on the road he led what he candidly described as a "malicious and predatory life,"[2] riding freight trains to Kansas, Wisconsin, Michigan, Louisiana, Florida and New York, occasionally working, engaging in petty crime, stealing food, clothes and money in small-time breaking-and-enterings. In that period he inevitably gained experience of the American jail, which in later life he referred to as "the cloacal region of American corrections."[3]

In 1941, Hans was drafted into the army, where he served more than four years, two of them overseas in Europe. When he was released from the army, he returned to Chicago ("to do something with my life") and enrolled as a student at the University of Chicago.[4] After graduating, he spent a year with the Committee on Social Thought, where Edward Shils was one of his tutors, and then entered the Department of Sociology, where he again met Joseph Lohman, who at that time was adjunct professor in the department. There he attended courses taught not only by Lohman but also by Ernest Burgess, Louis Wirth, William Ogburn, Herbert Blumer, and Everett Hughes, "some of the persons," he said later, "that made the University of Chicago Department of Sociology the renowned place of historical event, so to speak, that it was."[5]

Through Lohman he got actively involved in criminology and did his thesis on parolees in the army.[6] Gerald Suttles has suggested that for Hans military service was a sort of moratorium during which he was able to lay his past to rest and contemplate his future and that this is reflected in the subject he selected for study for his M.A. "It is," says Suttles, "a very fine study, still one of the most persuasive when attempting to single out how nearly our past can determine our future. It is still read, tho' not as widely as it deserves."[7]

It was also through Lohman, who held a number of political offices, including sheriff of Cook County and Illinois state treasurer, that Mattick was appointed to a series of jobs: sociologist actuary at Stateville Penitentiary (1950–55); assistant warden of the Cook County Jail (1955–58), from which he resigned a few days before an execution because he did not want to participate or be involved in it in any way; and supervisor of unemployment compensation (1959–60), during which period he was president of the Illinois Academy of Criminology as well. Then in 1960, he was appointed field director of research for the Chicago Youth Development Project, a position which he held until he joined the Center for Studies in Criminal Justice in 1965.[8]

On those who came to know him during his six years at the center, he made so striking and profound an impression that his death in 1978 called forth a peculiarly poignant sense of loss, which the passage of time has done little to diminish. He seemed at first meeting a slightly forbidding figure with his powerful physique, his battered physiognomy, and his gruff, laconic, deadpan delivery of sardonic assessments of the current scene. He had the appearance of a retired heavyweight boxer, an old-time police chief or political boss, and his apparent cynicism and lack of illusion matched his appearance.

Yet it seldom took long to discover that this carapace masked a disposition of great sensitivity and kindness. It was clear that he had few illusions, but it was evident also that he was no misanthrope. He loved music (both classical and traditional jazz), literature, the fine arts and good food. After a meal, which, perhaps as a result of his experience during the Depression, he always seemed to eat as if it might be his last, he would relax and, wreathed in smoke—he chain-smoked unfiltered cigarettes with the highest nicotine and tar content on the market—demonstrate his matchless ability as a raconteur.

Something of the flavor of his conversation is captured in "Dialogue with Hans W. Mattick," an interview published in the Winter 1979 issue of the *University of Toledo Law Review*, which was devoted to essays on reform of the criminal justice system and dedicated to Mattick's memory.[9] In that interview conducted in the last month of his life, Hans ranged reflectively over his whole career and incidentally answered a question which must have occurred to many who met him: How did so harsh a background produce a person of such wide culture?

His father Walter Rheiner, a leading member of the avant-garde movement known as German Expressionism (circa 1915–1925) and the author of a novella, *Kokain*, and a number of volumes of poetry, died in Berlin in 1925 when Hans was five years old. His mother, an artist's model who had voice and music training, remarried in 1926 and the family emigrated to the United States. Her second husband, Paul Mattick, was a Marxist active in the Spartacus League and subsequently the author of numerous pamphlets and a number of books.[10]

Hans gives a colorful account of the Chaplinesque squalor of his immigrant childhood on the near-northside of Chicago. But he emphasizes the fact that despite material poverty the family was not totally deprived: "I grew up in a home that was always full of books and the male adult figure was constantly reading and writing. . . . He almost never made any money . . . although we did have intellectual, artistic and spiritual resources in our home."[11] Much of his remembered experience and many of his conclusions are sombre, but they are vividly recounted and illuminated by the wit, pugnacity, candor, and forthrightness that distinguished the expression of his thought on any subject.

He had a natural dignity and also a great integrity. The latter is well exemplified in his final report on the Chicago Youth Development Project, which he directed and which cost over $1,400,000. He had invested all his energy through six years of his life on the project, but he made no attempt at all to claim, as is commonly done in such circumstances, that despite the apparent failure, some kind of unquantifiable success had been achieved. "[T]he project failed to achieve its goals," he wrote, "despite the expenditure of time, effort and money. The basic situation remained largely the same. No matter how the research team measured it, there were no 'significant differences' as the social scientists put it."[12]

As a criminologist his interests were extremely diverse, as the items under his name in our Cumulative Bibliography reveal. But it was on the subject of the American jail that he was unquestionably the ultimate authority. His combined experience of that institution as an inmate, administrator, and researcher gave him an unrivaled command of the subject. His writings on that subject, as Norval Morris has noted, carry forward "the great traditions of accuracy and controlled fervor for reform of John Howard."[13]

The analogy does not end there. Howard too had suffered imprisonment, as sheriff of Bedford he had been involved in the administration of jails, and in *The State of Prisons in England and Wales* (1777), he produced a detailed survey of jail conditions curiously similar in style, scope, and substance to Mattick's Illinois Jails Survey.[14] Both were men of unsentimental but deep compassion, great physical and moral courage, tenacity of purpose, and sober realism in their assessment of the possibilities of change. Both set out to shatter the complacence of their compatriots by the compilation of a massive and meticulous record of the details of intolerable abuse, and in that enterprise both acknowledged their failure. The similarities are remarkable. This is not to claim for Mattick equality of stature with John Howard. Yet it tells us something about him that he is the only criminologist in this century in regard to whom so close a comparison can be drawn with the father of penal reform.

Hans Mattick had neither the talent nor taste for self-advertisement, so he was not one of the best-known American criminologists. But in the streets of Chicago, a city he both loved and deplored, in which he passed the greater part of his life, he was well known and highly respected. On the day following his death the *Chicago Daily News* ran the following obituary in its editorial column.[15]

Hans Mattick—The Limitless Man

Hans Mattick was a big, burly bear of a man with a gravelly voice and heart huge enough to care for all the cripples of our complicated society. People who suffered from crime and people who committed crime; kids tortured and abused by their parents and parents so tortured that they abused their kids. Bad schools, bad prisons, slums that grow worse no matter how many urban improvement projects are launched. He cared and fought with limitless energy and optimism. At least, he made us think it was limitless. Mattick, ex-street gang worker, nationally known criminologist, died Thursday at 57. Police said he shot himself in the head.

Notes

1. John H. Laub, interviewer, "Dialogue with Hans W. Mattick," *University of Toledo Law Review* 10 (Winter 1979): 278.

2. Norval Morris, "Hans Mattick and the Death Penalty: Sentimental Notes on Two Topics." *University of Toledo Law Review* 10 (Winter 1979): 300. Reprinted as essay 4 in this volume.

3. See Hans W. Mattick and H. B. Aikman, "The Cloacal Region of American Corrections," *Annals of the American Academy of Political and Social Science* 381 (1969): 109–18.

4. Laub, "Dialogue," 278.

5. Ibid., 271.

6. See Hans W. Mattick, "Parolees in the Army during World War II," *Federal Probation* (September 1960): 49.

7. Personal communication from Professor Gerald D. Suttles, Dept. of Sociology, University of Chicago, 3 October 1980.

8. In 1972 he was appointed professor of criminal justice and director of the Center for Research in Criminal Justice at the University of Illinois at Chicago Circle, where he remained until his death in January 1978.

9. Laub, "Dialogue."

10. Including *Marx and Keynes* (Boston: Sargent, 1969); *Critique of Marcuse* (New York: Herder and Herder, 1972); and *Economic Crisis and Crisis Theory* (White Plains, N.Y.: Sharpe, 1981).

11. Laub, "Dialogue," 273–74.

12. Hans W. Mattick, Introduction to Frank J. Carney, Hans W. Mattick, and John D. Callaway, *Action on the Streets* (New York: Association Press, 1969), 16–17.

13. Morris, "Hans Mattick and the Death Penalty," 300.

14. Hans Mattick and Ronald Sweet, *Illinois Jails: Challenge and Opportunity for the 1970's* (Chicago: John Howard Association, 1970).

15. *Chicago Daily News*, Friday, 27 January 1978, 10.

Cumulative
Bibliography

Publications from the Center for
Studies in Criminal Justice 1965–1982

Corrections

Andenaes, Johannes, and Georg Stürup. *The Greenland Criminal Code.* The American Series of Foreign Penal Codes no. 16. South Hackensack, N.J.: Fred B. Rothman and Co., 1970.

Center for Studies in Criminal Justice. *A Selected Bibliography on the American Jail with Special Emphasis on Illinois Jails.* Chicago: Center for Studies in Criminal Justice, University of Chicago Law School, 1972.

Hawkins, Gordon. "Thomas Mott Osborne, 1859–1962: Pioneer in Penology." In N. Morris and M. Perlman, eds., *Law and Crime: Essays in Honor of Sir John Barry*, 155–80. New York: Gordon and Breach, 1972.

———. "Prisoner's Rights." *Australian Journal of Forensic Sciences* 6 (1974): 266–74.

———. *The Prison: Policy and Practice.* Studies in Crime and Justice. Chicago: University of Chicago Press, 1976.

———. "The Dangerous Offender in Prison." *Australian Journal of Forensic Science* 10 (1977): 23–29.

———. "The New Penology." In E. Kamenka, R. Brown, and A. E. Tay, eds., *Law and Society*, 108–27. London: Edward Arnold, 1978.

———. "The Prison." In G. G. Killinger, P. F. Cromwell, and J. M. Wood, eds., *Penology: The Evolution of Corrections in America*, 1–21. St. Paul: West Publishing Co., 1979.

———. "Correctional Officer Selection and Training." In B. M. Crouch, ed., *The Keepers: Prison Guards and Contemporary Corrections*, 49–62. Springfield, Ill.: Charles C. Thomas, 1980.

———. Review of *Prisons, Education, and Work* by John Braithwaite. *Australian and New Zealand Journal of Criminology* 14 (1981): 59–60.

Hawkins, Gordon, and Norval Morris. "Dangerousness and Prediction." In R. J. Gerber and P. F. McAnany, eds., *Contemporary Punishment*, 158–63. South Bend, Ind.: University of Notre Dame Press, 1972.

Jacobs, James B. "Participant Observation in Prison." *Urban Life and Culture* 3 (1974): 221–40.

———. "Street Gangs behind Bars." *Social Problems* 21 (1974): 359–409.

———. "The Politics of Corrections: Town/Prison Relations as a Determinant of Reform." *Social Service Review* 50 (1976): 623–31.

———. "Prison Violence and Formal Organization." In A. Cohen, G. Cole, and R. Bailey, eds., *Prison Violence*, 79–88. Lexington, Mass.: Lexington Books, 1976.

———. "The Stateville Counsellors: Symbol of Reform in Search of a Role." *Social Service Review* 50 (1976): 138–47.

———. "Stratification and Conflict among Prison Inmates." *Journal of Criminal Law and Criminology* 66 (1976): 476–82.

———. "Macrosociology and Imprisonment." In D. F. Greenburg, ed., *Corrections and Punishment*, 89–110. Beverly Hills: Sage Publications, 1977.

———. Review of *The Prison* by Gordon Hawkins, *Changing Prisons* by J. E. Hall Williams, and *Work Furlough and the County Jail* by Alvin Rudoff. *American Journal of Sociology* 83 (1977): 244–47.

———. Review of *Prison Life and Human Worth* by Paul Kleve, *The Dilemma of Prison Reform* by Tom Murton. *Crime and Delinquency* 23 (1977): 338–41.

———. *Stateville: The Penitentiary in Mass Society.* Studies in Crime and Justice. Chicago: University of Chicago Press, 1977.

———. "Review Essay; *American Prisons: A History of Good Intentions* by Blake McKelvey." *Reviews in American History* 6 (1978): 184–89.

———. Review of *Prison Reform and State Elites* by Richard Berk and Peter Rossi. *Social Forces* 56 (1978): 1267–68.

———. "What Prison Guards Think: A Profile of the Illinois Force." *Crime and Delinquency* 24 (1978): 185–96.

———. *Individual Rights and Institutional Authority: Prisons, Mental Hospitals, Schools, and Military.* Charlottesville, Va.: Miche Bobbs-Merrill, 1979.

———. "Race Relations and the Prison Subculture." In N. Morris and M. Tonry, eds., *Crime and Justice: An Annual Review of Research* 1 (1979): 1–28.

———. "The Sexual Integration of the Prison's Guard Force: A Few Comments on *Dothard v. Rawlinson.*" *University of Toledo Law Review* 10 (1979): 389–418.

———. "The Prisoners' Rights Movement and Its Impacts." In N. Morris and M. Tonry, eds., *Crime and Justice: An Annual Review of Research* 2 (1980): 429–70.

———. "The Limits of Racial Integration in Prison." *Criminal Law Bulletin* 18 (1982): 117–53.

Jacobs, James B., and Norma Crotty. *Guard Unions and the Future of Prisons.* Ithaca, N.Y.: Cornell University Industrial and Labor Relations Press, 1978.

Jacobs, James B., and Mary Greer. "Drop Outs and Rejects: An Analysis of the Prison Guard's Revolving Door." *Criminal Justice Review* 2 (1977): 57–70.

Jacobs, James B., and Lawrence J. Kraft. "Integrating the Keepers: A Comparison of Black and White Prison Guards in Illinois." *Social Problems* 25 (1978): 304–18.

Jacobs, James B., and Norval Morris. *Proposals for Prison Reform.* Public Affairs Pamphlet No. 510. New York: Public Affairs Committee, 1974.

Jacobs, James B., and Harold Retsky, "Prison Guard." *Urban Life* 4 (1975): 221–40.

Jacobs, James B., and Eric H. Steele. "A Theory of Prison Systems." *Crime and Delinquency* 21 (1975): 149–62.

———. "Prisons: Instruments of Law Enforcement or Social Welfare?" *Crime and Delinquency* 21 (1976): 348–55.

———. "Minimum Security: Untangling the Concepts and Realities." *Journal of Research in Crime and Delinquency* 14 (1977): 68–83.

———. "Sexual Deprivation and Penal Policy." *Cornell Law Review* 62 (1977): 289–312.

Jacobs, James B., and Lynn Zimmer. "Challenging the Taylor Law: Prison Guards on Strike." *Industrial and Labor Relations Review* 34 (1981): 531–44.

Keller, Oliver J., Jr., and Benedict S. Alper. *Halfway Houses: Community-Centered Corrections and Treatment.* Lexington, Mass.: Heath-Lexington Books, 1970.

Kerstetter, Wayne A. Contribution in *Tentative Final Draft of the Illinois Unified Code of Corrections.* Council on the Diagnosis and Evaluation of Criminal Defendants. St. Paul: West Publishing Co., 1971.

Mattick, Hans W. "Foreword: A Discussion of the Key Issues." In H. W. Mattick, ed., *Key Issues: The Future of Imprisonment in a Free Society*, 4–10. Chicago: St. Leonard's House, 1965.

———. "Ex-Cons Proved to be Good Soldiers: Prison Returns Fell to Record Low." *Menard Times* 17 (1966): 8.

———. "The Future of Imprisonment in a Free Society." *British Journal of Criminology* 7 (1967): 450–53.

———. "The Form and Content of Recent Riots." *University of Chicago Law Review* 35 (1968): 660–85.

———. "What's in a Prison." In *Law Enforcement, Science, and Technology III*, 45–50. Chicago: Thompson Book Co. and Chicago–I.I.T. Research Institute, 1970.

———. "Prevention, Detention, and the Disorder Problem." In *Preventive Detention*, 192–94. Chicago: Urban Research Corporation, 1971.

———. "The Prosaic Sources of Prison Violence." *Occasional Papers*, no. 3. Chicago: University of Chicago Law School, 1972.

———. "The Roots of Attica: Turmoil in the Prisons." *The Americana Annual: Yearbook of the Encyclopaedia Americana*, 38–41, 44–47. New York: Americana Annual Corp., 1972.

———. "The Contemporary Jails of the United States: An Unknown and Neglected Area of Justice." In D. Glaser, ed., *Handbook of Criminology*, 777–848. Chicago: Rand-McNally, 1974.

———, ed. *Para-Professionals in Probation and Parole: A Manual for Their Selection, Training, Induction, and Supervision in Day-to-Day Tasks*, by Raymond D. Clements. Chicago: Center for Studies in Criminal Justice, University of Chicago Law School, 1972.

Mattick, Hans W., and Alexander B. Aikman. "The Cloacal Region of American Corrections." *Annals of the American Academy of Political and Social Science* 381 (1969): 109–18.

Mattick, Hans W., and Richard Chused. "The Misdemeanor Offender." Paper given at the Professional Conference in Corrections and Criminal Justice in Illinois, Illinois Committee of the National Council on Crime and Delinquency, 26 April 1967. MS on deposit at the University of Chicago Law Library.

Mattick, Hans W., and Ronald Sweet. *Illinois Jails: Challenge and Opportunity for the 1970s.* Chicago: John Howard Association, 1970.

Meeker, Ben. "The Federal Probation System: The Second Twenty-Five Years, 1950–1975." *Federal Probation* 39 (1975): 16–25.

———. Review of *Prison Life and Human Worth* by Paul W. Kleve, *An Introduction to Criminal Justice* by N. C. Chamelin, V. Fox, and P. M. Whisenand. *Social Work* 20 (1975): 334–35.

Morris, Norval. "Prison in Evolution." *Federal Probation* 29 (1965): 20–32.

———. Review of *On the Penitentiary System in the United States and Its Application in France* by G. deBeaumont and A. de Tocqueville." *The Nation* 201 (1965): 168–71.

———. "Some Problems in the Evolution of Prison." in J. Ll. J. Edwards, ed., *Modern Advances in Criminology*, 1–23. Toronto: Center of Criminology, University of Toronto, 1964–65.

———. "Impediments to Penal Reform." *University of Chicago Law Review* 33 (1966): 627–56.

———. "Lessons from the Adult Correctional System of Sweden." *Federal Probation* 30 (1966): 3–13.

———. Foreword to B. Alper and O. Keller, *Halfway Houses: Community-Centered Correction and Treatment*, ix–x. Lexington, Mass.: Heath-Lexington Books, 1970.

———. "From the Outside Looking In: Or the Snail's Pace of Penal Reform." In *Outside Looking In*, 21–36. Washington, D.C.: Department of Justice, Law Enforcement Assistance Administration, 1970.

———. "Corrections Lurches Forward." *Proceedings of the First National Conference on Corrections*, 20–24. December, 1971.

———. "Correctional Change: The Snail Sprints." In D. Baker, ed., *Corrections in Context: The Criminal Justice System and the Corrective Function*, 51–62. Madison: University of Wisconsin Press, 1972.

———. "Corrections and the Community." In N. Morris and M. Perlman, eds., *Law and Crime: Essays in Honor of Sir John Barry*, 120–34. New York: Gordon and Breach, 1972.

———. "Prison Reform." *Encyclopaedia Yearbook 1972*, 364. New York: Grolier, 1972.

———. Foreword to Marcello Maestro, *Cesare Beccaria and the Origins of Penal Reform*, vii–xii. Philadelphia: Temple University Press, 1973.

———. "Minimum Standards for Medical Services in Prisons and Jails." In *Medical Care for Prisoners and Detainees*, 37–42. CIBA Foundation Symposium 16. The Hague: ASP Elsevier-Excerpta Medica North Holland, 1973.

———. "The Future of Imprisonment: Toward a Punitive Philosophy." *Michigan Law Review* 72 (1974): 1161–80.

———. *The Future of Imprisonment*. Studies in Crime and Justice. Chicago: University of Chicago Press, 1974.

———. "The Prison Boom." *Washington Post*, 30 May 1975, B-8.

———. "Taking an Optimistic View on Prisons." *Chicago Sun Times*, 3 August 1975.

———. "Punishment, Desert, and Rehabilitation." In *Equal Justice under Law*, 137–67. U.S. Department of Justice Bicentennial Lecture series. Washington, D.C.: Government Printing Office, 1976.

———. "Punishment and Prisons." In J. B. Cederblom and L. W. Blizek, eds., *Justice and Punishment*, 157–72. Cambridge, Mass.: Ballinger Publishing Co., 1977.

———. "Who Should Go to Prison." In B. Sales, ed., *Perspectives in Law and Psychology: The Criminal Justice System*, 151–60. New York: Plenum Press, 1977.

Morris, Norval, and Michael Mills. "Prisoners as Laboratory Animals." *Society* 11 (1974): 60–66.

O'Reilly, Charles, and John Flanagan. *Men in Detention*. Chicago: Citizen's Committee for Employment, 1967.

Salomon, Richard A. "Lessons from the Swedish Criminal Justice System: A Reappraisal." *Federal Probation* 40 (1976): 40–48.

Sherman, Michael, and Gordon Hawkins. *Imprisonment in America: Choosing the Future*. Studies in Crime and Justice. Chicago: University of Chicago Press, 1981.

Steele, Eric H. *A Model for the Imprisonment of Repetitively Violent Criminals*. Chicago: Center for Studies in Criminal Justice, University of Chicago Law School and Law Enforcement Assistance Administration, U.S. Department of Justice, 1974.

Stürup Georg. *Treating the Untreatable: The Chronic Criminal at Herstedvester*. Baltimore: Johns Hopkins Press, 1968.

———. *Treatment of Sexual Offenders in Herstedvester Denmark: The Rapists*. Third Issac Ray Lecture. Copenhagen: Munksgaard, 1968.

Tonry, Michael H. Review of *After Conviction* by Ronald Goldfarb and Linda Singer. *Federal Probation* 38 (1974): 76.

Tonry, Michael H., and William Reynolds. "Professional Mediation Services for Prisoners' Complaints." *American Bar Association Journal* 67 (1981): 294–97.

Zimring, Franklin E. "Taking a Tour of America's Prisons." *Chicago Tribune*, sec. 2, p. 4, 14 September 1980.

Courts

Alschuler, Albert W. "The Prosecutor's Role in Plea Bargaining." *University of Chicago Law Review* 36 (1968): 50–112.

Banfield, Laura, and C. David Anderson. "Continuances in the Cook County Criminal Courts." *University of Chicago Law Review* 35 (1968): 259–316.

Frase, Richard S. "The Speedy Trial Act of 1974." *University of Chicago Law Review* 43 (1976): 667–723.

Geller, William A. "Enforcing the Fourth Amendment: The Exclusionary Rule and Its Alternatives." *Washington University Law Quarterly* (1976): 621–722.

Haller, Mark H. "Plea Bargaining: The Nineteenth-Century Context." *Law and Society Review* 13 (1979): 273–79.

Hawkins, Gordon. *Beyond Reasonable Doubt*. Sydney: Australian Broadcasting Commission, 1977.

Kerstetter, Wayne A. "Letting Light into Plea Bargaining." *The Judge's Journal* 16 (1977): 38–42.

———. "Reforms in Plea Bargaining: The Effects of Changing the Rules." In B. Galway and J. Hudson, eds., *Perspectives on Crime Victims*, 266–76. St. Louis: C. V. Mosby Press, 1980.

———. "Police Participation in Plea Negotiations." *Journal of Criminal Justice* 9 (1980): 151–64.

Kerstetter, Wayne A., and Anne M. Heinz. *Pretrial Settlement Conference: An Evaluation*. Washington, D.C.: National Institute of Law Enforcement and Criminal Justice, U.S. Department of Justice, Government Printing Office, 1979.

————. "The Pretrial Settlement Conference: Evaluation of a Reform in Plea Bargaining." *Law and Society Review* 13 (1979): 349–66.

————. "Victim Participation in Plea Bargaining: A Field Experiment." In W. McDonald, ed., *Plea Bargaining*, 167–77. Lexington, Mass: Lexington Books, 1980.

Morris, Norval. Review of *The Defendant's Rights under English Law* by Fellman. *Journal of Criminal Law, Criminology, and Police Science* 59 (1969): 411–12.

————. "Probation and Plea Bargaining in Metropolitan Jurisdictions." *Journal of the American Judicature Society* 53 (1970): 231–34.

————. "The Judges Declining Role in the Criminal Justice System." *Law and the Social Order* 55 (1972): 373–81.

————. "Keynote Address." In *Final Report of the 1975 Conference on Pretrial Release and Diversion*, 17–23. Denver: National Center for State Courts, 1976.

————. Review of *Denial of Justice: Criminal Process in the United States* by L. Weinreb. *Harvard Law Review* 91 (1978): 1367–71.

————. Review of *The Grand Jury: An Institution on Trial* by M. Frankel and G. Naftalis. *Yale Law Journal* 87 (1978): 680–84.

————. "Hired Guns." Review of *Partisan Justice* by M. Frankel. *Michigan Law Review* 79 (1981): 642–44.

Oaks, Dallin. *The Criminal Justice Act in the Federal District Courts*. Chicago: Center for Studies in Criminal Justice, University of Chicago Law School and National Legal Aid and Defender Association, 1967.

Patner, Marshall. *Appointed Counsel's Guide for Illinois Crime Appeals*. Mundelein, Ill.: Callaghan and Co., 1968.

Spiotto, James E. "Search and Seizure: An Empirical Study of the Exclusionary Rule and Its Alternatives." *Journal of Legal Studies* 2 (1973): 243–78.

Zeisel, Hans. "Six Man Juries, Majority Verdicts: What Difference Do They Make?" *Occasional Papers*, no. 5. Chicago: University of Chicago Law School, 1973.

————. "Bail Revisited." *American Bar Foundation Research Journal* (1979): 769–89.

————. Foreword to "The American Jury." Special Issue of *Law and Contemporary Problems* 43 (1980): 1–7.

————. "The Disposition of Felony Arrests." *American Bar Foundation Research Journal* (1981): 407–62.

Zeisel, Hans, and Gerhard Casper. "Law Judges in the German Criminal Courts." *Journal of Legal Studies* 1 (1972):135–91.

————. *Der Laienrichter in Strafprozess* [The lay judge in the criminal trial]. Heidelberg: C. F. Muller Vlg., 1977.

Zeisel, Hans, and Shari S. Diamond. "'Convincing Empirical Evidence' on the Six Member Jury." *University of Chicago Law Review* 41 (1974): 281–95.

————. "The Jury Selection in the Mitchell-Stans Conspiracy Trial." *American Bar Foundation Research Journal* 1 (1976):151–74.

————. Review of *Procedural Justice: A Psychological Analysis* by J. Thibaut and L. Walker." *Duke Law Journal* (1977): 1289–96.

————. "The Effect of Peremptory Challenges on Jury and Verdict." *Stanford Law Review* 30 (1978): 491–531.

Zimring, Franklin E. "Measuring the Impact of Pretrial Diversion from the Criminal Justice System." *University of Chicago Law Review* 41 (1974): 224–41.

——. "Review of Pretrial Intervention." In *Pretrial Services: An Evaluation of Policy Related Research*, vol. 2, 152–58. Cambridge, Mass.: ABT Associates, 1975.

——. "Illegally Seized Evidence: Exclude It?" *Los Angeles Times*, 20 April, 1976.

Zimring, Franklin E., and Richard S. Frase. *The Criminal Justice System: Materials on the Administration and Reform of the Criminal Law*. Boston: Little, Brown and Co., 1980.

Death Penalty

Center for Studies in Criminal Justice. *A Selected International Bibliography on Capital Punishment*. Center for Studies in Criminal Justice, University of Chicago Law School, 1968.

Hawkins, Gordon. "The Death Penalty and the Problem of Punishment." *Quadrant* 14 (1969): 69–73.

Hawkins, Gordon, and Franklin E. Zimring. "Review of *For Capital Punishment: Crime and the Morality of the Death Penalty*" by Walter Berns. *American Journal of Sociology* 86 (1981): 1171–74.

Mattick, Hans W. *The Unexamined Death*, 2d ed. Chicago: John Howard Association, 1966.

Mattick, Hans W., Willard J. Lassers, Robert P. Taylor, and Jordan M. Scher. "Capital Punishment: A Symposium." *Existential Psychiatry* 1 (1966): 7–16.

Morris, Norval. Introduction to H. Zeisel, *Some Data on Juror Attitudes towards Capital Punishment*, v–vii. Chicago: Center for Studies in Criminal Justice, University of Chicago Law School, 1968.

——. "Two Studies of Capital Punishment." In *Proceedings: Conference on Capital Punishment, Coimbra, Portugal*, 2 411–14.

——. "Hans Mattick and the Death Penalty: Sentimental Notes on Two Topics." *University of Toledo Law Review* 10 (1979): 299–316.

Morris, Norval, Charles Marson, and Douglas Fuson. *Capital Punishment: Developments, 1961–1965*. New York: United Nations Publications, 1967.

Zeisel, Hans. *Some Data on Juror Attitudes towards Capital Punishment*. Chicago: Center for Studies in Criminal Justice, University of Chicago Law School, 1968.

——. "Facts vs. Faith Concerning the Deterrent Effect of the Death Penalty." *Supreme Court Review* (1977): 317–43.

——. "The Death Penalty and the Insanity Defense." *Occasional Papers*, no. 14. Chicago: University of Chicago Law School, 1978.

——. "Race Bias in the Administration of the Death Penalty: The Florida Experience." *Harvard Law Review* 91 (1981): 456–68.

Zimring, Franklin E., Joel Eigen, and Sheila O'Malley. "Punishing Homicide in Philadelphia: Perspectives on the Death Penalty." *University of Chicago Law Review* 43 (1976): 227–52.

Deterrence

Andenaes, Johannes. "Deterrence and Specific Offenses." *University of Chicago Law Review* 38 (1971): 537–53.

———. "The Moral or Educative Influence of the Criminal Law." *Journal of Social Issues* 27 (1971): 17–31.

———. *Punishment and Deterrence.* Ann Arbor: University of Michigan Press, 1974.

Hawkins, Gordon. "Deterrence: The Problematic Postulate." *Australia and New Zealand Journal of Criminology* 2 (1969): 132–48.

———. "Punishment and Deterrence: The Educative, Moralizing, and Habituative Effects." *University of Wisconsin Law Review* (1969): 550–65.

Morris, Norval, and Franklin E. Zimring. "Deterrence and Corrections." *Annals of the American Academy of Political and Social Science* 381 (1969): 137–46.

Zimring, Franklin E. *Perspectives on Deterrence.* Washington, D.C.: National Institutes of Mental Health, 1971.

———. "Of Doctors, Deterrence, and the Dark Figure of Crime: A Note on Abortion in Hawaii." *University of Chicago Law Review* 39 (1972): 699–722.

———. "Threat of Punishment as an Instrument of Crime Control." *Proceedings of the American Philosophical Society* 118 (1974): 231–34.

———. "Field Experiments in General Deterrence: Preferring the Tortoise to the Hare." *Evaluation* 31 (1976): 132–35.

———. "Bad Checks in Nebraska: A Study in Complex Threats." In D. Greenberg, ed., *Corrections and Punishment*, 173–92. Beverly Hills, Ca.: Sage Publications, 1977.

———. "Policy Experiments in General Deterrence, 1970–1975." In *National Academy of Science Report of the Panel on Deterrence and Incapacitation*, 140–86. Washington, D.C.: National Academy of Science, 1978.

Zimring, Franklin E., and Gordon Hawkins. "Deterrence and Marginal Groups." *Journal of Research in Crime and Delinquency* 5 (1968): 100–114.

———. "The Legal Threat as an Instrument of Social Change." *Journal of Social Issues* 27 (1971): 33–48.

———. *Deterrence: The Legal Threat in Crime Control.* Studies in Crime and Justice. Chicago: University of Chicago Press, 1973.

Zimring, Franklin E., and Edward Hunvald. "Whatever Happened to Implied Consent? A Sounding." *University of Missouri Law Review* 33 (1968): 323–99.

Drug Abuse

Kerstetter, Wayne A., and H. Joo Shin. *Report on the Evaluation of the Illinois Drug Abuse Program: Changes in Patients' Arrest Rates.* Chicago: Center for Studies in Criminal Justice, University of Chicago Law School, 1971.

———. "The Illinois Experience: Arrest Rate Changes after Methadone Centered Multi-Modality Treatments." *Journal of Research in Crime and Delinquency* 10 (1973): 163–76.

Mattick, Hans W. "The Epidemology of Drug Addiction and Reflections on the Narcotic Problem and Public Policy in the United States." *Illinois Medical Journal* 130 (1966): 436–47.

———. "Narcotics and the Law." Review of *The Addict and the Law* by Alfred Lindesmith; *Crime without Victims: Deviant Behavior and Public Policy—Abortion, Homosexuality, Drug Addiction* by Edwin Schur; *Narcotics*, edited by Gene

Kassebaum and Daniel Wilner; and *The Drug Takers.*" *University of Chicago Law Review* 33 (1966): 603–14.

Morris, Norval. Foreword to K. Brunn, R. Pan, and I. Rexed, *The Gentlemen's Club: International Control of Drugs and Alcohol*, ix–x. Studies in Crime and Justice. Chicago: University of Chicago Press, 1975.

Tonry, Michael H. Review of *Cannabis*, a report to the Canadian Commission of Inquiry into the Non-Medical Use of Drugs; and *Marihuana: A Signal of Misunderstanding*, a report of the American National Commission on Marihuana and Drug Abuse. *Yale Law Journal* 82 (1973): 1736–44.

———. Review of *Not the Law's Business* by Gilbert Geis. *Federal Probation* 37 (1973): 74.

Mental Illness and the Criminal Law

Hawkins, Gordon, and Oliver Briscoe. "The Treatment of Sexual Offenders." *Australian Journal of Forensic Sciences* 2 (1969) 41–46.

Morris, Norval. "The Disturbed and Dangerous Criminal: Certain Aspects of the Future Role of the State." In *Proceedings of the Conference on Mental Health and the State.* Chicago: Northwestern University Law School, 1967.

———. "Introduction to the Habitual Criminal." *McGill Law Journal* 13 (1967):534–52.

———. Foreword to Rock, Jacobsen, and Janopaul, *Hospitalization and Discharge of the Mentally Ill*, xii–xv. Chicago: University of Chicago Press, 1968.

———. "Psychiatry and the Dangerous Criminal." *Southern California Law Review* 41 (1968): 514–47.

———. "The Criminal Justice System and Psychiatry: Past, Present, and Future." In L. M. Irvine and T. B. Brelje, eds., *Law, Psychiatry, and the Mentally Disordered Offender*, vol. 1, 3–13. Springfield, Ill.: Charles C. Thomas, 1972.

———. "Legal Aspects of the Prevention of Birth of Mentally Retarded Children." In Albert Dorfman, ed., *Antenatal Diagnosis*, 239–41. Chicago: University of Chicago Press, 1972.

———. "Special Doctrinal Treatment in Criminal Law." In M. Kindred, ed., *The Mentally Retarded Citizen and the Law*, 681–86. New York: Free Press, 1976.

———. "The Difficult to Manage Inmate: Mad or Mean." In *Mental Health for the Convicted Offender: Patient and Prisoner*, 163–66. Raleigh, N.C.: North Carolina Department of Corrections, 1977.

———. "Mental Health for Prisoners: The Magnitude of the Problem." In *Mental Health for the Convicted Offender: Patient and Prisoner*, 9–21. Raleigh, N.C.: North Carolina Department of Corrections, 1977.

———. "The Brothel Boy: A Fragment of a Manuscript." *Occasional Papers*, no. 18. Chicago: University of Chicago Law School, 1982.

———. "The Criminal Responsibility of the Mentally Ill." *Syracuse Law Review* 33 (1982): 477–531.

———. "Mental Illness and the Criminal Law." In P. T. Bean, ed., *Key Issues in Mental Illness*, 1–25. London: John Wiley and Sons, 1982.

———. "The Planter's Dream." *University of Chicago Law Review* 49 (1982): 609–45.

338   CUMULATIVE BIBLIOGRAPHY

Morris, Norval, and Robert A. Burt. "A Proposal for the Abolition of the Incompetency Plea." *University of Chicago Law Review* 40 (1972): 66–95.

Morris, Norval, and Faye Goldberg. "The Psychopath in South African Criminal and Mental Health Law, Part II." *Comparative and International Law Journal of Southern Africa* 9 (1976): 30–56.

Rubin, Bernard. "Prediction of Dangerousness in Mentally Ill Criminals." *Archives of General Psychiatry* 27 (1972): 397–407.

Wallach, Stephen D. "A Constitutional Right to Treatment: Past, Present, and Future." *Professional Psychology* 7 (1976): 453–67.

Wallach, Stephen D., and Robert Perrucci. "Models of Mental Illness and Duration of Hospitalization." *Community Mental Health Journal* 11 (1975) 271–79.

Organized Crime

Haller, Mark H. Introduction to John Landesco, *Organized Crime in Chicago*, vii–xviii. Chicago: University of Chicago Press, 1968.

———. "Urban Vice and Civic Reform: Chicago in the Early Twentieth Century." In K. Jackson and S. Schultz, eds., *Cities in American History*, 290–305. New York: Alfred A. Knopf, 1971.

———. "Organized Crime in Urban Society in the Twentieth Century." *Journal of Social History* 5 (1971–72): 210–34.

———. "The Changing Structure of American Gambling in the Twentieth Century." *Journal of Social Issues* (1979): 87–114.

———. "Illegal Enterprise: Historical Perspectives and Public Policy." In J. C. Inciardi and C. E. Faupel, eds., *History and Crime: Implications for Criminal Justice Policy*, 77–90. Beverly Hills, Ca.: Sage Publications, 1980.

Haller, Mark H., and John V. Alviti. "Loansharking in American Cities: Historical Analysis of a Marginal Enterprise." *American Journal of Legal History* 12 (1977): 125–56.

Hawkins, Gordon. "God and the Mafia." *Public Interest* 14 (1969): 24–51.

Police

Fahey, Richard P., and Richard W. Harding. "Killings by Chicago Police, 1969–70: An Empirical Study." *Southern California Law Review* 46 (1973): 284–315.

Haller, Mark H. "The Historical Roots of Police Behavior, 1890–1925." *Law and Society Review* 10 (1976): 303–24.

———. "Police Reform in Chicago, 1905–1935." *American Behavioral Scientist* 13 (1970): 649–66.

———. "Introduction: The Nineteenth Century Police." In John J. Flinn, *History of the Chicago Police*, v–xix. Montclair, N.J.: Patterson-Smith Corp., 1973.

Hawkins, Gordon, and Paul Ward. "Armed and Disarmed Police: Police Firearms Policy and Levels of Violence." *Journal of Research in Crime and Delinquency* 7 (1970): 188–97.

Jacobs, James B., and Jay Cohen. "The Impact of Racial Integration on the Police." *Journal of Police Science and Administration* 6 (1978): 168–73.

Jacobs, James B., and Samuel B. Magdovitz. "At LEEP's End? A Review of the Law Enforcement Education Program." *Journal of Police Science and Administration* 5 (1977): 1–18.

Kerstetter, Wayne A. *Citizen Review of Police Misconduct; or, Who Will Watch the Watchmen?* Chicago: Center for Studies in Criminal Justice, University of Chicago Law School, 1971.

———. "Peer Accountability as the Primary Control Mechanisms in Police Agencies." *Criminal Justice Review* 4 (1979): 113–20.

———. "The Police in 1984." *Journal of Criminal Justice* 7 (1979): 1–9.

———. Review of *Big City Police* by Robert Fogelson. *Journal of Inter-Disciplinary History* 9 (1979): 774–76.

———. "Patrol Decentralization: An Assessment." *Journal of Police Science and Administration* 9 (1981): 48–60.

Mattick, Hans W., and Jerome Skolnick. "The Cities and the Police." *University of Chicago Roundtable*, no. 6. Chicago: University of Chicago, 1968.

Morris, Norval. "And Yet, Grass-Eaters Are the Heart of the Problem." *Arizona Statesman* 34 (1974): 6.

———. "Don't Be a Grass-Eater of the Law." *Learning and the Law* 1 (1975): 66–71.

———. Foreword to H. Treger et al., *The Police–Social Work Team*, vii. Springfield, Ill.: Charles C. Thomas, 1975.

———. Foreword to W. A. Geller and K. J. Karales, *Split Second Decisions: Shootings of and by Chicago Police*, iii–v. Chicago: Chicago Law Enforcement Study Group, 1981.

Skolnick, Jerome H. *The Police and the Urban Ghetto.* Chicago: Research Contributions of the American Bar Foundation no. 3, 1968.

Politics of Change

Force, Robert. "Decriminalization of Breach of the PEACE Statutes: A Nonpenal Approach to Order Maintenance." *Tulane Law Review* 46 (1972): 367–493.

Gordon, Margaret T. *Involving Paraprofessionals in the Helping Process: The Case of Federal Probation.* Cambridge, Mass.: Ballinger Publishing Co., 1976.

Hawkins, Gordon. "Humanism and the Crime Problem." In I. S. Edwards, ed., *A Human View*, 170–81. Sydney: Angus and Robertson, 1968.

———. Foreword to P. Ward and G. Woods, *Law and Order in Australia*, vi–ix. Sydney: Angus and Robertson, 1972.

———. "In Defense of Decriminalization." University of Chicago Law School, *Law Alumni Journal* 2 (1976): 3–11.

———. "Criminology and Ideology." *Quadrant* 23 (1979): 112–13.

Kerstetter, Wayne A. "Practical Problems of Law Enforcement." In A. E. Evans and J. F. Murphy, eds., *Legal Aspects of International Terrorism*, 535–51. Lexington, Mass.: American Society of International Law and Lexington Books, 1978.

Mattick, Hans W. "The Politics of Criminal Justice." In *An Invitational Conference on Planning for Juvenile Delinquency Prevention and Control*, 32–40. Chicago: Center for the Study of Welfare Policy, University of Chicago School of Social Service Administration, 1970.

———. "The Pessimistic Hypothesis: An Immodest Proposal." *Public Welfare* 31 (1973): 2–6.

Morris, Norval. "Crime Prevention and Professional Education." In *Law Enforce-*

ment, Science, and Technology, 63–66. Chicago: Thompson Book Company, 1967.

———. "Crime." In D. Szabo, ed., *Criminology in Action*, 313–70. Montreal: University of Montreal Press, 1968.

———. "The Plight of the Good Samaritan." *Hartwick Review* (1968): 48–51.

———. "Politics and Pragmatism in Crime Control." *Federal Probation* 32 (1968): 9–16.

———. "Should Law Students Encounter the New Research Techniques?" *Law and the Social Order* (1969): 55–67.

———. *The Businessman's Guide to Crime Control.* Chicago: University of Chicago Graduate School of Business, 1971.

———. "The Proper Role of the Criminal Law." In *The Great Ideas Today*, 22–39. Chicago: Encyclopaedia Britannica, 1972.

———. "Reforming the Criminal Justice System." *Center Magazine* 5 (1972): 40–41.

———. "Crimes without Victims." *New York Times Magazine*, 1 April, 1973, 10.

———. "Criminal Law: The State's Largest Power." *Center Magazine* 8 (1975): 43–47.

———. "Reordering Priorities Would Free Police and Criminal Courts to Deal with Predatory Crimes." *Center Magazine* 10 (1977): 39–41.

Morris, Norval, Francis L. Filas, Langdon B. Gilkey, and Kenneth Northcott. "Morality and the Law." *University of Chicago Roundtable*, no. 18. Chicago: University of Chicago, 1968.

Morris, Norval, and Gordon Hawkins. "From Murder and from Violence, Good Lord, Deliver Us." *Midway* 10 (1969): 63–95.

———. *The Honest Politician's Guide to Crime Control.* Chicago: University of Chicago Press, 1970.

———. *Letter to the President on Crime Control.* Chicago: University of Chicago Press, 1977.

Morris, Norval, and Tom Wicker. "Us vs. Them." *Barrister* 2 (1975):17–23.

Oaks, Dallin. "The Popular Myth of the Victimless Crime." University of Chicago Law School, *Law Alumni Journal* 1 (1975): 3–14.

Skolnick, Jerome. "Coercion to Virtue: The Legal Enforcement of Morals." *Southern California Law Review* 41 (1968): 588–641.

Tonry, Michael H. Review of *Crime, Power, and Morality* by Stuart L. Hills; *The Right to be Different: Deviance and Enforced Therapy* by Nicholas Kittrie; and *The Emergence of Deviant Minorities* by Robert W. Winslow. *Federal Probation* 36 (1972): 72–74.

Weiss, Kurt. "Politics and Measures of Success in the War on Crime." *Crime and Delinquency* 21 (1975): 1–10.

Weiss, Kurt, and Michael Milakovich. "Who's Afraid of Crime? or, How to Finance a Decrease Rate of Increase." In S. Sylvester and E. Sagarin, eds., *Politics and Crime*, 31–42. New York: Praeger, 1974.

Zimring, Franklin E., and Gordon Hawkins. "Ideology and Euphoria in Crime Control." *University of Toledo Law Review* 10 (1979): 370–88.

Zimring, Franklin E. "Poland's 'Real' Problem." *Chicago Tribune*, Perspective Wednesday, 13 January 1982, p. 15.

———. "Uncle Sam's Wars on Crime." *The New Republic* 186, no. 17 (April 1982): 38–40.

———. "Crime: The 120 Day Solution." *Chicago Tribune*, Perspective, Monday, 28 September 1982, p. 25.

Sentencing

Morris, Norval. Review of *Sentencing: The Decisions as to Type, Length, and Conditions of Sentence* by R. O. Dawson. *Southern California Law Review* 44 (1971): 524–27.

———. "Towards Principled Sentencing." *Maryland Law Review* 37 (1977): 267–85.

———. "Sentencing and Parole." *Australian Law Journal* 51 (1977): 523–31.

———. "Sentencing and Prison Reform." In *New Directions for Federal Involvement in Crime Control* (Subcommittee on Crime of the Committee on the Judiciary, House of Representatives, 1977).

———. "Conceptual Overview and Commentary on the Movement toward Determinacy." In *Determinate Sentencing: Reform or Regression?* 1–12. Washington, D.C.: Government Printing Office, 1978.

———. "Prison Sentencing: A Way Out of Anarchy." *Los Angeles Times*, 5 January 1978, pt. 2, p. 7.

Tonry, Michael H. "The Sentencing Commission in Sentencing Reform." *Hofstra Law Review* 7 (1979): 315–54.

———. "Real Offense Sentencing: The Model Sentencing and Corrections Act." *Journal of Criminal Law and Criminology* 72 (1981): 1550–96.

———. "More Sentencing Reform in America." *Criminal Law Review* (1982): 157–67.

Tonry, Michael H., and Norval Morris. "Sentencing Reform in America." In P. R. Glazebrook, ed., *Re-Shaping the Criminal Law: A Festschrift in Honor of Glanville Williams*, 434–48. London: Stevens, 1978.

Zeisel, Hans, and Shari S. Diamond. "Sentencing Councils: A Study of Sentencing Disparity and Its Reduction." *University of Chicago Law Review* 43 (1976): 109–49.

———. "Search for Sentencing Equity: Sentence Review in Massachusetts and Connecticut." *American Bar Foundation Research Journal* 2 (1977): 883–940.

Zimring, Franklin E. "Making the Punishment Fit the Crime: A Consumer's Guide to Sentencing Reform." *Hastings Center Reports* 6 (1976): 13–21.

———. "Comment." *Hastings Center Reports* 7 (1977): 44.

———. Remarks as commentator. In "Current Developments in Judicial Administration: Papers Presented at the Plenary Session of the American Association of Law Schools," December 1977. Published in *Federal Rules Decisions* 80 (1979): 163–66.

Violence

Block, Richard. "Homicide in Chicago: A Nine-Year Study (1965–1973)." *Journal of Criminal Law and Criminology* 66 (1975): 496–510.

———. *Violent Crime: Environment, Interaction, and Death.* Lexington, Mass.: Lexington Books, 1977.

———. "Community Environment, Interaction, and Violent Crime." *Criminology* 17 (1979): 46–57.

Block, Richard, and Carolyn Block. "Decisions and Data: The Transformation of Robbery Incidents into Robbery Statistics." *Journal of Criminal Law and Criminology* 72 (1981): 743–61.

Block, Richard, and Franklin E. Zimring. "Homicide in Chicago, 1965–1970." *Journal of Research in Crime and Delinquency* 10 (1973): 1–12.

Dardick, Nathan. *A Comprehensive Bibliography on Gun Control.* Chicago: Center for Studies in Criminal Justice, University of Chicago Law School, 1972.

Haller, Mark H. "Theories of Criminal Violence and Their Impact on the Criminal Justice System." In National Commission on the Causes and Prevention of Violence, Task Force Report, *Crimes of Violence* 13: 1327–57. Washington, D.C.: Government Printing Office, 1970.

Hawkins, Gordon. "The Greater Felon." In J. Birman, ed., *Democracy: The Issues of Law and Order*, 32–41. Perth: University of Western Australia, 1975.

———. "Skyjacking." *Australian Journal of Forensic Sciences* 7 (1975): 157–68.

Morris, Norval. "Compensation and the Good Samaritan." In J. M. Ratcliffe, ed., *The Good Samaritan and the Law*, 135–39. Garden City, N.Y.: Doubleday, 1966.

———. Review of *In Cold Blood* by Truman Capote. *Washington Law Review* 41 (1966): 920–24.

———. "Predicting Violence with Statistics." Review of *The Clinical Prediction of Violent Behavior* by J. Monahan. *Stanford Law Review* 34 (1981): 249–53.

Morris, Norval, and Gordon Hawkins. "Controlling Violence: Toward a Less Lethal Environment." *Current* 111 (1969): 48–53.

Morris, Norval, and Michael H. Tonry. "Black Crime, Black Victims." Editorial serial in *Chicago Tribune*, 18–21 August 1980.

Zimring, Franklin E. "Games with Guns and Statistics." *University of Wisconsin Law Review* 4 (1968): 1113–26.

———. "Is Gun Control Likely to Reduce Violent Killings?" *University of Chicago Law Review* 35 (1968): 721–37.

———. "Firearms and the Federal Criminal Law. A Consultant's Report to the National Commission on Reform of the Federal Criminal Laws." In *Working Papers of the National Commission on Reform of the Federal Criminal Laws* 2: 1031–46. Washington, D.C.: Government Printing Office, 1970.

———. "Eight Myths about Gun Control in the United States." *Christian Science Monitor*, 24 July 1972, 7.

———. "Firearms Control: Hard Choices." *Trial* 8 (1972): 53.

———. "Getting Serious about Guns." *The Nation* 214 (1972): 457–61.

———. "The Medium is the Message: Firearms Caliber as a Determinant of the Death Rate from Assault." *Journal of Legal Studies* 1 (1972): 97–123.

———. "Some Facts about Homicide." *The Nation* 214 (1972): 303–5.

———. "A Tale of Two Cities." *Wall Street Journal*, 12 December, 1974, 12.

———. "Firearms and the Federal Law: The Gun Control Act of 1968." *Journal of Legal Studies* 4 (1975): 133–98.

———. "Street Crimes and New Guns: Some Implications for Firearms Control." *Journal of Criminal Justice* 4 (1976): 95–107.

———. "Determinants of the Death Rate from Robbery: A Detroit Time Study." *Journal of Legal Studies* 6 (1977): 317–32.

———. Foreword to R. Block, *Violent Crime: Environment, Interaction, and Death*, xi. Lexington, Mass.: Lexington Books, 1977.

———. Review of *Code Name Zorro* by Richard Lane and Dick Gregory. *Chicago Sun Times Bookweek*, 8 May 1977.

———. Review of *Victims* by J. L. Barkas. *Chicago Sun Times Bookweek*, 27 November 1977, 14.

———. Review of *Criminal Justice, Criminal Violence* by Charles Silberman. *Chicago Tribune*, 5 November 1978, sec. 7, p. 1.

———. Foreword to P. Cook and D. Nagin, *Does the Weapon Matter?*, iii. Institute for Law and Social Research Publication no. 8. Washington, D.C.: 1979.

———. "Handguns in the Twenty-First Century: Alternative Policy Futures." *Annals of the American Academy of Political and Social Sciences* 455 (1981): 1–10.

———. "Will the 21st Century Be Safer?" *Chicago Tribune*, Monday, 13 April 1981, sec. 1, p. 22.

Zimring, Franklin E., and George Newton. *Firearms and Violence in American Life*. Staff report to the National Commission on the Causes and Prevention of Violence. Washington, D.C.: Government Printing Office, 1969.

Youth Crime

McGee, Henry W., Jr. "Juvenile Justice and the Ghetto Law Office." *University of Chicago Magazine* 60 (1967): 12–16.

Mattick, Hans W. "Juvenile Delinquency." In *The World Book Year Book, 1965: An Annual Supplement to the World Book Encyclopaedia*, 382–84. Chicago: Field Enterprises Education Corporation, 1965.

———. "Organization of the Chicago Youth Development Project: Action and Research Programs." In *Report Conference: Chicago Youth Development Project*. Chicago: Chicago Boys Club, 1966.

Mattick, Hans W., and Nathan S. Caplan. "Stake Animals, Loud-Talking, and Leadership in Do-Nothing and Do-Something Situations." In J. Klein and B. Meyerhoff, eds., *Juvenile Gangs in Context*, 1–14. Englewood Cliffs, N.J.: Prentice-Hall, 1967.

Mattick, Hans W., Nathan S. Caplan, Dennis J. Deshaies, and Gerald D. Suttles. "The Nature, Variety, and Patterns of Street Club Work in an Urban Setting." In J. Klein and B. Meyerhoff, eds., *Juvenile Gangs in Context*, 135–69. Englewood Cliffs, N.J.: Prentice-Hall, 1967.

Mattick, Hans W., Frank J. Carney, and John D. Callaway. "Street Club Work Practices." Chicago: Chicago Boys Club, 1968. Mimeograph.

———. "Street Workers and Gangs." *Reports Digests*, no. 38. Washington, D.C.: United States Office of Education, 1968.

———. *Action on the Streets: A Handbook for Inner City Youth Work*. New York: Association Press, 1969.

Mattick, Hans W., Warner Saunders, and Leonard Unterberger. "Gangs: Their Evolution and Essence." *Hyde Park Kenwood Voices, Special Supplement*, February 1969, 1ff.

Morris, Norval. "The Balance between Family and Public Control: Correction." In A. Dorfman, ed., *Child Care in Health and Disease*, 92–98. Chicago: Yearbook Medical Publishers, 1968.

―――. "In Re Gault: A Comparative Background." In V. D. Norin, ed., *Gault: What Now for the Juvenile Court?*, 25–38. Ann Arbor, Michigan: Institute for Continuing Legal Education, 1970.

―――. Foreword to M. Wolfgang, R. Figlio, and T. Sellin, *Delinquency in a Birth Cohort*, vii–viii. Studies in Crime and Justice. Chicago: University of Chicago Press, 1972.

Platt, Anthony. Critical notice on *Organisation for Treatment: A Comparative Study of Institutions for Delinquency* by Street, Vinter, and Perrow. *British Journal of Criminology* 7 (1967): 456–59.

―――. Review of *Law Enforcement and the Youthful Offender: Juvenile Procedures* by E. Eldefonso. *British Journal of Criminology* 8 (1968): 98–100.

―――. *The Child Savers: The Invention of Delinquency*. Chicago: University of Chicago Press, 1969.

―――. "The Rise of the Child Saving Movement: A Study in Social Policy and Correctional Reform." *Annals of the American Academy of Political and Social Sciences* 381 (1969): 21–38.

Platt, Anthony, Howard Schechter, and Phyllis Tiffany. "In Defense of Youth: A Case Study of the Public Defender in Juvenile Court." *Indiana Law Journal* 43 (1968): 619–40.

Rosenheim, Margaret, ed. *Pursuing Justice for the Child*. Studies in Crime and Justice. Chicago: University of Chicago Press, 1976.

Seymour, John A. *The Current Status of Youth Services Bureaus: A Report on a Seminar*. Chicago: Center for Studies in Criminal Justice and Center for the Study of Welfare Policy, University of Chicago, 1971.

―――. *Youth Services Bureaus*. Seminar Background Paper. Chicago: Center for Studies in Criminal Justice and the Center for the Study of Welfare Policy, Univeristy of Chicago, 1971.

Tonry, Michael H. "Juvenile Justice and the National Crime Commissions." In M. Rosenheim, ed., *Pursuing Justice for the Child*, 281–98. Chicago: University of Chicago Press, 1976.

―――. Introduction to Institute of Judicial Administration and American Bar Foundation, Juvenile Justice Standards Project, *Transfer between Courts*, 1–7. Cambridge: Ballinger Publishing Co., 1977.

Zimring, Franklin E. "Dealing with Youth Crime: National Needs and Federal Priorities." A policy paper prepared for the Federal Co-ordinating Council on Juvenile Justice and Delinquency Prevention. Chicago: Center for Studies in Criminal Justice, University of Chicago, 1975. Mimeograph.

―――. *Confronting Youth Crime: Report of the Twentieth Century Fund Task Force on Sentencing Policy toward Young Offenders*. New York: Holmes and Meier, 1978.

―――. "Pursuing Juvenile Justice: Comments on Some Recent Reform Proposals." *University of Detroit Journal of Urban Law* 55 (1978): 631–48.

―――. "The Serious Juvenile Offender: Notes on an Unknown Quantity." In *The Serious Juvenile Offender*. Proceedings of a national symposium held in Minneapolis, Minnesota, 19–20 September 1977, 15–31. Washington, D.C.: Government Printing Office, 1978.

———. Review of *Juvenile Justice Standards Project* by the Institute of Judicial Administration and American Bar Association. *Harvard Law Review* 91 (1978): 1934–40.

———. "American Youth Violence: Issues and Trends." In N. Morris and M. Tonry, eds., *Crime and Justice: An Annual Review of Research* 1 (1979): 67–108.

———. "Privilege, Maturity, and Responsibility: Notes on the Emerging Jurisprudence of Adolescence." In L. T. Empey, ed., *The Future of Childhood and Juvenile Justice*, 312–35. Charlottesville: University Press of Virginia, 1980.

———. "Kids, Groups, and Crime: Some Implications of a Well-Known Secret." *Journal of Criminal Law and Criminology* 72 (1981): 867–85.

———. "Notes toward a Jurisprudence of Waiver." In J. C. Hall et al., eds., *Major Issues in Juvenile Justice Information and Training*, 193–206. Columbus, Ohio: Academy of Contemporary Problems.

———. Review of *The Child Savers: Juvenile Justice Observed* by Peter Prescott. *New York Times Book Reviews*, 14 June 1981, 14.

———. *The Changing Legal World of Adolescence*. New York: Free Press, 1982.

Zimring, Franklin E., Peter Greenwood, and Joan Petersilia. *Age, Crime, and Sanctions: The Transition from Juvenile to Adult Court*. Rand Report no. R-2642-NIJ, October, 1980.

Supplement

Haller, Mark H. "Urban Crime and Criminal Justice: The Chicago Case." *Journal of American History* 42 (1970): 619–35.

———. "Recurring Themes." In Haller and Davis, eds., *The Peoples of Philadelphia: A History of Ethnic Groups and Lower Class Life*, 227–90. Philadelphia: Temple University Press, 1973.

Hawkins, Gordon. Review of *Crime, Criminology, and Public Policy*, edited by R. Hood. *Journal of Research in Crime and Delinquency* 14 (1977): 129–34.

Kerstetter, Wayne A. "Terrorism and Intelligence." *Terrorism: An International Journal* 3 (1979): 109–15.

Mallin, Michael. "In Warm Blood: Some Historical and Procedural Aspects of *Regina v. Dudley and Stephens*." *University of Chicago Law Review* 34 (1967): 387–407.

Mattick, Hans W. Review of *Comparative Criminology* by Hermann Mannheim. *Social Service Review* 40 (1966): 460–61.

———. *SRA Occupational Brief: Criminologists*, no. 385. Chicago: Research Associates Inc., 1971.

———. Review of *Crime and Justice*, volumes 1–3, edited by Leon Radzinowicz and Marvin Wolfgang. *Chicago Daily News Panorama*, 24 June 1972, p. 8.

———, ed. *Proceedings of the Second Conference of Directors of Criminological Research Institutions in the United States and Canada*, 1968.

Meeker, Ben. Review of *Social Work Practices and Social Justice*, edited by Bernard Ross and Charles Shireman. *Social Service Review* 48 (1974): 302–4.

Morris, Norval. Foreword to M. Wolfgang, R. Figlio, and R. Thornberry, *Evaluating Criminology*, ix. New York: Elsevier North-Holland, 1978.

Morris, Norval, and Michael H. Tonry. Introduction to *Crime and Justice: An Annual Review of Research* 1: vii–xi; 2: vii–ix. Chicago: University of Chicago Press, 1979–80.

Tonry, Michael H. Review of *The New Criminology* by P. Walton, I. Taylor, and J. Young. *Criminal Law Bulletin* 12 (1976): 493–97.

Tonry, Michael H., and Norval Morris. Introduction to *Crime and Justice: An Annual Review of Research* 3: vii–viii. Chicago: University of Chicago Press, 1981.

Studies in Crime and Justice

University of Chicago Press

Marvin E. Wolfgang, Robert M. Figlio, and Thorsten Sellin
Delinquency in a Birth Cohort   1972

Franklin E. Zimring and Gordon Hawkins
Deterrence: The Legal Threat in Crime Control   1973

Norval Morris
The Future of Imprisonment   1974

Kettil Bruun, Lynn Pan, and Ingemar Rexed
*The Gentlemen's Club: International Control of Drugs and
Alcohol*   1975

Paul Lerman
*Community Treatment and Social Control: A Critical Analysis of
Juvenile and Correctional Policy*   1975

Gordon Hawkins
The Prison   1976

Margaret Rosenheim, editor
Pursuing Justice for the Child   1976

James B. Jacobs
Stateville: The Penitentiary in Mass Society   1977

Henry J. Steadman
Beating a Rap? Defendants Found Incompetent to Stand Trial   1979

Terence Thornberry and Joseph E. Jacoby
*The Criminally Insane: A Community Follow-up of Mentally Ill
Offenders*   1979

Michael Sherman and Gordon Hawkins
Imprisonment in America   1981

Norval Morris
Madness and the Criminal Law   1982

John Kaplan
Heroin: The Most Dangerous Drug   1983

Michael H. Tonry and Franklin E. Zimring, editors
Reform and Punishment: Essays on Criminal Sentencing   1983

Diane Vaughan
Controlling Unlawful Organizational Behavior   1983

Gordon Hawkins and Franklin E. Zimring, editors
The Pursuit of Criminal Justice   1984

Crime and Justice
An Annual Review of Research

349

Volume 5 (1983)

Incapacitation as a Strategy for Crime Control
Jacqueline Cohen

Prison Labor and Prison Industries
Gordon Hawkins

Prisons for Women, 1790–1980
Nicole Hahn Rafter

Sex Offenses and Offending
Donald J. West

The Organization of Criminological Research

Australia
David Biles

Canada
Anthony N. Doob

Great Britain and the Council of Europe
John Croft

Netherlands
Josine Junger-Tas

Federal Republic of Germany
Günther Kaiser

Index